The Ruby Way

Hal Fulton

201 West 103rd St., Indianapolis, Indiana 46290 USA

The Ruby Way

Copyright © 2002 by Sams Publishing

International Standard Book Number: 0-672-32083-5

Library of Congress Catalog Card Number: 2001089585

Printed in the United States of America

First Printing: December 2001

04   03   02   01   4   3   2   1

Trademarks

Warning and Disclaimer

ASSOCIATE PUBLISHER
Jeff Koch

ACQUISITIONS EDITOR
William E. Brown

DEVELOPMENT EDITOR
Scott Meyers

MANAGING EDITOR
Matt Purcell

PROJECT EDITOR
Christina Smith

PRODUCTION EDITORS
Seth Kerney
Bart Reed
Rhonda Tinch-Mize

INDEXER
Erika Millen

PROOFREADER
Suzanne Thomas

TECHNICAL EDITOR
Chad Fowler
Dave Thomas

TEAM COORDINATOR
Denni Bannister

MEDIA DEVELOPER
Dan Scherf

INTERIOR DESIGNER
Gary Adair

COVER DESIGNER
Alan Clements

PAGE LAYOUT
Rebecca Harmon
Michelle Mitchell

Overview

Contents

5   OOP and Dynamicity in Ruby   243

Foreword

Shortly after I first met with computers in the early 80s, I became interested in programming languages. Since then, I have been a "language geek." I think the reason for this interest is that programming languages are ways to express human thought. They are fundamentally human-oriented.

Despite this fact, programming languages have tended to be rather machine-oriented. Many languages were designed for the convenience of the computer.

However, as computers become more powerful and cheaper, this situation has gradually changed. For example, look at structured programming. Machines do not care whether programs are structured well. They just execute them bit by bit. Structured programming is not for machines, but for humans. This is true of object-oriented programming as well.

The time for language design that focuses on humans has been coming.

In 1993, I was talking with my colleague about scripting languages—about their power and future. I felt scripting to be the way future programming should be. It is human-oriented programming.

However, I was not satisfied with existing languages such as Perl and Python. I wanted a language that was more powerful than Perl and more object-oriented than Python. I couldn't find the ideal language, so I decided to make my own.

Ruby is not the simplest language, but the human soul is not simple at all in its natural state. It loves simplicity and complexity at the same time. It can't handle too many complex things, nor too many simple things. It's a matter of balance.

Therefore, to design Ruby, a human-oriented language, I followed the Principle of Least Surprise. I consider that everything that surprises me less is good. As a result, I've developed a very natural feeling, even a kind of joy, when programming in Ruby. Since the first release of Ruby in 1995, many programmers worldwide agreed with me about the joy of Ruby programming.

As always, I'd like to express my very greatest appreciation to the people in the Ruby community. They are the heart of Ruby's success.

I am also thankful to the author of this book, Hal E. Fulton, for declaring the Ruby Way to help people.

This book explains the philosophy behind Ruby, distilled from my brain and the Ruby community. I wonder how it was possible for Hal to read my mind to know and reveal the secret of the Ruby Way. I have never met him face to face, but I hope to meet him soon.

I hope this book and Ruby both serve to make your programming fun and happy.

Yukihiro "Matz" Matsumoto
September 2001, Japan

まつもと ゆきひろ

About the Author

Hal Fulton has two degrees in computer science. He has taught at the community college level and also has more than a decade of industry experience as a programmer. He is a member of the ACM and the IEEE Computer Society.

Dedication

To my parents, without whom I would not be possible.

Acknowledgments

Writing a book is truly a team effort; this is a fact I could not fully appreciate until I wrote one myself. I recommend the experience, although it is a humbling one. It is a simple truth that without the assistance of many other people, this book would not have existed.

Thanks and appreciation must first go to Matz (Yukihiro Matsumoto), who created the Ruby language in the first place. *Domo arigato gozaimasu!*

Thanks go to Conrad Schneiker for conceiving the overall idea for the book and helping to create its overall structure. He also did me the service of introducing me to the Ruby language in 1999.

Several individuals have contributed material to the body of the book. The foremost of these is Guy Hurst, who wrote substantial parts of the earlier chapters as well as two of the appendixes. His assistance was absolutely invaluable.

Thanks also go to the other contributors, whom I'll name in no particular order. Kevin Smith did a great job on the GTK section of Chapter 6, "Graphical Interfaces in Ruby," saving me from a potentially steep learning curve on a tight schedule. Patrick Logan, in the same chapter, shed light on the mysteries of the FOX GUI. Chad Fowler, in Chapter 9, "Network and Web Programming," plumbed the depths of XML and also contributed to the CGI section.

Thanks also goes to those who assisted in proofreading, reviewing, or in other miscellaneous ways—Don Muchow, Mike Stok, Miho Ogishima, and others already mentioned. Thanks to David Eppstein, the mathematics professor, for answering questions about graph theory.

One of the great things about Ruby is the support of the community. Many people on the mailing list and the newsgroup answered questions and gave me ideas and assistance. Again, in no particular order, these are Dave Thomas, Andy Hunt, Hee-Sob Park, Mike Wilson, Avi Bryant, Yasushi Shoji ("Yashi"), Shugo Maeda, Jim Weirich, "arton," and Masaki Suketa. I'm sorry to say I have probably overlooked someone.

To state the obvious, a book would never be published without a publisher. Many people behind the scenes worked hard to produce this book. Primarily I have to thank William Brown, who worked closely with me and was a constant source of encouragement, and Scott Meyers, who delved deeply into the details of putting the material together. I also want to thank all the others whom I cannot even name because I have never heard of them. You know who you are.

I have to thank my parents, who watched this project from a distance, encouraged me along the way, and even bothered to learn a little bit of computer science for my sake.

A writer friend of mine once told me, "If you write a book and nobody reads it, you haven't really written a book." So, finally, I want to thank you, the reader. This book is for you. I hope it is of some value.

Tell Us What You Think!

As the reader of this book, *you* are our most important critic and commentator. We value your opinion and want to know what we're doing right, what we could do better, what areas you'd like to see us publish in, and any other words of wisdom you're willing to pass our way.

As an Associate Publisher for Sams Publishing, I welcome your comments. You can fax, e-mail, or write me directly to let me know what you did or didn't like about this book—as well as what we can do to make our books stronger.

Please note that I cannot help you with technical problems related to the topic of this book, and that due to the high volume of mail I receive, I might not be able to reply to every message.

When you write, please be sure to include this book's title and author's name as well as your name and phone or fax number. I will carefully review your comments and share them with the author and editors who worked on the book.

Fax: 317-581-4770
E-mail: feedback@samspublishing.com
Mail: Jeff Koch
           Associate Publisher
           Sams Publishing
           201 West 103rd Street
           Indianapolis, IN 46290 USA

Introduction

The way that can be named is not the true Way.

—Lao Tse, *Tao Te Ching*

The title of this book is *The Ruby Way*. This is a title that begs for a disclaimer.

It has been my aim to align this book with the philosophy of Ruby as well as I could. That has also been the aim of the other contributors. Credit for success must be shared with these others, but the blame for any mistakes must rest solely with me.

Of course, I can't presume to tell you with exactness what the spirit of Ruby is all about. That is primarily for Matz to say—and I think even he would have difficulty communicating all of it in words.

In short, *The Ruby Way* is only a book, but the Ruby Way is the province of the language creator and the community as a whole. This is something difficult to capture in a book.

Still, I have tried in this introduction to pin down a little of the ineffable spirit of Ruby. The wise student of Ruby will not take it as authoritative.

How This Book Works

You won't learn Ruby from this book. There is relatively little in the way of introductory or tutorial information. If you are totally new to Ruby, I suggest you start with another book.

Having said that, programmers are a tenacious bunch, and I grant that it might be possible to learn Ruby from this book. Chapter 1, "Ruby in Review," does contain a brief introduction and some tutorial information.

Chapter 1 also contains a fairly comprehensive "gotcha" list (which has been hard to keep up-to-date). The usefulness of this list will vary widely from one reader to another because we cannot all agree on what is intuitive.

This book is largely intended to answer questions of the form of "How do I...?" As such, you can expect to do a lot of skipping around. I'd be honored if everyone read every page from front to back, but I don't expect that. It's more my expectation that you will browse the table of contents in search of techniques you need or topics you find interesting.

Some areas this book covers are very elementary. That's because people vary in background and experience; what is obvious to one person may not be to another. I have tried to err on the side of completeness. On the other hand, I have tried to keep the book at a reasonable size (obviously a competing goal).

This book can be viewed as a sort of "inverted reference." Rather than looking up the name of a method or a class, you will look things up by function or purpose. For example, the `String` class has four methods for manipulating case: `capitalize`, `upcase`, `downcase`, and `swapcase`. In a reference work, these would quite properly be listed alphabetically, but in this book they are all listed together.

Of course, in striving for completeness, I have sometimes wandered onto the turf of the reference books. In many cases, I have tried to compensate for this by offering more unusual or diverse examples than you might find in a reference.

I have tried for a very high code-to-commentary ratio. Overlooking the initial chapter, I think I've achieved this. Writers may grow chatty, but programmers always want to see the code. (If not, they *should* want to.)

The examples here are sometimes very contrived, for which I must apologize. To illustrate a technique or principle in isolation from a real-world problem can be very difficult. However, the more complex or "high level" the task was, the more I attempted a real-world solution. Therefore, if the topic is concatenating strings, you may find an unimaginative code fragment involving `"foo"` and `"bar"`, but when the topic is parsing XML, for example, you will usually find a much more meaningful and realistic piece of code.

This book has two or three small quirks to which I'll confess up front. One is the avoidance of the "ugly" Perl-like global variables such as `$_` and others. These are present in Ruby, and they work fine; they are used daily by most or all Ruby programmers. However, in nearly all cases, their use can be avoided, and I have taken the liberty of omitting them in most of the examples.

Another quirk is that I avoid using standalone expressions when they don't have side effects. Ruby is expression oriented, and that is a good thing. I have tried to take advantage of that feature. However, in a code fragment, I prefer not to write expressions that merely return a value that is not usable. For example, the expression `"abc" + "def"` can illustrate string concatenation, but I would write something like `str = "abc" + "def"` instead. This may seem wordy to some, but it may seem more natural to you if you are a C programmer who really notices when functions are void or non-void (or an old-time Pascal programmer who thinks in procedures and functions).

My third quirk is that I don't like the "pound" notation to denote instance methods. Many Rubyists will think I am being verbose in saying "instance method `crypt` of class `String`" rather than saying "`String#crypt`," but I think no one will be confused.

I have tried to include "pointers" to outside resources whenever appropriate. Time and space did not allow putting everything into this book that I wanted, but I hope I have partially made up for that by telling you where to find related materials. The Ruby Application Archive on the Web is probably the foremost of these sources; you will see it referenced many times in this book.

Here, at the front of the book, is usually where you'll find a gratuitous reference to the typefaces used for code and how to tell code fragments from ordinary text. However, I won't insult your intelligence; you've read computer books before.

And now a word about personal pronouns. Here in the introduction, I've used the singular first person consistently, but throughout most of the book, I've used *we*, in the manner of kings and editors. This is not (just) my pompous nature revealing itself; it's a very real concession to the fact that a little over 10 percent of this book was written by other people. (Most readers skip the acknowledgements in a book. Go read them now. They're good for you, like vegetables.)

What Is the Ruby Way?

Let us prepare to grapple with the ineffable itself, and see if we may not eff it after all.

—Douglas Adams, *Dirk Gently's Holistic Detective Agency*

What do we mean by the Ruby Way? My belief is that there are two related aspects: One is the philosophy of the *design* of Ruby; the other is the philosophy of its usage. It is natural that design and use should be interrelated, whether in software or hardware; why else should there be such a field as ergonomics? If I build a device and put a handle on it, it is because I expect someone to grab that handle.

Ruby has a nameless quality that makes it what it is. We see that quality present in the design of the syntax and semantics of the language, but it is also present in the programs written for that interpreter. Yet, as soon as we make this distinction, we blur it.

Clearly, Ruby is not just a tool for creating software but is a piece of software in its own right. Why should the workings of Ruby *programs* follow laws different from those that guide the workings of the *interpreter*? After all, Ruby is highly dynamic and extensible. There might be reasons why the two levels should differ here and there—probably for accommodating to the inconvenience of the real world. However, in general, the thought processes can and should be the same. Ruby could be implemented in Ruby, in true Hofstadter-like fashion, although it is not at the time of this writing.

We don't often think of the etymology of the word *way*, but there are two important senses in which it is used. On the one hand, it means a *method* or *technique*, but it can also mean a *road* or *path*. Obviously, these two meanings are interrelated, and I think when I say "the Ruby Way," I mean both of them.

So what we are talking about is a thought process, but it is also a path that we follow. Even the greatest software guru cannot claim to have reached perfection, but only to follow the path. And there may be more than one path, but here I can only talk about one.

The conventional wisdom says that "form follows function." And the conventional wisdom is, of course, conventionally correct. However, Frank Lloyd Wright (speaking of his own field) once said, "Form follows function—that has been misunderstood. Form and function should be one, joined in a spiritual union."

What did Wright mean? I would say that this truth is not something you learn from a book, but from experience.

However, I would argue that Wright expressed this truth elsewhere in pieces easier to digest. He was a great proponent of simplicity, saying once, "An architect's most useful tools are an eraser at the drafting board and a wrecking bar at the site."

So one of Ruby's virtues is simplicity. Shall I quote other thinkers on the subject? According to Antoine de St. Exupéry, "Perfection is achieved, not when there is nothing left to add, but when there is nothing left to take away."

But Ruby is a complex language. How can I say that it is simple?

If we understood the universe better, we might find a "law of conservation of complexity"—a fact of reality that disturbs our lives like entropy so that we cannot avoid it but can only redistribute it.

And that is the key. We can't avoid complexity, but we can push it around. We can bury it out of sight. This is the old "black box" principle at work; a black box performs a very complex task, but it possesses simplicity *on the outside*.

If you haven't already lost patience with my quotations, a word from Albert Einstein is appropriate here: "Everything should be as simple as possible, but no simpler."

So, in Ruby we see simplicity embodied from the programmer's view (if not from the view of those maintaining the interpreter). Yet we also see the capacity for compromise. In the real world, we must bend a little. For example, every entity in a Ruby program should be a true object, but certain values such as integers are stored as immediate values. In a tradeoff familiar to computer science students for decades, we have traded elegance of design for practicality of implementation. In effect, we have traded one kind of simplicity for another.

What Larry Wall said about Perl holds true: "When you say something in a small language, it comes out big. When you say something in a big language, it comes out small." The same is true for English. The reason that biologist Ernst Haeckel could say "Ontogeny recapitulates phylogeny" in only three words was that he had these powerful words with highly specific meanings at his disposal. We allow inner complexity of the language because it enables us to shift the complexity away from the individual utterance.

I would state this guideline this way: *Don't write 200 lines of code when 10 will do.*

I'm taking it for granted that brevity is generally a good thing. A short program fragment will take up less space in the programmer's brain; it will be easier to grasp as a single entity. As a happy side effect, fewer bugs will be injected while the code is written.

Of course, we must remember Einstein's warning about simplicity. If we put it too high on our list of priorities, we will end up with code that is hopelessly obfuscated. Information theory teaches us that compressed data is statistically similar to random noise; if you have looked at C or APL or regular expression notation—especially badly written—you have experienced this truth firsthand. Simple, but not too simple; that is the key. Embrace brevity, but do not sacrifice readability.

It is a truism that both brevity and readability are good. However, there is an underlying reason for this—one so fundamental that we sometimes forget it. The reason is that *computers exist for humans, not humans for computers.*

In the old days, it was almost the opposite. Computers cost millions of dollars and ate electricity at the rate of many kilowatts. People acted as though the computer were a minor deity and the programmers were humble supplicants. An hour of the computer's time was more expensive than an hour of a person's time.

When computers became smaller and cheaper, high-level languages also became more and more popular. These were inefficient from the computer's point of view but efficient from the human perspective. Ruby is simply a later development in this line of thought. Some, in fact, have called it a *VHLL* (very high-level language); although this term is not well-defined, I think its use is justified here.

The computer is supposed to be the servant, not the master; and, as Matz has said, a smart servant should do a complex task with a few short commands. This has been true through all the history of computer science. We started with machine languages and progressed to assembly language and then to high-level languages.

What we are talking about here is a shift from a machine-centered paradigm to a human-centered one. In my opinion, Ruby is an excellent example of human-centric programming.

I'll now shift gears a little. There was a wonderful little book from the 1980s called *The Tao of Programming*, by Geoffrey James. Nearly every line is quotable, but I'll repeat only one: "A program should follow the 'Law of Least Astonishment.' What is this law? It is simply that the program should always respond to the user in the way that astonishes him least." (Of course, in the case of a language interpreter, the *user* is the programmer.)

I don't know whether James coined this term, but his book was my first introduction to the phrase. This is a principle that is well known and often cited in the Ruby community, although it is usually called the *Principle of Least Surprise*, or POLS. (I myself stubbornly prefer the acronym LOLA.)

Whatever you call it, this rule is a valid one, and it has been a guideline throughout the ongoing development of the Ruby language. It is also a useful guideline for those who develop libraries or user interfaces.

The only problem, of course, is that different people are surprised by different things; there is no universal agreement on how an object or method "ought" to behave. However, we can strive for consistency and to justify our design decisions, and each person can train his own intuition.

No matter how logically constructed a system may be, your intuition needs to be trained. Each programming language is a world unto itself, with its own set of assumptions; and human languages are the same. When I took German, I learned that all nouns were capitalized; but the word *deutsch* was not. I complained to my professor; after all, this was the *name* of the language, wasn't it? And he smiled and said, "Don't fight it."

What he taught me was to *let German be German*—and by extension, that is good advice for anyone coming to Ruby from some other language. Let Ruby be Ruby. Don't expect it to be Perl, because it isn't; don't expect it to be LISP or Smalltalk, either. On the other hand, Ruby has common elements with all three of these. Start by following your expectations, but when they are violated, don't fight it. (Unless Matz agrees it's a needed change.)

Every programmer today knows the orthogonality principle (which would better be termed the *orthogonal completeness* principle). Suppose we have an imaginary pair of axes with a set of comparable language entities on one and a set of attributes or capabilities on the other. When we talk of "orthogonality," we usually mean that the space defined by these axes is as "full" as we can logically make it.

Part of the Ruby Way is to strive for this orthogonality. An array is in some ways similar to a hash, so the operations on each of them should be similar. The limit is reached when we enter the areas where they are different.

Matz has said that "naturalness" is to be valued over orthogonality. But to fully understand what is natural and what is not may take some thinking and some coding.

Ruby strives to be friendly to the programmer. For example, there are aliases or synonyms for many method names; `size` and `length` will both return the number of entries in an array. The variant spellings `indexes` and `indices` both refer to the same method. Some consider this sort of thing to be an annoyance or "anti-feature," but I consider it a good design.

Ruby strives for consistency and regularity. There is nothing mysterious about this; in every aspect of life, we yearn for things to be regular and parallel. What makes it a little more tricky is learning when to violate this principle.

For instance, Ruby has the habit of appending a question mark (?) to the name of a predicate-like method. This is well and good; it clarifies the code and makes the namespace a little more manageable. But what is more controversial is the similar use of the exclamation point in marking methods that are "destructive" or "dangerous" in the sense that they modify their receivers. The controversy arises because *not all* of the destructive methods are marked in this way. Shouldn't we be consistent?

No, in fact we should not. Some of the methods by their very nature change their receiver (such as the `Array` methods `replace` and `concat`). Some of them are "writer" methods, allowing assignment to a class attribute. We should *not* append an exclamation point to the attribute name or the equal sign. There are some methods that arguably change the state of the receiver, such as `read`; this occurs too frequently to be marked in this way. If every destructive method name ended in !, very soon our programs would look like sales brochures for a multilevel marketing firm.

Do you notice a kind of tension between opposing forces, a tendency for all rules to be violated? Let me state this as Fulton's Second Law: *Every rule has an exception, except Fulton's Second Law.*

What we see in Ruby is not a "foolish consistency" or a rigid adherence to a set of simple rules. In fact, perhaps part of the Ruby Way is that it is *not* a rigid and inflexible approach. In language design, as Matz once said, you should "follow your heart."

Yet another aspect of this philosophy is this: Do not fear change at runtime; do not fear what is dynamic. The world is dynamic; why should a programming language be static? Ruby is one of the more dynamic languages in existence.

I would also argue another aspect: Do not be a slave to performance issues. When performance is unacceptable, the issue must be addressed, but it should normally not be the first thing you think about. Prefer elegance over efficiency where efficiency is less than critical. Then again, if you are writing a library that may be used in unforeseen ways, performance may be critical from the start.

When I look at Ruby, I perceive a balance between different design goals—a complex interaction reminiscent of the *n*-body problem in physics. I can imagine it might be modeled as an Alexander Calder mobile. It is perhaps this interaction itself, the harmony, that embodies Ruby's philosophy rather than just the individual parts. Programmers know that their craft is not just science and technology, but art. I hesitate to say that there is a spiritual aspect to computer science, but just between you and me, there certainly is. (If you have not read Robert Pirsig's *Zen and the Art of Motorcycle Maintenance*, I recommend that you do so.)

Ruby arose from the human urge to create things that are useful and beautiful. Programs written in Ruby should spring from that same God-given source. That, to me, is the essence of the Ruby Way.

Ruby in Review

IN THIS CHAPTER

Language shapes the way we think and determines what we can think about.

—Benjamin Lee Whorf

It is worth remembering that a new programming language is sometimes viewed as a panacea, especially by its adherents; however, there is no one language that will supplant all the others, no one tool that is unarguably the best for every possible task. There are many different problem domains in the world, and there are many possible constraints on problems within those domains.

Above all, there are different ways of *thinking* about these problems, stemming from the diverse backgrounds and personalities of the programmers themselves. For these reasons, no foreseeable end to the proliferation of languages is in site. As long as there is a multiplicity of languages, there will be a multiplicity of personalities defending and attacking them. In short, there will always be "language wars." In this book, however, we do not intend to participate in them.

Yet, in the constant quest for what is newer and better program notations, we have stumbled across ideas that endure, that transcend the context in which they were created. Just as Pascal borrowed from Algol, just as Java borrowed from C, so will every language borrow from its predecessors. A language is both a toolbox and a playground; it has its extremely practical side, but it also serves as a test bed for new ideas that may or may not be widely accepted by the computing community.

One of the most far reaching of these ideas is the concept of object-oriented programming (OOP). Although many would argue that the overall significance of OOP is evolutionary rather than revolutionary, no one can say that it has not had an impact on the industry. Twenty years ago, object orientation was for the most part an academic curiosity; today it is a universally accepted paradigm.

In fact, the ubiquitous nature of OOP has led to a significant amount of "hype" in the industry. In a classic paper of the late 80s, Roger King observed, "If you want to sell a cat to a computer scientist, you have to tell him it's object-oriented." Additionally, there are differences of opinion about what OOP really is, and even among those who are essentially in agreement there are differences in terminology.

It is not our purpose here to contribute to the hype. We do find OOP to be a useful tool and a meaningful way of thinking about problems; however, we do not claim that it cures cancer.

As for the exact nature of OOP, we have our pet definitions and favorite terminology, but we make these known only in order to communicate effectively, not to quibble over semantics.

We mention all this because it is necessary to have a basic understanding of OOP in order to proceed to the bulk of this book and understand the examples and techniques. Whatever else might be said about Ruby, it is definitely an object-oriented language.

Some Words on Object Orientation

Before talking about Ruby specifically, it is a good idea to talk about object-oriented programming in the abstract. These first few pages will provide a review of those concepts with only cursory references to Ruby, before we proceed in a few pages to the review of the Ruby language itself.

In object-oriented programming, the fundamental unit is the *object*, which is an entity that serves as a container for data and also controls access to the data. Associated with an object is a set of *attributes*, which are essentially no more than variables belonging to the object. (In this book, we will loosely use the ordinary term *variable* for an attribute.) Also associated with an object is a set of functions that provide an interface to the functionality of the object. These functions are called *methods*.

It is essential that any OOP language provide *encapsulation*. As the term is commonly used, it means first that the attributes and methods of an object are associated specifically with that object or bundled with it. Secondly, it means that the scope of those attributes and methods is by default the object itself (an application of the well-known principle of *data hiding*, which is not specific to OOP).

An object is considered to be an instance or manifestation of an *object class* (usually simply called a *class*). The class may be thought of as the blueprint or pattern; the object itself is the thing created from that blueprint or pattern. A class is often thought of as an *abstract type*—a more complex type than, for example, an integer or character string.

When an object (an instance of a class) is created, it is said to be *instantiated*. Some languages have the notion of an explicit *constructor* and *destructor* for an object—functions that perform whatever tasks are needed to initialize an object and, respectively, to "destroy" it. We may as well mention prematurely that Ruby has what might be considered a constructor but certainly does not have any concept of a destructor (because of its well-behaved garbage-collection mechanism).

Occasionally a situation arises in which a piece of data is more "global" in scope than a single object, and it is inappropriate to put a copy of the attribute into each instance of the class. For example, consider a class called `MyDogs`, from which three objects are created: `fido`, `rover`, and `spot`. For each dog, there might be such attributes as age and date of vaccination. But suppose we want to store the owner's name. We could certainly put it in each object, but that is wasteful of memory and at the very least a misleading design. Clearly the `owner_name` attribute belongs not to any individual object but rather to the class itself. When it is defined that way (and the syntax will vary from one language to another), it is called a *class attribute* (or *class variable*).

Of course, there are many situations in which a class variable might be needed. For example, suppose we want to keep a count of how many objects of a certain class have been created. We could use a class variable that was initialized to zero and incremented with every instantiation; the class variable would be associated with the class and not with any particular object. In scope, this variable would be just like any other attribute, but there would only be one copy of it for the entire class and the entire set of objects created from that class.

To distinguish between class attributes and ordinary attributes, the latter are sometimes explicitly called *object attributes* (or *instance attributes*). We will use the convention that any attribute is assumed to be an instance attribute unless we explicitly call it a class attribute.

Just as an object's methods are used to control access to its attributes and provide a clean interface to them, so is it sometimes appropriate or necessary to define a method that is associated with a class. A *class method*, not surprisingly, controls access to the class variables and also performs any tasks that might have class-wide effects rather than merely object-wide effects. As with data attributes, methods are assumed to belong to the object rather than the class, unless stated otherwise.

It is worth mentioning that there is a sense in which all methods are class methods. We should not suppose that when a hundred objects are created, we actually copy the code for the methods a hundred times! However, the rules of scope assure us that each object method operates only on the object whose method is being called, providing us with the extremely necessary illusion that object methods are associated strictly with their objects.

We come now to one of the real strengths of object-oriented programming: inheritance. *Inheritance* is a mechanism that allows us to extend a previously existing entity by adding features to create a new entity. In short, inheritance is a way of reusing code. (Easy, effective code reuse has long been the Holy Grail of computer science, resulting in the invention decades ago of parameterized subroutines and code libraries. OOP is only one of the later efforts in realizing this goal.)

Typically we think of inheritance at the class level. If we have a specific class in mind and there is a more general case already in existence, we can define our new class to inherit the features of the old one. For example, suppose we have the class `Polygon`, which describes convex polygons. If we then find ourselves wanting to deal with the `Rectangle` class, we can inherit from `Polygon` so that `Rectangle` now has all the attributes and methods that `Polygon` has. For example, there might be a method that would calculate perimeter by iterating over all the sides and adding their lengths. Assuming everything is implemented properly, this method would automatically work for the new class; the code would not have to be rewritten.

When class B inherits from class A, we say that B is a *subclass* of A—or conversely, A is the *superclass* of B. In slightly different terminology, we may say that A is a *base class* or *parent class*, and B is a *derived class* or *child class*.

A derived class, as you have seen, may treat a method inherited from its base class as if it were its own. On the other hand, it may redefine that method entirely, if it is necessary to provide a different implementation; this is referred to as *overriding* a method. In addition, most languages provide a way for an overridden method to call its namesake in the parent class; that is, the method foo in B knows how to call method foo in A if it wants to. (Any language not providing this feature is under suspicion of not being truly object oriented.) Essentially the same is true for data attributes.

The relationship between a class and its superclass is an interesting and important one; it is usually described as the *is-a* relationship, because a Square "is a" Rectangle, and a Rectangle "is a" Polygon, and so on. Therefore, if we create an inheritance hierarchy (which tends to exist in one form or another in any OOP language), we see that the more specific entity "is a" subclass of the more general entity at any given point in the hierarchy. Note that this relationship is transitive—in the preceding example, you can easily see that a Square "is a" Polygon. Note also that the relationship is not commutative—we know that every Rectangle is a Polygon, but not every Polygon is a Rectangle.

This brings us to the topic of *multiple inheritance*. It is conceivable that there might be more than one class from which a new class could inherit. For example, the classes Dog and Cat can both inherit from the class Mammal, and Sparrow and Raven can inherit from WingedCreature. But what if we want to define the class Bat? It can reasonably inherit from both Mammal and WingedCreature. This corresponds well with our experience in real life, in which things are not members of just one category but of many non-nested categories.

Multiple inheritance (MI) is probably the most controversial area in OOP. One camp will point out the potential for ambiguity that must be resolved. For example, if Mammal and WingedCreature both have an attribute called size (or a method called eat), which one will be referenced when we refer to it from a Bat object? Another related difficulty is the "diamond inheritance problem" (so called because of the shape of its inheritance diagram), with both superclasses inheriting from a single common superclass. For example, imagine that Mammal and WingedCreature both inherit from Organism; the hierarchy from Organism to Bat forms a diamond. But what about the attributes that the two intermediate classes both inherit from their parent? Does Bat get two copies of each of them, or are they merged back into single attributes because they come from a common ancestor in the first place?

These are both issues for the language designer rather than the programmer. Different OOP languages deal with the issues in different ways. Some will provide rules allowing one definition of an attribute to "win out," or a way to distinguish between attributes of the same name, or even a way of aliasing or renaming the identifiers. This in itself is considered by many to be an argument against MI—the mechanisms for dealing with name clashes and the like are not universally agreed upon but are very much language dependent. C++ offers a fairly minimal set of features for dealing with ambiguities; those of Eiffel are probably better, and those of Perl are different from both.

The alternative, of course, is to disallow MI altogether. This is the approach taken by such languages as Java and Ruby. This sounds like a drastic compromise; however, as you'll see later, it is not as bad as it sounds. We will look at a viable alternative to traditional multiple inheritance, but we must first discuss yet another OOP buzzword: polymorphism.

Polymorphism is the term that perhaps inspires the most semantic disagreement in the field. Everyone seems to know what it is, but everyone has a different definition. (In recent years, "What is polymorphism?" has become a popular interview question. If it is asked of you, I recommend quoting an expert like Bertrand Meyer or Bjarne Stroustrup; that way, if the interviewer disagrees, his beef is with the expert and not with you.)

The literal meaning of polymorphism is "the ability to take on multiple forms or shapes." In its broadest sense, this refers to the ability of different objects to respond in different ways to the same message (or method invocation).

Damian Conway, in his book *Object-Oriented Perl*, distinguishes meaningfully between two kinds of polymorphism. The first, *inheritance polymorphism*, is what most programmers are referring to when they talk about polymorphism.

When a class inherits from its superclass, we know (by definition) that any method present in the superclass is also present in the subclass. Therefore, a chain of inheritance represents a linear hierarchy of classes that can respond to the same set of methods. Of course, we must remember that any subclass can redefine a method; that is what gives inheritance its power. If I call a method on an object, typically it will be either the one it inherited from its superclass or a more appropriate (more specialized) method tailored for the subclass.

In strongly typed languages such as C++, inheritance polymorphism establishes type compatibility down the chain of inheritance (but not in the reverse direction). For example, if B inherits from A, then a pointer to an A object can also point to a B object. However, the reverse is not true. This type compatibility is an essential OOP feature in such languages—indeed it almost sums up polymorphism—but polymorphism certainly exists in the absence of static typing (as in Ruby).

The second kind of polymorphism Conway identifies is *interface polymorphism*. This does not require any inheritance relationship between classes; it only requires that the interfaces of the objects have methods of a certain name. The treatment of such objects as being the same "kind" of thing is therefore a type of polymorphism (although in most writings it is not explicitly referred to as such).

Readers familiar with Java will recognize that it implements both kinds of polymorphism. A Java class can extend another class, inheriting from it via the `extends` keyword, or it may implement an interface, acquiring a known set of methods (which must then be overridden) via the `implements` keyword. Because of the syntax requirements, the Java interpreter is able to determine at compile time whether a method can be invoked on a particular object.

Ruby supports interface polymorphism but in a different way, providing *modules* whose methods may be *mixed in* to existing classes (interfacing to user-defined methods that are expected to exist). This, however, is not the way modules are usually used. A module consists of methods and constants that may be used as though they were actual parts of that class or object; when a module is mixed in via the `include` statement, this is considered to be a restricted form of multiple inheritance. (According to the language designer Yukihiro Matsumoto, this can be viewed as "single inheritance with implementation sharing.") This is a way of preserving the benefits of MI without suffering all the consequences.

It's worth noting that Ruby supports implicit interface polymorphism by virtue of the simple fact that any class can "masquerade" as another class. In many cases, the only type information we care about is whether a certain set of methods is implemented—that is, whether an object responds to certain messages. Sometimes we write code for a `Duck` object when really all we care about is for it to implement a `quack` method. Yet, if something "quacks" like a `Duck`, for our purposes it *is* a `Duck` (with no need to inherit from that class at all). The set of available methods is arguably the most important type information.

Languages such as C++ contain the concept of *abstract classes*—classes that must be inherited from and cannot be instantiated on their own. This concept does not exist in the more dynamic Ruby language, although if the programmer really wants, it is possible to fake this kind of behavior by forcing the methods to be overridden. Whether this is useful or not is left as an exercise for you, the reader.

The creator of C++, Bjarne Stroustrup, also identifies the concept of a concrete type. This is a class that exists only for convenience; it is not designed to be inherited from, nor is it expected that there will ever be another class derived from it. In other words, the benefits of OOP are basically limited to encapsulation. Ruby does not specifically support this concept through any special syntax (nor does C++), but it is naturally well suited for the creation of such classes.

Some languages are considered to be more "purely" object-oriented than others. (We also use the term *radically object oriented*.) This refers to the concept that *every* entity in the language is an object; every primitive type is represented as a full-fledged class, and variables and constants alike are recognized as object instances. This is in contrast to such languages as Java, C++, and Eiffel. In these, the more primitive data types (especially constants) are not first-class objects, although they may sometimes be treated that way with "wrapper" classes.

Most object-oriented languages are fairly static; the methods and attributes belonging to a class, the global variables, and the inheritance hierarchy are all defined at compile time. Perhaps the largest conceptual leap for a Ruby programmer is that these are all handled *dynamically* in Ruby. Definitions and even inheritance can happen at runtime—in fact, we can truly say that every declaration or definition is actually *executed* during the running of the program. Among many other benefits, this obviates the need for conditional compilation and can produce more efficient code in many circumstances.

This sums up the whirlwind tour of OOP. Throughout the rest of the book, we have tried to make consistent use of the terms introduced here. Let's proceed now to a brief review of the Ruby language itself.

Basic Ruby Syntax and Semantics

Bring forth that ruby gem of Badakhshan,
That heart's delight, that balm of Turkestan....

—*The Rubaiyat*, Omar Khayyam
  (trans. E. H. Whinfield)

In the previous pages, you have already seen that Ruby is a pure, dynamic, OOP language. Let's now look briefly at some other attributes before summarizing the syntax and semantics.

Ruby is a scripting language. This should not be construed as meaning that it is not powerful. It can serve as a "glue language" in the tradition of KornShell and others, or it can serve as an environment for creating larger self-contained applications. Readers who are interested in the industry trend toward scripting languages should refer to John Ousterhout's article "Scripting: Higher-Level Programming for the 21st Century" in the March 1998 issue of *IEEE Computer*. (Ousterhout is the creator of the Tcl language.)

Ruby is an interpreted language. Of course, there may be later implementations of a Ruby compiler for performance reasons, but we maintain that an interpreter yields great benefits not only in rapid prototyping but in the shortening of the development cycle overall.

Ruby is an expression-oriented language. Why use a statement when an expression will do? This means, for instance, that code becomes more compact as the common parts are factored out and repetition is removed.

Ruby is a very high-level language (VHLL). One principle behind the language design is that the computer should work for the programmer rather than vice versa. The "density" of Ruby means that sophisticated and complex operations can be carried out with relative ease as compared to lower-level languages.

Having said all that, let's look more closely at Ruby. This section and the rest of the chapter concentrate on the Ruby language itself. As mentioned before, this is only a quick summary, so if you haven't learned it somewhere else, you won't learn it here.

Our first look at Ruby will not concentrate on the language's more complex features. These are covered in the next two sections. Here, we are concerned with the overall look and feel of the language and some of its terminology. We'll briefly examine the nature of a Ruby program before looking at examples.

To begin with, Ruby is essentially a line-oriented language—more so than languages such as C but not so much as antique languages such as FORTRAN. Tokens can be crowded onto a single line as long as they are separated by whitespace, as needed. Statements may occur more than one to a line if they are separated by semicolons; this is the only time the terminating semicolon is really needed. A line may be continued to the next line by ending it with a backslash or by letting the parser know that the statement is not complete—for example, by ending a line with a comma.

There is no main program as such; execution proceeds in general from top to bottom. In more complex programs, there may be numerous definitions at the top, followed by the (conceptual) main program at the bottom. However, even in that case, execution proceeds from the top down because definitions in Ruby are executed.

Keywords and Identifiers

The keywords (or reserved words) in Ruby typically cannot be used for other purposes. These are as follows:

BEGIN	END	alias	and	begin
break	case	class	def	defined
do	else	elsif	end	ensure
false	for	if	in	module

next	nil	not	or	redo
rescue	retry	return	self	super
then	true	undef	unless	until
when	while	yield		

Variables and other identifiers normally start with an alphabetic letter or a special modifier. The basic rules are as follows:

- Local variables (and pseudo-variables such as `self` and `nil`) begin with a lowercase letter.
- Global variables begin with a dollar sign ($).
- Instance variables (within an object) begin with an "at" sign (@).
- Class variables (within a class) begin with two "at" signs (@@).
- Constants begin with capital letters.

For purposes of forming identifiers, the underscore (_) may be used as a lowercase letter. Special variables starting with a dollar sign (such as $1 and $/) are not dealt with here.

The following list provides some examples:

- Local variables: `alpha`, `_ident`, `some_var`
- Pseudo-variables: `self`, `nil`, `__FILE__`
- Constants: `K6chip`, `Length`, `LENGTH`
- Instance variables: `@foobar`, `@thx1138`, `@NOT_CONST`
- Class variable: `@@phydeaux`, `@@my_var`, `@@NOT_CONST`
- Global variables: `$beta`, `$B12vitamin`, `$NOT_CONST`

Comments and Embedded Documentation

Comments in Ruby begin with a pound sign (#) outside of a string or character constant and proceed to the end of the line:

```
x = y + 5 # This is a comment.
# This is another comment.
print "# But this isn't."
```

Embedded documentation is intended to be retrieved from the program text by an external tool such as RDTOOL. From the point of view of the interpreter, it is like a comment and can be used as such. Given two lines starting with =begin and =end, everything between those lines (inclusive) is ignored by the interpreter:

```
=begin
The purpose of this program
is to cure cancer
and instigate world peace.
=end
```

Constants, Variables, and Types

In Ruby, variables do not have types, but the data they contain still has types. The simplest data types are numeric, character, and string.

Some numeric constants are shown in the following list:

- Integer: 237
- Integer (with sign): -123
- Integer (with underscore spacing): 1_048_576
- Octal integer: 0377
- Hexadecimal integer: 0xBEEF
- Floating point: 3.14159
- Floating point (scientific notation): 6.02e23

Character constants in Ruby actually evaluate to integers according to the ASCII code and are therefore interchangeable with the corresponding integer constants. Here are some character constants:

- Lowercase x (120): ?x
- Newline: ?\n
- Backslash: ?\\
- Ctrl+D: ?\cd
- Ctrl+X: ?\C-x
- Meta+X (x ORed with 0x80): ?\M-x
- Meta+Ctrl+X: ?\M-\C-x

Note that all these forms (and some others) can also be embedded in strings, as you'll see shortly.

Ruby has a wealth of notations available for representing strings; different ones may be convenient in different situations. Most commonly, a string constant in Ruby is enclosed between double quotes, as in C.

It is possible to embed "escaped" character constants in a Ruby string in order to express control characters and the like:

```
"This is a single line.\n"
"Here are three tabs\t\t\tand then more text."
"A backslash (\\) must be doubled."
```

It is also possible to embed variables or even expressions inside these strings. The pound sign (#) is used to signal that this is being done; typically the variable or expression is enclosed in braces, but they may be omitted if the expression consists of a single variable beginning with $ or @. Here are examples:

```
"The tax rate is #{taxrate}."
"Hello, #@yourname; my name is #{myname}."
"The sum is #{a+b+c}."
"#$num1 times #$num2 equals #{$num1*$num2}."
```

A single-quoted string in Ruby is the same except that no expression substitution is performed and no backslash processing is done, except \\ and \'. Single-quoted strings are useful when the strings are to be used more "as is," without the special interpretations. Here are examples:

```
'The notation #{alpha} will not be expanded.'
'We can embed the \\ (backslash) character'
'or the \' (single quote) character.'
```

For cases where the strings contain punctuation that would normally have to be escaped, there is a more general form of quote. The percent sign (%) introduces a string delimited according to rules determined by the character following the percent sign. Basically this character may be a lowercase *q*, an uppercase *Q*, a brace or parenthesis, or some other character. In the first two cases, there is still a delimiter character following the letter. We'll discuss each case briefly.

A %q string is a generalized single-quoted string; as such, there is no expression substitution and minimal backslash processing. The delimiter may be any character, including newline. If an opening brace or parenthesis is used, the corresponding closing brace or parenthesis closes the string; otherwise, the same character opens and closes the string. Here are examples:

```
%q(The notation #{alpha} will not be expanded.)
%q{We can embed \\ and \} in this string.}
%q/These characters are not special: " ' # () {}/
```

A %Q string is a generalized double-quoted string, meaning that substitution and backslash processing both occur as they normally would. The delimiters behave as with the %q string. Here are examples:

```
%Q(We can embed tabs \t\t and newlines and so on.)
%Q/Here, these characters are not special: () " '/
%Q("Hello, #{name}," I said to her.)
%Q(He said, "She said, 'Hello.'")
```

The q or Q may be left out entirely so that the delimiter immediately follows the percent sign. This delimiter obviously may not be q or Q but also may not be r, w, or x, for reasons you'll see shortly. In this case, the string once again acts like a double-quoted string. Here are examples:

```
%(The variable alpha = #{alpha}.)
%/Tab \t  Carriage return \r  Newline \n/
%{Using a brace makes substitution hard: #\{beta\}}
%<Less-than greater-than will also work.>
%[As will square brackets.]
```

Note once again that the closing delimiter is the same as the opening delimiter for most characters, but a "paired character" used as a delimiter requires the opposite paired character to close the string. The paired characters are parentheses, brackets, braces, and the so-called "angle brackets": (), [], {}, and <>, respectively. Note, however, that the grave accent (`) and single quote (') are *not* paired characters as some might think.

A special kind of string is worth mentioning here that's primarily useful in small scripts used to glue together larger programs. The command output string will be sent to the operating system as a command to be executed, whereupon the output of the command is substituted back into the string. The simple form of this string uses the grave accent (sometimes called a *back tick* or *back quote*) as a beginning and ending delimiter; the more complex form uses the %x notation:

```
`whoami`
`ls -l`
%x[grep -i meta *.html | wc -l]
```

Regular expressions in Ruby look similar to character strings, but they are used differently. Many operations in Ruby make sense with regular expressions but not with strings.

For those familiar with Perl, regular expression handling is similar in Ruby. Incidentally, we'll use the abbreviation *regex* throughout the remainder of the book; many abbreviate it as *regexp*, but that is not as pronounceable.

The typical regex is delimited by a pair of slashes; the %r form can also be used. Here are some simple regular expressions:

- /Ruby/   Matches the single word *Ruby*
- /[Rr]uby/   Matches *Ruby* or *ruby*
- /^abc/   Matches an instances of *abc* at the beginning of a line
- %r(xyz$)   Matches an instance of *xyz* at the end of a line
- %r|[0-9]*| Matches any sequence of (zero or more) digits

It is also possible to place a modifier, consisting of a single letter, immediately after a regex. The modifiers are as follows:

- i   Ignores case in regex
- o   Performs expression substitution only once
- m   Multiline mode (dot matches newline)
- x   Extended regex (allows whitespace and comments)

To complete our introduction to regular expressions, here's a list of the most common symbols and notations available:

- ^   Beginning of a line or string
- $ End of a line or string
- .   Any character except newline (unless POSIX)
- \w   Word character (digit, letter, or underscore)
- \W   Non-word character
- \s   Whitespace character (space, tab, newline, and so on)
- \S   Non-whitespace character
- \d   Digit (same as [0-9])
- \D   Non-digit
- \A   Beginning of a string
- \Z   End of a string or before newline at the end
- \z   End of a string
- \b   Word boundary (outside [ ] only)
- \B   Non-word boundary
- \b   Backspace (inside [ ] only)
- [ ]   Any single character of set
- *   Zero or more of the previous subexpression
- *?   Zero or more of the previous subexpression (non-greedy)
- +   One or more of the previous subexpression
- +?   One or more of the previous subexpression (non-greedy)
- {m,n} M to n instances of the previous subexpression
- {m,n}? M to n instances of the previous subexpression (non-greedy)

- ? Zero or one instance of the previous regular expression
- | Alternatives
- ( ) Grouping of subexpressions
- (?#) Comment

An understanding of regex handling is a powerful tool for the modern programmer. A complete discussion is far beyond the scope of this book. Instead, we refer you to the definitive work *Mastering Regular Expressions* by Jeffrey Friedl.

An *array* in Ruby is a very powerful construct; it may contain data of any type or even mixed types. As you'll see in a later section, all arrays are instances of the class Array and therefore have a rich set of methods that can operate on them. An array constant is delimited by brackets. The following are all valid array expressions:

```
[1, 2, 3]
[1, 2, "buckle my shoe"]
[1, 2, [3,4], 5]
["alpha", "beta", "gamma", "delta"]
```

The second example shows an array containing both integers and strings, the third example shows a nested array, and the fourth shows an array of strings. As in most languages, arrays are "zero indexed;" for instance, in the last array, "gamma" is element number 2. Arrays are dynamic and do not need to have a size specified when they are created.

Because the array of strings is so common (and so inconvenient to type), a special syntax has been set aside for it, similar to what you have seen before:

```
%w[alpha beta gamma delta]
%w(Jan Feb Mar Apr May Jun Jul Aug Sep Oct Nov Dec)
%w/am is are was were be being been/
```

In these examples, the quotes and commas are not needed; only whitespace separates the individual elements. In the case of an element that contains whitespace, of course, this would not work.

An array variable can use brackets to index into the array. The resulting expression can be both examined and assigned to:

```
val = myarray[0]
print stats[j]
x[i] = x[i+1]
```

Another extremely powerful construct in Ruby is the *hash*, which is also commonly called an *associative array* or *dictionary*. A hash is a set of associations between paired pieces of data; it is typically used as a lookup table or a kind of generalized array in which the index need not be an integer. Each hash is an instance of the class Hash.

A hash constant is typically represented between delimiting braces, with the symbol => separating the individual keys and values. The key can be thought of as an index where the corresponding value is stored. There is no restriction on the types of the keys or the corresponding values. Here are some hashes:

```
{1=>1, 2=>4, 3=>9, 4=>16, 5=>25, 6=>36}
{"cat"=>"cats", "ox"=>"oxen", "bacterium"=>"bacteria"}
{"hydrogen"=>1, "helium"=>2, "carbon"=>12}
{"odds"=>[1,3,5,7], "evens"=>[2,4,6,8]}
{"foo"=>123, [4,5,6]=>"my array", "867-5309"=>"Jenny"}
```

A hash variable can have its contents accessed by essentially the same bracket notation that arrays use:

```
print phone_numbers["Jenny"]
plurals["octopus"] = "octopi"
```

It should be stressed, however, that both arrays and hashes have many methods associated with them; these methods give them their real usefulness. The next section, covering Ruby OOP, will expand on this a little more.

Operators and Precedence

Now that we have established our most common data types, let's look at Ruby's operators. They are arranged here in order from highest to lowest precedence:

- Scope   ::
- Indexing   []
- Exponentiation   **
- Unary positive/negative, etc.   +   -   !   ~
- Multiplication, etc.   *   /   %
- Addition/subtraction   +   -
- Logical shifts, etc.   <<   >>
- Bitwise and   &
- Bitwise or, xor | ^
- Comparison   >   >=   <   <=
- Equality, etc.   ==   ===   <=>   !=   =~   !~
- Boolean and   &&
- Boolean or ||
- Range operators   ..   ...

- Assignment   = (also +=, -=, *=, etc.)
- Ternary decision   ?:
- Boolean negation   not
- Boolean and, or   and   or

Some of these operators serve more than one purpose; for example, the operator << is a bitwise left shift but is also an append operator (for arrays, strings, and so on) and a marker for a here-document. Likewise, the plus sign (+) is for addition and for string concatenation. As you'll see later, many of these operators are just shortcuts for method names.

Now we have defined most of the data types and many of the possible operations on them. Before going any further, let's look at an actual sample program.

A Sample Program

In a tutorial, the first program is always "Hello, World!" But in a whirlwind tour like this one, let's start with something slightly more advanced. Here's a small program to convert between Fahrenheit and Celsius temperatures:

```
print "Please enter a temperature and scale (C or F): "
str = gets
exit if not str or not str[0]

str.chomp!
temp, scale = str.split(" ")
if temp !~ /-?[0-9]+/
  print temp, " is not a valid number.\n"
  exit 1
end
temp = temp.to_f

case scale
  when "C", "c"
    f = 1.8*temp + 32
  when "F", "f"
    c = (5.0/9.0)*(temp-32)
  else
    print "Must specify C or F.\n"
    exit 2
end

if c != nil then
  print "#{c} degrees C\n"
else
  print "#{f} degrees F\n"
end
```

Here are some examples of running this program. These show that the program can convert from Fahrenheit to Celsius and from Celsius to Fahrenheit and that it can handle an invalid scale or an invalid number:

```
Please enter a temperature and scale (C or F): 98.6 F
37.0 degrees C

Please enter a temperature and scale (C or F): 100 C
212.0 degrees F

Please enter a temperature and scale (C or F): 92 G
Must specify C or F.

Please enter a temperature and scale (C or F): junk F
junk is not a valid number.
```

Now, as for the mechanics of the program, we begin with a `print` statement, which is actually a call to the predefined function `print`, to write to standard output. Following this, we call `gets` (get string from standard input), assigning the value to `str`.

Note that any apparently "free-standing" function calls such as `print` and `gets` are actually methods of various predefined classes or objects. In the same way, `chomp` is a method that is called with `str` as a receiver. Method calls in Ruby generally can omit the parentheses; for example, `print "foo"` is the same as `print("foo")`.

The variable `str` holds a character string, but there is no reason it could not hold some other type instead. In Ruby, data has types but variables do not.

The special method call `exit` will terminate the program. On this same line is a control structure called an `if` *modifier*. This is like the `if` statement that exists in most languages, but backwards; it comes after the action, does not permit an `else`, and does not require closing. As for the condition, we are checking two things: Does `str` have a value, and is it non-null? In the case of an immediate end-of-file, our first condition will hold; in the case of a newline with no preceding data, the second condition will hold.

The reason these tests work is that a variable that is undefined has a `nil` value, and `nil` evaluates to false in Ruby. In fact, `nil` and `false` evaluate as false, and everything else evaluates as true. Specifically, the null string `""` does *not* evaluate as false, as it does in some other languages.

The next statement performs a `chomp!` operation on the string (to remove any trailing newline characters). The exclamation point as a prefix serves as a warning that the operation actually changes the value of its receiver rather than just returning a value. The exclamation point is used in many such instances to remind the programmer that a method has a side effect or is more "dangerous" than its unmarked counterpart. The method `chomp`, for example, will return the same result but will not modify its receiver.

The next statement is an example of multiple assignment. The `split` method splits the string into an array of values, using the space as a delimiter. The two assignable entities on the left side will be assigned the respective values resulting on the right side.

The `if` statement that follows uses a simple regex to determine whether the number is valid; if the string fails to match a pattern consisting of an optional minus sign followed by one or more digits, it is an invalid number and the program exits. Note that the `if` statement is terminated by the keyword `end`; although it's not needed here, we could have had an `else` clause before `end`. The keyword `then` is optional; this statement does not use `then`, but the one below it does. As for the output, recall that the variable `temp` could also have been embedded in the string (as below).

The `to_f` method is used to convert the string to a floating-point number. We are actually assigning this floating-point value back to `temp`, which originally held a string.

The `case` statement chooses between three alternatives: the case in which the user specifies a C, specifies an F, or uses an invalid scale. In the first two instances, a calculation is done; in the third, we print an error and exit.

Ruby's `case` statement, by the way, is far more general than the example shown here. There is no limitation on the data types, and the expressions used are all arbitrary and may even be ranges or regular expressions.

There is nothing mysterious about the computation. However, consider the fact that the variables c and f are referenced first inside the branches of the case. There are no declarations as such in Ruby; a variable comes into existence when it is assigned. This means that when we fall through the `case` statement, only one of these variables will have a value.

We use this to determine after the fact which branch was followed so that we can create a slightly different output in each instance. The comparison of c with `nil` is effectively a test of whether c has a value. We do this here only to show that it can be done; obviously two different `print` statements could be used inside the `case` statement if we wished.

You may have noticed that we've used only "local" variables here. This might be somewhat confusing, because their scope certainly appears to cover the entire program. What's happening here is that the variables are all local to the *top level* of the program (written as *toplevel* by some). The variables appear "global" because there are no lower-level contexts in a program this simple; however, if we declared classes and methods, these top-level variables would not be accessible within them.

Looping and Branching

Let's spend some time looking at control structures. We have already seen the simple `if` statement and the `if` modifier; there are also corresponding structures based on the keyword unless (which also has an optional else) as well as expression-oriented forms of if and unless. We summarize all these as follows:

```
if x < 5 then
  statement1
end

unless x >= 5 then
  statement1
end

if x < 5 then
  statement1
else
  statement2
end

unless x < 5 then
  statement2
else
  statement1
end

statement1 if y == 3

statement1 unless y != 3

x = if a>0 then b else c end

x = unless a<=0 then c else b end
```

In this summary, the if and unless forms behave exactly the same. Note that the keyword then may be omitted except in the final (expression-oriented) cases. Note also that the modifier forms cannot have an else clause.

The case statement in Ruby is more powerful than in most languages. This multiway branch can even test for conditions other than equality—for example, a matched pattern. The test done by the case statement corresponds to the relationship operator (===), which has a behavior that varies from one object to another. Let's look at an example:

```
case "This is a character string."
  when "some value"
    print "Branch 1\n"
  when "some other value"
    print "Branch 2\n"
  when /char/
    print "Branch 3\n"
  else
    print "Branch 4\n"
end
```

This code will print `Branch 3`. Why? It first tries to check for equality between the tested expression and one of the strings `"some value"` or `"some other value"`. This fails, so it proceeds. The third test is for the presence of a pattern within the tested expression; that pattern is there, so the test succeeds and the third `print` statement is performed. The `else` clause will always handle the default case in which none of the preceding tests succeeds.

If the tested expression is an integer, the compared value can be an integer range (for example, `3..8`). In this case, the expression will be tested for membership in that range. In all instances, the first successful branch will be taken.

As for looping mechanisms, Ruby has a rich set. The `while` and `until` control structures are both pretest loops, and both work as expected: One specifies a continuation condition for the loop, and the other specifies a termination condition. They also occur in "modifier" form like `if` and `unless`. There is also the `loop` method of the `Kernel` module (by default an infinite loop), and iterators (described later) are associated with various classes.

The following examples assume an array called `list`, defined something like this:

```
list = %w[alpha bravo charlie delta echo]
```

They all step through the array and write out each element:

```
# Loop 1 (while)
i=0
while i < list.size do
  print "#{list[i]} "
  i += 1
end

# Loop 2 (until)
i=0
until i == list.size do
  print "#{list[i]} "
  i += 1
end

# Loop 3 (post-test while)
i=0
begin
  print "#{list[i]} "
  i += 1
end while i < list.size

# Loop 4 (post-test until)
i=0
begin
```

```
    print "#{list[i]} "
    i += 1
end until i == list.size

# Loop 5 (for)
for x in list do
  print "#{x} "
end

# Loop 6 ('each' iterator)
list.each do |x|
  print "#{x} "
end

# Loop 7 ('loop' method)
i=0
n=list.size-1
loop do
  print "#{list[i]} "
  i += 1
  break if i > n
end

# Loop 8 ('loop' method)
i=0
n=list.size-1
loop do
  print "#{list[i]} "
  i += 1
  break unless i <= n
end

# Loop 9 ('times' iterator)
n=list.size
n.times do |i|
  print "#{list[i]} "
end

# Loop 10 ('upto' iterator)
n=list.size-1
0.upto(n) do |i|
  print "#{list[i]} "
end

# Loop 11 (for)
n=list.size-1
```

```
for i in 0..n do
  print "#{list[i]} "
end

# Loop 12 ('each_index')
list.each_index do |x|
  print "#{list[x]} "
end
```

Let's examine these in a little detail. Loops 1 and 2 are the "standard" forms of the while and until loops; they behave essentially the same, but their conditions are negations of each other. Loops 3 and 4 are the same thing in "post-test" versions; the test is performed at the end of the loop rather than at the beginning. Note that the use of begin and end in this context is strictly a kludge or hack; what is really happening is that a begin/end block (used for exception handling) is followed by a while or until modifier. For someone really wanting a post-test loop, however, this is effectively the same.

Loops 5 and 6 are arguably the "proper" ways to write this loop. Note the simplicity of these two compared with the others; there is no explicit initialization and no explicit test or increment. This is because an array "knows" its own size, and the standard iterator each (loop 6) handles such details automatically. Indeed, loop 5 is merely an indirect reference to this same iterator because the for loop will work for any object having the iterator each defined. The for loop is only shorthand for a call to each; such shorthand is frequently called *syntax sugar* because it offers a more convenient alternative to another syntactic form.

Loops 7 and 8 both make use of the loop construct; as mentioned earlier, loop looks like a keyword introducing a control structure, but it is really a method of the module Kernel, not a control structure at all.

Loops 9 and 10 take advantage of the fact that the array has a numeric index; the times iterator will execute a specified number of times, and the upto iterator will carry its parameter up to the specified value. Neither of these is truly suitable for this instance.

Loop 11 is a for loop that operates specifically on the index values, using a range, and loop 12 likewise uses the each_index iterator to run through the list of array indexes.

In the preceding examples, we have not laid enough emphasis on the "modifier" form of the while and until loops. These are frequently useful, and they have the virtue of being concise. We offer these additional examples, both of which mean the same thing:

```
perform_task() until finished
perform_task() while not finished
```

One fact is largely ignored here: Loops do not always run smoothly from beginning to end, in a predictable number of iterations, or ending in a single predictable way. We need ways to control these loops further.

The first of these is the break keyword, which you see in loops 7 and 8. This is used to "break out" of a loop; in the case of nested loops, only the innermost one is halted. This will be intuitive for C programmers.

The keyword retry is used in two contexts: in the context of an iterator and in the context of a begin/end block (exception handling). Within the body of any iterator (or for loop) it will force the iterator to restart, reevaluating any arguments passed to the iterator. Note that it will not work for loops in general (while and until).

The redo keyword is the generalized form of retry for loops. It works for while and until loops just as retry works for iterators.

The next keyword will effectively jump to the end of the innermost loop and resume execution from that point. It works for any loop or iterator.

The iterator is an important concept in Ruby, as you have already seen. What you have not seen is that the language allows user-defined iterators in addition to the predefined ones.

The default iterator for any object is called each. This is significant because it allows the for loop to be used. However, iterators may be given different names and used for varying purposes.

As a crude example, consider this multipurpose iterator, which mimics a post-test loop (like C's do-while or Pascal's repeat-until):

```
def repeat(condition)
  yield
  retry if not condition
end
```

In this example, the keyword yield is used to call the block that is specified when the iterator is called in this way:

```
j=0
repeat (j<10) do { j+=1; print j,"\n"}
```

It is also possible to pass parameters via yield, which will be substituted into the block's parameter list (between vertical bars). As a somewhat contrived example, the following iterator does nothing but generate integers from 1 to 10, and the call of the iterator generates the first 10 cubes:

```
def my_sequence
  for i in 1..10 do
    yield i
  end
```

```
end

my_sequence {|x| print x**3, "\n"}
```

Note that do and end may be substituted for the braces that delimit a block. There are differences, but they are fairly subtle.

Exceptions

Like many other modern programming languages, Ruby supports *exceptions*. An exception is a means of handling errors that has significant advantages over older methods. Return codes are avoidable, as is the "spaghetti logic" that results from checking them. Also, the code that detects the error can be distinguished from the code that knows how to handle the error (because these are often separate anyway).

The raise statement will raise an exception. Note that raise is not a reserved word but rather a method of the module Kernel. (Its alias is named fail.) Here are examples:

```
raise                                    # Example 1
raise "Some error message."              # Example 2
raise ArgumentError                      # Example 3
raise ArgumentError, "Invalid data."     # Example 4
raise ArgumentError.new("Invalid data.") # Example 5
raise ArgumentError, "Invalid data.", caller[0] # Example 6
```

In example 1, the last exception encountered is re-raised. In example 2, a RuntimeError (the default error) is created using the message "Some error message." In example 3, an ArgumentError is raised; in example 4, this same error is raised with the message "Invalid data." Example 5 behaves exactly the same as example 4. Finally, example 6 adds traceback information of the form "filename:line" or "filename:line:in `method'" (as stored in the array returned by the caller method or stored in the $a special variable).

Now, how do we handle exceptions in Ruby? The begin-end block is used for this purpose. The simplest form is a begin-end block with nothing but our code inside:

```
begin  # No real purpose.
  # ...
end
```

This, however, is of no value in catching errors. The block, however, may have one or more rescue clauses in it. If an error occurs at any point in the code, between begin and rescue, control will be passed immediately to the appropriate rescue clause. Here's an example:

```
begin
  x = Math.sqrt(y/z)
  # ...
```

```
rescue ArgumentError
  print "Error taking square root.\n"
rescue ZeroDivisionError
  print "Attempted division by zero.\n"
end
```

Essentially the same thing can be accomplished by this fragment:

```
begin
  x = Math.sqrt(y/z)
  # ...
rescue => err
  print err, "\n"
end
```

Here, the variable err is used to store the value of the exception; printing it causes it to be translated to some meaningful character string. Note that because the error type is not specified, the rescue clause will catch every kind of error. The notation rescue => variable can be used with or without an error type before the => symbol.

In the event that error types are specified, it may be that an exception does not match any of these types. For that situation, we are allowed to use an else clause after all the rescue clauses:

```
begin
  # Error-prone code...
rescue Type1
  # ...
rescue Type2
  # ...
else
  # Other exceptions...
end
```

In many cases, we will want to do some kind of recovery. In that event, the keyword retry (within the body of a rescue clause) will restart the begin block and try those operations again:

```
begin
  # Error-prone code...
rescue
  # Attempt recovery...
  retry
end
```

Finally, it is sometimes necessary to write code that "cleans up" after a begin-end block. In the event this is necessary, an ensure clause can be specified:

```
begin
  # Error-prone code...
rescue
  # Handle exceptions
ensure
  # This code is always executed
end
```

The code in an ensure clause is always executed before the begin-end block exits. This happens regardless of whether an exception occurred.

There are two other ways in which exceptions may be caught. First of all, there is a modifier form of the rescue clause:

```
x = a/b  rescue print "Division by zero!\n"
```

In addition, the body of a method definition is an implicit begin-end block; the begin is omitted, and the entire body of the method is subject to exception handling, ending with the end of the method:

```
def some_method
    # Code...
rescue
    # Recovery...
end
```

This sums up the discussion of exception handling as well as the discussion of fundamental syntax and semantics.

Numerous aspects of Ruby have not been discussed here. The next two sections are devoted to the more advanced features of the language, and the final section is mostly a collection of Ruby lore that will help the intermediate programmer learn to "think in Ruby."

OOP in Ruby

Ruby has all the elements more generally associated with OOP languages, such as objects with encapsulation and data hiding, methods with polymorphism and overriding, and classes with hierarchy and inheritance. It goes farther and adds limited metaclass features, singleton methods, modules, and mixins.

Similar concepts are known by other names in other OOP languages, but concepts of the same name may have subtle differences from one language to another. This section elaborates on the Ruby understanding and usage of these elements of OOP.

Objects

In Ruby, all numbers, strings, arrays, regular expressions, and many other entities are actually objects. Work is done by executing the methods belonging to the object:

```
3.succ                    # 4
"abc".upcase              # "ABC"
[2,1,5,3,4].sort          # [1,2,3,4,5]
someObject.someMethod     # some result
```

In Ruby, *every* object is an instance of some class; the class contains the implementation of the methods. The object's class is essentially its type:

```
"abc".type     # String
"abc".class    # String
```

In addition to encapsulating its own attributes and operations, an object in Ruby has an identity.

```
"abc".id     #  53744407
```

Built-in Classes

More than 30 built-in classes are predefined in the Ruby class hierarchy. Like many other OOP languages, Ruby does not allow multiple inheritance, but that does not necessarily make it any less powerful. Modern object-oriented languages frequently follow the single-inheritance model. Ruby does support modules and mixins, which are discussed in the next section. It also implements object IDs, which support the implementation of persistent, distributed, and relocatable objects.

To create an object from an existing class, the new method is typically used:

```
myFile = File.new("textfile.txt","w")
myString = String.new("this is a string object")
```

This is not always explicitly required, however, as shown here:

```
yourString = "this is also a string object"
aNumber = 5
```

Variables are used to hold references to objects. As previously mentioned, variables themselves have no type, nor are they objects themselves; they are simply references to objects. Here's an example:

```
x = "abc"
```

An exception to this is that small immutable objects of some built-in classes, such as Fixnum, are copied directly into the variables that refer to them. (These objects are no bigger than pointers, and it is more efficient to deal with them in this way.) In this case, the assignment makes a copy of the object, and the heap (memory allocation area) is not used.

Variable assignment causes object references to be shared:

```
y = "abc"
x = y
x               # "abc"
```

After x = y is executed, variables x and y both refer to the same object:

```
x.id       # 53732208
y.id       # 53732208
```

If the object is mutable, a modification done to one variable will be reflected in the other one:

```
x.gsub!(/a/,"x")
y                     # "xbc"
```

Reassigning one of these variables has no effect on the other, however:

```
x = "abc"
y                     # still has value "xbc"
```

A mutable object can be made immutable using the `freeze` method:

```
x.freeze
x.gsub!(/b/,"y")   # error
```

A symbol in Ruby refers to a variable by ID rather than by reference. When we say :x, we are saying basically the same as x.id (which you saw previously). A colon applied to an identifier results in a symbol; if the identifier does not already exist, it is created. Among other uses, a symbol may be used when we want to *mention* an identifier as opposed to *using* it (the classical use/mention distinction); for example, the special method method_missing, called when a method is not found, gets passed a symbol corresponding to the unknown method. Any Symbol object has a method called id2name that returns a string corresponding to the identifier name. Here are examples:

```
Hearts    = :Hearts   # This is one way of assigning
Clubs     = :Clubs    #    unique values to constants,
Diamonds  = :Diamonds #    somewhat like an enumeration
Spades    = :Spades   #    in Pascal or C.

print Hearts.id2name  # Prints "Hearts"
```

Modules and Mixins

Many built-in methods are available from class ancestors. Of special note are the Kernel methods mixed in to the Object superclass; because Object is universally available, the methods that are added to it from Kernel are also universally available. These methods form a very important part of Ruby.

The terms *module* and *mixin* are nearly synonymous. A module is a collection of methods and constants that is external to the Ruby program. It can be used simply for namespace management, but the most common use of a module is to have its features "mixed" in to a class (by using `include`). In this case, it is used as a mixin. (This term, apparently borrowed from Python, is sometimes written as *mix-in*, but we write it as a single word.)

An example of using a module for namespace management is the frequent use of the `Math` module. To make use of the definition of pi, for example, it is not necessary to include the `Math` module; you can simply use `Math::PI` as the constant.

A mixin provides a way of getting some of the benefits of multiple inheritance without dealing with all the difficulties. It can be considered a restricted form of multiple inheritance, but the language creator Matz has called it "single inheritance with implementation sharing."

Note that `include` appends features of a namespace (a module) to the current space. The `extend` method appends functions of a module to an object. With `include`, the module's methods become available as instance methods; with `extend`, they become available as class methods.

We should mention that `load` and `require` do not really relate to modules but rather to non-module Ruby sources and binaries (statically or dynamically loadable). A `load` operation essentially reads a file and inserts it at the current point in the source file so that its definitions become available at that point. A `require` operation is similar to a `load`, but it will not load a file if it has already been loaded.

Creating Classes

Ruby has numerous built-in classes, and additional classes may be defined in a Ruby program. To define a new class, the following construct is used:

```ruby
class ClassName
  # ...
end
```

The name of the class is itself a global constant and therefore must begin with an uppercase letter. The class definition can contain class constants, class variables, class methods, instance variables, and instance methods. Class data is available to all objects of the class, whereas instance data is only available to the one object. Here's an example:

```ruby
class Friend
  @@myname = "Fred"              # a class variable

  def initialize(name, sex, phone)
    @name, @sex, @phone = name, sex, phone
    # These are instance variables
  end
```

```
  def hello                       # an instance method
    print "Hi, I'm #{@name}.\n"
  end
  def Friend.our_common_friend  # a class method
    print "We are all friends of #{@@myname}.\n"
  end
end
f1 = Friend.new("Susan","F","555-0123")
f2 = Friend.new("Tom","M","555-4567")
f1.hello                    # Hi, I'm Susan.
f2.hello                    # Hi, I'm Tom.
Friend.our_common_friend    # We are all friends of Fred.
```

Because class-level data is accessible throughout the class, it can be initialized at the time the class is defined. If a method named `initialize` is defined, it is guaranteed to be executed right after an instance is allocated. The `initialize` method is similar to the traditional concept of a constructor, but it does not have to handle memory allocation. Allocation is handled internally by `new`, and deallocation is handled transparently by the garbage collector.

Now consider this fragment, paying attention to the `getmyvar`, `setmyvar`, and `myvar=` methods:

```
class MyClass

  NAME = "Class Name"  # class constant

  def initialize        # called when object is allocated
    @@count += 1
    @myvar = 10
  end

  def MyClass.getcount # class method
    @@count            # class variable
  end

  def getcount          # instance returns class variable!
    @@count             # class variable
  end

  def getmyvar          # instance method
    @myvar              # instance variable
  end

  def setmyvar(val)     # instance method sets @myvar
    @myvar = val
  end
```

```
      def myvar=(val)        # Another way to set @myvar
        @myvar = val
      end
   end

   foo = MyClass.new        # @myvar is 10
   foo.setmyvar 20          # @myvar is 20
   foo.myvar = 30           # @myvar is 30
```

Here, you see that `getmyvar` returns the value of `@myvar`, and `setmyvar` sets it. (In the terminology of many programmers, these would be referred to as a *getter* and a *setter*, respectively.) These work fine, but they do not exemplify the Ruby way of doing things. The method `myvar=` looks like assignment overloading (although strictly speaking, it isn't); it is a better replacement for `setmyvar`, but there is a better way yet.

The class `Module` contains methods called `attr`, `attr_accessor`, `attr_reader`, and `attr_writer`. These can be used (with symbols as parameters) to automatically handle controlled access to the instance data. For example, the three methods named previously can be replaced by a single line in the class definition:

```
attr_accessor :myvar
```

This will create the method `myvar`, which returns the value of `@myvar`, and the method `myvar=`, which enables the setting of the same variable. Methods `attr_reader` and `attr_writer` create read-only and write-only versions of an attribute, respectively. For more details, consult a Ruby reference.

Within the instance methods of a class, the pseudo-variable `self` can be used as needed. This is only a reference to the current receiver, the object on which the instance method is invoked.

The modifying methods `private`, `protected`, and `public` can be used to control the visibility of methods in a class. (Instance variables are always private and inaccessible from outside the class except by means of accessors.) Each of these modifiers takes a symbol such as `:foo` as a parameter; if this is omitted, the modifier applies to all subsequent definitions in the class. Here's an example:

```
class MyClass
   def method1
     # ...
   end
   def method2
     # ...
   end
   def method3
     # ...
   end
```

```
    private :method1
    public  :method2
    protected :method3
    private

    def my_method
      # ...
    end
    def another_method
      # ...
    end
  end
```

In this example, `method1` will be private, `method2` will be public, and `method3` will be protected. Because of the `private` method with no parameters, both `my_method` and `another_method` will be private.

The `public` access level is self-explanatory; there are no restrictions on access or visibility. The `private` level means that the method is accessible only within the class or its subclasses, and it is callable only in "function form," with `self` (implicit or explicit) as a receiver. The `protected` level means that a method is callable only from within its class, but unlike a private method, it can be called with a receiver other than `self`, such as another instance of the same class.

The default visibility for the methods defined in a class is `public`. The exception is the instance-initializing method `initialize`, which is private because it is intended to be called only from the `new` method. Methods defined at the top level are also public by default; if they are private, they can be called only in function form (as, for example, the methods defined in `Object`).

Ruby classes are themselves objects, being instances of the metaclass `Class`. Ruby classes are always concrete; there are no abstract classes. However, it is theoretically possible to implement abstract classes in Ruby if you really wish to do so.

The class `Object` is at the root of the hierarchy. It provides all the methods defined in the built-in `Kernel` module.

To create a class that inherits from another class, define it in this way:

```
class MyClass < OtherClass
  # ...
end
```

In addition to using built-in methods, it is only natural to define your own and also to redefine and override existing ones. When you define a method with the same name as an existing one, the previous method is overridden. If a method needs to call the "parent" method that it overrides (a frequent occurrence), the keyword `super` can be used for this purpose.

Operator overloading is not strictly an OOP feature, but it is very familiar to C++ programmers and certain others. Because most operators in Ruby are simply methods anyway, it should come as no surprise that these operators can be overridden or defined for user-defined classes. Overriding the meaning of an operator for an existing class may be rare, but it is common to want to define operators for new classes.

It is possible to create aliases or synonyms for methods. The syntax (used inside a class definition) is as follows:

```
alias newname oldname
```

The number of parameters will be the same as for the old name, and it will be called in the same way.

Methods and Attributes

In a previous section, methods were used with simple class instances and variables by separating the receivers from the methods with a period (*receiver.method*). In the case of method names that are punctuation, the period is omitted. Methods can take arguments:

```
Time.mktime( 2000, "Aug", 24, 16, 0 )
```

Because method calls return objects, method calls may typically be chained or stacked:

```
3.succ.to_s
    /(x.z).*?(x.z).*?/.match("x1z_1a3_x2z_1b3_").to_a[1..3]
    3+2.succ
```

Note that problems can arise if the cumulative expression is of a type that does not support that particular method. Specifically, some methods return `nil` under certain conditions, and this will usually cause any methods tacked onto that result to fail.

Certain methods may have blocks passed to them. This is true of all iterators, whether built in or user defined. A block is usually passed as a do-end block or a brace-delimited block; it is not treated like the other parameters preceding it, if any. See especially the `File.open` example:

```
my_array.each do |x|
  some_action
end

File.open(filename) { |f| some_action }
```

Named parameters will be supported in the future but are not supported at the time of this writing. These are called *keyword arguments* in the Python realm.

Methods may take a variable number of arguments:

```
receiver.method(arg1, *more_args)
```

In this case, the method called will treat `more_args` as an array that it deals with as it would any other array. In fact, an asterisk in the list of formal parameters (on the last or only parameter) can likewise "collapse" a sequence of actual parameters into an array:

```
def mymethod(a, b, *c)
  print a, b
  c.each do |x| print x end
end

mymethod(1,2,3,4,5,6,7)    # a=1, b=2, c=[3,4,5,6,7]
```

Ruby has the ability to define methods on a per-object basis (rather than per class). Such methods are called *singletons*; they belong solely to that object and have no effect on its class or superclasses. As an example, this might be useful in programming a GUI; you can define a button action for a widget by defining a singleton method for the button object.

It is theoretically possible to create a prototype-based object system using singleton methods. This is a less traditional form of OOP without classes. The basic structuring mechanism is to construct a new object using an existing object as a delegate; the new object is exactly like old except for the items that are overridden. This enables you to build prototype/delegation-based systems rather than inheritance based. Although we do not have experience in this area, we do feel that this demonstrates the power of Ruby.

Dynamic Aspects of Ruby

Ruby is a very dynamic language in the sense that objects and classes may be altered at runtime. It has the ability to construct and evaluate pieces of code in the course of executing the existing statically coded program. It has a sophisticated reflection API that makes it very "self-aware"; this enables the easy creation of debuggers, IDEs, and similar tools, and it also makes certain advanced coding techniques possible.

This is perhaps the most difficult area a programmer will encounter in learning Ruby. Here, we briefly examine some of the implications of Ruby's dynamic nature.

Coding at Runtime

We have already mentioned `load` and `require` earlier. However, it is important to realize that these are not built-in statements or control structures or anything of that nature; they are actual methods. Therefore, it is possible to call them with variables or expressions as parameters or to call them conditionally. Contrast with this the `#include` directive in C and C++, which is evaluated and acted on at compile-time.

Ruby also enables the program to get access to the names of its own variables. Here's a variable called foobar assigned the value 3; following that assignment, the print method prints out not only the value but the name of the variable:

```
foobar = 3
print "The value is ", foobar, "\n"
print "The variable name is ", :foobar.id2name, "\n"
```

Of course, this contrived example is not truly useful; the point is that the user's code can retrieve and manipulate internal names at will. Similar but much more sophisticated operations can be done with the reflection API, as you'll see in the next section.

Code can be constructed piecemeal and evaluated. As another contrived example, consider this calculate method and the code calling it:

```
def calculate(op1, operator, op2)
  string = op1.to_s + operator + op2.to_s
  # operator is assumed to be a string; make one big
  # string of it and the two operands
  eval(string)   # Evaluate and return a value
end

$alpha = 25
$beta = 12
puts calculate(2, "+", 2)            # Prints 4
puts calculate(5, "*", "$alpha")     # Prints 125
puts calculate("$beta", "**", 3)     # Prints 1728
```

As an even more extreme example, the following code will prompt the user for a method name and a single line of code; then it will actually define the method and call it:

```
puts "Method name: "
meth_name = gets.chomp
puts "Line of code: "
line = gets.chomp

# Build a string
string = %[def #{meth_name}\n #{line}\n end]
eval(string)         # Define the method
eval(meth_name)      # Call the method
```

Frequently, programmers wish to code for different platforms or circumstance and still maintain only a single code base. In such a case, a C programmer would use #ifdef directives; in Ruby, however, definitions are executed. There is no "compile time," and everything is dynamic rather than static. Therefore, if we want to make some kind of decision like this, we can simply evaluate a flag at runtime:

```
if platform == Windows
  action1
elsif platform == Linux
  action2
else
  default_action
end
```

Of course, there is a small runtime penalty for coding in this way, because the flag may be tested many times in the course of execution. However, the next example does essentially the same thing, enclosing the platform-dependent code in a method whose name is the same across all platforms:

```
if platform == Windows
  def my_action
    action1
  end
elsif platform == Linux
  def my_action
    action2
  end
else
  def my_action
    default_action
  end
end
```

In this way, the same result is achieved, but the flag is only evaluated *once*. When the user's code calls my_action, it will already have been defined appropriately.

Reflection

Languages such as Smalltalk, LISP, and Java implement the notion of a *reflective* programming language—one in which the active environment can query the objects that define it as well as extend or modify them at runtime.

Ruby allows reflection quite extensively but does not go as far as Smalltalk, which even represents control structures as objects. Ruby control structures and blocks are *not* objects (a Proc object can be used to "objectify" a block, but control structures are never objects).

The keyword defined (with an appended question mark) may be used to determine whether an identifier name is in use, as shown here:

```
if defined? some_var
  print "some_var = #{some_var}\n"
else
  print "The variable some_var is not known.\n"
end
```

In most if not all cases, this is equivalent to comparing the variable to `nil`.

In a similar way, the method `respond_to?` determines whether an object can respond to the specified method call (that is, whether that method is defined for that object). The `respond_to?` method is defined in class `Object`.

Ruby supports runtime type information in a radical way. The type (or class) of an object can be determined at runtime using the method `type` (defined in `Object`). Similarly, `is_a?` will tell whether an object is of a certain class (including the superclasses), and `kind_of?` is the alias. Here's an example:

```
print "abc".type          # Prints String
print 345.type            # Prints Fixnum
rover = Dog.new
print rover.type          # Prints Dog
if rover.is_a? Dog
  print "Of course he is.\n"
end
if rover.kind_of? Dog
  print "Yes, still a dog.\n"
end
if rover.is_a? Animal
  print "Yes, he's an animal, too.\n"
end
```

It is possible to retrieve an exhaustive list of all the methods that can be invoked for a given object; this is done by using the `methods` method, defined in `Object`. There are also variations such as `private_instance_methods`, `public_instance_methods`, and so on.

In a similar way, you can determine the class variables and instance variables associated with an object. By the very nature of OOP, the lists of methods and variables include the entities defined not only in the object's class but in its superclasses. The `Module` class has a method called `constants` that's used to list all the constants defined.

The class `Module` has a method `ancestors` that will return a list of modules that are included in the given module. This list is self-inclusive; `Mod.ancestors` will always have at least `Mod` in the list. The class `Object` has a method called `superclass` that returns the superclass of the object or returns `nil`. Because `Object` itself is the only object without a superclass, it is the only case in which `nil` will be returned.

The `ObjectSpace` module is used to access any and all "living" objects. The method `_idtoref` can be used to convert an object ID to an object reference; it can be considered the inverse of the colon notation. `ObjectSpace` also has an iterator called `each_object` that will iterate over all the objects currently in existence, including many that you will not otherwise explicitly know about. (Remember that certain small immutable objects, such as objects of class `Fixnum`, `NilClass`, `TrueClass`, and `FalseClass` are not kept on the stack for optimization reasons.)

Missing Methods

When a method is invoked (myobject.mymethod), Ruby first searches for the named method according to this search order:

1. Singleton methods in the receiver myobject.
2. Methods defined in myobject's class.
3. Methods defined among myobject's ancestors.

If the method mymethod is not found, Ruby searches for a default method called method_miss-ing. If this method is defined, it is passed the name of the missing method (as a symbol) and all the parameters that were passed to the nonexistent mymethod.

Garbage Collection

Managing memory on a low level is hard and error prone, especially in a dynamic environment such as Ruby. Having a garbage-collection facility is a very significant advantage. In languages such as C++, memory allocation and deallocation are handled by the programmer; in more recent languages such as Java, memory is reclaimed (when objects go out of scope) by a garbage collector.

Memory management done by the programmer is the source of two of the most common kinds of bugs. If an object is freed while still being referenced, a later access may find the memory in an inconsistent state. These so-called "dangling pointers" are difficult to track down because they often cause errors in code that is far removed from the offending statement. A related bug is a "memory leak," caused when an object is not freed even though there are no references to it. Programs with this bug typically use up more and more memory until they crash; this kind of error is also difficult to find. Ruby uses a GC facility that tracks down unused objects and reclaims the storage that was allocated to them. For those who care about such things, Ruby's GC is done using a "mark and sweep" algorithm rather than reference counting (which frequently has difficulties with recursive structures).

Certain performance penalties may be associated with garbage collection. There are some limited controls in the GC module so that the programmer can tailor garbage collection to the needs of the individual program.

Training Your Intuition: Things to Remember

It may truly be said that "everything is intuitive once you understand it." This verity is the heart of this section, because Ruby has many features and personality quirks that may be different from what the traditional programmer is used to.

Some readers may feel their time is wasted by a reiteration of some of these points; if that is the case for you, you are free to skip the paragraphs that seem obvious to you. Programmers' backgrounds vary widely; an old-time C hacker and a Smalltalk guru will each approach Ruby from different viewpoints. We hope, however, that a perusal of these following paragraphs will assist many readers in following what some call the Ruby Way.

Syntax Issues

The Ruby parser is very complex and relatively forgiving. It tries to make sense out of what it finds, rather than forcing the programmer into slavishly following a set of rules. However, this behavior may take some getting used to. Here's a list of things you should know about Ruby syntax:

- Parentheses are usually optional with a method call. These calls are all valid:

```
foobar
foobar()
foobar(a,b,c)
foobar a, b, c
```

- Given that parentheses are optional, what does x y z mean, if anything? As it turns out, this means, "Invoke method y, passing z as a parameter, and then pass the result as a parameter to method x." In short, the statement x(y(z)) means the same thing.

- Let's try to pass a hash to a method: my_method {a=>1, b=>2}

  This results in a syntax error, because the left brace is seen as the start of a block. In this instance, parentheses are necessary: my_method({a=>1, b=>2})

- Now let's suppose that the hash is the *only* parameter to a method. Ruby very forgivingly lets us omit the braces: my_method(a=>1, b=>2)

  Some people might think that this looks like a method invocation with named parameters, which it emphatically is not.

- Now consider this method call:

```
foobar.345
```

  Looking at it, one might think that foobar is an object and 345 is a method being invoked, but obviously a method name can't start with a digit! The parser interprets this as a call to method foobar, passing the number 0.345 as a parameter. Here, you see that the parentheses and the intervening space have all been omitted. Needless to say, the fact that you can code this way does not imply that you should.

- There are other cases in which blank spaces are somewhat significant. For example, these expressions may all seem to mean the same:

```
x = y + z
x = y+z
```

```
x = y+ z
x = y +z
```

In fact, the first three do mean the same. However, in the fourth case, the parser thinks that y is a method call and +z is a parameter passed to it! It will then give an error message for that line if there is no method named y. The moral is to use blank spaces in a reasonable way.

- Similarly, x = y*z is a multiplication of y and z, whereas x = y *z is an invocation of method y, passing an expansion of array z as a parameter.

- In constructing identifiers, the underscore is considered to be lowercase. Therefore, an identifier may start with an underscore, but it will *not* be a constant even if the next letter is uppercase.

- In linear, nested if statements, the keyword elsif is used rather than else if or elif, as in some languages.

- Keywords in Ruby are not really "reserved words." In many circumstances, a keyword can actually be used as an identifier as long as the parser is not confused. We won't attempt to state the conditions under which this may and may not be done; we mention this only to say that it can often be done if you really need to do it—and as a warning to those who might be confused by this. In general, using a keyword as an identifier should be done with caution, keeping readability in mind.

- The keyword then is optional (in if and case statements). Those who wish to use it for readability may do so. The same is true for do in while and until loops.

- The question mark and exclamation point are not really part of the identifier that they modify but should be considered as suffixes. Therefore, although chop and chop!, for example, are considered different identifiers, it is not permissible to use these characters in any other position in the word. Likewise, we use defined? in Ruby, but defined is the keyword.

- Inside a string, the pound sign (#) is used to signal expressions to be evaluated. That means that in some circumstances, when a pound sign occurs in a string, it has to be escaped with a backslash, but this is *only* when the next character is a left brace ({), a dollar sign ($), or an "at" sign (@).

- The ternary decision operator (?:), which originated in the C language, has sometimes been said to be "undocumented" in Ruby. For this reason, programmers may wish not to use it (though we personally do not shy away from it).

- Because of the fact that the question mark may be appended to an identifier, care should be taken with spacing around the ternary operator. For example, suppose we have the variable my_flag, which stores either true or false. Then the first line of code shown here will be correct, but the second will give a syntax error:

```
x = my_flag ? 23 : 45    # OK
x = my_flag? 23 : 45     # Syntax error
```

- The ending marker =end for embedded documentation should not be considered a token. It marks the entire line; therefore, any characters on the rest of that line are not considered part of the program text but belong to the embedded document.

- There are no arbitrary blocks in Ruby; that is, you can't start a block whenever you feel like it, as in C. Blocks are allowed only where they are needed (for example, attached to an iterator). That is why any post-test loops in Ruby are kludged by using a begin-end pair even though no exception handling is being done.

- Remember that the keywords BEGIN and END are completely different from the begin and end keywords.

- When strings bump together (static concatenation), the concatenation is of a higher precedence than a method call. Here's an example:

```
# These three all give the same result.
str1 = "First " 'second'.center(20)
str2 = ("First " + 'second').center(20)
str3 = "First second".center(20)
```

Precedence is different.

- Ruby has several pseudo-variables that look like local variables but really serve specialized purposes. These are self, nil, true, false, __FILE__, and __LINE__.

Perspectives in Programming

Presumably everyone who knows Ruby (at this point in time) has been a student or user of other languages in the past. This of course makes learning Ruby easy, in the sense that numerous features in Ruby are just like the corresponding features in other languages. On the other hand, the programmer may be lulled into a false sense of security by some of the familiar constructs in Ruby and may draw unwarranted conclusions based on past experience—which we might term *geek baggage*.

Many people are coming to Ruby from Smalltalk, Perl, C/C++, and various other languages. Their presuppositions and expectations may all vary somewhat, but they will always be present. For this reason, here are a few of the things that some programmers may "trip over" in using Ruby:

- A character in Ruby truly is an integer. It is not a type of its own, as in Pascal, and is not the same as a string of length 1. Consider the following code fragment:

```
x = "Hello"
y = ?A
print "x[0] = #{x[0]}\n"  # Prints: x[0] = 72
```

```
print "y = #y\n"        # Prints: y = 65
if y == "A"             # Prints: no
  print "yes\n"
else
  print "no\n"
end
```

- There is no Boolean type such as many languages have. `TrueClass` and `FalseClass` are distinct classes, and their only instantiations are `true` and `false`.

  Many of Ruby's operators are similar or identical to those in C. Two notable exceptions are the increment and decrement operators (++ and --). These are not available in Ruby, either in "pre" or "post" forms.

- The modulus operator is known to work somewhat differently in different languages with respect to negative numbers. The two sides of this argument are beyond the scope of this book; suffice to say that Ruby's behavior is as follows:

```
print  5 % 3   # Prints 2
print -5 % 3   # Prints 1
print  5 % -3  # Prints -1
print -5 % -3  # Prints -2
```

- Some may be used to thinking that a false value may be represented as a zero, a null string, a null character, or various other things. However, in Ruby, all of these are true; in fact, *everything* is true except `false` and `nil`.

- Always recall that in Ruby, variables don't have types; only values have types.

- To say that a value is undefined (for example, a variable not declared) is essentially the same as saying that it is `nil`. Such a value will pass a test for equality with `nil` and will evaluate to `false` if used by itself in a condition. The principle exception relates to hashes; because `nil` is a valid value to be stored in a hash, it is not appropriate to compare against `nil` to find whether a value exists in a hash. (There are several correct ways to perform this test by means of method calls.)

- Recall that a post-test loop can be faked in Ruby by using a `begin-end` construct followed by the "modifier" form of `while` or `until`.

- Recall that there are no declarations of variables in Ruby. It is good practice, however, to assign `nil` to a variable initially. This certainly does not assign a type to the variable and does not truly initialize it, but it does inform the parser that this is a variable name rather than a method name. Ruby interprets an identifier as a method name unless it has seen a previous assignment indicating that the name refers to a variable.

- Recall that `ARGV[0]` is truly the first of the command-line parameters, numbering naturally from zero; it is not the file or script name preceding the parameters, such as `argv[0]` in C.

- Most of Ruby's operators are really methods; the "punctuation" form of these methods is provided for familiarity and convenience. The first exception is the set of reflexive assignment operators (+=, -=, *=, and so on); the second exception is the following set:

  ```
  =  ..  ...  !  not  &&  and  ||  or  !=  !~
  ```

- Like most (though not all) modern languages, Boolean operations are always short-circuited; that is, the evaluation of a Boolean expression stops as soon as its truth value is known. In a sequence of or operations, the first true will stop evaluation; in a string of and operations, the first false will stop evaluation.

- Recall that the prefix @@ is used for class variables (which are associated with the class rather than the instance).

- Recall that loop is not a keyword; it is a Kernel method, not a control structure.

- Some may find the syntax of unless-else to be slightly unintuitive. Because unless is the opposite of if, the else clause will be executed if the condition is *false*.

- Ordinarily a parameter passed to a method is really a reference to an object; as such, the parameter can potentially be changed from within the method.

- The simpler Fixnum type is passed as an immediate value and therefore may not be changed from within methods. The same is true for true, false, and nil.

- Do not confuse the && and || operators with the & and | operators. These are used as in C; the former are for Boolean operations, and the latter are for arithmetic or bitwise operations.

- There are interesting differences between the &&-|| operators and the and-or operators. The former are more general purpose and may result in an expression other than true or false. The latter always result in true or false; they are specifically for joining Boolean expressions in conditions (and therefore are susceptible to syntax errors if an operand does not evaluate to true or false). See the following code fragment:

  ```
  print (false || "string1\n")      # Prints string1
  # print (false or "string2\n")    #   Syntax error!
  print (true && "string3\n")       # Prints string3
  # print (true and "string4\n")    #   Syntax error!
  print (true || "string5\n")       # Prints true
  # print (true or "string6\n")     #   Syntax error!
  print (false && "string5\n")      # Prints false
  # print (false or "string6\n")    #   Syntax error!
  ```

- The and-or operators also have lower precedence than the &&-|| operators. See the following code fragment:

  ```
  a = true
  b = false
  c = true
  ```

```
d = true
a1 = a && b or c && d    # &&'s are done first
a2 = a && (b or c) && d  # or is done first
print a1                 # Prints false
print a2                 # Prints true
```

- Additionally, be aware that the assignment operator has a *higher* precedence than the and and or operators! (This is also true for the reflexive assignment operators +=, -=, and the others.) For example, line 3 of the following code looks like a normal assignment statement, but it is really a free-standing expression (equivalent to line 5, in fact). Line 7 is a real assignment statement, which may be what the programmer really intends:

```
y = false
z = true
x = y or z      # Line 3: = is done BEFORE or!
print x, "\n"   # Prints false
(x = y) or z    # Line 5: Same as line 3
print x, "\n"   # Prints false
x = (y or z)    # Line 7: or is done first
print x, "\n"   # Prints true
```

- Don't confuse object attributes and local variables. If you are accustomed to C++ or Java, you might forget this. The variable @my_var is an instance variable (or attribute) in the context of whatever class you are coding; but my_var, used in the same circumstance, is only a local variable within that context.

- Many languages have some kind of for loop, as does Ruby. The question sooner or later arises as to whether the index variable can be modified. Some languages do not allow the control variable to be modified at all (printing a warning or error either at compile time or runtime); and some will cheerfully allow the loop behavior to be altered in midstream by such a change. Ruby takes yet a third approach. When a variable is used as a for loop control variable, it is an ordinary variable and can be modified at will; however, such a modification does not affect the loop behavior! The for loop sequentially assigns the values to the variable on each iteration without regard for what may have happened to that variable inside the loop. For example, this loop will execute exactly 10 times and print the values 1 through 10:

```
for var in 1..10
  print "var = #{var}\n"
  if var > 5
    var = var + 2
  end
end
```

- Recall that variable names and method names are not always distinguishable "by eye" in the immediate context. How does the parser decide whether an identifier is a variable or a method? The rule is that if the parser sees the identifier being assigned a value prior to its being used, it will be considered a variable; otherwise, it is considered to be a method name.

- The `while` and `until` modifiers are *not* post-test loops. These two loops will not execute:

```
puts "looping" while false
puts "still looping" until true
```

Ruby's case Statement

Every modern language has some kind of multiway branch, such as the `switch` statement in C/C++ and Java or the `case` statement in Pascal. These serve basically the same purpose, and they function much the same in most languages.

Ruby's case statement is superficially similar to these others, but on closer examination it is so unique that it makes C and Pascal look like close friends. The `case` statement in Ruby has no precise analogue in any other language that we (the authors) are familiar with, and this makes it worth additional attention here.

You have already seen the syntax of this statement. We will concentrate here on its actual semantics:

- To begin with, consider the trivial `case` statement shown here. The expression shown is compared with the value, not surprisingly, and if they correspond, `some_action` is performed:

```
case expression
  when value
    some_action
end
```

But what do we mean by "compare" and "correspond"? As it turns out, Ruby uses the special operator === (sometimes called the *relationship operator*) for this. This operator is also referred to (somewhat inappropriately) as the *case equality operator*.

Therefore, the preceding simple statement is equivalent to this statement:

```
if value === expression
  some_action
end
```

However, do not confuse the relationship operator with the equality operator (==). They are utterly different, although their behavior may be the same in many circumstances. The relationship operator is defined differently for different classes, and for a given class, it may behave differently for different operand types passed to it.

- Also, do not fall into the trap of thinking that the tested expression is the receiver and the value is passed as a parameter to it. The opposite is true.

- This brings up the fact that x `===` y is *not* typically the same as y `===` x! There will be situations in which this is true, but overall the relationship operator is not commutative. (That is why we do not favor the term *case equality operator*, because equality is always commutative.) In other words, reversing our original example, this code does not behave the same way:

```
case value
  when expression
    some_action
end
```

- As an example, consider the string str and the pattern (regular expression) pat, which matches that string. The expression str `=~` pat is true, just as in Perl. Because Ruby defines the opposite meaning for `=~` in Regexp, one can also say that pat `=~` str is true. Following this logic further, we find that (because of how `Regexp::===` is defined) pat `===` str is also true. However, note that str `===` pat is *not* true. This means that the code fragment

```
case "Hello"
  when /Hell/
    print "We matched.\n"
  else
    print "We didn't match.\n"
end
```

does not do the same thing as this fragment:

```
case /Hell/
  when "Hello"
    print "We matched.\n"
  else
    print "We didn't match.\n"
end
```

If this confuses you, just memorize the behavior. If it does not confuse you, so much the better.

- Programmers accustomed to C may be puzzled by the absence of break statements in the case statement; such a usage of break in Ruby is unnecessary (and illegal). This is due to the fact that "falling through" is very rarely the desired behavior in a multiway branch. There is an implicit jump from each when clause (or *case limb*, as it is sometimes called) to the end of the case statement. In this respect, Ruby's case statement resembles the one in Pascal.

- The values in each case limb are essentially arbitrary. They are not limited to any certain type. They need not be constants but can be variables or complex expressions. Ranges or multiple values can be associated with each case limb.
- Case limbs may have empty actions (null statements) associated with them. The values in the limbs need not be unique but may overlap. Look at this example:

```
case x
  when 0
  when 1..5
    print "Second branch\n"
  when 5..10
    print "Third branch\n"
  else
    print "Fourth branch\n"
end
```

Here, a value of 0 for x will do nothing, and a value of 5 will print Second branch, even though 5 is also included in the next limb.

- The fact that case limbs may overlap is a consequence of the fact that they are evaluated in sequence *and* that short-circuiting is done. In other words, if evaluation of the expressions in one limb results in success, then the limbs that follow are never evaluated. Therefore, it is a bad idea for case limb expressions to have method calls that have side effects. (Of course, such calls are questionable in most circumstances anyhow.) Also, be aware that this behavior may mask runtime errors that would occur if expressions were evaluated. Here's an example:

```
case x
  when 1..10
    print "First branch\n"
  when foobar()            # Possible side effects?
    print "Second branch\n"
  when 5/0                 # Dividing by zero!
    print "Third branch\n"
  else
    print "Fourth branch\n"
end
```

As long as x is between 1 and 10, foobar() will not be called, and the expression 5/0 (which would naturally result in a runtime error) will not be evaluated.

Rubyisms and Idioms

Much of this material will overlap conceptually with the preceding pages. Don't worry too much about why we divided it as we did; many of these tidbits are hard to classify or organize. Our most important motivation is simply to break the information into digestible chunks.

Ruby was designed to be consistent and orthogonal. However, it is also a very complex entity. Therefore, like every language, it has its own set of idioms and quirks. We discuss some of these here:

- Remember that `alias` can be used to give alternate names for global variables and methods. Remember that the numbered global variables $1, $2, $3, and so on cannot be aliased.

- We do not recommend the use of the "special variables," such as $=, $_, $/, and the rest. Although they can sometimes make code more compact, they rarely make it any clearer; we use them very sparingly in this book and recommend the same practice. In many cases, the names can be clarified by using the `English.rb` library; in other cases, a more explicit coding style makes them unnecessary.

- Do not confuse the `..` and `...` range operators. The former is *inclusive* of the upper bound, and the latter is *exclusive*. For example, `5..10` includes the number `10`, but `5...10` does not.

- There is a small detail relating to ranges that may cause slight confusion. Given the range `m..n`, the method `end` will return the endpoint of the range; its alias, `last`, will do the same thing. However, these methods will return the same value, n, for the range `m...n`, even though n is not included in the latter range. The method `end_excluded?` is provided to distinguish between these two situations.

- Do not confuse ranges with arrays. These two assignments are entirely different:

  ```
  x = 1..5
  x = [1, 2, 3, 4, 5]
  ```

  However, there is a convenient method, `to_a`, for converting ranges to arrays. (Many other types also have such a method.)

- Keep a clear distinction in your mind between *class* and *instance*. For example, a class variable such as `@@foobar` has a class-wide scope, but an instance variable such as `@foobar` has a separate existence in each object of the class.

- Similarly, a class method is associated with the class in which it is defined; it does not belong to any specific object and cannot be invoked as though it did. A class method is invoked with the name of a class, and an instance method is invoked with the name of an object.

- In writing about Ruby, the "pound notation" is sometimes used to indicate an instance method—for example, we use `File.chmod` to denote the class method `chmod` of class `File`, and we use `File#chmod` to denote the instance method that has the same name. This notation is not part of Ruby syntax, but only Ruby folklore. We have tried to avoid it in this book.

- In Ruby, constants are not truly *constant*. They cannot be changed from within instance methods, but otherwise their values *can* be changed.

- In writing about Ruby, the word *toplevel* is common as both an adjective and a noun. We prefer to use *top level* as a noun and *top-level* as an adjective, but our meaning is the same as everyone else's.

- The keyword `yield` comes from CLU and may be misleading to some programmers. It is used within an iterator to invoke the block with which the iterator is called. It does not mean "yield," as in producing a result or returning a value, but is more like the concept of "yielding a timeslice."

- Remember that the reflexive assignment operators +=, -=, and the rest are not methods (nor are they really operators); they are only "syntax sugar" or "shorthand" for their longer forms. Therefore, to say x += y is really identical to saying x = x + y, and if the + operator is overloaded, the += operator is defined "automagically" as a result of this predefined shorthand.

- Because of the way the reflexive assignment operators are defined, they cannot be used to initialize variables. If the first reference to x is x += 1, an error will result. This will be intuitive to most programmers, unless they are accustomed to a language where variables are initialized to some sort of zero or null value.

- It is actually possible in some sense to get around this behavior. One can define operators for `nil` such that the initial `nil` value of the variable produces the desired result. Here is a method (`nil.+`) that will allow += to initialize a `String` or a `Fixnum` value, basically just returning `other` and thus ensuring that `nil + other` is equal to `other`:

  ```
  def nil.+(other)
    other
  end
  ```

  This illustrates the power of Ruby, but whether it is useful or appropriate to code this way is left as an exercise for the reader.

- It is wise to recall that `Class` is an *object* and that `Object` is a *class*. We will try to make this clear in a later chapter; for now, simply recite it every day as a mantra.

- Some operators can't be overloaded because they are built in to the language rather than implemented as methods. These operators are as follows:

  ```
  =    ..    ...    and    or    not    &&    ||    !    !=    !~
  ```

  Additionally, the reflexive assignment operators (+=, -=, and so on) cannot be overloaded. These are not methods, and it can be argued they are not true operators either.

- Be aware that although assignment is not overloadable, it is still possible to write an instance method with a name such as `foo=` (thus allowing statements such as x.foo = 5). Consider the equal sign to be like a suffix.

- Recall that a "bare" scope operator has an implied `Object` before it, so that `::Foo` means `Object::Foo`.

- Recall that `fail` is an alias for `raise`.

- Recall that definitions in Ruby are executed. Because of the dynamic nature of the language, it's possible, for example, to define two methods completely differently based on a flag that is tested at runtime.

- Remember that the `for` construct (`for x in a`) is really calling the default iterator `each`. Any class having this iterator can be walked through with a `for` loop.

- Recall that the term *iterator* is sometimes a misnomer. Any method that invokes a block passed as a parameter is an iterator. Some of the predefined ones do not really look like looping mechanisms at all (see `File.open`).

- Be aware that a method defined at the top level is a member of `Object`.

- A setter method (such as `foo=`) must be called with a receiver; otherwise, it will look like a simple assignment to a local variable of that name.

- Recall that `retry` can be used in iterators but not in general loops. In iterators, it causes the reassignment of all the parameters and the restarting of the current iteration.

- The keyword `retry` is also used in exception handling. Don't confuse the two usages.

- An object's `initialize` method is always private.

- Where an iterator ends in a left brace (or in `end`) and results in a value, that value can be used as the receiver for further method calls. Here's an example:

  ```
  squares = [1,2,3,4,5].collect do |x| x**2 end.reverse
  # squares is now [25,16,9,4,1]
  ```

- The idiom `if $0 == __FILE__` is sometimes seen near the bottom of a Ruby program. This is a check to see whether the file is being run as a standalone piece of code (`true`) or is being used as some kind of auxiliary piece of code such as a library (`false`). A common use of this is to put a sort of "main program" (usually with test code in it) at the end of a library.

- Recall that normal subclassing or inheritance is done with the < symbol:

  ```
  class Dog < Animal
     # ...
  end
  ```

  However, creation of a singleton class (an anonymous class that extends a single instance) is done with the << symbol:

  ```
  class << platypus
     # ...
  end
  ```

- When a block is passed to an iterator, the difference between braces ({ }) and a do-end pair is a matter of precedence, as shown here:

```
mymethod param1, foobar do ... end
# Here, do-end binds with mymethod
mymethod param1, foobar { ... }
# Here, {} binds with foobar, assumed to be a method
```

- It is somewhat traditional in Ruby to put single-line blocks in braces and multiline blocks in do-end pairs. Here are examples:

```
my_array.each {|x| print x, "\n"}

my_array.each do |x|
  print x
  if x % 2 == 0
    print " is even\n"
  else
    print " is odd\n"
  end
end
```

This habit is not required, and there may conceivably be occasions where it is inappropriate to follow this rule.

- Bear in mind that strings are in a sense two-dimensional; they can be viewed as sequences of characters or sequences of lines. Some may find it surprising that the default iterator each operates on lines (where a *line* is a group of characters terminated by a record separator that defaults to newline); an alias for each is each_line. If you want to iterate by characters, you can use each_byte. The iterator sort also works on a line-by-line basis. There is no iterator called each_index because of the ambiguity involved—do we want to handle the string by character or by line? This all becomes habitual with repeated use.

- A closure remembers the context in which it was created. One way to create a closure is by using a Proc object. As a crude example, consider the following:

```
def power(exponent)
  proc {|base| base**exponent}
end

square = power(2)
cube   = power(3)

a = square(11)     # Result is 121
b = square(5)      # Result is  25
c = cube(6)        # Result is 216
d = cube(8)        # Result is 512
```

Observe that the closure "knows" the value of exponent that it was given at the time it was created.

- However, let's assume that a closure uses a variable defined in an outer scope (which is perfectly legal). This property can be useful, but here we show a misuse of it:

```
$exponent = 0

def power
  proc {|base| base**$exponent}
end

$exponent = 2
square = power
$exponent = 3
cube    = power

a = square.call(11)    # Wrong! Result is 1331
b = square.call(5)     # Wrong! Result is  125
# The above two results are wrong because the CURRENT value
# of $exponent is being used, since it is still in scope.
c = cube.call(6)       # Result is 216
d = cube.call(8)       # Result is 512
```

- Finally, consider this somewhat contrived example. Inside the block of the `times` iterator, a new context is started, so that x is a local variable. The variable `closure` is already defined at the top level, so it will not be defined as local to the block:

```
closure = nil    # Define closure so the name will be known
1.times {        # Start a new context
  x = 5          # x is local to this block
  closure = Proc.new {
    print "In closure, x = #{x}\n"
  }
}

x = 1            # Define x at top level

closure.call     # Prints: In closure, x = 5
```

Now note that the variable x that is set to 1 is a new variable, defined at the top level. It is not the same as the other variable of the same name. The closure therefore prints 5 because it remembers its creation context, with the previous variable x and its previous value.

- Variables starting with a single @, defined inside a class, are generally instance variables. However, if they are defined outside of any method, they are really *class instance* variables. (This usage is somewhat contrary to most OOP terminology, in which a class instance is regarded to be the same as an instance or an object.) Here's an example:

```
class Myclass
  @x = 1        # A class instance variable
  @y = 2        # Another one

  def mymethod
    @x = 3      # An instance variable
    # Note that @y is not accessible here.
  end

end
```

The preceding class instance variable `@y` is really an attribute of the class object `Myclass`, which is an instance of the class `Class`. (Remember, `Class` is an object and `Object` is a class.) Class instance variables cannot be referenced from within instance methods and, in general, are not very useful.

- Remember that `attr`, `attr_reader`, `attr_writer`, and `attr_accessor` are shorthand for the actions of defining setters and getters; they take symbols as arguments.

- Remember that there is never any assignment with the scope operator; for example, the assignment `Math::PI = 3.2` is illegal.

- Note that closures have to return values implicitly (by returning the value of the last expression evaluated). The `return` statement can be used only in actual method returns.

- A closure is associated with a block at the time it is created. Therefore, it is never useful to associate a block with the `call` method; this will result in a warning.

- To recognize an identifier as a variable, Ruby only has to *see* an assignment to it; the assignment does not have to be executed. This can lead to a seeming paradox, as shown here:

```
name = "Fred" if ! defined? name
```

Here, the assignment to `name` is seen, so that the variable is defined. Because it is defined (and the test is false), it is never assigned, and it will be `nil` after this statement is executed.

- Some of the "bang" methods (with names ending in an exclamation point) behave in a slightly confusing way. Normally they return `self` as a return value, but some of them return `nil` in certain circumstances (to indicate that no work was actually done). In particular, this means that these cannot always be chained safely. Here's an example:

```
str = "defghi"
str.gsub!(/def/,"xyz").upcase!
#   str is now "XYZGHI"

str.gsub!(/abc/,"klm").downcase!
# Error (since nil has no downcase! method)
```

Other such methods are `sort!` and `sub!` (although `sort!` may change soon).

Expression Orientation and Other Miscellaneous Issues

In Ruby, expressions are nearly as significant as statements. If you are a C programmer, this will be of some familiarity to you; if your background is in Pascal, it may seem utterly foreign. However, Ruby carries expression orientation even further than C.

In addition, we use this section to remind you of few little issues regarding regular expressions. Consider them to be tiny bonuses:

- In Ruby, any kind of assignment returns the same value that was assigned. Therefore, we can sometimes take little shortcuts, as shown here:

```
x = y = z = 0    # All are now zero.
a = b = c = []   # Danger! a, b, and c now all refer
                 #   to the SAME empty array.

x = 5
y = x += 2       # Now x and y are both 7
```

  Be very careful when you are dealing with objects! Remember that these are nearly always *references* to objects.

- Many control structures, such as if, unless, and case, return values. The code shown here is all valid; it demonstrates that the branches of a decision need not be statements but can simply be expressions:

```
a = 5
x = if a < 8 then 6 else 7 end  # x is now 6
y = if a < 8                    # y is 6 also; the
      6                         # if-statement can be
    else                        # on a single line
      7                         # or on multiple lines.
    end
# unless also works; z will be assigned 4
z = unless x == y then 3 else 4 end
t = case a                      # t gets assigned
      when 0..3                 # the value
        "low"                   # "medium"
      when 4..6
        "medium"
      else
        "high"
    end
```

- Note, however, that the while and until loops do *not* return usable values. For example, this fragment is not valid:

```
i  = 0
x = while (i < 5)        # Error!
      print "#{i}\n"
    end
```

- Note that the ternary decision operator can be used with statements or expressions. For syntactic reasons, the parentheses here are necessary:

```
x = 6
y = x == 5 ? 0 : 1                          # y is now 1
x == 5 ? print("Hi\n") : print("Bye\n") # Prints Bye
```

- The `return` at the end of a method can be omitted. A method will always return the last expression evaluated in its body, regardless of where that happens.

- When an iterator is called with a block, the last expression evaluated in the block will be returned as the value of the block. Therefore, if the body of an iterator has a statement such as x = `yield`, that value can be captured.

- When necessary, we can use parentheses to convert a statement into an expression, as shown here:

```
a = [1, 2, 3 if x==0]      # Illegal syntax
a = [1, 2, (3 if x==0)]    # Valid syntax

mymeth(a, b, if x>5 then c else d end)    # Illegal
mymeth(a, b, (if x>5 then c else d end)) # Valid
```

- For regular expressions, recall that the multiline modifier /m can be appended to a regex, in which case a dot (.) will match a newline character.

- For regular expressions, beware of zero-length matches. If all elements of a regex are optional, then "nothingness" will match that pattern, and a match will always be found at the very beginning of a string. This is a common error for regex users, particularly novices.

Simple Data Tasks

IN THIS CHAPTER

Theory attracts practice as the magnet attracts iron.
—Karl Friedrich Gauss

One measure of the sophistication of a programming language is: What kinds of data will it directly support? The earliest computers were programmed strictly in machine language with purely numeric data. Soon after, the concept of character data and strings of characters was invented, which was crucial to the development of general-purpose languages.

As time goes by, we find ourselves dealing with data of increasing complexity. Modern languages frequently include support for many kinds of data. Note that we don't say types here because the usual notion of a type might be somewhat different. For example, a regular expression might be stored essentially in the form of a character string, but we don't really consider them to be strings because of their special uses.

We could easily add things like arrays and hashes to this list because these are, for Ruby, fairly low-level entities. In fact, there are some incidental uses of these in this chapter. But arrays and hashes (and more complex data structures) deserve a chapter of their own.

This chapter, then, is devoted to four of the most common kinds of data in Ruby. These are strings, regular expressions, numbers, and times and dates.

A *string*, as in other languages, is simply a sequence of characters. Similar to most entities in Ruby, strings are first-class objects.

Regular expressions form a very condensed notation for describing patterns within text. These have been around for decades and have become even more commonly used in the last 10 years.

Numbers need little explanation; they comprise both integers and floating-point numbers. In Ruby, integers can be of class Fixnum or Bignum, depending on their magnitude.

Times and dates are problematic in any language. Ruby strives to sort through the confusion with an object-oriented interface to the traditional time and date routines.

The alert reader might notice that we don't include the Range class in this discussion. This isn't because ranges aren't useful, but because they aren't that complex; that class is far less rich and interesting than the others covered here. But ranges are certainly covered in incidental code throughout the entire book.

Let's look at some sample code now. We'll begin with strings.

Strings

Atoms were once thought to be fundamental, elementary building blocks of nature; protons were then thought to be fundamental, then quarks. Now we say the string is fundamental.

—David Gross, professor of theoretical physics, Princeton University

We offer an anecdote here. In the early 1980s, a computer science professor started out his data structures class with a single question. He didn't introduce himself or state the name of the course; he didn't hand out a syllabus or give the name of the textbook. He walked to the front of the class and asked, "What is the most important data type?"

There were one or two guesses. Someone guessed, "Pointers." He brightened, but said no, that wasn't it. Then he offered his opinion: The most important data type was *character data*.

He had a valid point. Computers are supposed to be our servants, not our masters, and character data has the distinction of being human readable. (Some humans can read binary data easily, but we will ignore them.) The existence of characters (and thus strings) enables communication between humans and computers. Every kind of information we can imagine, including natural language text, can be encoded in character strings.

What do we find ourselves wanting to do with strings? We want to concatenate them, tokenize them, analyze them, perform searches and substitutions, and more. Ruby makes most of these tasks easy.

Performing Specialized String Comparisons

Ruby has built-in ideas about comparing strings; comparisons are done lexicographically as we have come to expect (that is, based on character set order). But if we want, we can introduce rules of our own for string comparisons, and these can be of arbitrary complexity.

As an example, suppose that we want to ignore the English articles *a*, *an*, and *the* at the front of a string, and we also want to ignore most common punctuation marks. We can do this by overriding the built-in method <=>, which is called for <, <=, >, and >= (see Listing 2.1).

LISTING 2.1 Specialized String Comparisons

```
class String

   alias old_compare <=>

   def <=>(other)
     a = self.dup
```

LISTING 2.1   Continued

```
    b = other.dup
    # Remove punctuation
    a.gsub!(/[\,\.\?\!\:\;]/, "")
    b.gsub!(/[\,\.\?\!\:\;]/, "")
    # Remove initial articles
    a.gsub!(/^(a |an |the )/i, "")
    b.gsub!(/^(a |an |the )/i, "")
    # Remove leading/trailing whitespace
    a.strip!
    b.strip!
    # Use the old <=>
    a.old_compare(b)
  end

end


title1 = "Calling All Cars"
title2 = "The Call of the Wild"

# Ordinarily this would print "yes"

if title1 < title2
  puts "yes"
else
  puts "no"          # But now it prints "no"
end
```

Note that we save the old <=> with an alias and then call it at the end. This is because if we tried to use the < method, it would call the new <=> rather than the old one, resulting in infinite recursion and a program crash.

Note also that the == operator doesn't call the <=> method (mixed in from comparable). This means that if we need to check equality in some specialized way, we will have to override the == method separately. But in this case, == works as we want it to anyhow.

Tokenizing a String

The split method will parse a string and return an array of tokens. It accepts two parameters, a delimiter, and a field limit, which is an integer.

The delimiter defaults to whitespace. Actually, it uses $; or the English equivalent $FIELD_SEPARATOR. If the delimiter is a string, the explicit value of that string is used as a token separator.

```
s1 = "It was a dark and stormy night."
words = s1.split              # ["It", "was", "a", "dark", "and",
                              #  "stormy", "night"]
s2 = "apples, pears, and peaches"
list = s2.split(", ")        # ["apples", "pears", "and peaches"]

s3 = "lions and tigers and bears"
zoo = s3.split(/ and /)  # ["lions", "tigers", "bears"]
```

The limit parameter places an upper limit on the number of fields returned, according to these rules:

1. If it is omitted, trailing null entries are suppressed.

2. If it is a positive number, the number of entries will be limited to that number (stuffing the rest of the string into the last field as needed). Trailing null entries are retained.

3. If it is a negative number, there is no limit to the number of fields, and trailing null entries are retained.

These three rules are illustrated here:

```
str = "alpha,beta,gamma,,"
list1 = str.split(",")     # ["alpha","beta","gamma"]
list2 = str.split(",",2)   # ["alpha", "beta,gamma,,"]
list3 = str.split(",",4)   # ["alpha", "beta", "gamma", ","]
list4 = str.split(",",8)   # ["alpha", "beta", "gamma", "", ""]
list5 = str.split(",",-1)  # ["alpha", "beta", "gamma", "", ""]
```

Formatting a String

String formatting is done in Ruby as it is in C—with the sprintf method. It takes a string and a list of expressions as parameters and returns a string. The format string contains essentially the same set of specifiers that are available with C's sprintf (or printf).

```
name = "Bob"
age = 28
str = sprintf("Hi, %s... I see you're %d years old.", name, age)
```

You might ask why we would use this instead of simply interpolating values into a string using the #{expr} notation. The answer is that sprintf makes it possible to do extra formatting such as specifying a maximum width, specifying a maximum number of decimal places, adding or suppressing leading zeroes, left-justifying, right-justifying, and more.

```
str = sprintf("%-20s  %3d", name, age)
```

The `String` class has a method `%`, which will do much the same thing. It takes a single value or an array of values of any type.

```
str = "%-20s  %3d" % [name, age]  # Same as previous example
```

We also have the methods `ljust`, `rjust`, and `center`; these take a length for the destination string and pad with spaces as needed.

```
str = "Moby-Dick"
s1 = str.ljust(13)            # "Moby-Dick    "
s2 = str.center(13)           # "  Moby-Dick  "
s3 = str.rjust(13)            # "    Moby-Dick"
```

For more information, see any reference.

Controlling Uppercase and Lowercase

Ruby's `String` class offers a rich set of methods for controlling case. We offer an overview of them here.

The `downcase` method will convert a string to all lowercase. Likewise `upcase` will convert it to all uppercase.

```
s1 = "Boston Tea Party"
s2 = s1.downcase              # "boston tea party"
s3 = s2.upcase               # "BOSTON TEA PARTY"
```

The `capitalize` method will capitalize the first character of a string while forcing all the remaining characters to be lowercase.

```
s4 = s1.capitalize           # "Boston tea party"
s5 = s2.capitalize           # "Boston tea party"
s6 = s3.capitalize           # "Boston tea party"
```

The `swapcase` method will exchange the case of each letter in a string.

```
s7 = "THIS IS AN ex-parrot."
s8 = s7.swapcase             # "this is an EX-PARROT."
```

Each of these has its in-place equivalent (`upcase!`, `downcase!`, `capitalize!`, `swapcase!`).

There are no built-in methods for detecting case, but this is easy to do with regular expressions.

```
if string =~ /[a-z]/
  puts "string contains lowercase charcters"
end

if string =~ /[A-Z]/
```

```
    puts "string contains uppercase charcters"
end

if string =~ /[A-Z]/ and string =~ /a-z/
  puts "string contains mixed case"
end

if string[0..0] =~ /[A-Z]/
  puts "string starts with a capital letter"
end
```

Note that all these methods ignore locale.

Accessing and Assigning Substrings

In Ruby, substrings can be accessed in several different ways. Normally the bracket notation is used, as for an array; but the brackets can contain a pair of Fixnums, a range, a regex, or a string. Each case is discussed in turn.

If a pair of Fixnum values is specified, they are treated as an offset and a length, and the corresponding substring is returned:

```
str = "Humpty Dumpty"
sub1 = str[7,4]          # "Dump"
sub2 = str[7,99]         # "Dumpty" (overrunning is OK)
sub3 = str[10,-4]        # nil (length is negative)
```

It is important to remember that these are an offset and a length (number of characters), not beginning and ending offsets.

A negative index counts backward from the end of the string. In this case, the index is one-based, not zero-based. The length is still added in the forward direction.

```
str1 = "Alice"
sub1 = str1[-3,3]    # "ice"
str2 = "Through the Looking-Glass"
sub3 = str2[-13,4]   # "Look"
```

A range can be specified. In this case, the range is taken as a range of indices into the string. Ranges can have negative numbers, but the numerically lower number must still be first in the range. If the range is backward or if the initial value is outside the string, nil is returned.

```
str = "Winston Churchill"
sub1 = str[8..13]    # "Church"
sub2 = str[-4..-1]   # "hill"
sub3 = str[-1..-4]   # nil
sub4 = str[25..30]   # nil
```

If a regular expression is specified, the string matching that pattern will be returned. If there is no match, `nil` will be returned.

```ruby
str = "Alistair Cooke"
sub1 = str[/l..t/]    # "list"
sub2 = str[/s.*r/]    # "stair"
sub3 = str[/foo/]     # nil
```

If a string is specified, that string will be returned if it appears as a substring (or `nil` if it doesn't).

```ruby
str = "theater"
sub1 = str["heat"]  # "heat"
sub2 = str["eat"]   # "eat"
sub3 = str["ate"]   # "ate"
sub4 = str["beat"]  # nil
sub5 = str["cheat"] # nil
```

Finally, in the trivial case, a single `Fixnum` as index will yield an ASCII code (or `nil` if out of range).

```ruby
str = "Aaron Burr"
ch1 = str[0]      # 65
ch1 = str[1]      # 97
ch3 = str[99]     # nil
```

It is important to realize that the notations we have described here will serve for assigning values as well as for accessing them.

```ruby
str1 = "Humpty Dumpty"
str1[7,4] = "Moriar"      # "Humpty Moriarty"

str2 = "Alice"
str2[-3,3] = "exandra"   # "Alexandra"

str3 = "Through the Looking-Glass"
str3[-13,13]  = "Mirror" # "Through the Mirror"

str4 = "Winston Churchill"
str4[8..13] = "H"         # "Winston Hill"

str5 = "Alistair Cooke"
str5[/e$/] ="ie Monster" # "Alistair Cookie Monster"

str6 = "theater"
str6["er"] = "re"         # "theatre"
```

```
str7 = "Aaron Burr"
str7[0] = 66                # "Baron Burr"
```

Assigning to an expression evaluating to `nil` will have no effect.

Substituting in Strings

You've already seen how to perform simple substitutions in strings. The sub and gsub methods provide more advanced pattern-based capabilities. There are also sub! and gsub!, which are their in-place counterparts.

The sub method will substitute the first occurrence of a pattern with the given substitute string or the given block.

```
s1 = "spam, spam, and eggs"
s2 = s1.sub(/spam/,"bacon")                 # "bacon, spam, and eggs"

s3 = s2.sub(/(\w+), (\w+),/,'\2, \1,')   # "spam, bacon, and eggs"

s4 = "Don't forget the spam."
s5 = s4.sub(/spam/) { |m| m.reverse }     # "Don't forget the maps."

s4.sub!(/spam/) { |m| m.reverse }
# s4 is now "Don't forget the maps."
```

As this example shows, the special symbols \1, \2, and so on can be used in a substitute string. However, special variables such as $& (or the English version $MATCH) might not.

If the block form is used, the special variables can be used. However, if all you need is the matched string, it will be passed into the block as a parameter. If it isn't needed at all, the parameter can of course be omitted.

The gsub method (global substitution) is essentially the same except that all matches are substituted rather than just the first.

```
s5 = "alfalfa abracadabra"
s6 = s5.gsub(/a[bl]/,"xx")      # "xxfxxfa xxracadxxra"
s5.gsub!(/[lfdbr]/) { |m| m.upcase + "-" }
# s5 is now "aL-F-aL-F-a aB-R-acaD-aB-R-a"
```

The method `Regexp.last_match` is essentially identical to $& or $MATCH.

Searching a String

Besides the techniques for accessing substrings, there are other ways of searching within strings. The `index` method will return the starting location of the specified substring, character, or regex. If the item isn't found, the result is `nil`.

```
str = "Albert Einstein"
pos1 = str.index(?E)     # 7
pos2 = str.index("bert") # 2
pos3 = str.index(/in/)   # 8
pos4 = str.index(?W)     # nil
pos5 = str.index("bart") # nil
pos6 = str.index(/wein/) # nil
```

The method `rindex` (right index) will start from the right side of the string (that is, from the end). The numbering, however, proceeds from the beginning as usual.

```
str = "Albert Einstein"
pos1 = str.rindex(?E)     # 7
pos2 = str.rindex("bert") # 2
pos3 = str.rindex(/in/)   # 13 (finds rightmost match)
pos4 = str.rindex(?W)     # nil
pos5 = str.rindex("bart") # nil
pos6 = str.rindex(/wein/) # nil
```

The `include?` method simply tells whether the specified substring or character occurs within the string.

```
str1 = "mathematics"
flag1 = str1.include? ?e       # true
flag2 = str1.include? "math"   # true
str2 = "Daylight Saving Time"
flag3 = str2.include? ?s       # false
flag4 = str2.include? "Savings"  # false
```

The `scan` method will repeatedly scan for occurrences of a pattern. If called without a block, it will return an array. If the pattern has more than one (parenthesized) group, the array will be nested.

```
str1 = "abracadabra"
sub1 = str1.scan(/a./)
# sub1 now is ["ab","ac","ad","ab"]

str2 = "Acapulco, Mexico"
sub2 = str2.scan(/(.)(c.)/)
# sub2 now is [ ["A","ca"], ["l","co"], ["i","co"] ]
```

If a block is specified, the method will pass the successive values to the block:

```
str3 = "Kobayashi"
str3.scan(/[^aeiou]+[aeiou]/) do |x|
  print "Syllable: #{x}\n"
end
```

This code will produce the following output:

```
Syllable: Ko
Syllable: ba
Syllable: ya
Syllable: shi
```

Converting Between Characters and ASCII Codes

In Ruby, a character is already an integer.

```
str = "Martin"
print str[0]        # 77
```

If a `Fixnum` is appended directly onto a string, it is converted to a character.

```
str2 = str << 111   # "Martino"
```

The method `length` can be used for finding the length of a string. A synonym is size.

```
str1 = "Carl"
x = str1.length     # 4
str2 = "Doyle"
x = str2.size       # 5
```

Processing a Line at a Time

A Ruby string can contain newlines. For example, a small enough file can be read into memory and stored in a single string. The default iterator `each` will process such a string one line at a time.

```
str = "Once upon\na time...\nThe End\n"
num = 0
str.each do |line|
  num += 1
  print "Line #{num}: #{line}"
end
```

This code produces three lines of output:

```
Line 1: Once upon
Line 2: a time...
Line 3: The End
```

The method `each_with_index` could also be used in this case.

Processing a Byte at a Time

Because Ruby isn't fully internationalized at the time of this writing, a character is essentially the same as a byte. To process these in sequence, use the each_byte iterator.

```
str = "ABC"
str.each_byte do |char|
  print char, " "
end
# Produces output: 65 66 67
```

Appending an Item onto a String

The append operator << can be used to append strings onto another string. It is *stackable* in that multiple operations can be performed in sequence on a given receiver.

```
str = "A"
str << [1,2,3].to_s << " " << (3.14).to_s
# str is now "A123 3.14"
```

If a Fixnum in the range 0–255 is specified, it will be converted to a character.

```
str = "Marlow"
str << 101 << ", Christopher"
# str is now "Marlowe, Christopher"
```

Removing Trailing Newlines and Other Characters

Often we want to remove extraneous characters from the end of a string. The prime example is a newline on a string read from input.

The chop method will remove the last character of the string (typically, a trailing newline character). If the character before the newline is a carriage return (\r), it will be removed also. The reason for this behavior is the discrepancy between different systems' concept of what a newline is. On some systems such as UNIX, the newline character is represented internally as a linefeed (\n). On others, such as DOS and Windows, it is stored as a carriage return followed by a linefeed (\r\n).

```
str = gets.chop        # Read string, remove newline
s2 = "Some string\n"   # "Some string" (no newline)
s3 = s2.chop!          # s2 is now "Some string" also
s4 = "Other string\r\n"
s4.chop!               # "Other string" (again no newline)
```

Note that the in-place version of the method (chop!) will modify its receiver.

It is also very important to note that in the absence of a trailing newline, the last character will be removed anyway.

```
str = "abcxyz"
s1 = str.chop              # "abcxy"
```

Because a newline might not always be present, the chomp method might be a better alternative.

```
str = "abcxyz"
str2 = "123\n"
s1 = str.chomp             # "abcxyz"
s2 = str2.chomp            # "123"
```

There is also a chomp! method as we would expect.

If a parameter is specified for chomp, it will remove the set of characters specified from the end of the string rather than the default record separator. Note that if the record separator appears in the middle of the string, it is ignored.

```
str1 = "abcxyz"
str2 = "abcxyz"
s1 = str1.chomp("yz")    # "abcx"
s2 = str2.chomp("x")     # "abcxyz"
```

Trimming Whitespace from a String

The strip method will remove whitespace from the beginning and end of a string. Its counterpart strip! will modify the receiver in place.

```
str1 = "\t \nabc  \t\n"
str2 = str1.strip          # "abc"
str3 = str1.strip!         # "abc"
# str1 is now "abc" also
```

Whitespace, of course, consists mostly of blanks, tabs, and end-of-line characters.

If we want to remove whitespace only from the beginning of a string, it is better to do it another way. Here we do substitution with the sub method. (Here \s matches a whitespace character.)

```
str1 = "\t \nabc  \t\n"
# Remove from beginning of string
str2 = str1.sub(/^\s*/,"")   # "abc  \t\n"
```

However, note that removing whitespace from the end of a string is problematic. If we only remove spaces and tabs, we are fine; but if we try to remove a newline, we run into difficulties. This is because a newline is considered to mark the end of a string; the dollar sign ($) will match the earliest newline even if multiline mode is being used. So the naive method of using $ won't work. Here we show a technique that will work even for newlines; it is unconventional but effective.

```
str3 = str2.reverse.sub(/^[ \t\n]*/,"").reverse
# Reverse the string; remove the whitespace; reverse it again
# Result is "\t  \nabc"
```

Repeating Strings

In Ruby, the multiplication operator (or method) is overloaded to enable repetition of strings. If a string is multiplied by *n*, the result is *n* copies of the original string concatenated together.

```
yell = "Fight! "*3    # "Fight! Fight! Fight! "
ruler = "+" + ("."*4+"5"+"."*4+"+")*3
# "+....5....+....5....+....5....+"
```

Expanding Variables in Input

This is a case of the *use-mention* distinction that is so common in computer science: Am I *using* this entity or only *mentioning* it? Suppose that a piece of data from outside the program (for example, from user input) is to be treated as containing a variable name or expression. How can we evaluate that expression?

The `eval` method comes to our rescue. Suppose that we want to read in a variable name and tell the user what its value is. The following fragment demonstrates this idea:

```
alpha=10
beta=20
gamma=30
print "Enter a variable name: "
str = gets.chop!
result = eval(str)

puts "#{str} = #{result}"
```

If the user enters alpha, for instance, the program will respond with `alpha = 10`.

However, we will point out a potential danger here. It is conceivable that a malicious user could enter a string specifically designed to run an external program and produce side effects that the programmer never intended or dreamed of. For example, on an UNIX system, one might enter `%x[rm -rf *]` as an input string. When the program evaluated that string, it would recursively remove all the files under the current directory!

For this reason, you must exercise caution when doing an `eval` of a string you didn't build yourselves. (This is particularly true in the case of Web-based software that is accessible by anyone on the Internet.) For example, you could scan the string and verify that it didn't contain backticks, the %x notation, the method name `system`, and so on.

Embedding Expressions Within Strings

The #{} notation makes embedding expressions within strings easy. You need not worry about converting, appending, and concatenating; you can interpolate a variable value or other expression at any point in a string.

```
puts "#{temp_f} Fahrenheit is #{temp_c} Celsius"
puts "The discriminant has the value #{b*b - 4*a*c}."
puts "#{word} is #{word.reverse} spelled backward."
```

Some shortcuts for global, class, and instance variables can be used so that the braces can be dispensed with.

```
print "$gvar = #$gvar and ivar = #@ivar."
```

Note that this technique isn't applicable for single-quoted strings (because their contents aren't expanded), but it does work for double-quoted documents and regular expressions.

Parsing Comma-separated Data

Comma-delimited data is common in computing. It is a kind of lowest common denominator of data interchange, which is used (for example) to transfer information between incompatible databases or applications that know no other common format.

We assume here that we have a mixture of strings and numbers and all strings are enclosed in quotes. We further assume that all characters are escaped as necessary (commas and quotes inside strings, and so on).

The problem becomes simple because this data format looks suspiciously like a Ruby array of mixed types. In fact, we can simply add brackets to enclose the whole expression, and we have an array of items.

```
string = gets.chop!
# Suppose we read in a string like this one:
# "Doe, John", 35, 225, "5'10\"", "555-0123"
data = eval("[" + string + "]")   # Convert to array
data.each {|x| puts "Value = #{x}"}
```

This fragment will produce the following output:

```
Value = Doe, John
Value = 35
Value = 225
Value = 5' 10"
Value = 555-0123
```

Converting Strings to Numbers (Decimal and Otherwise)

Frequently, we need to capture a number that is embedded in a string. For the simple cases, we can use to_f and to_i to convert to floating point numbers and integers, respectively. Each will ignore extraneous characters at the end of the string, and each will return a zero if no number is found.

```
num1 = "237".to_i                # 237
num2 = "50 ways to leave...".to_i   # 50
num3 = "You are number 6".to_i    # 0
num4 = "no number here at all".to_i  # 0

num5 = "3.1416".to_f             # 3.1416
num6 = "0.6931 is ln 2".to_f     # 0.6931
num7 = "ln 2 is 0.6931".to_f     # 0.0
num8 = "nothing to see here".to_f   # 0.0
```

Octal and hexadecimal can similarly be converted with the oct and hex methods as shown in the following. Signs are optional as with decimal numbers.

```
oct1 = "245".oct                # 165
oct2 = "245 Days".oct           # 165
# Leading zeroes are irrelevant.
oct3 = "0245".oct               # 165
oct4 = "-123".oct               # -83
# Non-octal digits cause a halt
oct4 = "23789".oct              # 237

hex1 = "dead".hex               # 57005
# Uppercase is irrelevant
hex2 = "BEEF".hex               # 48879
# Non-hex letter/digit causes a halt
hex3 = "beefsteak".hex          # 48879
hex4 = "0x212a".hex             # 8490
hex5 = "unhexed".hex            # 0
```

There is no bin method to convert from binary, but you can write your own (see Listing 2.2). Notice that it follows all the same rules of behavior as oct and hex.

LISTING 2.2   Converting from Binary

```
class String

  def bin
    val = self.strip
    pattern = /^([+-]?)(0b)?([01]+)(.*)$/
    parts = pattern.match(val)
```

Listing 2.2   Continued

```
      return 0 if not parts
      sign = parts[1]
      num  = parts[3]
      eval(sign+"0b"+num)
    end

  end

a = "10011001".bin        # 153
b = "0b10011001".bin      # 153
c = "0B1001001".bin       # 0
d = "nothing".bin         # 0
e = "0b100121001".bin     # 9
```

Encoding and Decoding `rot13` Text

The `rot13` method is perhaps the weakest form of encryption known to humankind. Its historical use is simply to prevent people from accidentally reading a piece of text. It is commonly seen in Usenet; for example, a joke that might be considered offensive might be encoded in `rot13`, or you could post the entire plot of *Star Wars: Episode II* the day before the premiere.

The encoding method consists simply of rotating a string through the alphabet, so *A* becomes *N*, *B* becomes *O*, and so on. Lowercase letters are rotated in the same way; digits, punctuation, and other characters are ignored. Because 13 is half of 26 (the size of our alphabet), the function is its own inverse; applying it a second time will decrypt it.

The following is an implementation as a method added to the `String` class. We present it without further comment.

```
class String

  def rot13
    self.tr("A-Ma-mN-Zn-z","N-Zn-zA-Ma-m")
  end

end

joke = "Y2K bug"
joke13 = joke.rot13     # "L2X oht"

episode2 = "Fcbvyre: Nanxva qbrfa'g trg xvyyrq."
puts episode2.rot13
```

Obscuring Strings

Sometimes we don't want strings to be immediately legible. For example, passwords shouldn't be stored in plain text, no matter how tight the file permissions are.

The standard method `crypt` uses the standard function of the same name in order to DES-encrypt a string. It takes a "salt" value as a parameter (similar to the seed value for a random number generator).

A trivial application for this is shown in the following, where we ask for a password that Tolkien fans should know.

```
coded = "hfCghHIE5LAM."

puts "Speak, friend, and enter!"

print "Password: "
password = gets.chop

if password.crypt("hf") == coded
  puts "Welcome!"
else
  puts "What are you, an orc?"
end
```

There are other conceivable uses for hiding strings. For example, we sometimes want to hide strings inside a file so that they aren't easily read. Even a binary file can have readable portions easily extracted by the UNIX strings utility or the equivalent, but a DES encryption will stop all but the most determined crackers.

It is worth noting that you should never rely on encryption of this nature for a server-side Web application. That is because a password entered on a Web form is still transmitted over the Internet in plaintext. In a case like this, the easiest security measure is the *Secure Sockets Layer (SSL)*. Of course, you could still use encryption on the server side, but for a different reason—to protect the password as it is stored rather than during transmission.

Counting Characters in Strings

The `count` method will count the number of occurrences of any set of specified characters.

```
s1 = "abracadabra"
a  = s1.count("c")      # 1
b  = s1.count("bdr")    # 5
```

The `string` parameter is similar to a very simple regular expression. If it starts with a caret, the list is negated.

```
c = s1.count("^a")      # 6
d = s1.count("^bdr")    # 6
```

A hyphen indicates a range of characters.

```
e = s1.count("a-d")     # 9
f = s1.count("^a-d")    # 2
```

Reversing a String

A string can be reversed very simply with the reverse method (or its in-place counterpart reverse!).

```
s1 = "Star Trek"
s2 = s1.reverse         # "kerT ratS"
s1.reverse!             # s1 is now "kerT ratS"
```

Suppose that you have a sentence and need to reverse the word order (rather than character order). Use the %w operator to make it an array of words, reverse the array, and then use join to rejoin them.

```
words = %w( how now brown cow )
# ["how", "now", "brown", "cow"]
words.reverse.join(" ")
# "cow brown now how"
```

This can be generalized with String#split, which allows you to divide the words based on your own pattern.

```
phrase = "Now here's a sentence"
phrase.split(" ").reverse.join(" ")
# "sentence a here's Now"
```

Removing Duplicate Characters

Runs of duplicate characters can be removed using the squeeze method.

```
s1 = "bookkeeper"
s2 = s1.squeeze         # "bokeper"
s3 = "Hello..."
s4 = s3.squeeze         # "Helo."
```

If a parameter is specified, only those characters will be squeezed.

```
s5 = s3.squeeze(".")    # "Hello."
```

This parameter follows the same rules as the one for the count method (see "Counting Characters in Strings"); that is, it understands the hyphen and the caret.

There is also a squeeze! method.

Removing Specific Characters from Within a String

The `delete` method will remove characters from a string if they appear in the list of characters passed as a parameter.

```
s1 = "To be, or not to be"
s2 = s1.delete("b")            # "To e, or not to e"
s3 = "Veni, vidi, vici!"
s4 = s3.delete(",!")           # "Veni vidi vici"
```

This parameter follows the same rules as the one for the `count` method (see "Counting Characters in Strings"); that is, it understands the hyphen and the caret.

There is also a `delete!` method.

Printing Special Characters

The `dump` method will provide explicit printable representations of characters that might ordinarily be invisible or print differently.

```
s1 = "Listen" << 7 << 7 << 7    # Add three ASCII BEL characters
puts s1.dump                    # Prints: Listen\007\007\007
s2 = "abc\t\tdef\tghi\n\n"
puts s2.dump                    # Prints: abc\t\tdef\tghi\n\n
s3 = "Double quote: \""
puts s3.dump                    # Prints: Double quote: \"
```

Generating Successive Strings

On rare occasions we might want to find the successor value for a string; for example, the successor for `"aaa"` is `"aab"` (then `"aac"`, `"aad"`, and so on).

Ruby provides the method `succ` for this purpose.

```
droid = "R2D2"
improved = droid.succ      # "R2D3"
pill  = "Vitamin B"
pill2 = pill.succ          # "Vitamin C"
```

We don't recommend the use of this feature unless the values are predictable and reasonable. If you start with a string that is esoteric enough, you will eventually get strange and surprising results.

There is also an `upto` method that will apply `succ` repeatedly in a loop until the desired final value is reached.

```
"Files, A".upto "Files, X" do |letter|
  puts "Opening: #{letter}"
```

```
end

# Produces 24 lines of output
```

Again, we stress that this isn't used very frequently, and you use it at your own risk. Also we want to point out that there is no corresponding predecessor function at the time of this writing.

Calculate the Levenstein Distance Between Two Strings

The concept of distance between strings is important in inductive learning (AI), cryptography, proteins research, and in other areas.

The Levenstein distance (see Listing 2.3) is the minimum number of modifications needed to change one string into another, using three basic modification operations: del (deletion), ins (insertion), and sub (substitution). A substitution is also considered to be a combination of a deletion and insertion (indel). There are various approaches to this, but we will avoid getting too technical. Suffice it to say that this Ruby implementation allows you to provide optional parameters to set the cost for the three types of modification operations, and defaults to a single indel cost basis (cost of insertion=cost of deletion).

LISTING 2.3   Levenstein Distance

```
class String

  def levenstein(other, ins=2, del=2, sub=1)
    # ins, del, sub are weighted costs
    return nil if self.nil?
    return nil if other.nil?
    dm = []          # distance matrix

    # Initialize first row values
    dm[0] = (0..self.length).collect { |i| i * ins }
    fill = [0] * (self.length - 1)

    # Initialize first column values
    for i in 1..other.length
      dm[i] = [i * del, fill.flatten]
    end

    # populate matrix
    for i in 1..other.length
      for j in 1..self.length
        # critical comparison
```

LISTING 2.3   Continued

```
            dm[i][j] = [
                dm[i-1][j-1] +
                  (self[j-1] == other[i-1] ? 0 : sub),
                dm[i][j-1] + ins,
                dm[i-1][j] + del
              ].min
          end
        end

        # The last value in matrix is the
        # Levenstein distance between the strings
        dm[other.length][self.length]
      end

    end


    s1 = "ACUGAUGUGA"
    s2 = "AUGGAA"
    d1 = s1.levenstein(s2)     # 9


    s3 = "pennsylvania"
    s4 = "pencilvaneya"
    d2 = s3.levenstein(s4)     # 7


    s5 = "abcd"
    s6 = "abcd"
    d3 = s5.levenstein(s6)     # 0
```

Now that we have the Levenstein distance defined, it's conceivable that we could define a similar? method, giving it a threshold for similarity.

```
class String

  def similar?(other, thresh=2)
    if self.levenstein(other) < thresh
      true
    else
      false
```

```
      end
    end

  end


  if "polarity".similar?("hilarity")
    puts "Electricity is funny!"
  end
```

Of course, it would also be possible to pass in the three weighted costs to the `similar?` method so that they could in turn be passed into the Levenstein method. We have omitted these for simplicity.

Using Strings as Stacks and Queues

These routines make it possible to treat a string as a stack or a queue (see Listing 2.4), adding the operations `shift`, `unshift`, `push`, `pop`, `rotate_left`, and `rotate_right`. The operations are implemented both at the character and the word level. These have proved useful in one or two programs that we have written, and they might be useful to you also. Use your imagination.

There might be some confusion as to what is returned by each method. In the case of a retrieving operation such as `pop` or `shift`, the return value is the item that was retrieved. In a storing operation such as `push` or `unshift`, the return value is the new string. All rotate operations return the value of the new string. And we will state the obvious: Every one of these operations modifies its receiver, although none of them is marked with an exclamation point as suffix.

LISTING 2.4   String as Queues

```
  class String

    def shift
      # Removes first character from self and
      #   returns it, changing self
      return nil if self.empty?
      item=self[0]
      self.sub!(/^./,"")
      return nil if item.nil?
      item.chr
    end

    def unshift(other)
      # Adds last character of provided string to
```

LISTING 2.4   Continued

```ruby
      #    front of self
      newself = other.to_s.dup.pop.to_s + self
      self.replace(newself)
    end

    def pop
      # Pops last character off self and
      #    returns it, changing self
      return nil if self.empty?
      item=self[-1]
      self.chop!
      return nil if item.nil?
      item.chr
    end

    def push(other)
      # Pushes first character of provided
      #    string onto end of self
      newself = self + other.to_s.dup.shift.to_s
      self.replace(newself)
    end

    def rotate_left(n=1)
      n=1 unless n.kind_of? Integer
      n.times do
        char = self.shift
        self.push(char)
      end
      self
    end

    def rotate_right(n=1)
      n=1 unless n.kind_of? Integer
      n.times do
        char = self.pop
        self.unshift(char)
      end
      self
    end

    @@first_word_re = /^(\w+\W*)/
    @@last_word_re = /(\w+\W*)$/
```

LISTING 2.4   Continued

```ruby
def shift_word
  # Shifts first word off of self
  #   and returns; changes self
  return nil if self.empty?
  self=~@@first_word_re
  newself= $' || ""          # $' is POSTMATCH
  self.replace(newself) unless $'.nil?
  $1
end

def unshift_word(other)
  # Adds provided string to front of self
  newself = other.to_s + self
  self.replace(newself)
end

def pop_word
  # Pops and returns last word off
  # self; changes self
  return nil if self.empty?
  self=~@@last_word_re
  newself= $` || ""          # $` is PREMATCH
  self.replace(newself) unless $`.nil?
  $1
end

def push_word(other)
  # Pushes provided string onto end of self
  newself = self + other.to_s
  self.replace(newself)
end

def rotate_word_left
  word = self.shift_word
  self.push_word(word)
end

def rotate_word_right
  word = self.pop_word
  self.unshift_word(word)
end

alias rotate_Left rotate_word_left
alias rotate_Right rotate_word_right
```

LISTING 2.4   Continued

```
end

# -----------

str = "Hello there"
puts str.rotate_left                # "ello thereH"
puts str.pop                        # "H"
puts str.shift                    # "e"
puts str.rotate_right                # "ello ther"
puts str.unshift("H")                # "Hello ther"
puts str.push("e")                 # "Hello there"

puts str.push_word(", pal!")        # "Hello there, pal!"
puts str.rotate_Left                # "there, pal!Hello "

puts str.pop_word                  # str is "there, pal!"
                                   # result is "Hello "

puts str.shift_word                # str is "pal!"
                                   # result is "there, "

puts str.unshift_word("Hi there, ") # "Hi there, pal!"
puts str.rotate_Right                # "pal!Hi there, "
puts str.rotate_left(4)             # "Hi there, pal!"

puts "Trying again..."
str = "pal! Hi there, "
puts str.rotate_left(5)             # "Hi there, pal!"
```

Note that the [] operator with a range might be used to gain a window onto a string that is being rotated.

```
str = ".....duck....*...*..*..........*......*..."
loop do
  print str.rotate_left[0..7],"\r"}
end

# speed reading
string="See Bill run. Run Bill run! See Jane sit. Jane sees Bill."
loop{print string.rotate_Left[0..4],"\r"}
```

Creating an Abbreviation or Acronym

Suppose that we have a string and we want to create an abbreviation from the initial letters of each word in it. The code fragment shown in Listing 2.5 accomplishes that. We have added a threshold value such that any word fewer than that number of letters will be ignored. The threshold value defaults to zero, including all words.

Note that this uses the `shift_word` function, defined in "Using Strings as Stacks and Queues."

LISTING 2.5   Acronym Creator

```
class String

  def acronym(thresh=0)
    acro=""
    str=self.dup.strip
    while !str.nil? && !str.empty?
      word = str.shift_word
      if word.length >= thresh
        acro += word.strip[0,1].to_s.upcase
      end
    end
    acro
  end

end


s1 = "Same old, same old"
puts s1.acronym        #  "SOSO"

s2 = "three-letter abbreviation"
puts s2.acronym        #  "TLA"

s3 = "light amplification by stimulated emission of radiation"
puts s3.acronym        #  "LABSEOR"
puts s3.acronym(3)     #  "LASER"
```

Here is a less readable but perhaps more instructive version of the same method.

```
def acro(thresh=0)
  self.split.find_all {|w| w.length > thresh }.
      collect {|w| w[0,1].upcase}.join
end
```

Don't fail to notice the trailing dot on the `find_all` call.

Encoding and Decoding Base64 Strings

Base64 is frequently used to convert machine-readable data into a text form with no special characters in it. For example, newsgroups that handle binary files, such as program executables, frequently will use base64.

The easiest way to do a base64 encode/decode is to use the built-in features of Ruby. The Array class has a pack method that will return a base64 string (given the parameter "m"). The String class has a method unpack that will likewise unpack the string (decoding the base64).

```
str = "\007\007\002\abdce"

new_string = [str].pack("m")          # "BwcCB2JkY2U="
original   = new_string.unpack("m") # ["\a\a\002\abdce"]
```

Note that an array is returned by unpack.

Encoding and Decoding Strings (uuencode/uudecode)

The *uu* in these names means UNIX-to-UNIX. The uuencode and uudecode utilities are a time-honored way of exchanging data in text form (similar to the way base64 is used).

```
str = "\007\007\002\abdce" new_string = [str].pack("u") #
'(!P<"!V)D8V4`' original = new_string.unpack("u") # ["\a\a\002\abdce"]
```
Note that an array is returned by unpack.

Expanding and Compressing Tab Characters

Occasionally we have a string with tabs in it and we want to convert them to spaces (or vice versa). The two methods shown in Listing 2.6 will do these operations.

LISTING 2.6   Convert Tabs to Spaces

```
class String

  def detab(ts=8)
    str = self.dup
    while (leftmost = str.index("\t")) != nil
      space = " "*(ts-(leftmost%ts))
      str[leftmost]=space
    end
    str
  end

  def entab(ts=8)
```

LISTING 2.6   Continued

```
      str = self.detab
      areas = str.length/ts
      newstr = ""
      for a in 0..areas
        temp = str[a*ts..a*ts+ts-1]
        if temp.size==ts
          if temp =~ / +/
            match=Regexp.last_match[0]
            endmatch = Regexp.new(match+"$")
            if match.length>1
             temp.sub!(endmatch,"\t")
            end
          end
        end
        newstr += temp
      end
      newstr
    end

  end

  foo = "This      is      only   a     test.          "

  puts foo
  puts foo.entab(4)
  puts foo.entab(4).dump
```

Note that this code isn't smart enough to handle backspaces.

Wrapping Lines of Text

Occasionally, we might want to take long text lines and print them within margins of our own
choosing. Listing 2.7 accomplishes this, splitting only on word boundaries and honoring tabs
(but not honoring backspaces or preserving tabs).

LISTING 2.7   Line Wrap

```
  str = "When in the Course of human events it becomes necessary\n
  for one people to dissolve the political bands which have\n
  connected them with another, and to assume among the powers\n
  of the earth the separate and equal station to which the Laws\n
  of Nature and of Nature's God entitle them, a decent respect\n
  for the opinions of mankind requires that they should declare\n
  the causes which impel them to the separation."
```

LISTING 2.7   Continued

```
max = 20

line = 0
out = [""]

input = str.gsub("\n"," ")
# input.detab!

while input != ""
  word = input.shift_word
  break if not word
  if out[line].length + word.length > max
    out[line].squeeze!(" ")
    line += 1
    out[line] = ""
  end
  out[line].push_word(word)
end

out.each {|line| puts line}  # Prints 24 very short lines
```

Regular Expressions

I would choose
To lead him in a maze along the patterned paths...
—Amy Lowell, "Patterns"

The power of regular expressions as a computing tool has often been underestimated. From their earliest theoretical beginnings in the 1940s, they found their way onto computer systems in the 1960s and thence into various tools in the UNIX operating system. In the 1990s, the popularity of Perl helped make regular expressions a household item rather than the esoteric domain of bearded gurus.

The beauty of regular expressions is that everything in our experience can be understood in terms of patterns. Where there are patterns that we can describe, we can detect matches; we can find the bits of reality that correspond to those matches; and we can replace those bits with others of our own choosing.

Escaping Special Characters

The class method `Regexp.escape` will escape any special characters that are used in regular expressions. Such characters include the asterisk, question mark, and brackets.

```
str1 = "[*?]"
str2 = Regexp.escape(str1)   # "\[\*\?\]"
```

The method `Regexp.quote` is an alias.

Compiling Regular Expressions

Regular expressions can be compiled using the class method `Regexp.compile`, which is really only a synonym for `Regexp.new`. The first parameter is required and can be a string or a regex. (Note that if the parameter is a regex with options, the options won't carry over into the newly compiled regex.)

```
pat1 = Regexp.compile("^foo.*")   # /^foo.*/
pat2 = Regexp.compile(/bar$/i)    # /bar/ (i not propagated)
```

The second parameter, if present, is normally a bitwise `OR` of any of the following constants: `Regexp::EXTENDED`, `Regexp::IGNORECASE`, and `Regexp::MULTILINE`. Additionally, any non-nil value will have the result of making the regex not case sensitive; we don't recommend this practice.

```
options = Regexp::MULTILINE || Regexp::IGNORECASE
pat3 = Regexp.compile("^foo", options)
pat4 = Regexp.compile(/bar/, Regexp::IGNORECASE)
```

The third parameter, if specified, is the language parameter, which enables multibyte character support. It can take any of the following four string values:

```
"N" or "n" means None
"E" or "e" means EUC
"S" or "s" means Shift-JIS
"U" or "u" means UTF-8
```

Accessing Backreferences

The class method `Regexp.last_match` will return an object of class `MatchData` (as will the instance method `match`). This object has instance methods that enable the programmer to access backreferences.

The `MatchData` object is manipulated with a bracket notation as though it were an array of matches. The special element 0 contains the text of the entire matched string. Thereafter, element n refers to the nth match.

```
pat = /(.+[aiu])(.+[aiu])(.+[aiu])(.+[aiu])/i
# Four identical groups in this pattern
refs = pat.match("Fujiyama")
# refs is now: ["Fujiyama","Fu","ji","ya","ma"]
x = refs[1]
y = refs[2..3]
refs.to_a.each {|x| print "#{x}\n"}
```

Note that the object refs isn't a true array. Thus, when we want to treat it as one by using the iterator each, we must use to_a (as shown previously) to convert it to an array.

We can use more than one technique to locate a matched substring within the original string. The methods begin and end will return the beginning and ending offsets of a match. (It is important to realize that the ending offset is really the index of the next character after the match.)

```
str = "alpha beta gamma delta epsilon"
#        0....5....0....5....0....5....
#        (for  your counting convenience)

pat = /(b[^ ]+ )(g[^ ]+ )(d[^ ]+ )/
# Three words, each one a single match
refs = pat.match(str)

# "beta "
p1 = refs.begin(1)        # 6
p2 = refs.end(1)          # 11
# "gamma "
p3 = refs.begin(2)        # 11
p4 = refs.end(2)          # 17
# "delta "
p5 = refs.begin(3)        # 17
p6 = refs.end(3)          # 23
# "beta gamma delta"
p7 = refs.begin(0)        # 6
p8 = refs.end(0)          # 23
```

Similarly, the offset method will return an array of two numbers, which are the beginning and ending offsets of that match. To continue the preceding example:

```
range0 = refs.offset(0)    # [6,23]
range1 = refs.offset(1)    # [6,11]
range2 = refs.offset(2)    # [11,17]
range3 = refs.offset(3)    # [17,23]
```

The portions of the string before and after the matched substring can be retrieved by the instance methods pre_match and post_match, respectively. To continue the preceding example:

```
before = refs.pre_match    # "alpha "
after  = refs.post_match   # "epsilon"
```

Using Character Classes

Ruby regular expression might contain references to character classes, which are basically named patterns (of the form [[:name:]]). For example, [[:digit:]] means the same as [0-9] in a pattern. In most cases, this turns out to be shorthand.

Some others are [[:print:]] (printable characters) and [[:alpha:]] (alphabetic characters).

```
s1 = "abc\007def"
/[[:print:]]*/.match(s1)
m1 = Regexp::last_match[0]            # "abc"

s2 = "1234def"
/[[:digit:]]*/.match(s2)
m2 = Regexp::last_match[0]            # "1234"

/[[:digit:]]+[[:alpha:]]/.match(s2)
m3 = Regexp::last_match[0]           # "1234d"
```

Treating Newline as a Character

Ordinarily a dot will match any character except a newline. When the m (multiline) modifier is used, a newline will be matched by a dot. The same is true when the Regexp::MULTILINE option is used in creating a regex.

```
str = "Rubies are red\nAnd violets are blue.\n"
pat1 = /red./
pat2 = /red./m

str =~ pat1     # false
str =~ pat2     # true
```

Matching an IP Address

Suppose that we want to determine whether a string is a valid IPv4 address. The standard form of such an address is a *dotted quad* or *dotted decimal* string. This is, in other words, four decimal numbers separated by periods, each number ranging from 0 to 255.

The pattern given here will do the trick (with a few exceptions such as 127.1). We break the pattern up a little just for readability. Note that the \d symbol is double escaped so that the slash in the string will get passed on to the regex.

```
num = "(\\d|[01]?\\d\\d|2[0-4]\\d|25[0-5])"
pat = "^#{num}\.#{num}\.#{num}\.#{num}$"
ip_pat = Regexp.new(pat)

ip1 = "9.53.97.102"

if ip1 =~ ip_pat              # Prints "yes"
  puts "yes"
else
  puts "no"
end
```

IPv6 addresses aren't in widespread use yet, but we include them for completeness. These consist of eight colon-separated 16-bit hex numbers with zeroes suppressed.

```
num = "[0-9A-Fa-f]{0,4}"
pat = "^" + "#{num}:"*7 + "#{num}$"
ipv6_pat = Regexp.new(pat)

v6ip = "abcd::1324:ea54::dead::beef"

if v6ip =~ ipv6_pat           # Prints "yes"
  puts "yes"
else
  puts "no"
end
```

Matching a Keyword-Value Pair

Occasionally, we want to work with strings of the form "*attribute=value*" (for example, when we parse some kind of configuration file for an application).

This code fragment will extract the keyword and the value. The assumptions are that the keyword or attribute is a single word; the value extends to the end of the line; and the equal sign can be surrounded by whitespace.

```
pat = /(\w+)\s*=\s*(.*?)$/
str = "color = blue"

matches = pat.match(str)

puts matches[1]          # "color"
puts matches[2]          # "blue"
```

For additional information see the section "Adding a Keyword-Value String to a Hash."

Matching Roman Numerals

Here we match against a complex pattern to determine whether a string is a valid Roman number (up to decimal 3999). As before, the pattern is broken up into parts for readability.

```
rom1 = "m{0,3}"
rom2 = "(d?c{0,3}|c[dm])"
rom3 = "(l?x{0,3}|x[lc])"
rom4 = "(v?i{0,3}|i[vx])"
rom_pat = "^#{rom1}#{rom2}#{rom3}#{rom4}$"

roman = Regexp.new(rom_pat, Regexp::IGNORECASE)

year1985 = "MCMLXXXV"

if year1985 =~ roman       # Prints "yes"
  puts "yes"
else
  puts "no"
end
```

Matching Numeric Constants

A simple decimal integer is the easiest number to match. It has an optional sign and consists thereafter of digits (except that Ruby allows an underscore as a digit separator). Note that the first digit shouldn't be a zero; then it would be interpreted as an octal constant.

```
int_pat = /^[+-]?[1-9][\d_]*/
```

Integer constants in other bases are similar. Note that the hex and binary patterns are not case sensitive because they contain at least one letter.

```
hex_pat = /^[+-]?0x[\da-f_]+$/i
oct_pat = /^[+-]?0[0-7_]+$/
bin_pat = /^[+-]?0b[01_]+/i
```

A normal floating-point constant is a little tricky; the number sequences on each side of the decimal point are optional, but one or the other must be included.

```
float_pat = /^(\d[\d_]*)*\.[\d_]*$/
```

Finally, scientific notation builds on the ordinary floating-point pattern.

```
sci_pat = /^(\d[\d_]*)?\.[\d_]*(e[+-]?)?(_*\d[\d_]*)$/i
```

These patterns can be useful if, for instance, you have a string and you want to verify its validity as a number before trying to convert it.

Matching a Date/Time String

Suppose that we want to match a date/time in the form mm/dd/yy hh:mm:ss. This pattern is a good first attempt: datetime_re=/(\d\d)\/(\d\d)\/(\d\d) (\d\d):(\d\d):(\d\d)/.

However, that will also match invalid date/times, and miss valid ones. A pickier pattern is shown in Listing 2.8.

LISTING 2.8   Matching Date/Time Strings

```ruby
class String

  def scan_datetime(flag=2)
    datetime_re=/((\d\d)\/(\d\d)\/(\d\d) (\d\d):(\d\d):(\d\d))/

    month_re=/(0?[1-9]|1[0-2])/
    # 01 to 09 or 1 to 9 or 10-12
    day_re=/([0-2]?[1-9]|[1-3][01])/
    # 1-9 or 01-09 or 11-19 or 21-29 or 10,11,20,21,30,31
    year_re=/(\d\d)/
    # 00-99
    hour_re=/([01]?[1-9]|[12][0-4])/
    # 1-9 or 00-09 or 11-19 or 10-14 or 20-24
    minute_re=/([0-5]\d)/
    # 00-59, both digit required
    second_re=/(:[0-6]\d)?/
    # leap seconds ;-) both digits required if present

    date_re=/(#{month_re.source}\/#{day_re.source}\
/#{year_re.source})/
    time_re=/(#{hour_re.source}
:#{minute_re.source}#{second_re.source})/

    datetime_re2 = /(#{date_re.source} #{time_re.source})/

    if flag==2
      self.scan(datetime_re2)     # returns arrays
    else
      self.scan(datetime_re)
    end
  end
end


str="Recorded on 11/18/00 20:31:00, viewed 11/18/00 8:31 PM "
str.scan_datetime
```

LISTING 2.8 Continued

```
# [ ["11/18/00 20:31:00", "11", "18", "00", "20", "31", "00"] ]
str.scan_datetime(2)
# [ ["11/18/00 20:31:00", "11/18/00", "11", "18", "00",
#   "20:31:00", "20", "31", ":00"],
# ["11/18/00 8:31", "11/18/00", "11", "18", "00", "8:31",
#   "8", "31", nil]  ]
```

Detecting Doubled Words in Text

Here, we implement the famous double-word detector. Typing the same word twice in succession is one of the most common typing errors. The code we show here will detect instances of that occurrence.

```
double_re = /\b(['A-Z]+) +\1\b/i

str="There's there's the the pattern."
str.scan(double_re)  #  [["There's"],["the"]]
```

Note that the trailing i in the regex is for not case sensitive matching. There is an array for each grouping, hence the resulting array of arrays.

Matching All-caps Words

This one is simple if we assume no numerics, underscores, and so on.

```
allcaps = /\b[A-Z]+\b/

string = "This is ALL CAPS"
string[allcaps]              #  "ALL"
```

Suppose that you want to simply extract every word in all-caps.

```
string.scan(allcaps)   #  ["ALL", "CAPS"]
```

If we wanted, we could extend this concept to include Ruby identifiers and similar items.

Numbers

> *On two occasions I have been asked [by members of Parliament], 'Pray, Mr. Babbage, if you put into the machine wrong figures, will the right answers come out?' I am not able rightly to apprehend the kind of confusion of ideas that could provoke such a question.*
>
> —Charles Babbage

Numeric data is the original data type, the native language of the computer. We would be hard-pressed to find areas of our experience in which numbers aren't applicable. It doesn't matter whether you're an accountant or an aeronautical engineer; you can't survive without numbers. We present here a few ways to process, manipulate, convert, and analyze numeric data.

Performing Bit-level Operations on Numbers

Occasionally, we might need to operate on a Fixnum as a binary entity. This is less common in application level programming, but the need still arises.

Ruby has a relatively full set of capabilities in this area. For convenience, numeric constants can be expressed in binary, octal, or hexadecimal. The usual operators AND, OR, XOR, and NOT are expressed by the Ruby operators &, |, ^, and ~, respectively.

```
x = 0377            # Octal   (decimal 255)
y = 0b00100110      # Binary (decimal  38)
z = 0xBEEF          # Hex     (decimal 48879)

a = x | z           # 48895 (bitwise OR)
b = x & z           #   239 (bitwise AND)
c = x ^ z           # 48656 (bitwise XOR)
d = ~ y             #   -39 (negation or 1's complement)
```

The instance method size can be used to determine the wordsize of the specific architecture on which the program is running.

```
bytes = 1.size      # Returns 4 for one particular machine
```

There are left-shift and right-shift operators (<< and >>, respectively). These are logical shift operations; they don't disturb the sign bit (although >> does propagate it).

```
x = 8
y = -8

a = x >> 2          # 2
b = y >> 2          # -2
c = x << 2          # 32
d = y << 2          # -32
```

Of course, anything shifted far enough to result in a zero value will lose the sign bit because -0 is merely 0.

Brackets can be used to treat numbers as arrays of bits. The 0th bit is the least significant bit regardless of the bit order (endianness) of the architecture.

```
x = 5               # Same as 0b0101
a = x[0]            # 1
b = x[1]            # 0
c = x[2]            # 1
d = x[3]            # 0
# Etc.              # 0
```

It isn't possible to assign bits using this notation (because a Fixnum is stored as an immediate value rather than an object reference). However, you can always fake it by left-shifting a 1 to the specified bit position and then doing an OR or AND operation.

```
# We can't do x[3] = 1
# but we can do:
x |= (1<<3)
# We can't do x[4] = 0
# but we can do:
x &= ~(1<<4)
```

Finding Cube Roots, Fourth Roots, and So On

Ruby has a built-in square root function (Math.sqrt) because that function is so commonly used. But what if you need higher-level roots? If you remember your math, this is easy.

One way is to use logarithms. Recall that e to the x is the inverse of the natural log of x. When multiplying numbers, that is equivalent to adding their logarithms.

```
x = 531441
cuberoot = Math.exp(Math.log(x)/3.0)      # 81.0
fourthroot = Math.exp(Math.log(x)/4.0)    # 27.0
```

However, it is just as easy and perhaps clearer to use fractions with an exponentiation operator (which can take any integer or floating-point value).

```
y = 4096
cuberoot = y**(1.0/3.0)        # 16.0
fourthroot = y**(1.0/4.0)      # 8.0
fourthroot = sqrt(sqrt(y))     # 8.0 (same thing)
twelfthroot = y**(1.0/12.0)    # 2.0
```

Note that in all of these examples, we have used floating-point numbers when dividing (to avoid truncation to an integer).

Rounding Floating-Point Values

If you want to round a floating-point value to an integer, the method round will do the trick.

```
pi = 3.14159
new_pi = pi.round   # 3
temp = -47.6
temp2 = temp.round  # -48
```

Sometimes we want to round not to an integer, but to a specific number of decimal places. In this case, we could use sprintf (which knows how to round) and eval to do this.

```
pi = 3.1415926535
pi6 = eval(sprintf("%8.6f",pi))  # 3.141593
```

```
pi5 = eval(sprintf("%8.5f",pi))   # 3.14159
pi4 = eval(sprintf("%8.4f",pi))   # 3.1416
```

Of course, this is somewhat ugly. Let's encapsulate this behavior in a method that we'll add to Float.

```
class Float

  def roundf(places)
    temp = self.to_s.length
    sprintf("%#{temp}.#{places}f",self).to_f
  end

end
```

Occasionally, we follow a different rule in rounding to integers. The tradition of rounding $n+0.5$ upward results in slight inaccuracies at times; after all, $n+0.5$ is no closer to $n+1$ than it is to n. So there is an alternative tradition that rounds to the nearest even number in the case of 0.5 as a fractional part. If we wanted to do this, we might extend the Float class with a method of our own called round2, as shown here.

```
class Float

  def round2
    whole = self.floor
    fraction = self - whole
    if fraction == 0.5
      if (whole % 2) == 0
        whole
      else
        whole+1
      end
    else
      self.round
    end
  end

end

a = (33.4).round2  # 33
b = (33.5).round2  # 34
c = (33.6).round2  # 34
d = (34.4).round2  # 34
e = (34.5).round2  # 34
f = (34.6).round2  # 35
```

Obviously round2 differs from round only when the fractional part is exactly 0.5; note that 0.5 can be represented perfectly in binary, by the way. What is less obvious is that this method will work fine for negative numbers also. (Try it.) Also note that the parentheses used here aren't actually necessary, but rather they are used for readability.

Now, what if we wanted to round to a number of decimal places, but we wanted to use the even rounding method? In this case, we could add a method called roundf2 to Float.

```
class Float

  # round2 definition as before

  def roundf2(places)
    shift = 10**places
    (self * shift).round2 / shift.to_f
  end

end

a = 6.125
b = 6.135
x = a.roundf(2)    # 6.12
y = b.roundf(2)    # 6.12
```

The code shown here (roundf and roundf2) has certain limitations, in that a large floating-point number will naturally cause problems when it is multiplied by a large power of ten. For these occurrences, error-checking should be added.

Formatting Numbers for Output

To output numbers in a specific format, you can use the printf method in the Kernel module. It is virtually identical to its C counterpart. For more information, see the documentation for the printf method.

```
x = 345.6789
i = 123
printf("x = %6.2f\n", x)    # x = 345.68
printf("x = %9.2e\n", x)    # x = 3.457e+02
printf("i = %5d\n", i)      # i =   123
printf("i = %05d\n", i)     # i = 00123
printf("i = %-5d\n", i)     # i = 123
```

To store a result in a string rather than printing it immediately, sprintf can be used in much the same way. This method returns a string.

```
str = sprintf("%5.1f",x)    # "345.7"
```

Finally, the String class has a % method that performs this same task. The % method has a format string as a receiver; it takes a single argument (or an array of values) and returns a string.

```
# Usage is 'format % value'
str = "%5.1" % x            # "345.7"
str = "%6.2, %05d" % [x,i]  # "345.68, 00123"
```

Working with Large Integers

The control of large numbers is possible, and like unto that of small numbers, if we subdivide them.

—Sun Tzu

In the event it becomes necessary, Ruby programmers can work with integers of arbitrary size. The transition from a Fixnum to a Bignum is handled automatically and transparently.

```
num1 = 1000000        # One million (10**6)
num2 = num1*num1      # One trillion (10**12)
puts num1             # 1000000
puts num1.type        # Fixnum
puts num2             # 1000000000000
puts num2.type        # Bignum
```

The size of a Fixnum will vary from one architecture to another.

Swapping Two Values

This item isn't strictly concerned with numeric data, but we did want to mention it somewhere. In many languages, swapping or exchanging two values requires a temporary variable; in Ruby (as in Perl and some others), this isn't needed. The following statement

```
x, y = y, x
```

will exchange x and y using multiple assignment. Note, of course, that in the case of numbers, we are exchanging the actual values. In the case of most other objects, we are only swapping what amounts to a pointer or reference—that is, changing which variable refers to which object.

Determining the Architecture's Byte Order

It is an interesting fact of the computing world that we cannot all agree on the order in which binary data ought to be stored. Is the most significant bit stored at the higher-numbered address or the lower? When we shove a message over a wire, do we send the most significant bit first, or the least significant?

Believe it or not, it's not entirely arbitrary. There are good arguments on both sides, which we won't delve into here.

For at least 20 years, the terms "little-endian" and "big-endian" have been applied to the two extreme opposites. These apparently were first used by Danny Cohen; refer to his classic article "On Holy Wars and a Plea for Peace" (*IEEE Computer*, October 1981). The actual terms are derived from the novel *Gulliver's Travels* by Jonathan Swift.

Most of the time, we don't care what byte order our architecture uses. But what if we do need to know?

Here's one little method that will determine this for us. It will return a string that is LITTLE, BIG, or OTHER. It depends on the fact that the l directive packs in native mode and the N directive unpacks in network order (or big-endian).

```ruby
def endianness
  num=0x12345678
  little = "78563412"
  big    = "12345678"
  native = [num].pack('l')
  netunpack = native.unpack('N')[0]
  str = "%8x" % netunpack
  case str
    when little
      "LITTLE"
    when big
      "BIG"
    else
      "OTHER"
  end
end

puts endianness   # In this case, prints "LITTLE"
```

This technique might come in handy if, for example, you are working with binary data (such as scanned image data) imported from another system.

Calculating the MD5 Hash of a String

The MD5 message-digest algorithm produces a 128-bit fingerprint or *message digest* of a message of arbitrary length. This is in the form of a hash, so the encryption is one way and doesn't allow for the discovery of the original message from the digest. Ruby has an extension for a class to implement MD5; for those interested in the source code, it's in the ext/md5 directory of the standard Ruby distribution.

There are two class methods, new and md5, to create a new MD5 object. There is really no difference in them.

```
require 'md5'
cryptic = MD5.md5
password = MD5.new
```

There are four instance methods: clone, digest, hexdigest, and update. The clone method simply copies the object; update is used to add content to the object as follows:

```
cryptic.update("Can you keep a secret?")
```

You can also create the object and add to the message at the same time:

```
secret = MD5.new("Sensitive data")
```

If a string argument is given, it is added to the object using update. Repeated calls are equivalent to a single call with concatenated arguments.

```
# These two statements...
cryptic.update("Shhh! ")
cryptic.update("Be very, very quiet!")

# ...are equivalent to this one.
cryptic.update("Shhh! Be very, very quiet!").
```

The digest method provides a 16-byte binary string containing the 128-bit digest.

The hexdigest method is what we actually find most useful. It provides the digest as an ASCII string of 32 hex characters representing the 16 bytes. This method is equivalent to the following:

```
def hexdigest
  ret = ''
  digest.each_byte {|i| ret << sprintf('%02x', i) }
  ret
end

secret.hexdigest  #  "b30e77a94604b78bd7a7e64ad500f3c2"
```

In short, you can get an md5 hash as follows:

```
require 'md5'
m = MD5.new("sensitive data").hexdigest
```

Calculating a 32-bit CRC

The *Cyclic Redundancy Checksum (CRC)* is a well-known way of obtaining a signature for a file or other collection of bytes. The CRC has the property that the chance of data being changed and keeping the same CRC is 1 in $2^{**}N$, where N is the number of bits in the result (most often 32 bits).

We refer you to the Zlib library for this. This library, created by Ueno Katsuhiro, isn't part of the standard distribution, but is still well known.

The method `crc32` will compute a CRC given a string as a parameter:

```
crc = Zlib::crc32("hello")  # 907060870
```

A previous CRC can be specified as an optional second parameter; the result will be as if the strings were concatenated and a single CRC was computed. This can be used, for example, to compute the checksum of a file so large that we can only read it in chunks.

Numerical Computation of a Definite Integral

> *I'm very good at integral and differential calculus...*
> —W. S. Gilbert, *The Pirates of Penzance*, Act I

If you want to estimate the value of a definite integral, there is a time-tested technique for doing so. Essentially we are performing what the calculus student will remember as a Riemann sum.

The `integrate` method shown here will take beginning and ending values for the dependent variable as well as an increment. The fourth parameter (which isn't really a parameter) is a block. This block should evaluate a function based on the value of the dependent variable passed into that block. (Here we are using *variable* in the mathematical sense, not in the computing sense.) It isn't necessary to define a function to call in this block, but we do so here for clarity.

```ruby
def integrate(x0, x1, dx=(x1-x0)/1000.0)
  x = x0
  sum = 0
  loop do
    y = yield(x)
    sum += dx * y
    x += dx
    break if x > x1
  end
  sum
end

def f(x)
  x**2
end
```

```
z = integrate(0.0,5.0) {|x| f(x) }

puts z, "\n"              # 41.7291875
```

Note that in the preceding example, we are relying on the fact that a block returns a value that yield can retrieve. We also make certain assumptions here. First, we assume that x0 is less than x1 (otherwise an infinite loop will result); you can easily improve the code in details such as this one. Second, we assume that the function can be evaluated at arbitrary points in the specified domain. If at any time we try to evaluate the function at any other point, chaos will ensue. (Such functions generally aren't integrable anyway, at least over that set of x values. Consider the function $f(x)=x/(x-3)$, when x is 3.)

Drawing on our faded memories of calculus, we might compute the result here to be 41.666 or thereabout (5 cubed divided by 3). Why is the answer not as exact as we might like? It is because of the size of the slice in the Riemann sum; a smaller value for dx will result in greater accuracy (at the expense of an increase in runtime).

Finally, we will point out that a function like this is more useful when we have a variety of functions of arbitrary complexity, not just a simple function such as $f(x) = x**2$.

Trigonometry in Degrees, Radians, and Grads

When it comes to measuring arc, the mathematical or natural unit is the radian, defined in such a way that an angle of one radian will correspond to an arclength equal to the radius of the circle. A little thought will show that there are 2π radians in a circle.

The degree of arc that we use in everyday life is a holdover from ancient Babylonian base-60 units; this system divides the circle into 360 degrees. The less-familiar *grad* is a pseudo-metric unit defined in such a way that there are 100 grads in a right angle (or 400 in a circle).

Programming languages often default to the radian when calculating trigonometric functions, and Ruby is no exception. But we show here how to do these calculations in degrees or grads, in the event that any of you are engineers.

Because the number of units in a circle is a simple constant, it follows that there are simple conversion factors between all these units. We will define these here and simply use the constant names in subsequent code. As a matter of convenience, we'll stick them in the Math module.

```
module Math

  RAD2DEG  = 360.0/(2.0*PI)  # Radians to degrees
  RAD2GRAD = 400.0/(2.0*PI)  # Radians to grads

end
```

Now we can define new trig functions if we want. Because we are converting to radians in each case, we will divide by the conversion factor we calculated previously. We could place these in the Math module if we wanted, although we don't show it here.

```
def sin_d(theta)
  Math.sin (theta/Math::RAD2DEG)
end

def sin_g(theta)
  Math.sin (theta/Math::RAD2GRAD)
end
```

Of course, the corresponding cos and tan functions can be similarly defined.

The atan2 function is a little different. It takes two arguments (the opposite and adjacent legs of a right triangle) and returns an angle. Thus we convert the result, not the argument, handling it this way:

```
def atan2_d(y,x)
  Math.atan2(y,x)/Math::RAD2DEG
end

def atan2_g(y,x)
  Math.atan2(y,x)/Math::RAD2GRAD
end
```

More Advanced Trig: Arcsin, Arccos, and Hyperbolic Functions

Ruby's Math module doesn't provide arcsin and arccos functions, but you can always define your own. Here we don't provide the theory but only the code.

```
def arcsin(x)
  Math.atan2(x, Math.sqrt(1.0-x*x))
end

def arccos(x)
  Math.atan2(Math.sqrt(1.0-x*x), x)
end
```

Note that because we used atan2, we don't have to worry about dividing by zero. This is a compelling reason to use atan2, by the way, along with other issues regarding floating-point error and the speed of floating-point division.

Of course, if you prefer the traditional arctan function that is so familiar to mathematicians, you can define it this way.

```
def arctan(x)
```

```
    Math.atan2(x,1.0)
  end
```

All the preceding functions could be modified (as you have already seen) to use degrees or grads rather than radians.

The hyperbolic trig functions aren't defined in Math, but they can be defined as follows. We assume here that you're working with real (not complex) numbers.

```
def sinh(x)
  (Math.exp(x)-Math.exp(-x))/2.0
end

def cosh(x)
  (Math.exp(x)+Math.exp(-x))/2.0
end

def tanh(x)
  sinh(x)/cosh(x)
end
```

The inverses of these functions can also be defined.

```
def asinh(x)
  Math.log(x + Math.sqrt(1.0+x**2))
end

def acosh(x)
  2.0 * Math.log(Math.sqrt((x+1.0)/2.0)+Math.sqrt((x-1)/2.0))
end

def atanh(x)
  (Math.log (1.0+x) - Math.log(1.0-x)) / 2.0
end
```

Finding Logarithms with Arbitrary Bases

When working with logarithms, we frequently use the *natural* logarithms (or base e, which is sometimes written ln); we can also use the *common* or base 10 logarithms. These are defined in Ruby as Math.log and Math.log10, respectively.

In computer science, specifically in such areas as coding and information theory, a base 2 log isn't unusual. For example, this tells the minimum number of bits needed to store a number. We define this function here as log2:

```
def log2(x)
  Math.log(x)/Math.log(2)
end
```

The inverse is obviously $2**x$ just as the inverse of log x is Math::E**x or Math.exp(x).

Furthermore, this same technique can be extended to any base. In the unlikely event that you ever need a base 7 logarithm, this will do the trick.

```
def log7(x)
  Math.log(x)/Math.log(7)
end
```

In practice, the denominator should be calculated once and kept around as a constant.

Comparing Floating-Point Numbers

It is a sad fact of life that computers don't represent floating-point values exactly. The following code fragment, in a perfect world, would print "yes"; on every architecture we have tried, it prints "no" instead.

```
x = 1000001.0/0.003
y = 0.003*x
if y == 1000001.0
  puts "yes"
else
  puts "no"
end
```

The reason, of course, is that a floating-point number is stored in some finite number of bits; and no finite number of bits is adequate to store a repeating decimal with an infinite number of digits.

Because of this inherent inaccuracy in floating-point comparisons, we might find ourselves in situations (like the one we just saw) in which the values we are comparing are the same for all practical purposes, but the hardware stubbornly thinks they are different.

Here is a simple way to ensure that floating-point comparisons are done with a fudge factor; that is, the comparisons will be done to within any tolerance specified by the programmer.

```
class Float

  EPSILON = 1e-6    # 0.000001

  def ==(x)
    (self-x).abs < EPSILON
  end

end
```

```
x = 1000001.0/0.003
y = 0.003*x
if y == 1.0          # Using the new ==
  puts "yes"         # Now we output "yes"
else
  puts "no"
end
```

We might find that we want different tolerances for different situations. For this case, we define a new method equals? as a member of Float. (We name it this in order to avoid confusion with the standard methods equal? and eql?; the latter in particular shouldn't be overridden.)

```
class Float

  EPSILON = 1e-6

  def equals?(x, tolerance=EPSILON)
    (self-x).abs < tolerance
  end

end

flag1 = (3.1416).equals? Math::PI          # false
flag2 = (3.1416).equals?(Math::PI, 0.001)  # true
```

We could also use a different operator entirely to represent approximate equality; the =~ operator might be a good choice.

We'll also mention here that there is a BigFloat class (created by Shigeo Kobayashi) that isn't part of the standard Ruby distribution; this extension allows essentially infinite-precision floating-point math. The library can be found in the Ruby Application Archive.

Finding the Mean, Median, and Mode of a Data Set

Given an array x, let's find the mean of all the values in that array. Actually, there are three common kinds of mean. The ordinary or *arithmetic* mean is what we call the average in everyday life. The *harmonic* mean is the number of terms divided by the sum of all their reciprocals. And finally, the *geometric* mean is the nth root of the product of the n values. Each of these is shown as follows:

```
def mean(x)
  sum=0
  x.each {|v| sum += v}
  sum/x.size
end
```

```ruby
def hmean(x)
  sum=0
  x.each {|v| sum += (1.0/v)}
  x.size/sum
end

def gmean(x)
  prod=1.0
  x.each {|v| prod *= v}
  prod**(1.0/x.size)
end

data = [1.1, 2.3, 3.3, 1.2, 4.5, 2.1, 6.6]

am = mean(data)    # 3.014285714
hm = hmean(data)   # 2.101997946
gm = gmean(data)   # 2.508411474
```

The median value of a data set is the value that occurs approximately in the middle of the set. For this value, half the numbers in the set should be less and half should be greater. Obviously, this statistic will be more appropriate and meaningful for some data sets than others.

```ruby
def median(x)
  sorted = x.sort
  mid = x.size/2
  sorted[mid]
end

data = [7,7,7,4,4,5,4,5,7,2,2,3,3,7,3,4]
puts median(data)          # 4
```

The mode of a data set is the value that occurs most frequently. If there is only one such value, the set is unimodal; otherwise it is multimodal. A multimodal data set is a more complex case that we don't consider here. If interested, you can extend and improve the code shown here.

```ruby
def mode(x)
  sorted = x.sort
  a = Array.new
  b = Array.new

  sorted.each do |x|
    if a.index(x) == nil
      a << x                 # Add to list of values
      b << 1                 # Add to list of frequencies
    else
      b[a.index(x)] += 1   # Increment existing counter
    end
```

2

SIMPLE DATA
TASKS

```
  end
  maxval = b.max          # Find highest count
  where  = b.index(maxval) # Find index of highest count
  a[where]                # Find corresponding data value
end

data = [7,7,7,4,4,5,4,5,7,2,2,3,3,7,3,4]
puts mode(data)          # 7
```

Variance and Standard Deviation

The variance of a set of data is a measure of how spread out the values are. (Here we don't distinguish between biased and unbiased estimates.) The standard deviation, usually represented by a sigma (ε) is simply the square root of the variance.

```
data = [2, 3, 2, 2, 3, 4, 5, 5, 4, 3, 4, 1, 2]

def variance(x)
  m = mean(x)
  sum = 0.0
  x.each {|v| sum += (v-m)**2 }
  sum/x.size
end

def sigma(x)
  Math.sqrt(variance(x))
end

puts variance(data)   # 1.461538462
puts sigma(data)      # 1.20894105
```

Note that the preceding variance function makes use of the mean function defined earlier.

Finding a Correlation Coefficient

The correlation coefficient is one of the simplest and most universal of statistical measures. It is a measure of the "linearity" of a set of x-y pairs, ranging from -1.0 (complete negative correlation) to +1.0 (complete positive correlation).

We compute this using the mean and sigma (standard deviation) functions that we defined previously. For an explanation of this tool, consult any statistics text.

The first version we show assumes two arrays of numbers (of the same size).

```
def correlate(x,y)
  sum = 0.0
  x.each_index do |i|
    sum += x[i]*y[i]
```

```
    end
    xymean = sum/x.size.to_f
    xmean  = mean(x)
    ymean  = mean(y)
    sx = sigma(x)
    sy = sigma(y)
    (xymean-(xmean*ymean))/(sx*sy)
  end


  a = [3, 6, 9, 12, 15, 18, 21]
  b = [1.1, 2.1, 3.4, 4.8, 5.6]
  c = [1.9, 1.0, 3.9, 3.1, 6.9]

  c1 = correlate(a,a)          # 1.0
  c2 = correlate(a,a.reverse)  # -1.0
  c3 = correlate(b,c)          # 0.8221970228
```

The next version is similar, but it operates on a single array, each element of which is an array containing an x-y pair.

```
  def correlate2(v)
    sum = 0.0
    v.each do |a|
      sum += a[0]*a[1]
    end
    xymean = sum/v.size.to_f
    x = v.collect {|a| a[0]}
    y = v.collect {|a| a[1]}
    xmean  = mean(x)
    ymean  = mean(y)
    sx = sigma(x)
    sy = sigma(y)
    (xymean-(xmean*ymean))/(sx*sy)
  end


  d = [[1,6.1], [2.1,3.1], [3.9,5.0], [4.8,6.2]]

  c4 = correlate2(d)          # 0.2277822492
```

Finally we show a version that assumes the x-y pairs are stored in a hash. It simply builds on the previous example.

```
  def correlate_h(h)
    correlate2(h.to_a)
  end


  e = { 1 => 6.1, 2.1 => 3.1, 3.9 => 5.0, 4.8 => 6.2}

  c5 = correlate_h(e)          # 0.2277822492
```

Performing Base Conversions

Obviously any integer can be represented in any base because they are all stored internally in binary. Further, we know that Ruby can deal with integer constants in any of the four commonly-used bases. This means that if we are concerned about base conversions, we must be concerned with strings in some fashion.

If you are concerned with converting a string to an integer, that is covered in "Converting Strings to Numbers (Decimal and Otherwise)."

If you are concerned with converting numbers to strings, that is another matter. The best way to do it is with the % method of the String class. This method formats its argument according to the printf directive found in the string.

```
hex = "%x" % 1234      # "4d2"
oct = "%o" % 1234      # "2322"
bin = "%b" % 1234      # "10011010010"
```

Converting from one nondecimal base to another can be done with a combination of these techniques.

```
oct = "2322"
hex = "%x" % oct.oct   # "4d2"
```

Converting to and from oddball bases such as 5 or 11 is unsupported by Ruby. This is rare enough that we will leave it as an exercise for you.

Generating Random Numbers

If a pseudorandom number is good enough for you, you're in luck. This is what most language implementations supply you with, and Ruby is no exception.

The Kernel method rand will return a pseudorandom floating-point number x such that $x>=0.0$ and $x<1.0$.

```
a = rand       # 0.6279091137
```

If it is called with an integer parameter max, it will return an integer in the range $0...max$ (non-inclusive of the upper bound).

```
n = rand(10)   # 7
```

If we want to seed the random number generator, we can do so with the Kernel method srand, which takes a single numeric parameter. If we pass no value to it, it will construct its own using (among other things) the time of day. If we pass a number to it, it will use that number as the seed. This can be useful in testing, when we want a repeatable sequence of pseudorandom numbers from one script invocation to the next.

```
srand(5)
i, j, k = rand(100), rand(100), rand(100)
# 26, 45, 56

srand(5)
l, m, n = rand(100), rand(100), rand(100)
# 26, 45, 56
```

Caching Functions for Speed

Suppose that you have a computationally expensive mathematical function that will be called repeatedly in the course of execution. If speed is critical and you can afford to sacrifice a little memory and accuracy, it might be effective to store values in a table and look them up.

In this example, we define an arbitrary function called zeta, which we want to call over a domain of 0.0 to 90.0. The function zeta is defined to be 2 sin x cos x (in degrees). Let's assume that our parameters will be no more accurate than a tenth of a degree. This means that if we want to store these values, we will need a table of about 900 elements.

Let's look at a code fragment.

```
def zeta(x)
  r2d  = 360.0/(2.0*Math::PI)  # Radians to degrees
  2.0*(Math.sin (x/r2d))*(Math.cos (x/r2d))
end

$fast_zeta = []

(0..900).each {|x| $fast_zeta[x]=zeta(x/10.0)}

def fast_zeta(x)
  $fast_zeta[(x*10).round]
end

y1 = zeta(37.5)                 # Slow

y2 = fast_zeta(37.5)            # Somewhat faster

y3 = $fast_zeta[(37.5*10).round] # Still faster
```

We define an array called $fast_zeta, using a global variable; we then populate it with all the values from zeta(0.0) to zeta(90.0). We define a function called fast_zeta, which will take a parameter, convert it to an index, and find the appropriate entry in the array. As an alternative, we also access the array directly (in the computation of y3).

In our tests, we put each calculation in a tight loop that ran for millions of iterations. We found that, compared with the calculation of y1, the calculation of y2 was about 66% faster. In addition, the calculation of y3 (which avoided the method call overhead) was about 72.5% faster.

At times, this method won't be practical at all. But we present it to you as a simple demonstration of what can be done to increase speed without dropping into C code.

Matrix Manipulation

There is a standard library `matrix.rb` for this purpose. It is fairly full-featured, with class methods to create matrices in various forms (including identity and zero matrices) and an accessor method to get at the elements in standard *x[i,j]* form. There are methods to find a determinant, to transpose a matrix, to multiply by another matrix or by a scalar, and so on.

This is a standard library. It is too elaborate to document here in detail.

Complex Numbers

The standard library `complex.rb` provides most of the functionality anyone would need for working with numbers in the complex plane. Be warned that some of the methods are named with exclamation points when there isn't necessarily a compelling reason to do so.

This is a well-known standard library. We won't document it here because it is too complex (no pun intended).

Formatting Numbers with Commas

There might be better ways to do it, but this one works. We reverse the string to make it easier to do global substitution, and then reverse it again at the end.

```
def commas(x)
  str = x.to_s.reverse
  str.gsub!("([0-9]{3})","\\1,")
  str.gsub(",$","").reverse
end

puts commas(123)        # "123"
puts commas(1234)       # "1,234"
puts commas(12345)      # "12,435"
puts commas(123456)     # "123,456"
puts commas(1234567)    # "1,234,567"
```

Times and Dates

> *Does anybody really know what time it is?*
> —Chicago, *Chicago IV*

One of the most complex and confusing areas of human life is that of measuring time. To come to a complete understanding of the subject, you would need to study physics, astronomy, history, law, business, and religion. Astronomers know (as most of us don't!) that solar time and sidereal time aren't quite the same thing, and why a leap second is occasionally added to the end of the year. Historians know that the calendar skipped several days in October 1582, when Italy converted from the Julian calendar to the Gregorian. Very few people know the difference between astronomical Easter and ecclesiastical Easter (which are almost always the same). Many people don't know that century years not divisible by 400 (such as the year 1900) aren't leap years.

Performing calculations with times and dates is common in computing, but it has traditionally been somewhat tedious in most programming languages. It is tedious in Ruby, too, because of the nature of the data. However, Ruby has taken some incremental steps toward making these operations easier.

As a courtesy to you, we'll go over a few terms that might not be familiar to you. Most of these come from standard usage or from other programming languages.

Greenwich Mean Time (GMT) is an old term not really in official use anymore. The new global standard is *Coordinated Universal Time (or UTC)*, which is from the French version of the name. GMT and UTC are virtually the same thing; over a period of years, the difference will be on the order of seconds. Much of the software in the industry doesn't distinguish between the two at all (nor does Ruby).

Daylight Saving Time is a semiannual shift in the official time, amounting to a difference of one hour. Thus the U.S. time zones usually end in "ST" (standard time) or "DT" (daylight savings time). This annoying trick is used in most (although not all) of the U.S.A. Other countries need not worry about it.

The epoch is a term borrowed from UNIX lore. In this realm, a time is typically stored internally as a number of seconds from a specific point in time (called the *epoch*), which was midnight January 1, 1970 GMT. (Note that in U.S. time zones, this will actually be the preceding December 31.) The same term is used to denote not only the point of origin, but also the distance in time from that point.

The `Time` class is used for most operations. The Date and ParseDate libraries extend its capabilities somewhat. We will look at the basic techniques and the problems they enable us to solve.

Determining the Current Time

The most fundamental problem in time/date manipulation is to answer the question: What is the time and date right now? In Ruby, when we create a `Time` object with no parameters, it is set to the current date and time.

```
t0 = Time.new
```

`Time.now` is a synonym.

```
t0 = Time.now
```

Note that the resolution of system clocks varies from one architecture to another. It might include microseconds; in which case, two `Time` objects created in succession might actually record different times.

Working with Specific Times (Post-epoch)

Most software only needs to work with dates in the future or in the recent past. For these circumstances, the `Time` class is adequate. The relevant class methods are `mktime`, `local`, `gm`, and `utc`.

The `mktime` method will create a new `Time` object based on the parameters passed to it. These time units are given in reverse from longest to shortest: year, month, day, hours, minutes, seconds, microseconds. All but the year are optional; they default to the lowest possible value. The microseconds can be ignored on many architectures. The hours must be between 0 and 23 (that is, a 24-hour clock).

```
t1 = Time.mktime(2001)                  # January 1, 2001 at 0:00:00
t2 = Time.mktime(2001,3)
t3 = Time.mktime(2001,3,15)
t4 = Time.mktime(2001,3,15,21)
t5 = Time.mktime(2001,3,15,21,30)
t6 = Time.mktime(2001,3,15,21,30,15)    # March 15, 2001 9:30:15 pm
```

Note that `mktime` assumes the local time zone. In fact, `Time.local` is a synonym for it.

```
t7 = Time.local(2001,3,15,21,30,15)     # March 15, 2001 9:30:15 pm
```

The `Time.gm` method is basically the same, except that it assumes GMT (or UTC). Because the authors are in the U.S. Central time zone, we would see an eight-hour difference here.

```
t8 = Time.gm(2001,3,15,21,30,15)        # March 15, 2001 9:30:15 pm
# This is only 1:30:15 pm in Central time!
```

The `Time.utc` method is a synonym.

```
t9 = Time.utc(2001,3,15,21,30,15)       # March 15, 2001 9:30:15 pm
# Again, 1:30:15 pm Central time.
```

There is one more important item to note. All these methods can take an alternative set of parameters. The instance method to_a (which converts a time to an array of relevant values) returns a set of values in this order: seconds, minutes, hours, day, month, year, day of week (0..6), day of year (1..366), daylight saving (true or false), and time zone (as a string).

Thus, these are also valid calls:

```
t0 = Time.local(0,15,3,20,11,1979,2,324,false,"GMT-8:00")
t1 = Time.gm(*Time.now.to_a)
```

However, in the first example, don't fall into the trap of thinking that you can change the computable parameters such as the day of the week (in this case, 2 meaning Tuesday). A change like this simply contradicts the way our calendar works, and it will have no effect on the time object created. November 20, 1979, was a Tuesday regardless of how we might write our code.

Finally, note that there are obviously many ways to attempt coding incorrect times, such as a thirteenth month or a 35th day of the month. In cases like these, an ArgumentError will be raised.

Determining Day of the Week

There are several ways to do this. First of all, the instance method to_a will return an array of time information. You can access the seventh element, which is a number from 0 to 6 (0 meaning Sunday and 6 meaning Saturday).

```
time = Time.now
day = time.to_a[6]          # 2 (meaning Tuesday)
```

It's better to use the instance method wday as shown here:

```
day = time.wday             # 2 (meaning Tuesday)
```

But both these techniques are a little cumbersome. Sometimes we want the value coded as a number, but more often we don't. To get the actual name of the weekday as a string, we can use the strftime method. This name will be familiar to C programmers. There are nearly two dozen different specifiers that it recognizes, enabling us to format dates and times more or less as we please. (See the section "Formatting and Printing Date/Time Values.")

```
day = time.strftime("%a")    # "Tuesday"
```

It's also possible to obtain an abbreviated name.

```
long  = time.strftime("%A")  # "Tuesday"
```

Determining the Date of Easter

Traditionally, this holiday is one of the hardest to compute because it is tied to the lunar cycle. The lunar month doesn't go evenly into the solar year, and thus anything based on the moon can be expected to vary from year to year.

The algorithm we present here is a well-known one that has made the rounds. We have seen it coded in BASIC, Pascal, and C. We now present it to you in Ruby.

```ruby
def easter(year)
  c = year/100
  n = year - 19*(year/19)
  k = (c-17)/25
  i = c - c/4 - (c-k)/3 + 19*n + 15
  i = i - 30*(i/30)
  i = i - (i/28)*(1 -(i/28)*(29/(i+1))*((21-n)/11))
  j = year + year/4 + i + 2 - c + c/4
  j = j - 7*(j/7)
  l = i - j
  month = 3 + (l+40)/44
  day = l + 28 - 31*(month/4)
  [month, day]
end
```

```ruby
date = easter 2001      # Find month/day for 2001
date = [2001] + date    # Tack year on front
t = Time.local *date    # Pass parameters to Time.local
puts t                  # Sun Apr 15 01:00:00 GMT-8:00 2001
```

We would love to explain this algorithm to you, but we don't understand it ourselves. Some things must be taken on faith, and in the case of Easter, this might be especially appropriate.

Finding the *N*th Weekday in a Month

Sometimes for a given month and year, we want to find the date of the third Monday in the month, or the second Tuesday, and so on. Listing 2.9 makes that calculation simple.

If we are looking for the *nth* occurrence of a certain weekday, we pass *n* as the first parameter. The second parameter is the number of that weekday (*0* meaning Sunday, *1* meaning Monday, and so on). The third and fourth parameters are the month and year, respectively.

LISTING 2.9   Finding the *N*th Weekday

```ruby
def nth_wday(n, wday, month, year)
  if (!n.between? 1,5) or
     (!wday.between? 0,6) or
```

LISTING 2.9   Continued

```
      (!month.between? 1,12)
      raise ArgumentError
  end
  t = Time.local year, month, 1
  first = t.wday
  if first == wday
      fwd = 1
    elsif first < wday
      fwd = wday - first + 1
    elsif first > wday
      fwd = (wday+7) - first + 1
    end
    target = fwd + (n-1)*7
    begin
      t2 = Time.local year, month, target
    rescue ArgumentError
      return nil
    end
    if t2.mday == target
      t2
    else
      nil
    end
  end

  puts nth_wday(ARGV[0].to_i, ARGV[1].to_i, ARGV[2].to_i, ARGV[3].to_i)
```

The peculiar-looking code near the end of the method is put there to counteract a long-standing tradition in the underlying time-handling routines. You might expect that trying to create a date of November 31 would result in an error of some kind. You would be mistaken. Most systems would happily (and silently) convert this to December 1. If you are an old-time UNIX hacker, you might think this is a feature; otherwise, you might consider it a bug.

We won't venture an opinion here as to what the underlying library code ought to do or whether Ruby ought to change that behavior. But we don't want to have this routine perpetuate the tradition. If you are looking for the date of, say, the fifth Friday in November 2000, you will get a `nil` value back (rather than December 1, 2000).

Converting Between Seconds and Larger Units

Sometimes we want to take a number of seconds and convert to days, hours, minutes, and seconds. This little routine will do just that.

```ruby
def sec2dhms(secs)
  time = secs.round         # Get rid of microseconds
  sec = time % 60           # Extract seconds
  time /= 60                # Get rid of seconds
  mins = time % 60          # Extract minutes
  time /= 60                # Get rid of minutes
  hrs = time % 24           # Extract hours
  time /= 24                # Get rid of hours
  days = time               # Days (final remainder)
  [days, hrs, mins, sec]    # Return array [d,h,m,s]
end

t = sec2dhms(1000000)       # A million seconds is...

puts "#{t[0]} days,"              # 11 days,
puts "#{t[1]} hours,"            # 13 hours,
puts "#{t[2]} minutes,"         # 46 minutes,
puts " and #{t[3]} seconds."  # and 40 seconds.
```

We could, of course, go up to higher units. But a week isn't an overly useful unit, a month isn't a well-defined term, and a year is far from being an integral number of days.

We also present here the inverse of that function.

```ruby
def dhms2sec(days,hrs=0,min=0,sec=0)
  days*86400 + hrs*3600 + min*60 + sec
end
```

Converting to and from the Epoch

For various reasons, we might want to convert back and forth between the internal (or traditional) measure and the standard date form. Internally, dates are stored as a number of seconds since the epoch.

The Time.at class method will create a new time given the number of seconds since the epoch.

```ruby
epoch = Time.at(0)            # Find the epoch (1 Jan 1970 GMT)
newmil = Time.at(978307200) # Happy New Millennium! (1 Jan 2001)
```

The inverse is the instance method to_i, which converts to an integer.

```ruby
now = Time.now        # 16 Nov 2000 17:24:28
sec = now.to_i        # 974424268
```

If you need microseconds and your system supports that resolution, you can use to_f to convert to a floating-point number.

Working with Leap Seconds: Don't!

Ah, but my calculations, people say,
Reduced the year to better reckoning? Nay,
'Twas only striking from the calendar
Unborn Tomorrow and dead Yesterday.

—Omar Khayyam, *The Rubaiyat* (translation by Fitzgerald)

You want to work with leap seconds? Our advice is: Don't do it.

Although leap seconds are very real and for years the library routines have for years allowed for the possibility of a 61-second minute, our experience has been that most systems don't keep track of leap seconds. By most, we mean all the ones we've ever checked.

For example, a leap second is known to have been inserted at the end of the last day of 1998. Immediately following 23:59:59 came that rare event 23:59:60. But the underlying C libraries on which Ruby is built are ignorant of this.

```
t0 = Time.gm(1998, 12, 31, 23, 59, 59)
t1 = t0 + 1
puts t1      # Fri Jan 01 00:00:00 GMT 1999
```

It is (barely) conceivable that Ruby could add a layer of intelligence to correct for this. At the time of this writing, however, there are no plans to add such functionality.

Finding the Day of the Year

The day number within the year is sometimes called the Julian date, which isn't directly related to the Julian calendar that has gone out of style. Other people insist that this usage isn't correct, so we won't use it from here on.

No matter what you call it, there will be times you want to know what day of the year it is, from 1 to 366. This is easy in Ruby; we use the yday method.

```
t = Time.now
day = t.yday      # 315
```

Validating a Date/Time

As you saw in "Finding the *N*th Weekday in a Month," the standard date/time functions don't check the validity of a date, but roll it over as needed. For example, November 31 will be translated to December 1.

At times, this might be the behavior you want. If it isn't, you will be happy to know that the standard library date doesn't regard such a date as valid. We can use this fact to perform validation of a date as we instantiate it.

```ruby
class Time

  def Time.validate(year, month=1, day=1,
                    hour=0, min=0, sec=0, usec=0)
    require "date"

    begin
      d = Date.new(year,month,day)
    rescue
      return nil
    end
    Time.local(year,month,day,hour,min,sec,usec)
  end

end

t1 = Time.validate(2000,11,30)  # Instantiates a valid object
t2 = Time.validate(2000,11,31)  # Returns nil
```

Here we have taken the lazy way out; we simply set the return value to nil if the parameters passed in don't form a valid date (as determined by the Date class). We have made this method a class method of Time by analogy with the other methods that instantiate objects.

Note that the Date class can work with dates prior to the epoch. This means that passing in a date such as 31 May 1961 will succeed as far as the Date class is concerned. But when these values are passed into the Time class, an ArgumentError will result. We don't attempt to catch that exception here because we think it's appropriate to let it be caught at the same level as (for example) Time.local, in the user code.

Speaking of Time.local, we used that method in the preceding; but if we wanted GMT instead, we could have called the gmt method. It would be a good idea to implement both flavors.

Finding the Week of the Year

The definition of week number isn't absolute and fixed. Various businesses, coalitions, government agencies, and standards bodies have differing concepts of what it means. This stems, of course, from the fact that the year can start on any day of the week; we might or might not want to count partial weeks, and we might start on Sunday or Monday.

We offer only three alternatives here. The first two are made available by the Time method `strftime`. The %U specifier numbers the weeks starting from Sunday, and the %W specifier starts with Monday.

The third possibility comes from the Date class. It has an accessor called `cweek`, which returns the week number based on the ISO 8601 definition (which says that week 1 is the week containing the first Thursday of the year).

If none of these three suits you, you might have to roll your own. We present these three in a single code fragment.

```
require "date"

# Let's look at May 1 in the years
# 2002 and 2005.

t1 = Time.local(2002,5,1)
d1 = Date.new(2002,5,1)

week1a = t1.strftime("%U").to_i    # 17
week1b = t1.strftime("%W").to_i    # 17
week1c = d1.cweek                  # 18

t2 = Time.local(2005,5,1)
d2 = Date.new(2005,5,1)

week2a = t2.strftime("%U").to_i    # 18
week2b = t2.strftime("%W").to_i    # 18
week2c = d2.cweek                  # 17
```

Detecting Leap Years

The Date class has two class methods `julian_leap?` and `gregorian_leap?`; only the latter is of use in recent years. It also has a method `leap?`, which is an alias for the `gregorian_leap?` method.

```
require "date"
flag1 = Date.julian_leap? 1700     # true
flag2 = Date.gregorian_leap? 1700  # false
flag3 = Date.leap? 1700            # false
```

Every child knows the first rule for leap years: The year number must be divisible by four. Fewer people know the second rule, that the year number must not be divisible by 100; and fewer still know the exception, that the year can be divisible by 400. In other words: A century year is a leap year only if it is divisible by 400, so 1900 wasn't a leap year, but 2000 was.

The `Time` class doesn't have a method like this, but if we needed one, it would be simple to create.

```ruby
class Time

  def Time.leap? year
    if year % 400 == 0
      true
    elsif year % 100 == 0
      false
    elsif year % 4 == 0
      true
    else
      false
  end

end
```

We implement this as a class method by analogy with the `Date` class methods. It could also be implemented as an instance method.

Obtaining the Time Zone

The accessor zone in the `Time` class will return a String representation of the time zone name.

```ruby
z1 = Time.gm(2000,11,10,22,5,0).zone      # "GMT-6:00"
z2 = Time.local(2000,11,10,22,5,0).zone   # "GMT-6:00"
```

Unfortunately, times are stored relative to the current time zone, not the one with which the object was created.

Working with Hours and Minutes Only

We might want to work with times of day as strings. Once again, `strftime` comes to our aid.

We can print the time with hours, minutes, and seconds if we want.

```ruby
t = Time.now
puts t.strftime("%H:%M:%S")    # Prints 22:07:45
```

We can print hours and minutes only (and, using the trick of adding 30 seconds to the time, we can even round to the nearest minute).

```ruby
puts t.strftime("%H:%M")       # Prints 22:07
puts (t+30).strftime("%H:%M")  # Prints 22:08
```

Finally, if we don't like the standard 24-hour (or military) clock, we can switch to the 12-hour clock. It's appropriate to add a meridian indicator then (AM/PM).

```
puts t.strftime("%I:%M %p")    # Prints 10:07 PM
```

There are other possibilities, of course. Use your imagination.

Comparing Date/Time Values

The Time class conveniently mixes in the Comparable module, so dates and times might be compared in a straightforward way.

```
t0 = Time.local(2000,11,10,22,15)    # 10 Nov 2000 22:15
t1 = Time.local(2000,11,9,23,45)     #  9 Nov 2000 23:45
t2 = Time.local(2000,11,12,8,10)     # 12 Nov 2000  8:10
t3 = Time.local(2000,11,11,10,25)    # 11 Nov 2000 10:25

if t0 < t1 then puts "t0 < t1" end
if t1 != t2 then puts "t1 != t2" end
if t1 <= t2 then puts "t1 <= t2" end
if t3.between?(t1,t2)
  puts "t3 is between t1 and t2"
end

# All four if statements test true
```

Adding Intervals to Date/Time Values

We can obtain a new time by adding an interval to a specified time. The number is interpreted as a number of seconds.

```
t0 = Time.now
t1 = t0 + 60       # Exactly one minute past t0
t2 = t0 + 3600     # Exactly one hour past t0
t3 = t0 + 86400    # Exactly one day past t0
```

The function dhms2sec (defined in "Converting Between Seconds and Larger Units") might be helpful here. Recall that the hours, minutes, and seconds all default to 0.

```
t4 = t0 + dhms2sec(5,10)       # Ahead 5 days, 10 hours
t5 = t0 + dhms2sec(22,18,15)   # Ahead 22 days, 18 hrs, 15 min
t6 = t0 - dhms2sec(7)          # Exactly one week ago
```

Don't forget that we can move backward in time by subtracting. This is shown in the preceding calculation of t6.

Computing the Difference in Two Date/Time Values

We can find the interval of time between two points in time. Subtracting one `Time` object from another gives us a number of seconds.

```
today = Time.local(2000,11,10)
yesterday = Time.local(2000,11,9)
diff = today - yesterday              # 86400 seconds
```

Once again, the function `sec2dhms` comes in handy. (This is defined in "Converting Between Seconds and Larger Units.")

```
past = Time.local(1998,9,13,4,15)
now = Time.local(2000,11,10,22,42)
diff = now - past
unit = sec2dhms(diff)
puts "#{unit[0]} days,"              # 789 days,
puts "#{unit[1]} hours,"            # 18 hours,
puts "#{unit[2]} minutes,"         # 27 minutes,
puts "and #{unit[3]} seconds."     # and 0 seconds.
```

Working with Specific Dates (Pre-epoch)

The standard library Date provides a class of the same name for working with dates that precede midnight GMT, January 1, 1970.

Although there is some overlap in functionality with the `Time` class, there are significant differences. Most notably, the `Date` class doesn't handle the time of day at all. Its resolution is a single day. Also, the `Date` class performs more rigorous error-checking than the `Time` class; if you attempt to refer to a date such as June 31 (or even February 29 in a nonleap year), you will get an error. The code is smart enough to know the different cutoff dates for Italy and England switching to the Gregorian calendar (in 1582 and 1752, respectively), and it can detect nonexistent dates that are a result of this switchover. This standard library is a tangle of interesting and arcane code. We don't have space to document it further here.

Retrieving a Date/Time Value from a String

A date and time can be formatted as a string in many different ways because of abbreviations, varying punctuation, different orderings, and so on. Because of the various ways of formatting, writing code to decipher such a character string can be daunting. Consider these examples:

```
s1 = "9/13/98 2:15am"
s2 = "1961-05-31"
s3 = "11 July 1924"
s4 = "April 17, 1929"
s5 = "20 July 1969 16:17 EDT"  # That's one small step...
```

```
s6 = "Mon Nov 13 2000"
s7 = "August 24, 79"              # Destruction of Pompeii
s8 = "8/24/79"
```

Fortunately, much of the work has already been done for us. The `ParseDate` module has a single class of the same name, which has a single method called `parsedate`. This method returns an array of elements in this order: year, month, day, hour, minute, second, time zone, day of week. Any fields that cannot be determined are returned as `nil` values.

```
require "parsedate.rb"
include ParseDate

p parsedate(s1)        # [98, 9, 13, 2, 15, nil, nil, nil]
p parsedate(s2)        # [1961, 5, 31, nil, nil, nil, nil, nil]
p parsedate(s3)        # [1924, 7, 11, nil, nil, nil, nil, nil]
p parsedate(s4)        # [1929, 4, 17, nil, nil, nil, nil, nil]
p parsedate(s5)        # [1969, 7, 20, 16, 17, nil, "EDT", nil]
p parsedate(s6)        # [2000, 11, 13, nil, nil, nil, nil, 1]
p parsedate(s7)        # [79, 8, 24, nil, nil, nil, nil, nil]
p parsedate(s8,true)   # [1979, 8, 24, nil, nil, nil, nil, nil]
```

The last two strings illustrate the purpose of `parsedate`'s second parameter `guess_year`; because of our cultural habit of representing a year as two digits, ambiguity can result. Thus the last two strings are interpreted differently because we parse `s8` with `guess_year` set to `true`, resulting in its conversion to a four-digit year. On the other hand, `s7` refers to the eruption of Vesuvius in 79 A.D., so we definitely want a two-digit year there.

The rule for `guess_year` is this: If the year is less than 100 and `guess_year` is `true`, convert to a four-digit year. The conversion will be done as follows: If the year is 70 or greater, add 1900 to it; otherwise add 2000. Thus 75 will translate to 1975, but 65 will translate to 2065. This rule isn't uncommon in the computing world.

What about `s1`, where we probably intended 1998 as the year? All is not lost as long as we pass this number to some other piece of code that interprets it as 1998.

Note that `parsedate` does virtually no error checking. For example, if you feed it a date with a weekday and a date that don't correspond correctly, it won't detect this discrepancy. It is only a parser, and it does this job pretty well, but no other.

Also note an American bias in this code. An American writing 3/4/2001 usually means March 4, 2001; in Europe and most other places, this would mean April 3 instead. But if all the data is consistent, this isn't a huge problem. Because the return value is simply an array, you can mentally switch the meaning of elements 1 and 2. Be aware also that this bias happens even with a date such as 15/3/2000, where it is clear (to us) that 15 is the day. The `parsedate` method will happily return 15 as the month value.

2

SIMPLE DATA TASKS

Although this method is very flexible, it is far from perfect. We have observed that it tends not to capture the time zone if it follows a meridian indicator such as p.m. We have also noted that it doesn't recognize a year such as '79 (with a leading apostrophe).

Formatting and Printing Date/Time Values

You can obtain the canonical representation of the date and time by calling the asctime method (ASCII time); it has an alias called *ctime*, for those who already know it by that name.

You can obtain a similar result by calling the to_s method. This is the same as the result you would get if doing a simple puts of a date/time value.

The strftime method of class Time will format a date and time in almost any form you can think of. Other examples in this chapter have shown the use of the directives %a, %A, %U, %W, %H, %M, %S, %I, and %p; we list here all the remaining directives that strftime recognizes.

```
%b    Abbreviated month name ("Jan")
%B    Full month name ("January")
%c    Preferred local date/time representation
%d    Day of the month (1..31)
%j    Day of the year (1..366); so-called "Julian date"
%m    Month as a number (1..12)
%w    Day of the week as a number (0..6)
%x    Preferred representation for date (no time)
%y    Two-digit year (no century)
%Y    Four-digit year
%Z    Time zone name
%%    A literal "%" character
```

For more information, consult a Ruby reference.

Time Zone Conversions

It is only convenient to work with two time zones: GMT (or UTC) is one, and the other is whatever time zone you happen to be in.

The gmtime method will convert a time to GMT (changing the receiver in place). There is an alias named utc.

You might expect that it would be possible to convert a time to an array, tweak the time zone, and convert it back. The trouble with this is that all the class methods such as local and gm (or their aliases mktime and utc) want to create a Time object using either your local time zone or GMT.

It is possible to fake time zone conversions. This does require that you know the time difference in advance.

```
mississippi = Time.local(2000,11,13,9,35) # 9:35 am CST
california  = mississippi - 2*3600         # Minus two hours

time1 = mississippi.strftime("%X CST")    # 09:35:00 CST
time2 = california.strftime("%X PST")     # 07:35:00 PST
```

The %X directive to strftime that we see here simply uses the hh:mm:ss format as shown.

Finding the Internet Time (@nnn)

Time is an illusion created by the Swiss to sell watches.

—Douglas Adams

We offer this next item mostly as a curiosity. The Swiss watch manufacturer Swatch has created a trendy way of measuring time in cyberspace, a metric-like time that they call Internet Time. This time standard has no time zones and is thus usable, for example, by people meeting each other in chat rooms when they are physically thousands of miles apart. It was inaugurated on October 23, 1998, in the presence of Nicholas Negroponte, founder and director of MIT's Media Lab.

Not surprisingly, Internet Time is based on the meridian of Biel, Switzerland. The day is divided into 1000 beats, each 86.4 seconds long (or 1 minute, 26.4 seconds). The three digit number representing the time of day is prefixed by an at (@) sign.

This method will find the current time in Internet Time. It returns a number, unless true is passed in; then it returns a string, with an @ and any leading zeroes. Mimicking the behavior of the applications we have seen, we truncate any fractional part rather than rounding up.

```
def internet_time(str=false)
  t = Time.now.gmtime + 3600   # Biel, Switzerland
  midnight = Time.gm(t.year, t.month, t.day)
  secs = t - midnight
  beats = (secs/86.4).to_i
  if str
    "@%03d" % beats
  else
    beats
  end
end

time_now = internet_time       # 27
now = internet_time(true)      # "@027"
```

Summary

That ends our discussion of the simpler tasks we might perform with numbers, strings, and so on. Now it's time to go on to bigger and better data structures and the algorithms that support them.

Manipulating Structured Data

IN THIS CHAPTER

All parts should go together without forcing. You must remember that the parts you are reassembling were disassembled by you. Therefore, if you can't get them together again, there must be a reason. By all means, do not use a hammer.

—IBM maintenance manual (1925)

Simple variables are not adequate for real-life programming. Every modern language supports more complex forms of structured data and also provides mechanisms for creating new abstract data types.

Historically, arrays are the earliest known and most widespread of the complex data structures. Long ago, in FORTRAN, they were called *subscripted variables*. Today they have changed somewhat, but the basic idea is the same in all languages.

More recently, the hash has become an extremely popular programming tool. Like an array, a *hash* is an indexed collection of data items; unlike an array, it may be indexed by any arbitrary object. (In Ruby, as in most languages, array elements are accessed by a numerical index.)

Finally, in this chapter we will look at more advanced data structures. Some of these are just special "views" of an array or hash; for example, stacks and queues can be implemented easily using arrays. Other structures such as trees and graphs may be implemented in different ways according to the situation and the programmer's preference.

But let's not get ahead of ourselves. We will begin with arrays.

Working with Arrays

Arrays in Ruby are indexed by integers and are zero based, just like C arrays. The resemblance ends there, however.

A Ruby array is dynamic. It is possible (but not necessary) to specify its size when you create it. After creation, it can grow as needed without any intervention by the programmer.

A Ruby array is *heterogeneous* in the sense that it can store multiple data types rather than just one type. Actually, it stores object references rather than the objects themselves, except in the case of immediate values such as Fixnum values.

An array keeps up with its own length so that we don't have to waste our time with calculating it or keeping an external variable in sync with the array. Also, iterators are defined so that, in practice, we rarely need to know the array length anyway.

Finally, the Array class in Ruby provides arrays with many useful functions for accessing, searching, concatenating, and otherwise manipulating arrays. We'll spend the remainder of this section exploring the built-in functionality and expanding on it.

Creating and Initializing an Array

The special class method [] is used to create an array; the data items listed within the brackets are used to populate the array. The three ways of calling this method are shown here (note that arrays a, b, and c will all be populated identically):

```
a = Array.[](1,2,3,4)
b = Array[1,2,3,4]
c = [1,2,3,4]
```

Also, the class method new can take zero, one, or two parameters. The first parameter is the initial size of the array (number of elements). The second parameter is the initial value of each of the elements. Here's an example:

```
d = Array.new              # Create an empty array
e = Array.new(3)           # [nil, nil, nil]
f = Array.new(3, "blah")   # ["blah", "blah", "blah"]
```

Accessing and Assigning Array Elements

Element reference and assignment are done using the class methods [] and []=, respectively. Each can take an integer parameter, a pair of integers (start and length), or a range. A negative index counts backward from the end of the array, starting at -1.

Also, the special instance method at works like a simple case of element reference. Because it can take only a single integer parameter, it is slightly faster. Here's an example:

```
a = [1, 2, 3, 4, 5, 6]
b = a[0]                  # 1
c = a.at(0)              # 1
d = a[-2]               # 5
e = a.at(-2)            # 5
f = a[9]                # nil
g = a.at(9)             # nil
h = a[3,3]              # [4, 5, 6]
i = a[2..4]             # [3, 4, 5]
j = a[2...4]            # [3, 4]

a[1] = 8                 # [1, 8, 3, 4, 5, 6]
a[1,3] = [10, 20, 30]    # [1, 10, 20, 30, 5, 6]
a[0..3] = [2, 4, 6, 8]   # [2, 4, 6, 8, 5, 6]
a[-1] = 12               # [2, 4, 6, 8, 5, 12]
```

Note in the following example how a reference beyond the end of the array causes the array to grow (note also that a subarray can be replaced with more elements than were originally there, also causing the array to grow):

```
k = [2, 4, 6, 8, 10]
k[1..2] = [3, 3, 3]      # [2, 3, 3, 3, 8, 10]
k[7] = 99                # [2, 3, 3, 3, 8, 10, nil, 99]
```

Finally, we should mention that an array assigned to a single element will actually insert that element as a nested array (unlike an assignment to a range), as shown here:

```
m = [1, 3, 5, 7, 9]
m[2] = [20, 30]          # [1, 3, [20, 30], 7, 9]

# On the other hand...
m = [1, 3, 5, 7, 9]
m[2..2] = [20, 30]       # [1, 3, 20, 30, 7, 9]
```

The method slice is simply an alias for the [] method:

```
x = [0, 2, 4, 6, 8, 10, 12]
a = x.slice(2)                 # 4
b = x.slice(2,4)               # [4, 6, 8, 10]
c = x.slice(2..4)              # [4, 6, 8]
```

The special methods first and last will return the first and last elements of an array, respectively. They will return nil if the array is empty. Here's an example:

```
x = %w[alpha beta gamma delta epsilon]
a = x.first      # "alpha"
b = x.last       # "epsilon"
```

We have seen that some of the element-referencing techniques actually can return an entire subarray. There are other ways to access multiple elements, which we'll look at now.

The method indices will take a list of indices (or *indexes*, if you prefer) and return an array consisting of only those elements. It can be used where a range cannot (when the elements are not all contiguous). The alias is called indexes. Here's an example:

```
x = [10, 20, 30, 40, 50, 60]
y = x.indices(0, 1, 4)         # [10, 20, 50]
z = x.indexes(2, 10, 5, 4)     # [30, nil, 60, 50]
```

Finding an Array's Size

The method length (or its alias size) will give the number of elements in an array. Note that this is one less than the index of the last item:

```
x = ["a", "b", "c", "d"]
a = x.length               # 4
b = x.size                 # 4
```

The method `nitems` is the same except that it does not count `nil` elements:

```
y = [1, 2, nil, nil, 3, 4]
c = y.size              # 6
d = y.length            # 6
e = y.nitems            # 4
```

Comparing Arrays

Comparing arrays is slightly tricky. If you do it at all, you should do it with caution.

The instance method `<=>` is used to compare arrays. It works the same as the other contexts in which it is used, returning either -1 (meaning "less than"), 0 (meaning "equal"), or 1 (meaning "greater than"). The methods `==` and `!=` depend on this method.

Arrays are compared in an "elementwise" manner; the first two elements that are not equal will determine the inequality for the whole comparison. (Therefore, preference is given to the leftmost elements, just as if we were comparing two long integers "by eye," looking at one digit at a time.) Here's an example:

```
a = [1, 2, 3, 9, 9]
b = [1, 2, 4, 1, 1]
c = a <=> b              # -1 (meaning a < b)
```

If all elements are equal, the arrays are equal. If one array is longer than another, and they are equal up to the length of the shorter array, the longer array is considered to be greater:

```
d = [1, 2, 3]
e = [1, 2, 3, 4]
f = [1, 2, 3]
if d == f
  puts "d equals f"    # Prints "d equals f"
end
```

Because the `Array` class does not mix in the `Comparable` module, the usual operators, `<`, `>`, `<=`, and `>=`, are not defined for arrays. However, we can easily define them ourselves if we choose:

```
class Array

  def <=> other)
    (self <=> other)== -1
  end

  def <=(other)
    (self < other) or (self == other)
  end

  def >(other)
```

```
    (self <=> other) == 1
  end

  def >=(other)
    (self > other) or (self == other)
  end

end
```

Having defined them, we can use them as you would expect:

```
if a < b
  print "a < b"        # Prints "a < b"
else
  print "a >= b"
end
if d < e
  puts "d < e"         # Prints "d < e"
end
```

It is conceivable that comparing arrays will result in the comparison of two elements for which <=> is undefined or meaningless. This will result in a runtime error (a TypeError) because the comparison 3 <=> "x" is problematic:

```
g = [1, 2, 3]
h = [1, 2, "x"]
if g < h               # Error!
  puts "g < h"         # No output
end
```

However, in case you are still not confused, equal and not-equal will still work in this case. This is because two objects of different types are naturally considered to be unequal, even though we can't say which is greater or less than the other:

```
if g != h              # No problem here.
  puts "g != h"        # Prints "g != h"
end
```

Finally, it is conceivable that two arrays containing mismatched data types will still compare with the < and > operators. In the case shown here, we get a result before we stumble across the incomparable elements:

```
i = [1, 2, 3]
j = [1, 2, 3, "x"]
if i < j               # No problem here.
  puts "i < j"         # Prints "i < j"
end
```

Sorting an Array

The easiest way to sort an array is to use the built-in `sort` method, as shown here:

```
words = %w(the quick brown fox)
list = words.sort  # ["brown", "fox", "quick", "the"]
# Or sort in place:
words.sort!        # ["brown", "fox", "quick", "the"]
```

This method assumes that all the elements in the array are comparable with each other. A mixed array, such as [1, 2, "three", 4], will normally give a type error.

In a case like this one, you can use the block form of the same method call. The example here assumes that there is at least a `to_s` method for each element (to convert it to a string):

```
a = [1, 2, "three", "four", 5, 6]
b = a.sort {|x,y| x.to_s <=> y.to_s}
# b is now [1, 2, 5, 6, "four", "three"]
```

Of course, such an ordering (in this case, depending on ASCII) may not be meaningful. If you have such a heterogeneous array, you may want to ask yourself why you are sorting it in the first place or why you are storing different types of objects.

This technique works because the block returns an integer (-1, 0, or 1) on each invocation. When a -1 is returned, meaning that x is less than y, the two elements are swapped. Therefore, to sort in descending order, we could simply swap the order of the comparison, like this:

```
x = [1, 4, 3, 5, 2]
y = x.sort {|a,b| b <=> a}     # [5, 4, 3, 2, 1]
```

The block style can also be used for more complex sorting. Let's suppose we want to sort a list of book and movie titles in a certain way: We ignore case, we ignore spaces entirely, and we want to ignore any certain kinds of embedded punctuation. Listing 3.1 presents a simple example. (Both English teachers and computer programmers will be equally confused by this kind of alphabetizing.)

Listing 3.1   Specialized Sorting

```
titles = ["Starship Troopers",
          "A Star is Born",
          "Star Wars",
          "Star 69",
          "The Starr Report"]
sorted = titles.sort do |x,y|
  # Delete leading articles
  a = x.sub(/^(a |an |the )/i, "")
  b = y.sub(/^(a |an |the )/i, "")
```

LISTING 3.1   Continued

```
      # Delete spaces and punctuation
      a.delete!(" .,-?!")
      b.delete!(" .,-?!")
      # Convert to uppercase
      a.upcase!
      b.upcase!
      # Compare a and b
      a <=> b
    end

    # sorted is now:
    # [ "Star 69", "A Star is Born", "The Starr Report"
    #    "Starship Troopers", "Star Wars"]
```

This example is not overly useful, and it could certainly be written more compactly. The point is that any arbitrarily complex set of operations can be performed on two operands in order to compare them in a specialized way. (Note, however, that we left the original operands untouched by manipulating copies of them.) This general technique can be useful in many situations—for example, sorting on multiple keys or sorting on keys that are computed at runtime.

Selecting from an Array by Criteria

Sometimes we want to locate an item or items in an array much as though we were querying a table in a database. There are several ways to do this; the ones we outline here are all mixed in from the Enumerable module.

The detect method will find at most a single element. It takes a block (into which the elements are passed sequentially) and returns the first element for which the block evaluates to a value that is not false. Here's an example:

```
x = [5, 8, 12, 9, 4, 30]
# Find the first multiple of 6
x.detect {|e| e % 6 == 0 }        # 12
# Find the first multiple of 7
x.detect {|e| e % 7 == 0 }        # nil
```

Of course, the objects in the array can be of arbitrary complexity, as can the test in the block.

The find method is a synonym for detect; the method find_all is a variant that will return multiple elements as opposed to a single element. Finally, the method select is a synonym for find_all. Here's an example:

```
# Continuing the above example...
x.find {|e| e % 2 == 0}           # 8
```

```
x.find_all {|e| e % 2 == 0}      # [8, 12, 4, 30]
x.select {|e| e % 2 == 0}        # [8, 12, 4, 30]
```

The grep method will invoke the relationship operator to match each element against the pattern specified. In its simplest form, it will simply return an array containing the matched elements. Because the relationship operator (===) is used, the so-called pattern need not be a regular expression. (The name *grep*, of course, comes from the Unix tool of the same name, historically meaning something like *general regular expression pattern-matcher*.) Here's an example:

```
a = %w[January February March April May]
a.grep(/ary/)      # ["January, "February"]
b = [1, 20, 5, 7, 13, 33, 15, 28]
b.grep(12..24)     # [20, 13, 15]
```

There is a block form that will effectively transform each result before storing it in the array; the resulting array contains the return values of the block rather than the values passed into the block:

```
# Continuing above example...
# Let's store the string lengths
a.grep(/ary/) {|m| m.length}     # [7, 8]
# Let's square each value
b.grep(12..24) {|n| n*n}         # {400, 169, 225}
```

The reject method is complementary to select. It excludes each element for which the block evaluates to true. The in-place mutator reject! is also defined:

```
c = [5, 8, 12, 9, 4, 30]
d = c.reject {|e| e % 2 == 0}    # [5, 9]
c.reject! {|e| e % 3 == 0}
# c is now [5, 8, 4]
```

The min and max methods may be used to find the minimum and maximum values in an array. There are two forms of each of these. The first form uses the "default" comparison, whatever that may be in the current situation (as defined by the <=> method). The second form uses a block to do a customized comparison. Here's an example:

```
a = %w[Elrond Galadriel Aragorn Saruman Legolas]
b = a.min                                # "Aragorn"
c = a.max                                # "Saruman"
d = a.min {|x,y| x.reverse <=> y.reverse} # "Elrond"
e = a.max {|x,y| x.reverse <=> y.reverse} # "Legolas"
```

Suppose we want to find the *index* of the minimum or maximum element (assuming it is unique). We could use the index method for tasks such as this, as shown here:

```
# Continuing above example...
i = a.index a.min    # 2
j = a.index a.max    # 3
```

This same technique can be used in other similar situations. However, if the element is not unique, the first one in the array will naturally be the one found.

Using Specialized Indexing Functions

The internals of a language handle the mapping of array indexes to array elements through what is called an *indexing function*. Because the methods that access array elements can be overridden, we can in effect index an array in any way we wish.

For example, in Listing 3.2, we implement an array that is "one-based" rather than "zero-based."

LISTING 3.2   Implementing a One-Based Array

```
class Array2 < Array

  def [](index)
    if index>0
      super(index-1)
    else
      raise IndexError
    end
  end

  def []=(index,obj)
    if index>0
      super(index-1,obj)
    else
      raise IndexError
    end
  end

end


x = Array2.new

x[1]=5
x[2]=3
x[0]=1  # Error
x[-1]=1 # Error
```

Note that the negative indexing (from the end of an array) is disallowed here. Also, be aware that if this were a real-life solution, there would be other changes to make, such as the `slice` method and others. However, this gives the general idea.

A similar approach can be used to implement multidimensional arrays (as you'll see later in the section "Using Multidimensional Arrays").

It is also possible to implement something like a triangular matrix (see Listing 3.3). This is like a special case of a two-dimensional array in which element x,y is always the same as element y,x (so that only one needs to be stored). This is sometimes useful, for example, in storing an undirected graph (as you'll see toward the end of this chapter).

LISTING 3.3   Triangular Matrix

```
class TriMatrix

  def initialize
    @store = []
  end

  def [](x,y)
    if x > y
      index = (x*x+x)/2 + y
      @store[index]
    else
      raise IndexError
    end
  end

  def []=(x,y,v)
    if x > y
      index = (x*x+x)/2 + y
      @store[index] = v
    else
      raise IndexError
    end
  end

end


t = TriMatrix.new

t[3,2] = 1
puts t[3,2]   # 1

puts t[2,3]   # IndexError
```

Here, we have chosen to implement the matrix so that the row number must be greater than or equal to the column number; we also could have coded it so that the same pair of indexes simply mapped to the same element. These design decisions will depend on your use of the matrix.

It would have been possible to inherit from Array, but we thought this solution was easier to understand. The indexing formula is a little complex, but 10 minutes with pencil and paper should convince anyone it is correct. Some enhancements could probably be made to this class to make it truly useful, but we will leave that to you, the reader.

Also, it is possible to implement a triangular matrix as an array containing arrays that increase in size as the row number gets higher. This is somewhat similar to what we have done in the section "Using Multidimensional Arrays." The only tricky part would be to make sure that a row does not accidentally grow past its proper size.

Implementing a Sparse Matrix

Sometimes we need an array that has very few of its elements defined; the rest of its elements can be undefined (or more often zero). This so-called "sparse matrix" has historically been a waster of memory that has led people to seek indirect ways of implementing it.

Of course, in most cases, a Ruby array will suffice, because modern architectures typically have large amounts of memory. An unassigned element will have the value nil, which takes only a few bytes to store.

On the other hand, assigning an array element beyond the previous bounds of the array also creates all the nil elements in between. For example, if elements 0 through 9 are defined, and we suddenly assign to element 1000, we have in effect caused elements 10 through 999 to spring into being as nil values. If this is unacceptable, you might consider an alternative.

The alternative we have to suggest, however, does not involve arrays at all. If you really need a sparse matrix, a hash might be the best solution. See the section "Using a Hash As a Sparse Matrix" for more information.

Using Arrays As Mathematical Sets

Most languages do not directly implement sets (Pascal being one exception). However, Ruby arrays have some features that make them usable as sets. We'll present these here and add a few of our own.

First of all, an array can have duplicate entries. If you specifically want to treat the array as a set, you can remove these entries (using uniq or uniq!).

The two most basic operations performed on sets are union and intersection. These are accomplished by the | (or) and & (and) operators, respectively. In accordance with the idea that a set does not contain duplicates, any duplicates will be removed. (This may be contrary to your expectations if you are used to array union and intersection operations in some other language.) Here's an example:

```
a = [1, 2, 3, 4, 5]
b = [3, 4, 5, 6, 7]
c = a | b              # [1, 2, 3, 4, 5, 6, 7]
d = a & b              # [3, 4, 5]
# Duplicates are removed...
e = [1, 2, 2, 3, 4]
f = [2, 2, 3, 4, 5]
g = e & f              # [2, 3, 4]
```

The concatenation operator + can be used for set union, but it does *not* remove duplicates.

The - method is a "set difference" operator that will produce a set with all the members of the first set except the ones appearing in the second set. (See the section "Finding Elements in One Array but Not Another" for more information.) Here's an example:

```
a = [1, 2, 3, 4, 5]
b = [4, 5, 6, 7]
c = a - b              # [1, 2, 3]
# Note that the extra items 6 and 7 are irrelevant.
```

To "accumulate" sets, you can use the |= operator; as expected, a |= b simply means a = a | b. Likewise &= can progressively "narrow down" the elements of a set.

There is no exclusive-or defined for arrays, but we can make our own very easily. In set terms, this corresponds to elements that are in the union of two sets but *not* in the intersection. Here's an example:

```
class Array

  def ^(other)
    (self | other) - (self & other)
  end

end

x = [1, 2, 3, 4, 5]
y = [3, 4, 5, 6, 7]
z = x ^ y              # [1, 2, 6, 7]
```

To check for the presence of an element in a set, we can use the method `include?` or `member?` (essentially an alias mixed in from `Comparable`), like so:

```
x = [1, 2, 3]
if x.include? 2
  puts "yes"      # Prints "yes"
else
  puts "no"
end
```

Of course, this is a little backward from what we are used to in mathematics, where the operator resembling a Greek epsilon denotes set membership. It is backward in the sense that the set is on the left rather than on the right; we are not asking "Is this element in this set?" but rather "Does this set contain this element?"

Many people will not be bothered by this at all. However, if you are used to Pascal or Python (or you have ingrained mathematical inclinations), you may want to use a different way. We present two options here:

```
class Object

  def in(other)
    other.include? self
  end

end

x = [1, 2, 3]
if 2.in x
  puts "yes"      # Prints "yes"
else
  puts "no"
end
```

This is still a trifle ugly, but at least the ordering is more familiar. As for making it look "more like an operator," Ruby's amazingly flexible parser allows you to write the expression `2.in x` instead as `2 .in x` or even `2. in x`, should you wish to go that far.

For those who can't stand the presence of that period, it is conceivable that we could overload an operator such as `<=` for that purpose. However, something like this should be done with caution.

There has been talk of a Python-like (or Pascal-like) in operator for Ruby. However, it is no more than talk at this time.

How do we tell whether a set is a subset or a superset of another? There are no built-in methods, but we can do it as demonstrated in Listing 3.4.

LISTING 3.4   Subset and Superset

```ruby
class Array

  def subset?(other)
    self.each  do |x|
      if !(other.include? x)
        return false
      end
    end
    true
  end

  def superset?(other)
    other.subset?(self)
  end

end

a = [1, 2, 3, 4]
b = [2, 3]
c = [2, 3, 4, 5]

flag1 = c.subset? a     # false
flag2 = b.subset? a     # true
flag3 = c.superset? b   # true
```

Note that we've chosen the "natural" ordering—that is, x.subset? y means "Is *x* a subset of *y*?" rather than vice versa.

To detect the null set (or empty set), we simply detect the empty array. The empty? method will do this.

The concept of set negation (or complement) depends on the concept of a *universal set*. Because in practical terms this will vary from one application or situation to another, the best way is the simplest—define the universe and then do a set difference, as shown here:

```ruby
universe = [1, 2, 3, 4, 5, 6]
a = [2, 3]
b = universe - a   # complement of a = [1, 4, 5, 6]
```

Of course, if you really feel the need, you could define a unary operator (such as - or ~) to do this.

You can iterate through a set just by iterating through the array. The only difference is that the elements will come out in order, which you may not want. To see how to iterate randomly, refer to the section "Iterating over an Array."

Finally, we may sometimes want to compute the powerset of a set. This is simply the set of all possible subsets (including the null set and the original set itself). Those familiar with discrete math, especially combinatorics, will see that there must be 2^n of these subsets. We can generate the powerset as demonstrated in Listing 3.5.

LISTING 3.5   Powerset of a Set

```ruby
class Array

  def powerset
    num = 2**size
    ps = Array.new(num, [])
    self.each_index do |i|
      a = 2**i
      b = 2**(i+1) - 1
      j = 0
      while j < num-1
        for j in j+a..j+b
          ps[j] += [self[i]]
        end
        j += 1
      end
    end
    ps
  end

end

x = [1, 2, 3]
y = x.powerset
# y is now:
#   [[], [1], [2], [1,2], [3], [1,3], [2,3], [1,2,3]]
```

Randomizing an Array

Sometimes we want to scramble an array into a random order. The first example that might come to mind is a card game, but there are other circumstances, such as presenting a list of questions to a user in a random order, in which we might use this.

To accomplish this task, we can use `rand` in the `Kernel` module. Here's one way to do this:

```ruby
class Array

  def randomize
    arr=self.dup
```

```
    arr.collect { arr.slice!(rand arr.length) }
  end

  def randomize!
    arr=self.dup
    result = arr.collect { arr.slice!(rand arr.length) }
    self.replace result
  end

end

x = [1, 2, 3, 4, 5]
y = x.randomize      # [3, 2, 4, 1 ,5]
x.randomize!         # x is now [3, 5, 4, 1, 2]
```

The key to understanding this solution is knowing that the slice! method will return the value of an array element and, at the same time, delete that element from the array (so that it cannot be used again).

There are other ways to perform this operation. If you find a better one, let us know.

If we wanted simply to pick an array element at random (without disallowing duplicates), we could do that as follows.

```
class Array

  def pick_random
    self[rand(self.length)]
  end

end
```

Finally, remember that any time you are using rand, you can generate a predictable sequence (for example, for testing) simply by seeding with a known seed using srand.

Using Multidimensional Arrays

If you want to use multidimensional arrays for numerical purposes, an excellent library in the Ruby Application Archive called NArray (by Masahiro Tanaka) is available. If you want to use matrixes, you can use the matrix.rb standard library, as mentioned in Chapter 2, "Simple Data Tasks."

In Listing 3.6, we present a way of handling multidimensional arrays by overloading the [] and []= methods to map elements onto a nested array. The class Array3 presented here will handle three-dimensional arrays in a rudimentary fashion, but it is far from complete.

LISTING 3.6   Three-dimensional Array

```ruby
class Array3

  def initialize
    @store = [[[]]]
  end

  def [](a,b,c)
    if @store[a]==nil ||
       @store[a][b]==nil ||
       @store[a][b][c]==nil
      return nil
    else
      return @store[a][b][c]
    end
  end

  def []=(a,b,c,x)
    @store[a] = [[]] if @store[a]==nil
    @store[a][b] = [] if @store[a][b]==nil
    @store[a][b][c] = x
  end

end


x = Array3.new
x[0,0,0] = 5
x[0,0,1] = 6
x[1,2,3] = 99

puts x[1,2,3]
```

Note that all we really gain here is the convenience of a "comma" notation [x,y,z] instead of the more C-like [x][y][z]. If the C-style notation is acceptable to you, you can just use nested arrays in Ruby. Another minor benefit is the prevention of the situation in which nil is the receiver for the bracket method.

Finding Elements in One Array but Not Another

Finding elements in one array but not another is simpler in Ruby than in many languages. It is a simple "set difference" problem:

```ruby
text = %w[the magic words are squeamish ossifrage]
dictionary = %w[an are magic the them these words]
```

```
# Find potential misspellings
unknown = text - dictionary    # ["squeamish", "ossifrage"]
```

Transforming or Mapping Arrays

The `collect` method (part of `Enumerable`) is a useful little tool that proves to be a time and labor saver in many circumstances. If you are a Smalltalk programmer, this may be more intuitive than if you come from a C background.

This method simply operates on each element of an array in some arbitrary way to produce a new array. In other words, it "maps" an array onto another array (hence the synonym `map`). Here's an example:

```
x = %w[alpha bravo charlie delta echo foxtrot]
# Get the initial letters
a = x.collect {|w| w[0..0]}      # %w[a b c d e f]
# Get the string lengths
b = x.collect {|w| w.length}      # [5, 5, 7, 5, 4, 7]
# map is just an alias
c = x.map {|w| w.length}          # [5, 5, 7, 5, 4, 7]
```

The in-place variant `collect!` (or `map!`) is also defined:

```
x.collect! {|w| w.upcase}
# x is now %w[ALPHA BRAVO CHARLIE DELTA ECHO FOXTROT]
x.map! {|w| w.reverse}
# x is now %w[AHPLA OVARB EILRAHC ATLED OHCE TORTXOF]
```

Removing `nil` Values from an Array

The `compact` method (or its in-place version `compact!`) will remove `nil` values from an array, leaving the rest untouched:

```
a = [1, 2, nil, 3, nil, 4, 5]
b = a.compact       # [1, 2, 3, 4, 5]
a.compact!          # a is now [1, 2, 3, 4, 5]
```

Removing Specific Array Elements

It is easy to delete elements from a Ruby array, and there are many ways to do it. If you want to delete one specific element by index, `delete_at` is a good way:

```
a = [10, 12, 14, 16, 18]
a.delete_at(3)                  # Returns 16
# a is now [10, 12, 14, 18]
a.delete_at(9)                  # Returns nil (out of range)
```

If you want to delete all instances of a certain piece of data, `delete` will do the job. It will return the value of the objects deleted or `nil` if the value was not found. Here's an example:

```
b = %w(spam spam bacon spam eggs ham spam)
b.delete("spam")                # Returns "spam"
# b is now ["bacon", "eggs", "ham"]
b.delete("caviar")              # Returns nil
```

The `delete` method will also accept a block. This may be a little counterintuitive, though. All that happens is that the block is evaluated (potentially performing a wide range of operations) if the object is not found and the value of the block is returned, as shown here:

```
c = ["alpha", "beta", "gamma", "delta"]
c.delete("delta") { "Nonexistent" }
# Returns "delta" (block is never evaluated)
c.delete("omega") { "Nonexistent" }
# Returns "Nonexistent"
```

The `delete_if` method will pass every element into the supplied block and delete the elements for which the block evaluates to `true`. It behaves similarly to `reject!`, except that the latter can return `nil` when the array remains unchanged. Here's an example:

```
email = ["job offers", "greetings", "spam", "news items"]
# Delete four-letter words
email.delete_if {|x| x.length==4 }
# email is now ["job offers", "greetings", "news items"]
```

The `slice!` method accesses the same elements as `slice` but deletes them from the array as it returns their values:

```
x = [0, 2, 4, 6, 8, 10, 12, 14, 16]
a = x.slice!(2)                       # 4
# x is now [0, 2, 6, 8, 10, 12, 14, 16]
b = x.slice!(2,3)                     # [6, 8, 10]
# x is now [0, 2, 12, 14, 16]
c = x.slice!(2..3)                    # [12, 14]
# x is now [0, 2, 16]
```

The `shift` and `pop` methods can be used for deleting array elements (for more about their intended uses, see the discussion of stacks and queues elsewhere in this chapter):

```
x = [1, 2, 3, 4, 5]
x.pop                   # Delete the last element
# x is now [1, 2, 3, 4]
x.shift                 # Delete the first element
# x is now [2, 3, 4]
```

Finally, the `clear` method will delete all the elements in an array. It is equivalent to assigning an empty array to the variable, but it's marginally more efficient. Here's an example:

```
x = [1, 2, 3]
x.clear
# x is now []
```

Concatenating and Appending onto Arrays

Very frequently we want to take an array and append an element or another array. There are many ways to do this with a Ruby array.

The "append" operator << will append an object onto an array; the return value is the array itself so that these operations can be "chained":

```
x = [1, 5, 9]
x << 13        # x is now [1, 5, 9, 13]
x << 17 << 21  # x is now [1, 5, 9, 13, 17, 21]
```

Similar to the append are the `unshift` and `push` methods, which add to the beginning and end of an array, respectively. See the section "Using an Array As a Stack or Queue" for more information.

Arrays may be concatenated with the `concat` method or by using the + and += operators:

```
x = [1,2]
y = [3,4]
z = [5,6]
b = y + z      # [3,4,5,6]
b += x         # [3,4,5,6,1,2]
z.concat y     # z is now [5,6,3,4]
```

Using an Array As a Stack or Queue

The basic stack operations are `push` and `pop`, which add and remove items, respectively, at the end of an array. The basic queue operations are `shift` (which removes an item from the beginning of an array) and `unshift` (which adds an element to the beginning). The append operator, can also be used to add an item to the end of an array (basically a synonym for `push`).

Don't get confused. The `shift` and `unshift` methods work on the *beginning* of an array; the `push`, `pop`, and << methods work on the *end*.

For a better discussion of this topic, see the section "Working with Stacks and Queues."

Iterating over an Array

The `Array` class has the standard iterator each, as is to be expected. However, it also has other useful iterators.

The `reverse_each` method will iterate in reverse order. It is equivalent to using `reverse` and then `each`, but it is faster. Here's an example:

```
words = %w(Son I am able she said)
str = ""
words.reverse_each { |w| str += "#{w} "}
# str is now "said she able am I Son "
```

If we only want to iterate over the indexes, we can use `each_index`. Saying `x.each_index` is equivalent to saying `(0..(x.size-1)).each` (that is, iterating over the range of indexes).

The iterator `each_with_index` (mixed in from `Comparable`) will pass both the element and the index into the block, as shown here:

```
x = ["alpha", "beta", "gamma"]
x.each_with_index do |x,i|
   puts "Element #{i} is #{x}"
end
# Produces three lines of output
```

Suppose you wanted to iterate over an array in random order? The following example uses the iterator `random_each` (which simply invokes the `randomize` method from section "Randomizing an Array"):

```
class Array

# Assumes we have defined randomize

  def random_each
    temp = self.randomize
    temp.each {|x| yield x}
  end

end

dwarves = %w(Sleepy Dopey Happy Sneezy Grumpy Bashful Doc)
list = ""
dwarves.random_each {|x| list += "#{x} "}
# list is now:
# "Bashful Dopey Sleepy Happy Grumpy Doc Sneezy "
# (Your mileage may vary.)
```

Interposing Delimiters to Form a String

Frequently we will want to insert delimiters in between array elements in a "fencepost" fashion; that is, we want to put delimiters between the elements, but not before the first one or after the last one. The method `join` will do this, as will the * operator:

```
been_there = ["Veni", "vidi", "vici."]
journal = been_there.join(", ")        # "Veni, vidi, vici."

# Default delimiter is space
letters = ["Phi","Mu","Alpha"]
musicians = letters.join               # "Phi Mu Alpha"

people = ["Bob","Carol","Ted","Alice"]
movie = people * " and "
# movie is now "Bob and Carol and Ted and Alice"
```

Note that if we really need to treat the last element differently, perhaps by inserting the word *and*, we can do it manually, like so:

```
list = %w[A B C D E F]
with_commas = list[0..-2]*", ", " + ", and " + list[-1]
# with_commas is now "A, B, C, D, E, and F"
```

Reversing an Array

To reverse the order of an array, use the `reverse` or `reverse!` method:

```
inputs = ["red", "green", "blue"]
outputs = inputs.reverse          # ["green","blue","red"]
priorities = %w(eat sleep code)
priorities.reverse!               # ["code","sleep","eat"]
```

Removing Duplicate Elements from an Array

If you want to remove duplicate elements from an array, the `uniq` method (or its in-place mutator `uniq!`) will do the job:

```
breakfast = %w[spam spam eggs ham eggs spam]
lunch = breakfast.uniq    # ["spam","eggs","ham"]
breakfast.uniq!           # breakfast has changed now
```

Interleaving Arrays

Suppose you want to take two arrays and "interleave" them so that the new array contains alternating elements from each of the two original ones. There must be a hundred ways to do this. Here is one way:

```
a = [1, 2, 3, 4]
b = ["a", "b", "c", "d"]
c = []
a.each_with_index { |x,i| c << x << b[i]}
# c is now [1, "a", 2, "b", 3, "c", 4, "d"]
```

Counting Frequency of Values in an Array

There is no count method for arrays as there is for strings (to count the occurrences of each data item). Therefore, we've created one here:

```
class Array

  def count
    k=Hash.new(0)
    self.each{|x| k[x]+=1 }
    k
  end

end

meal = %w[spam spam eggs ham eggs spam]
items = meal.count
# items is {"ham" => 1, "spam" => 3, "eggs" => 2}
spams = items["spam"]    # 3
```

Note that a hash is returned. No pun intended.

Inverting an Array to Form a Hash

An array is used to associate an integer index with a piece of data. However, what if you want to invert that association (that is, associate the data with the index, thus producing a hash)? The following method will do just that:

```
class Array

  def invert
    h={}
    self.each_with_index{|x,i| h[x]=i}
    h
  end

end

a = ["red","yellow","orange"]
h = a.invert    # {"orange"=>2, "yellow"=>1, "red"=>0}
```

Synchronized Sorting of Multiple Arrays

Suppose you want to sort an array, but you have other arrays that corresponded with this one on an element-for-element basis. In other words, you don't want to get them out of sync. How would you do this?

The solution we present in Listing 3.7 will sort an array and gather the resulting set of indexes. The list of indexes (itself an array) can be applied to any other array to put its elements in the same order.

LISTING 3.7   Synchronized Array Sorting

```
class Array

  def sort_index
    d=[]
    self.each_with_index{|x,i| d[i]=[x,i]}
    if block_given?
      d.sort {|x,y| yield x[0],y[0]}.collect{|x| x[1]}
    else
      d.sort.collect{|x| x[1]}
    end
  end

  def sort_by(ord=[])
    return nil if self.length!=ord.length
    self.indexes(*ord)
  end

end


a = [21, 33, 11, 34, 36, 24, 14]
p a
p b=a.sort_index
p a.sort_by b
p c=a.sort_index {|x,y| x%2 <=> y%2}
p a.sort_by c
```

Establishing a Default Value for New Array Elements

When an array grows and new (unassigned) elements are created, these elements default to nil values:

```
a = Array.new
a[0]="x"
```

```
a[3]="y"
# a is now ["x", nil, nil, "y"]
```

What if we want to set those new elements to some other value? As a specific instance of a general principle, we offer the ZArray class in Listing 3.8, which will default new unassigned elements to 0.

LISTING 3.8   Specifying a Default for Array Elements

```
class ZArray < Array

  def [](x)
    if x > size
      for i in size+1..x
        self[i]=0
      end
    end
    v = super(x)
  end

  def []=(x,v)
    max = size
    super(x,v)
    if size - max > 1
      (max..size-2).each do |i|
        self[i] = 0
      end
    end
  end

end


num = ZArray.new
num[1] = 1
num[2] = 4
num[5] = 25
# num is now [0, 1, 4, 0, 0, 25]
```

Working with Hashes

Hashes are known in some circles as *associative arrays*, *dictionaries*, and by various other names. Perl and Java programmers in particular will be familiar with this data structure.

Think of an array as an entity that creates an association between index *x* and data item *y*. A hash creates a similar association, with at least two exceptions. First, for an array, *x* is always an integer; for a hash, it need not be. Second, an array is an ordered data structure; a hash typically has no ordering.

A hash key can be of any arbitrary type. As a side effect, this makes a hash a nonsequential data structure. In an array, we know that element 4 follows element 3; but in a hash, the key may be of a type that does not define a real predecessor or successor. For this reason (and others), there is no notion in Ruby of the pairs in a hash being in any particular order.

You may think of a hash as an array with a specialized index, or as a database "synonym table" with two fields, stored in memory. Regardless of how you perceive it, it is a powerful and useful programming construct.

Creating a New Hash

As with `Array`, the special class method `[]` is used to create a hash. The data items listed in the brackets are used to form the mapping of the hash.

Six ways of calling this method are shown here (note that hashes a1 through c2 will all be populated identically):

```
a1 = Hash.[]("flat",3,"curved",2)
a2 = Hash.[]("flat"=>3,"curved"=>2)
b1 = Hash["flat",3,"curved",2]
b2 = Hash["flat"=>3,"curved"=>2]
c1 = {"flat",3,"curved",2}
c2 = {"flat"=>3,"curved"=>2}
# For a1, b1, and c1: There must be
# an even number of elements.
```

Also, the class method `new` can take a parameter specifying a *default* value. Note that this default value is not actually part of the hash; it is simply a value returned in place of `nil`. Here's an example:

```
d = Hash.new          # Create an empty hash
e = Hash.new(99)      # Create an empty hash
f = Hash.new("a"=>3)  # Create an empty hash
e["angled"]           # 99
e.inspect             # {}
f["b"]                # {"a"=>3} (default value is
                      #   actually a hash itself)
f.inspect             # {}
```

Specifying a Default Value for a Hash

The default value of a hash is an object that is referenced in place of nil in the case of a missing key. This is useful if you plan to use methods with the hash value that are not defined for nil. It can be assigned upon creation of the hash or at a later time using the default= method.

All missing keys point to the same default value object, so changing the default value has a side effect:

```
a = Hash.new("missing")  # default value object is "missing"
a["hello"]               # "missing"
a.default="nothing"
a["hello"]               # "nothing"
a["good"] << "bye"       # "nothingbye"
a.default                # "nothingbye"
```

The special instance method fetch raises an IndexError exception if the key does not exist in the Hash object. It takes a second parameter that serves as a default value. Also, fetch optionally accepts a block to produce a default value in case the key is not found. This is in contrast to default, because the block allows each missing key to have its own default. Here's an example:

```
a = {"flat",3,"curved",2,"angled",5}
a.fetch("pointed")                    # IndexError
a.fetch("curved","na")                # 2
a.fetch("x","na")                     # "na"
a.fetch("flat") {|x| x.upcase}        # 3
a.fetch("pointed") {|x| x.upcase}     # "POINTED"
```

Accessing and Adding Key/Value Pairs

Hash has class methods [] and []=, just as Array has; they are used much the same way, except that they accept only one parameter. The parameter can be any object, not just a string (although string objects are commonly used). Here's an example:

```
a = {}
a["flat"] = 3           # {"flat"=>3}
a.[]=("curved",2)       # {"flat"=>3,"curved"=>2}
a.store("angled",5)     # {"flat"=>3,"curved"=>2,"angled"=>5}
```

The method store is simply an alias for the []= method, both of which take two arguments, as shown in the example.

The method fetch is similar to the [] method, except that it raises an IndexError for missing keys. It also has an optional second argument (or alternatively a code block) for dealing with default values (see the section "Specifying a Default Value for a Hash"). Here's an example:

```
a["flat"]        # 3
a.[]("flat")     # 3
```

```
a.fetch("flat")  # 3
a["bent"]        # nil
```

Suppose you are not sure whether the Hash object exists, and you would like to avoid clearing an existing hash. The obvious way is to check whether the hash is defined, as shown here:

```
unless defined? a
  a={}
end
a["flat"] = 3
```

Another way to do this is as follows:

```
a ||= {}
a["flat"] = 3
```

The same problem can be applied to individual keys, where you only want to assign a value if the key does not exist:

```
a=Hash.new(99)
a[2]             # 99
a                # {}
a[2] ||= 5       # 99
a                # {}
b=Hash.new
b                # {}
b[2]             # nil
b[2] ||= 5       # 5
b                # {2=>5}
```

Note that nil may be used as either a key or an associated value:

```
b={}
b[2]       # nil
b[3]=nil
b          # {3=>nil}
b[2].nil? # true
b[3].nil? # true
b[nil]=5
b          # {3=>nil,nil=>5}
b[nil]     # 5
b[b[3]]    # 5
```

Deleting Key/Value Pairs

Key/value pairs of a Hash object can be deleted using clear, delete, delete_if, reject, reject!, and shift.

Use `clear` to remove all key/value pairs. This is essentially the same as assigning a new empty hash, but it's marginally faster.

Use `shift` to remove an unspecified key/value pair. This method returns the pair as a two-element array (or `nil` if no keys are left):

```
a = {1=>2, 3=>4}
b = a.shift        # [1,2]
# a is now {3=>4}
```

Use `delete` to remove a specific key/value pair. It accepts a key and returns the value associated with the key removed (if found). If the key is not found, the default value is returned. It also accepts a block to produce a unique default value rather than just a reused object reference. Here's an example:

```
a = {1=>1, 2=>4, 3=>9, 4=>16}
a.delete(3)                       # 9
# a is now {1=>1, 2=>4, 4=>16}
a.delete(5)                       # nil in this case
a.delete(6) { "not found" }       # "not found"
```

Use `delete_if`, `reject`, or `reject!` in conjunction with the required block to delete all keys for which the block evaluates to `true`. The method `reject` uses a copy of the hash, and `reject!` returns `nil` if no changes were made.

Iterating over a Hash

The `Hash` class has the standard iterator `each`, as is to be expected. It also has `each_key`, `each_pair`, and `each_value` (`each_pair` is an alias for each). Here's an example:

```
{"a"=>3,"b"=>2}.each do |key, val|
  print val, " from ", key, "; "    # 3 from a; 2 from b;
end
```

The other two provide only one or the other (the key or the value) to the block:

```
{"a"=>3,"b"=>2}.each_key do |key|
  print "key = #{key};"      # Prints: key = a; key = b;
end

{"a"=>3,"b"=>2}.each_value do |value|
  print "val = #{value};"    # Prints: val = 3; val = 2;
end
```

Inverting a Hash

Inverting a hash in Ruby is trivial with the `invert` method:

```
a = {"fred"=>"555-1122","jane"=>"555-7779"}
b = a.invert
b["555-7779"]      # "jane"
```

Because hashes have unique keys, there is potential for data loss when doing this—duplicate associated values will be converted to a unique key using only one of the associated keys as its value. There is no predictable way to tell which one will be used.

Detecting Keys and Values in a Hash

Determining whether a key has been assigned can be done with `has_key?` or any one of its aliases: `include?`, `key?`, or `member?`. Here's an example:

```
a = {"a"=>1,"b"=>2}
a.has_key? "c"         # false
a.include? "a"         # true
a.key? 2               # false
a.member? "b"          # true
```

You can also use `empty?` to see whether there are any keys at all left in the hash; `length` or its alias `size` can be used to determine how many there are, as shown here:

```
a.empty?        # false
a.length        # 2
```

Alternatively, you can test for the existence of an associated value using `has_value?` or `value?`:

```
a.has_value? 2        # true
a.value? 99           # false
```

Extracting Hashes into Arrays

To convert the entire hash into an array, use the `to_a` method. In the resulting array, keys will be even-numbered elements (starting with 0) and values will be odd-numbered elements of the array:

```
h = {"a"=>1,"b"=>2}
h.to_a          # ["a",1,"b",2]
```

It is also possible to convert only the keys or only the values of the hash into an array:

```
h.keys          # ["a","b"]
h.values        # [1,2]
```

Finally, you can extract an array of values selectively based on a list of keys, using the `indices` method. This works for hashes much as the method of the same name works for arrays (the alias is `indexes`):

```
h = {1=>"one",2=>"two",3=>"three",4=>"four","cinco"=>"five"}
h.indices(3,"cinco",4)      # ["three","five","four"]
h.indexes(1,3)              # ["one","three"]
```

Selecting Key/Value Pairs by Criteria

The `Hash` class mixes in the `Enumerable` module, so you can use `detect` (`find`), `select` (`find_all`), `grep`, `min`, `max`, and `reject` as with arrays.

The `detect` method (whose alias is `find`) finds a single key/value pair. It takes a block (into which the pairs are passed one at a time) and returns the first pair for which the block evaluates to `true`. Here's an example:

```
names = {"fred"=>"jones","jane"=>"tucker",
         "joe"=>"tucker","mary"=>"SMITH"}
# Find a tucker
names.detect {|k,v| v=="tucker" }     # ["joe","tucker"]
# Find a capitalized surname
names.find {|k,v| v==v.upcase }     # ["mary", "SMITH"]
```

Of course, the objects in the hash can be of arbitrary complexity, as can the test in the block, but comparisons between differing types can cause problems.

The `select` method (whose alias is `find_all`) will return multiple matches, as opposed to a single match:

```
names.select {|k,v| v=="tucker" }
# [["joe", "tucker"], ["jane", "tucker"]]
names.find_all {|k,v| k.count("r")>0}
# [["mary", "SMITH"], ["fred", "jones"]]
```

Sorting a Hash

Hashes are by their nature not ordered according to the value of their keys or associated values. In performing a sort on a hash, Ruby converts the hash to an array and then sorts that array. The result is naturally an array:

```
names = {"Jack"=>"Ruby","Monty"=>"Python",
         "Blaise"=>"Pascal", "Minnie"=>"Perl"}
list = names.sort
# list is now:
# [["Blaise","Pascal"], ["Jack","Ruby"],
#  ["Minnie","Perl"], ["Monty","Python"]]
```

Merging Two Hashes

Merging hashes may be useful sometimes. Ruby's `update` method will put the entries of one hash into the target hash, overwriting any previous duplicates:

```
dict = {"base"=>"foundation", "pedestal"=>"base"}
added = {"base"=>"non-acid", "salt"=>"NaCl"}
dict.update(added)
# {"base"=>"non-acid", "pedestal"=>"base", "salt"=>"NaCl"}
```

Creating a Hash from an Array

The easiest way to create a hash from an array is to remember the bracket notation for creating hashes. This works if the array has an even number of elements. Here's an example:

```
array = [2, 3, 4, 5, 6, 7]
hash = Hash[*array]
# hash is now: {2=>3, 4=>5, 6=>7}
```

Finding Difference or Intersection of Hash Keys

Because the keys of a hash can be extracted as a separate array, the extracted arrays of different hashes can be manipulated using the `Array` class methods & and - to produce the intersection and difference of the keys. The matching values can be generated with the `each` method performed on a third hash representing the merge of the two hashes (to ensure all keys can be found in one place):

```
a = {"a"=>1,"b"=>2,"z"=>3}
b = {"x"=>99,"y"=>88,"z"=>77}
intersection = a.keys & b.keys
difference = a.keys - b.keys
c = a.dup.update(b)
inter = {}
intersection.each {|k| inter[k]=c[k] }
# inter is {"z"=>77}
diff={}
difference.each {|k| diff[k]=c[k] }
# diff is {"a"=>1, "b"=>2}
```

Using a Hash As a Sparse Matrix

Often we want to make use of an array or matrix that is nearly empty. We could store it in the conventional way, but this is often wasteful of memory. A hash provides a way to store only the values that actually exist.

Here is an example in which we are assuming that the nonexistent values should default to zero:

```
values = Hash.new(0)
values[1001] = 5
values[2010] = 7
values[9237] = 9
x = values[9237]      # 9
y = values[5005]      # 0
```

Obviously in this example, an array would have created over 9,000 unused elements. This may not be acceptable.

What if we want to implement a sparse matrix of two or more dimensions? All we need do is use arrays as the hash keys, like so:

```
cube = Hash.new(0)
cube[[2000,2000,2000]] = 2
z = cube[[36,24,36]]       # 0
```

In this case, we see that literally *billions* of array elements would need to be created if this three-dimensional array were to be complete.

Implementing a Hash with Duplicate Keys

Purists would likely say that if a hash has duplicate keys, it isn't really a hash. We don't want to argue. Call it what you will, there might be occasions when you want a data structure that offers the flexibility and convenience of a hash but allows duplicate key values.

We offer a partial solution here (see Listing 3.9). It is partial for two reasons. First, we have not bothered to implement all the functionality that could be desired, but only a good representative subset. Second, the inner workings of Ruby are such that a hash literal is always an instance of the Hash class, and even though we were to inherit from Hash, a literal would not be allowed to contain duplicates. (We're thinking about this one further.)

But as long as you stay away from the hash-literal notation, this problem is doable. Here we implement a class that has a "store" (@store) that is a simple hash; each value in the hash is an array. We control access to the hash in such a way that when we find ourselves adding a key that already exists, we add the value to the existing array of items associated with that key.

What should size return? Obviously, the "real" number of key/value pairs *including* duplicates. Likewise, the keys method returns a value potentially containing duplicates. The iterators behave as expected; as with a normal hash, there is no predicting the order in which the pairs will be visited.

Besides the usual `delete`, we have implemented a `delete_pair` method. The former will delete *all* values associated with a key; the latter will delete only the specified key/value pair. (Note that it would have been difficult to make a single method such as `delete(k,v=nil)` because `nil` is a valid value for any hash.)

For brevity, we have not implemented the entire class; frankly, some of the methods, such as `invert`, would require some design decisions as to what their behavior should be. If you're interested, you can flesh out the rest as needed.

LISTING 3.9   Hash with Duplicate Keys

```ruby
class HashDup

  def initialize(*all)
    raise IndexError if all.size % 2 != 0
    @store = {}
    if all[0]  # not nil
      keyval = all.dup
      while !keyval.empty?
        key = keyval.shift
        if @store.has_key?(key)
          @store[key] += [keyval.shift]
        else
          @store[key] = [keyval.shift]
        end
      end
    end
  end

  def store(k,v)
    if @store.has_key?(k)
      @store[k] += [v]
    else
      @store[k] = [v]
    end
  end

  def [](key)
    @store[key]
  end

  def []=(key,value)
    self.store(key,value)
  end
```

LISTING 3.9   Continued

```ruby
def to_s
  @store.to_s
end

def to_a
  @store.to_a
end

def inspect
  @store.inspect
end

def keys
  result=[]
  @store.each do |k,v|
    result += ([k]*v.size)
  end
  result
end

def values
  @store.values.flatten
end

def each
  @store.each {|k,v| v.each {|y| yield k,y}}
end

alias each_pair each

def each_key
  self.keys.each {|k| yield k}
end

def each_value
  self.values.each {|v| yield v}
end

def has_key? k
  self.keys.include? k
end

def has_value? v
  self.values.include? v
end
```

LISTING 3.9 Continued

```ruby
  def length
    self.values.size
  end

  alias size length

  def delete k
    val = @store[k]
    @store.delete k
    val
  end

  def delete k,v
    @store[k] -= [v] if @store[k]
    v
  end

  # Other methods omitted here...

end



# This won't work... dup key will ignore
# first occurrence.
h = {1=>1, 2=>4, 3=>9, 4=>16, 2=>0}

# This will work...
h = HashDup.new(1,1, 2,4, 3,9, 4,16, 2,0)

k = h.keys        # [4, 1, 2, 2, 3]
v = h.values      # [16, 1, 4, 0, 9]

n = h.size        # 5

h.each {|k,v| puts "#{k} => #{v}"}
# Prints:
# 4 => 16
# 1 => 1
# 2 => 4
# 2 => 0
# 3 => 9
```

Working with Stacks and Queues

Stacks and queues are the first entities we have discussed that are not strictly built in to Ruby. By this we mean that Ruby does not have Stack and Queue classes as it has Array and Hash classes.

And yet, in a way, they are built in to Ruby after all. In fact, the Array class implements all the functionality we need to treat an array as a stack or a queue. You'll see this in detail shortly.

A *stack* is a last-in first-out (LIFO) data structure. The traditional everyday example is a stack of cafeteria trays on its spring-loaded platform; trays are added at the top and also taken away from the top.

There is a limited set of operations that can be performed on a stack. These include *push* and *pop* (to add and remove items) at the very least; usually there is a way to test for an empty stack, and there may be a way to examine the top element without removing it. A stack implementation never provides a way to examine an item in the middle of the stack.

You might ask how an array can implement a stack given that array elements may be accessed randomly and stack elements may not. The answer is simple: A stack sits at a higher level of abstraction than an array; it is a stack only so long as you treat it as one. The moment you access an element illegally, it ceases to be a stack.

Of course, you can easily define a Stack class so that elements can only be accessed legally. We will show how this is done.

It is worth noting that many algorithms that use a stack also have elegant recursive solutions. The reason for this becomes clear with a moment's reflection. Function or method calls result in data being pushed onto the system stack, and this data is popped upon return. Therefore, a recursive algorithm simply trades an explicit user-defined stack for the implicit system-level stack. Which is better? That depends on how you value readability, efficiency, and other considerations.

A *queue* is a first-in first-out (FIFO) data structure. It is analogous to a group of people standing in line at, for example, a movie theater. Newcomers go to the end of the line, whereas those who have waited longest are the next served. In most areas of programming, these are probably used less often than stacks.

Queues are useful in more real-time environments where entities are processed as they are presented to the system. They are useful in producer/consumer situations (especially where threads or multitasking is involved). A printer queue is a good example; print jobs are added to one end of the queue, and they "stand in line" until they are removed at the other end.

The two basic queue operations are usually called *enqueue* and *dequeue* in the literature. The corresponding instance methods in the Array class are called shift and unshift, respectively.

Note that `unshift` could serve as a companion for `shift` in implementing a stack, not a queue, because `unshift` adds to the same end from which `shift` removes. There are various combinations of these methods that could implement stacks and queues, but we will not concern ourselves with all the variations.

That ends our introductory discussion of stacks and queues. Now let's look at some examples.

Implementing a Stricter Stack

We promised earlier to show how a stack could be made "idiot-proof" against illegal access. We may as well do that now (see Listing 3.10). We present here a simple class that has an internal array and manages access to that array. (There are other ways of doing this—by delegating, for example—but what we show here is simple and works fine.)

LISTING 3.10   Stack

```
class Stack

  def initialize
    @store = []
  end

  def push(x)
    @store.push x
  end

  def pop
    @store.pop
  end

  def peek
    @store.last
  end

  def empty?
    @store.empty?
  end

end
```

We have added one more operation that is not defined for arrays; `peek` will simply examine the top of the stack and return a result without disturbing the stack.

Some of the rest of our examples will assume this class definition.

Converting Infix to Postfix

In writing algebraic expressions, we commonly use *infix* notation, with the operator in between the operands. Often it is more convenient to store an expression in *postfix* form, a parenthesis-free form in which the operator follows both the operands. (This is sometimes called *Reverse Polish Notation.*)

In Listing 3.11, we present a simple routine for converting infix to postfix notation using a stack. We make the simplifying assumptions that all operands are lowercase letters and the only operators are *, /, +, and -.

LISTING 3.11   Infix to Postfix

```ruby
# Define level of precedence

def level(opr)
  case opr
    when "*", "/"
      2
    when "+", "-"
      1
    when "("
      0
  end
end


# "Main"

infix = "(a+b)*(c-d)/(e-(f-g))"
postfix = ""

stack = Stack.new

infix.each_byte do |sym|
  sym = "" << sym    # Convert to string
  case sym
    when "("
      stack.push sym

    when /[a-z]/
      postfix += sym

    when "*", "/", "+", "-"
      finished = false
```

LISTING 3.11   Continued

```
            until finished or stack.empty?
              if level(sym) > level(stack.peek)
                finished = true
              else
                postfix += stack.pop
              end
            end
            stack.push sym

        when ")"
          while stack.peek != "("
            postfix += stack.pop
          end
          stack.pop   # Get rid of paren on stack
      end
    end

    while !stack.empty?
      postfix += stack.pop
    end

    puts postfix                # Prints "ab+cd-*efg--/"
```

Detecting Unbalanced Punctuation in Expressions

Because of the nature of grouped expressions, such as parentheses and brackets, their validity can be checked using a stack (see Listing 3.12). For every level of nesting in the expression, the stack will grow one level higher; when we find closing symbols, we can pop the corresponding symbol off the stack. If the symbol does not correspond as expected, or if there are symbols left on the stack at the end, we know the expression is not well formed.

LISTING 3.12   Detecting Unbalanced Punctuation

```
def paren_match str
  stack = Stack.new
  lsym = "{[(<"
  rsym = "}])>"
  str.each_byte do |byte|
    sym = byte.chr
    if lsym.include? sym
      stack.push(sym)
    elsif rsym.include? sym
      top = stack.peek
```

LISTING 3.12   Continued

```
        if lsym.index(top) != rsym.index(sym)
          return false
        else
          stack.pop
        end
        # Ignore non-grouped characters...
      end
    end
    # Ensure stack is empty...
    return stack.empty?
  end

str1 = "Hello (yes, [um] you) there!"
str2 = "(((a+b))*((c-d)-(e*f))"
str3 = "[[(a-(b-c))], [[x,y]]]"

paren_match str1          # true
paren_match str2          # false
paren_match str3          # true
```

Detecting Unbalanced Tags in HTML and XML

The example shown in Listing 3.13 is essentially the same as Listing 3.12. We include it only to give a hint that this task is possible (that is, that a stack is useful for validating HTML and XML).

In the old days, a string was considered, at best, a special case of an array. Your opinion may vary depending on your language background. In Ruby, strings are not arrays; however, it is a tribute to the orthogonality of the language when we see how similar these two examples turned out. This is because, after all, there is a certain isomorphism between strings and arrays. They are both ordered sequences of elements, where in the case of a string, the element is a character.

Because we are talking about stacks and not HTML/XML, we have made a huge truckload of simplifying assumptions here. (If you're interested in real-life HTML and XML examples, refer to later chapters.) First of all, we assume that the text has already been parsed and stuck into an array. Second, we only care about a limited subset of the many tags possible. Third, we ignore the possibility of attributes and values associated with the tags.

In short, this is not a real-life example at all; however, like the previous example, it shows the underlying principle.

LISTING 3.13   Detecting Unbalanced Tags

```ruby
def balanced_tags list
  stack = Stack.new
  opening = %w[ <html> <body> <b> <i> <u> <sub> <sup> ]
  closing = %w[ </html> </body> </b> </i> </u> </sub> </sup> ]
  list.each do |word|
    if opening.include? word
      stack.push(word)
    elsif closing.include? word
      top = stack.peek
      if closing.index(top) != opening.index(word)
        return false
      else
        stack.pop
      end
      # Ignore other words
    end
  end
  # Ensure stack is empty...
  return stack.empty?
end

text1 = %w[ <html> <body> This is <b> only </b>
            a test. </body> </html> ]

text2 = %w[ <html> <body> Don't take it <i> too </i>
            seriously... </html> ]

balanced_tags(text1)    # true
balanced_tags(text2)    # false
```

Understanding Stacks and Recursion

As an example of the isomorphism between stack-oriented algorithms and recursive algorithms, we will take a look at the classic "Tower of Hanoi" problem.

According to legend, there is a Buddhist temple somewhere in the Far East, where monks have the sole task of moving disks from one pole to another while obeying certain rules about the moves they can make. There were originally 64 disks on the first pole; when they finish the task, the world will come to an end.

As an aside, we like to dispel myths when we can. It seems that in reality, this puzzle originated with the French mathematician Edouard Lucas in 1883 and has no actual basis in eastern culture. What's more, Lucas himself named the puzzle the "Tower of Hanoi" (in the singular).

So if you were worried about the world ending, don't worry on that account. Anyway, 64 disks would take $2^{64}-1$ moves. A few minutes with a calculator will reveal that those monks would be busy for millions of years.

But on to the rules of the game. (We'll explain this even though every first-year computer science student in the world has already seen the puzzle.) We have a pole with a certain number of varying-sized disks stacked on it; call this the *source pole*. We want to move all these disks to the *destination pole*, using a third pole (called the *auxiliary pole*) as an intermediate resting place. The catch is that you can only move one disk at a time, and you cannot ever place a larger disk onto a smaller one.

The following example uses a stack to solve the problem. We use only three disks here because 64 would occupy a computer for centuries:

```
def towers2(list)
  while !list.empty?
    n, src, dst, aux = list.pop
    if n == 1
      puts "Move disk from #{src} to #{dst}"
    else
      list.push [n-1, aux, dst, src]
      list.push [1, src, dst, aux]
      list.push [n-1, src, aux, dst]
    end
  end
end


list = []
list.push([3, "a", "c", "b"])

towers2(list)
```

Here's the output that's produced:

```
Move disk from a to c
Move disk from a to b
Move disk from c to b
Move disk from a to c
Move disk from b to a
Move disk from b to c
Move disk from a to c
```

Of course, the classic solution to this problem is recursive. As we already pointed out, the close relationship between the two algorithms is no surprise because recursion implies the use of an invisible system-level stack. Here's an example:

```ruby
def towers(n, src, dst, aux)
  if n==1
    puts "Move disk from #{src} to #{dst}"
  else
    towers(n-1, src, aux, dst)
    towers(1, src, dst, aux)
    towers(n-1, aux, dst, src)
  end
end


towers(3, "a", "c", "b")
```

The output produced here is the same. And it may interest you to know that we tried commenting out the output statements and comparing the runtimes of these two methods. Don't tell anyone, but the recursive version is twice as fast.

Implementing a Stricter Queue

We define a queue here in much the same way we defined a stack earlier. If you want to protect yourself from accessing such a data structure in an illegal way, we recommend this practice (see Listing 3.14).

LISTING 3.14   A Stricter Queue

```ruby
class Queue

  def initialize
    @store = []
  end

  def enqueue(x)
    @store << x
  end

  def dequeue
    @store.shift
  end

  def peek
    @store.first
  end
```

LISTING 3.14   Continued

```
def length
  @store.length
end

def empty?
  @store.empty?
end

end
```

We should mention that there is a `Queue` class in the `thread` library that works very well in threaded code.

A Token Queue Example: Traffic Light Simulation

We offer here a fairly contrived example of using a queue. This code will simulate the arrival of cars at a traffic light and store the arrival times in four queues. At the end, it prints some (presumably meaningful) statistics about the queue lengths and wait times.

A number of simplifying assumptions have been made. Time is granularized at the level of one second. There are no threads involved; all car movements are serialized in a reasonable way. Cars turn neither left nor right, they never go through a yellow or red light, and so on. The code is shown in Listing 3.15.

LISTING 3.15   Traffic Light Simulation with a Queue

```
#
# Program: Traffic light simulation
#          (Queue example)
#
# The traffic light has this behavior:
# Green north/south for 40 seconds
# Pause 2 seconds
# Green east/west for 45 seconds
# Pause 2 seconds
# Repeat
#
# The traffic behaves this way:
# A northbound car arrives at the traffic light
#    every 3 seconds;
# Southbound, every 5 seconds;
# Eastbound, every 4 seconds;
# Westbound, every 6 seconds.
# All times are approximate (random).
```

LISTING 3.15 Continued

```ruby
# Assume no cars turn at the light.
#
# Cars pass through the light at a rate of
# one per second.
#
# Let's run for 8900 seconds (100 full cycles or
# more than two hours) and answer these questions:
# How long on the average is each line of cars
# when the light turns green? What is the average
# wait time in seconds? What is the longest wait
# time?
#


# Direction constants

NORTH, SOUTH, EAST, WEST = 0, 1, 2, 3
dirs = %w[North South East West]

# Probabilities for car arriving
# from each direction:

p = Array.new(4)
p[NORTH] = 1.0/3.0
p[SOUTH] = 1.0/5.0
p[EAST]  = 1.0/4.0
p[WEST]  = 1.0/6.0

# Queues:

waiting = Array.new(4)
waiting[NORTH] = Queue.new
waiting[SOUTH] = Queue.new
waiting[EAST]  = Queue.new
waiting[WEST]  = Queue.new

lengths = [0, 0, 0, 0]  # How long is queue
                        # when light turns green?
greens  = [0, 0, 0, 0]  # How many times did
                        # light turn green?
times   = [0, 0, 0, 0]  # How long did cars wait?
ncars   = [0, 0, 0, 0]  # Count cars through light.
maxtime = [0, 0, 0, 0]  # Max wait time?

# Looping...
```

LISTING 3.15   Continued

```
time=0
while time < 8900

  change = true  # Light changed
  for time in time..time+40          # North/south green
    # Enqueue all arrivals
    for dir in NORTH..WEST
      waiting[dir].enqueue(time) if rand < p[dir]
    end

    # Record queue lengths, counts
    if change
      for dir in NORTH..SOUTH
        lengths[dir] += waiting[dir].length
        greens[dir] += 1
      end
      change = false
    end

    # N/S can leave, one per second...
    for dir in NORTH..SOUTH
      if !waiting[dir].empty?
        car = waiting[dir].dequeue
        wait = time - car
        ncars[dir] += 1
        times[dir] += wait
        maxtime[dir] = [maxtime[dir],wait].max
      end
    end
  end

  for time in time..time+2           # Yellow/red
    # Nothing happens...
  end

  change = true  # Light changed
  for time in time..time+45          # East/west green
    # Enqueue all arrivals
    for dir in NORTH..WEST
      waiting[dir].enqueue(time) if rand < p[dir]
    end

    # Record queue lengths, counts
    if change
      for dir in EAST..WEST
```

LISTING 3.15   Continued

```ruby
        lengths[dir] += waiting[dir].length
        greens[dir] += 1
      end
      change = false
    end

    # N/S can leave, one per second...
    for dir in EAST..WEST
      if !waiting[dir].empty?
        car = waiting[dir].dequeue
        wait = time - car
        ncars[dir] += 1
        times[dir] += wait
        maxtime[dir] = [maxtime[dir],wait].max
      end
    end
  end

  for time in time..time+2          # Yellow/red
    # Nothing happens...
  end

end

# Display results...

puts "Average queue lengths:"
for dir in NORTH..WEST
  printf "  %-5s %6.1f\n", dirs[dir],
         lengths[dir]/greens[dir].to_f
end

puts "Max wait times:"
for dir in NORTH..WEST
  printf "  %-5s %4d\n", dirs[dir],
         maxtime[dir]
end

puts "Average wait times:"
for dir in NORTH..WEST
  printf "  %-5s %6.1f\n", dirs[dir],
         times[dir]/ncars[dir].to_f
end
```

Here is the output this example produces (which will vary because of the use of the pseudorandom number generator `rand`):

```
Average queue lengths:
  North   15.6
  South    9.5
  East    10.8
  West     7.3
Max wait times:
  North   51
  South   47
  East    42
  West    42
Average wait times:
  North   19.5
  South   16.2
  East    13.7
  West    12.9
```

You may at once see a dozen ways in which this program could be improved. However, it serves its purpose, which is to illustrate a simple queue.

Working with Trees

I think that I shall never see
A poem as lovely as a tree....

—[Alfred] Joyce Kilmer, "Trees"

A *tree* in computer science is a relatively intuitive concept (except that it is usually drawn with the "root" at the top and the "leaves" at the bottom). This is because we are familiar with so many kinds of hierarchical data in everyday life—from the family tree, to the corporate org chart, to the directory structures on our hard drives.

The terminology of trees is rich but easy to understand. Any item in a tree is a *node*; the first or topmost node is the *root*. A node may have *descendants* that are below it, and the immediate descendants are called *children*. Conversely, a node may also have a *parent* (only one) and *ancestors*. A node with no child nodes is called a *leaf*. A *subtree* consists of a node and all its descendants. To travel through a tree (for example, to print it out) is called *traversing the tree*.

We will look mostly at binary trees, although in practice a node can have any number of children. You will see how to create a tree, populate it, and traverse it. Also, we will look at a few real-life tasks that use trees.

We should mention here that in many languages, such as C and Pascal, trees are implemented using true address pointers. However, in Ruby (as in Java, for instance), we don't use pointers; object references work just as well or even better.

Implementing a Binary Tree

There is more than one way to implement a binary tree in Ruby. For example, we could use an array to store the values. Here, we use a more traditional approach, coding much as we would in C, except that pointers are replaced with object references.

What is required in order to describe a binary tree? Well, each node needs an attribute of some kind for storing a piece of data. Each node also needs a pair of attributes for referring to the left and right subtrees under that node.

We also need a way to insert into the tree and a way of getting information out of the tree. A pair of methods will serve these purposes.

The first tree we'll look at will implement these methods in a slightly unorthodox way. We will expand on the `Tree` class in later examples.

A tree is, in a sense, defined by its insertion algorithm and by how it is traversed. In this first example, shown in Listing 3.16, we define an `insert` method that inserts in a *breadth-first* fashion (that is, top to bottom and left to right). This guarantees that the tree grows in depth relatively slowly and is always balanced. Corresponding to the `insert` method, the `traverse` iterator will iterate over the tree in the same breadth-first order.

LISTING 3.16 Breadth-First Insertion and Traversal in a Tree

```
class Tree

attr_accessor :left
attr_accessor :right
attr_accessor :data

def initialize(x=nil)
  @left = nil
  @right = nil
  @data = x
end

def insert(x)
  list = []
  if @data == nil
    @data = x
  elsif @left == nil
```

LISTING 3.16   Continued

```ruby
        @left = Tree.new(x)
      elsif @right == nil
        @right = Tree.new(x)
      else
        list << @left
        list << @right
        loop do
          node = list.shift
          if node.left == nil
            node.insert(x)
            break
          else
            list << node.left
          end
          if node.right == nil
            node.insert(x)
            break
          else
            list << node.right
          end
        end
      end
    end

    def traverse()
      list = []
      yield @data
      list << @left if @left != nil
      list << @right if @right != nil
      loop do
        break if list.empty?
        node = list.shift
        yield node.data
        list << node.left if node.left != nil
        list << node.right if node.right != nil
      end
    end

  end


  items = [1, 2, 3, 4, 5, 6, 7]

  tree = Tree.new
```

LISTING 3.16   Continued

```
items.each {|x| tree.insert(x)}

tree.traverse {|x| print "#{x} "}
print "\n"

# Prints "1 2 3 4 5 6 7 "
```

This kind of tree, as defined by its insertion and traversal algorithms, is not especially interesting. However, it does serve as an introduction and something on which we can build.

Sorting Using a Binary Tree

For random data, using a binary tree is a good way to sort. (Although in the case of already-sorted data, it degenerates into a simple linked list.) The reason, of course, is that with each comparison, we are eliminating half the remaining alternatives as to where we should place a new node.

Although it might be fairly rare to sort using a binary tree nowadays, it can't hurt to know how. The code in Listing 3.17 builds on the previous example.

LISTING 3.17   Sorting with a Binary Tree

```
class Tree

  # Assumes definitions from
  # previous example...

  def insert(x)
    if @data == nil
      @data = x
    elsif x <= @data
      if @left == nil
        @left = Tree.new x
      else
        @left.insert x
      end
    else
      if @right == nil
        @right = Tree.new x
      else
        @right.insert x
      end
    end
  end
```

LISTING 3.17   Continued

```
    def inorder()
      @left.inorder {|y| yield y} if @left != nil
      yield @data
      @right.inorder {|y| yield y} if @right != nil
    end

    def preorder()
      yield @data
      @left.preorder {|y| yield y} if @left != nil
      @right.preorder {|y| yield y} if @right != nil
    end

    def postorder()
      @left.postorder {|y| yield y} if @left != nil
      @right.postorder {|y| yield y} if @right != nil
      yield @data
    end

  end

  items = [50, 20, 80, 10, 30, 70, 90, 5, 14,
           28, 41, 66, 75, 88, 96]

  tree = Tree.new

  items.each {|x| tree.insert(x)}

  tree.inorder {|x| print x, " "}
  print "\n"
  tree.preorder {|x| print x, " "}
  print "\n"
  tree.postorder {|x| print x, " "}
  print "\n"
```

Using a Binary Tree As a Lookup Table

Suppose we have a tree already sorted. Traditionally, this has made for a good lookup table; for example, a balanced tree of a million items would take no more than 20 comparisons (the depth of the tree or log base 2 of the number of nodes) to find a specific node. For this to be useful, we assume that the data for each node is not just a single value but has a key value and other information associated with it.

In most if not all situations, a hash or even an external database table will be preferable. However, we present this code to you anyhow (see Listing 3.18).

LISTING 3.18 Searching a Binary Tree

```
class Tree

  # Assumes definitions
  # from previous example...

  def search(x)
    if self.data == x
      return self
    else
      ltree = left != nil ? left.search(x) : nil
      return ltree if ltree != nil
      rtree = right != nil ? right.search(x) : nil
      return rtree if rtree != nil
    end
    nil
  end

end

keys = [50, 20, 80, 10, 30, 70, 90, 5, 14,
        28, 41, 66, 75, 88, 96]

tree = Tree.new

keys.each {|x| tree.insert(x)}

s1 = tree.search(75)    # Returns a reference to the node
                        # containing 75...

s2 = tree.search(100)   # Returns nil (not found)
```

Converting a Tree to a String or Array

The same old tricks that allow us to traverse a tree will allow us to convert it to a string or array if we wish, as shown in Listing 3.19. Here, we assume an *inorder* traversal, although any other kind could be used.

LISTING 3.19   Converting a Tree to a String or Array

```ruby
class Tree

  # Assumes definitions from
  # previous example...

  def to_s
    "[" +
    if left then left.to_s + "," else "" end +
    data.inspect +
    if right then "," + right.to_s else "" end + "]"
  end

  def to_a
    temp = []
    temp += left.to_a if left
    temp << data
    temp += right.to_a if right
    temp
  end

end

items = %w[bongo grimace monoid jewel plover nexus synergy]

tree = Tree.new
items.each {|x| tree.insert x}

str = tree.to_s * ","
# str is now "bongo,grimace,jewel,monoid,nexus,plover,synergy"
arr = tree.to_a
# arr is now:
# ["bongo",["grimace",[["jewel"],"monoid",[["nexus"],"plover",
#   ["synergy"]]]]]
```

Note that the resulting array is as deeply nested as the depth of the tree from which it came. You can, of course, use flatten to produce a non-nested array.

Storing an Infix Expression in a Tree

Here is another little contrived problem illustrating how a binary tree might be used (see Listing 3.20). We are given a prefix arithmetic expression and want to store it in standard infix form in a tree. (This is not completely unrealistic because the Ruby interpreter itself stores expressions in a tree structure, although it is a couple of orders of magnitude greater in complexity.)

We define a "standalone" method called `addnode` that will add a node to a tree in the proper place. The result will be a tree in which every leaf is an operand and every non-leaf node is an operator. We also define a new `Tree` method called `infix`, which will traverse the tree in order and act as an iterator. One twist is that it adds in parentheses as it goes, because prefix form is "parenthesis free" but infix form is not. The output would look more elegant if only necessary parentheses were added, but we added them indiscriminately to simplify the code.

LISTING 3.20   Storing an Infix Expression in a Tree

```
class Tree

  # Assumes definitions from
  # previous example...

  def infix()
    if @left != nil
      flag = %w[* / + -].include? @left.data
      yield "(" if flag
      @left.infix {|y| yield y}
      yield ")" if flag
    end
    yield @data
    if @right != nil
      flag = %w[* / + -].include? @right.data
      yield "(" if flag
      @right.infix {|y| yield y} if @right != nil
      yield ")" if flag
    end
  end

end

def addnode(nodes)
  node = nodes.shift
  tree = Tree.new node
  if %w[* / + -].include? node
    tree.left  = addnode nodes
    tree.right = addnode nodes
  end
  tree
end


prefix = %w[ * + 32 * 21 45 - 72 + 23 11 ]
```

LISTING 3.20   Continued

```
tree = addnode prefix

str = ""
tree.infix {|x| str += x}
# str is now "(32+(21*45))*(72-(23+11))" ·
```

Additional Notes on Trees

We'll mention a few more notes on trees here. First of all, a tree is a special case of a graph (as you will see shortly); in fact, it is a *directed acyclic graph* (DAG). Therefore, you can learn more about trees by researching graph algorithms in general.

There is no reason that a tree should necessarily be binary; this is a convenient simplification that frequently makes sense. However, it is conceivable to define a *multiway tree* in which each node is not limited to two children but may have an arbitrary number. In such a case, you would likely want to represent the child node pointers as an array of object references.

A *B-tree* is a specialized form of multiway tree. It is an improvement over a binary tree in that it is always balanced (that is, its depth is minimal), whereas a binary tree in a degenerate case can have a depth that is equal to the number of nodes it has. There is plenty of information on the Web and in textbooks if you need to learn about B-trees. Also, the principles we've applied to ordinary binary trees can be extended to B-trees as well.

A *red-black tree* is a specialized form of binary tree in which each node has a color (red or black) associated with it. In addition, each node has a pointer back to its parent (meaning that it is arguably not a tree at all because it isn't truly acyclic). A red-black tree maintains its balance through rotations of its nodes; that is, if one part of the tree starts to get too deep, the nodes can be rearranged so that depth is minimized (and in-order traversal ordering is preserved). The extra information in each node aids in performing these rotations.

Another tree that maintains its balance in spite of additions and deletions is the *AVL tree*. This structure is named for its discoverers, the two Russian researchers Adel'son-Vel'skii and Landis. An AVL tree is a binary tree that uses slightly more sophisticated insertion and deletion algorithms to keep the tree balanced. It performs rotation of subtrees similar to that done for red-black trees.

All these and more are potentially useful tree structures. If you need more information, search the Web or consult any book on advanced algorithms.

Working with Graphs

A *graph* is a collection of nodes that interconnect with each other arbitrarily. (A tree is a special case of a graph.) We will not get deeply into graphs because the theory and terminology can have a steep learning curve. Before long, we would find ourselves wandering out of the field of computer science entirely and into the province of mathematicians.

Yet, graphs do have many practical applications. Consider any ordinary highway map, with highways connecting cities, or consider a circuit diagram. These are both best represented as graphs. A computer network can be thought of in terms of graph theory, whether it is a LAN of a dozen systems or the Internet itself with its countless millions of nodes.

When we say "graph," we usually mean an *undirected graph*. In simplistic terms, this is a graph in which the connecting lines don't have arrows; two nodes are either connected or they are not. By contrast, a *directed graph* or *digraph* can have "one-way streets;" just because node *x* is connected to node *y* doesn't mean that the reverse is true. (A node is also commonly called a *vertex*.) Finally, a weighted graph has connections (or edges) that have weights associated with them; these weights may express, for instance, the "distance" between two nodes. We won't go beyond these basic kinds of graphs; if you're interested in learning more, you can refer to the numerous references in computer science and mathematics.

In Ruby, as in most languages, a graph can be represented in multiple ways—for example, as a true network of interconnected objects or as a matrix storing the set of edges in the graph. We will look at both of these as we show a few practical examples of manipulating graphs.

Implementing a Graph As an Adjacency Matrix

The example here builds on two previous examples. In Listing 3.21, we implement an undirected graph as an adjacency matrix, using the ZArray class to make sure new elements are zero and inheriting from TriMatrix to get a *lower triangular matrix* form.

Note that in the kind of graph we are implementing here, a node cannot be connected to itself, and two nodes can be connected by only one edge.

We provide a way to specify edges initially by passing pairs into the constructor. We also provide a way to add and remove edges and detect the presence of edges. The vmax method will return the highest-numbered vertex in the graph. The degree method will find the *degree* of the specified vertex (that is, the number of edges that connect to it).

Finally, we provide two iterators, each_vertex and each_edge. These will iterate over vertices and edges, respectively.

LISTING 3.21   Adjacency Matrix

```ruby
class LowerMatrix < TriMatrix

  def initialize
    @store = ZArray.new
  end

end


class Graph

  def initialize(*edges)
    @store = LowerMatrix.new
    @max = 0
    for e in edges
      e[0], e[1] = e[1], e[0] if e[1] > e[0]
      @store[e[0],e[1]] = 1
      @max = [@max, e[0], e[1]].max
    end
  end

  def [](x,y)
    if x > y
      @store[x,y]
    elsif x < y
      @store[y,x]
    else
      0
    end
  end

  def []=(x,y,v)
    if x > y
      @store[x,y]=v
    elsif x < y
      @store[y,x]=v
    else
      0
    end
  end

  def edge? x,y
    x,y = y,x if x < y
    @store[x,y]==1
  end
```

LISTING 3.21   Continued

```
def add x,y
  @store[x,y] = 1
end

def remove x,y
  x,y = y,x if x < y
  @store[x,y] = 0
  if (degree @max) == 0
    @max -= 1
  end
end

def vmax
  @max
end

def degree x
  sum = 0
  0.upto @max do |i|
    sum += self[x,i]
  end
  sum
end

def each_vertex
  (0..@max).each {|v| yield v}
end

def each_edge
  for v0 in 0..@max
    for v1 in 0..v0-1
      yield v0,v1 if self[v0,v1]==1
    end
  end
end

end


mygraph = Graph.new([1,0],[0,3],[2,1],[3,1],[3,2])

# Print the degrees of all the vertices: 2 3 3 2
mygraph.each_vertex {|v| puts mygraph.degree(v)}
```

LISTING 3.21 Continued

```ruby
# Print the list of edges
mygraph.each_edge do |a,b|
  puts "(#{a},#{b})"
end

# Remove a single edge
mygraph.remove 1,3

# Print the degrees of all the vertices: 2 2 2 2
mygraph.each_vertex {|v| p mygraph.degree v}
```

Determining Whether a Graph Is Fully Connected

Not all graphs are fully connected. That is, sometimes "you can't get there from here" (there may be vertices that are unreachable from other vertices no matter what path you try). Connectivity is an important property of a graph to be able to assess, telling whether the graph is "of one piece." If it is, every node is ultimately reachable from every other node.

We won't explain the algorithm; you can refer to any discrete math book. However, we offer the Ruby method in Listing 3.22.

LISTING 3.22 Determining Whether a Graph Is Fully Connected

```ruby
class Graph

  def connected?
    x = vmax
    k = [x]
    l = [x]
    for i in 0..@max
      l << i if self[x,i]==1
    end
    while !k.empty?
      y = k.shift
      # Now find all edges (y,z)
      self.each_edge do |a,b|
        if a==y || b==y
          z = a==y ? b : a
          if !l.include? z
            l << z
            k << z
          end
        end
```

LISTING 3.22   Continued

```
        end
      end
      if l.size < @max
        false
      else
        true
      end
    end

  end


mygraph = Graph.new([0,1], [1,2], [2,3], [3,0], [1,3])

puts mygraph.connected?     # true

puts mygraph.euler_path?    # true

mygraph.remove 1,2
mygraph.remove 0,3
mygraph.remove 1,3

puts mygraph.connected?     # false

puts mygraph.euler_path?    # false
```

A refinement of this algorithm could be used to determine the set of all connected components (or *cliques*) in a graph that is not overall fully connected. We won't do this here.

Determining Whether a Graph Has an Euler Circuit

There is no branch of mathematics, however abstract, which may not some day be applied to phenomena of the real world.

—Nikolai Lobachevsky

Sometimes we want to know whether a graph has an *Euler circuit*. This term comes from the mathematician Leonhard Euler who essentially founded the field of topology by dealing with a particular instance of this question. (A graph of this nature is sometimes called a *unicursive graph* because it can be drawn without lifting the pen from the paper or retracing.)

In the German town of Königsberg is an island in the middle of a river (near where the river splits into two parts). Seven bridges crisscross at various places between opposite shores and the island. The townspeople wondered whether it was possible to make a walking tour of the city in such a way that you would cross each bridge exactly once and return to your starting place. In 1735, Euler proved that this was impossible. This, then, is not just a classic problem, but the *original* graph theory problem.

And, as with many things in life, once you know the answer, it is easy. It turns out that for a graph to have an Euler circuit, it must possess only vertices with *even degree*. Here, we add a little method to check that property:

```ruby
class Graph

  def euler_circuit?
    return false if !connected?
    for i in 0..@max
      return false if degree(i) % 2 != 0
    end
    true
  end

end


mygraph = Graph.new([1,0],[0,3],[2,1],[3,1],[3,2])

flag1 =  mygraph.euler_circuit?    # false

mygraph.remove 1,3

flag2 =  mygraph.euler_circuit?    # true
```

Determining Whether a Graph Has an Euler Path

An *Euler path* is not quite the same as an Euler circuit. The word *circuit* implies that you must return to your starting point; with a *path*, we are really only concerned with visiting each edge exactly once. The following code fragment illustrates the difference:

```ruby
class Graph

  def euler_path?
    return false if !connected?
    odd=0
    each_vertex do |x|
      if degree(x) % 2 == 1
```

```
          odd += 1
        end
      end
      odd <= 2
    end

  end


  mygraph = Graph.new([0,1],[1,2],[1,3],[2,3],[3,0])

  flag1 =  mygraph.euler_circuit?   # false
  flag2 =  mygraph.euler_path?      # true
```

Hints for More Complex Graphs

It would be possible to write an entire book about graph algorithms. There are many good ones out there already, and we are certainly not going to range that far outside our realm of expertise.

However, we will offer a few hints for dealing with more sophisticated graphs. These hints should get you started if you need to tackle a more advanced problem.

Suppose you want a directed graph rather than an undirected one. Just because vertex *x* points to vertex *y* doesn't mean the converse is true. You should no longer use a lower triangular matrix form but rather a full-fledged two-dimensional array (see the section "Using Multidimensional Arrays"). You may still find ZArray useful (see the section "Establishing a Default Value for New Array Elements"). You will likely want to implement not just a degree method but rather a pair of them; in a directed graph, a vertex has an *in-degree* and an *out-degree*.

Suppose you have a directed graph in which a node or vertex is allowed to point to itself. Now you have potential nonzero numbers in the diagonal of your matrix rather than just zeroes. Be sure your code doesn't disallow access to the diagonal.

Suppose you want a *weighted graph*, where each edge has a weight associated with it. Now you would store the weight itself in the array rather than just a 1 or 0 (present or absent).

What about a *multigraph*, in which there can be multiple connections (edges) between the same pair of vertices? If it is undirected, a lower triangular matrix will suffice, and you can store the number of edges in each element (rather than just a 1 or 0). If it is directed, you will need a two-dimensional array, and you can still store the number of edges in each respective element.

What about bizarre combinations of these? For example, it is certainly conceivable to have a weighted, directed multigraph (and if you have a valid everyday need for one, let us know about your application). In this case, you would need a more complex data structure. One possibility would be to store a small array in each element of the matrix.

For example, suppose vertex 3 has five edges connecting it with vertex 4; then element 3,4 of the adjacency matrix might store an array containing the associated weights.

The possibilities are endless and are beyond the scope of this book.

Summary

In this chapter, we've taken a good look at arrays, hashes, and more complex data structures. You've seen some similarities between arrays and hashes (many of which are due to the fact that both mix in Enumerable) as well as some differences. We've looked at converting between arrays and hashes, and you've learned some interesting ways of extending their standard behavior.

Where more advanced data structures are concerned, you've seen examples of inheriting from an existing class and examples of limited delegation by encapsulating an instance of another class. You've seen ways to store data creatively, ways to make use of various data structures, and how to create iterators for these classes.

In the next chapter, we are again covering the topic of manipulation of data. However, where we have so far been concerned with objects stored in memory, we will now be looking at secondary storage—working with files (and I/O in general), databases, and persistent objects.

External Data Manipulation

IN THIS CHAPTER

On a clean disk you can seek forever.

—Thomas B. Steel, Jr.

Computers are good at computing. This tautology is more profound than it appears. If we only had to sit and chew up the CPU cycles and reference RAM as needed, life would be easy.

A computer that only sits and thinks to itself is of little use to us, however. Sooner or later we have to get information into it and out of it, and that is where life gets harder.

Several things make I/O complicated. First of all, input and output are rather different things, but we naturally lump them together. Second, the varieties of I/O operations (and their usages) are as diverse as species of insects.

History has seen such devices as drums, paper tapes, magnetic tapes, punched cards, and teletypes. Some operated with a mechanical component; others were purely electromagnetic. Some were read-only; others were write-only or read-write. Some writable media were erasable, and others were not. Some devices were inherently sequential; others were random access. Some media were permanent; others were transient or volatile. Some devices depended on human intervention; others did not. Some were character oriented; others were block oriented. Some block devices were fixed length; others were variable length. Some devices were polled; others were interrupt driven. Interrupts could be implemented in hardware or software, or both. We have seen both buffered and nonbuffered I/O. We have seen memory-mapped I/O, channel-oriented I/O, and with the advent of operating systems such as Unix, we have seen I/O devices mapped to files in a file system. We have done I/O in machine language, in assembly language, and in high-level languages. Some languages have the I/O capabilities firmly hardwired in place; others leave it out of the language specification completely. We have done I/O with and without suitable device drivers or layers of abstraction.

If this seems like a confusing mess, that's because it is. Part of the complexity is inherent in the concept of input/output, part of it is the result of design tradeoffs, and part of it is the result of legacies or traditions in computer science and the quirks of various languages and operating systems.

Ruby's I/O is complex because I/O in general is complex. However, we have tried to make it understandable and present a good overview of how and when to use various techniques.

The core of all Ruby I/O is the `IO` class, which defines behavior for every kind of input/output operation. Closely allied with `IO` (and inheriting from it) is the `File` class. There is a nested class within `File` called `Stat`, which is an object that encapsulates various details about a file that we might want to examine (such as its permissions and timestamps). The methods `stat` and `lstat` return objects of type `File::Stat`.

The module `FileTest` also has methods that allow us to test much the same set of properties. This is mixed into the `File` class and can also be used on its own.

Finally, there are I/O methods in the `Kernel` module that are mixed into `Object` (the ancestor of all objects). These are the simple I/O routines we have used all along without worrying about what their receiver was. These naturally default to standard input and standard output.

The beginner may find these classes to be a confused jumble of overlapping functionality. The good news is that you need only use small pieces of this framework at any given time.

On a higher level, Ruby offers features to make object persistence possible. The `Marshal` enables simple serialization of objects, and the more sophisticated `PStore` library is based on `Marshal`. We include the `DBM` library in this section, although it is only string based.

On the highest level of all, data access can be performed by interfacing to a separate database management system such as MySQL or Oracle. This issue is complex enough that one or more books could devoted to it. We will provide only a brief overview to get you started. In some cases, we provide only a pointer to an online archive.

Working with Files and Directories

When we say "file," we usually mean a disk file, although not always. We do use the concept of a file as a meaningful abstraction in Ruby as in other programming languages. When we say "directory," we mean a directory in the normal Windows or Unix sense.

The `File` class is closely related to the `IO` class from which it inherits. The `Dir` class is not so closely related, but we chose to discuss files and directories together because they are still conceptually related.

Opening and Closing Files

The class method `File.new`, which instantiates a `File` object, will also open that file. The first parameter is naturally the filename.

The optional second parameter is called the *mode string*, which tells how to open the file (for reading, writing, or whatever). The mode string has nothing to do with the mode as in permissions. This defaults to `"r"` for reading. Here's an example:

```
file1 = File.new("one")       # Open for reading
file2 = File.new("two", "w")  # Open for writing
```

There is another form for new that takes three parameters. In this case, the second parameter specifies the original permissions for the file (usually as an octal constant), and the third is a set of flags ORed together. The flags are constants such as File::CREAT (create the file when it is opened if it doesn't already exist) and File::RDONLY (open for reading only). This form will rarely be used. Here's an example:

```
file = File.new("three", 0755, File::CREAT|File::WRONLY)
```

As a courtesy to the operating system and the runtime environment, always close a file that you open. In the case of a file open for writing, this is more than mere politeness and can actually prevent lost data. Not surprisingly, the close method will serve this purpose:

```
out = File.new("captains.log", "w")
# Process as needed...
out.close
```

There is also an open method. In its simplest form, it is merely a synonym for new, as shown here:

```
trans = File.open("transactions","w")
```

However, open can also take a block; this is the form that is more interesting. When a block is specified, the open file is passed in as a parameter to the block. The file remains open throughout the scope of the block and is closed automatically at the end. Here's an example:

```
File.open("somefile","w") do |file|
  file.puts "Line 1"
  file.puts "Line 2"
  file.puts "Third and final line"
end
# The file is now closed
```

This is obviously an elegant way of ensuring that a file is closed when we've finished with it. In addition, the code that handles the file is grouped visually into a unit.

Updating a File

Suppose we want to open a file for reading and writing. This is done simply by adding a plus sign (+) in the file mode when we open the file (see the section titled "Opening and Closing Files" for more information). Here's an example:

```
f1 = File.new("file1", "r+")
  # Read/write, starting at beginning of file.

  f2 = File.new("file2", "w+")
  # Read/write; truncate existing file or create a new one.
```

```
f3 = File.new("file3", "a+")
# Read/write; start at end of existing file or create a
# new one.
```

Appending to a File

Suppose we want to append information onto an existing file. This is done simply by using `"a"` in the file mode when we open the file (see the section titled "Opening and Closing Files" for more information). Here's an example:

```
logfile = File.open("captains_log", "a")
  # Add a line at the end, then close.
  logfile.puts "Stardate 47824.1: Our show has been canceled."
  logfile.close
```

Random Access to Files

If you want to read a file randomly rather than sequentially, you can use the method `seek`, which `File` inherits from `IO`. The simplest usage is to seek to a specific byte position. The position is relative to the beginning of the file, where the first byte is numbered 0. Here's an example:

```
# myfile contains only: abcdefghi
file = File.new("myfile")
file.seek(5)
str = file.gets     # "fghi"
```

If you took care to ensure that each line is a fixed length, you could seek to a specific line, like so:

```
# Assume 20 bytes per line.
# Line N starts at byte (N-1)*20
file = File.new("fixedlines")
file.seek(5*20)                      # Sixth line!
# Elegance is left as an exercise.
```

If you want to do a relative seek, you can use a second parameter. The constant `IO::SEEK_CUR` will assume the offset is relative to the current position (which may be negative). Here's an example:

```
file = File.new("somefile")
file.seek(55)                    # Position is 55
file.seek(-22, IO::SEEK_CUR)     # Position is 33
file.seek(47, IO::SEEK_CUR)      # Position is 80
```

You can also seek relative to the end of the file. Only a negative offset makes sense here:

```
file.seek(-20, IO::SEEK_END)   # twenty bytes from eof
```

4

EXTERNAL DATA
MANIPULATION

There is also a third constant, IO::SEEK_SET, but it is the default value (seek relative to the beginning of file).

The method tell will report the file position (pos is an alias):

```
file.seek(20)
pos1 = file.tell               # 20
file.seek(50, IO::SEEK_CUR)
pos2 = file.pos                # 70
```

The rewind method can also be used to reposition the file pointer at the beginning. This terminology comes from the use of magnetic tapes.

If you are performing random access on a file, you may want to open it for updating (reading and writing). Updating a file is done by specifying a plus sign (+) in the mode string. See the section titled "Updating a File" for more information.

Working with Binary Files

In days gone by, C programmers would use the "b" character appended to the mode string in order to open a file as a binary. This character is still allowed for compatibility in most cases, but nowadays binary files are not as tricky as they used to be. A Ruby string can easily hold binary data, and a file need not be read in any special way.

The exception is the Windows family of operating systems. The chief difference between binary and text files on these platforms is that in binary mode, the end-of-line is not translated into a single linefeed but is kept as a carriage-return/linefeed pair.

The "b" character is indeed used in this circumstance:

```
# Input file contains a single line: Line 1.
file = File.open("data")
line = file.readline            # "Line 1.\n"
puts "#{line.size} characters."  # 8 characters
file.close

file = File.open("data","rb")
line = file.readline            # "Line 1.\r\n"
puts "#{line.size} characters."  # 9 characters
file.close
```

Note that the binmode method can switch a stream to binary mode. Once switched, it cannot be switched back. Here's an example:

```
file = File.open("data")
file.binmode
line = file.readline            # "Line 1.\r\n"
```

```
puts "#{line.size} characters."  # 9 characters
file.close
```

If you really want to do low-level input/output, you can use the `sysread` and `syswrite` methods. The former takes a number of bytes as a parameter; the latter takes a string and returns the actual number of bytes written. (You should *not* use other methods to read from the same stream; the results may be unpredictable.) Here's an example:

```
input = File.new("infile")
output = File.new("outfile")
instr = input.sysread(10);
bytes = output.syswrite("This is a test.")
```

Note that `sysread` raises `EOFError` at end-of-file. Either of these methods will raise `SystemCallError` when an error occurs.

Note that the `Array` method `pack` and the `String` method `unpack` can be very useful in dealing with binary data.

Locking Files

On operating systems where it is supported, the `flock` method of `File` will lock or unlock a file. The second parameter is one of these constants: `File::LOCK_EX`, `File::LOCK_NB`, `File::LOCK_SH`, `File::LOCK_UN`, or a logical OR of two or more of these. Note, of course, that many of these combinations will be nonsensical; primarily the nonblocking flag will be ORed in if anything is. Here's an example:

```
file = File.new("somefile")

file.flock(File::LOCK_EX)  # Lock exclusively; no other process
                           # may use this file.
file.flock(File::LOCK_UN)  # Now unlock it.

file.flock(File::LOCK_SH)  # Lock file with a shared lock (other
                           # processes may do the same).
file.flock(File::LOCK_UN)  # Now unlock it.

locked = file.flock(File::LOCK_EX | File::LOCK_NB)
# Try to lock the file, but don't block if we can't; in that case,
# locked will be false.
```

Performing Simple I/O

You are already familiar with some of the I/O routines in the `Kernel` module; these are the ones we have called all along without specifying a receiver for the methods. Calls such as `gets` and `puts` originate here; others are `print`, `printf`, and `p` (which calls the object's `inspect` method to display it in some way readable to humans).

There are some others that we should mention for completeness, though. For example, the `putc` method will output a single character. (The corresponding method `getc` is *not* implemented in `Kernel` for technical reasons; it can be found in any `IO` object, however.) If a `String` is specified, the first character of the string will be taken. Here's an example:

```
putc(?\n)    # Output a newline
putc("X")    # Output the letter X
```

A reasonable question is, where does output go when we use these methods without a receiver? Well, to begin with, three constants are defined in the Ruby environment corresponding to the three standard I/O streams we are accustomed to in Unix. These are `STDIN`, `STDOUT`, and `STDERR`. All are global constants of the type `IO`.

There is also a global variable called `$defout` that is the destination of all the output coming from `Kernel` methods. This is initialized (indirectly) to the value of `STDOUT` so that this output all gets written to standard output as we expect. The variable `$defout` can be reassigned to refer to some other `IO` object at any time. Here's an example:

```
diskfile = File.new("foofile","w")
puts "Hello..."  # prints to stdout
$defout = diskfile
puts "Goodbye!"  # prints to "foofile"
diskfile.close
```

Besides `gets`, `Kernel` also has the methods `readline` and `readlines` for input. The former is equivalent to `gets` except that it raises `EOFError` at the end of a file instead of just returning a `nil` value. The latter is equivalent to the `IO.readlines` method (that is, it reads an entire file into memory).

Where does input come from? Well, there is also the standard input stream `$stdin`, which defaults to `STDIN`. In the same way, there is a standard error stream (`$stderr` defaulting to `STDERR`).

Also, an interesting global object called `ARGF` represents the concatenation of all the files named on the command line. It is not really a `File` object, although it resembles one. Standard input is connected to this object in the event files are named on the command line.

Performing Buffered and Unbuffered I/O

Ruby does its own internal buffering in some cases. Consider this fragment:

```
print "Hello... "
sleep 10
print "Goodbye!\n"
```

If you run this, you will notice that the hello and goodbye messages both appear at the same time, *after* the sleep. The first output is not terminated by a newline.

This can be fixed by calling `flush` to flush the output buffer. In this case, we use the stream `$defout` (the default stream for all `Kernel` method output) as the receiver. It then behaves as we probably wanted, with the first message appearing earlier than the second one:

```
print "Hello... "
$defout.flush
sleep 10
print "Goodbye!\n"
```

This buffering can be turned off (or on) with the `sync=` method; the `sync` method will let us know the status:

```
buf_flag = $defout.sync       # true
$defout.sync = false
buf_flag = $defout.sync       # false
```

Also, at least one lower level of buffering is going on behind the scenes. Just as the `getc` method returns a character and moves the file or stream pointer, the `ungetc` method pushes a character back onto the stream:

```
ch = mystream.getc     # ?A
mystream.ungetc(?C)
ch = mystream.getc     # ?C
```

You should be aware of three things here. First of all, the buffering we're speaking of is unrelated to the buffering we mentioned earlier in this section; in other words, `sync=false` won't turn it off. Second, only one character can be pushed back; if you attempt more than one, only the last character will actually be pushed back onto the input stream. Finally, the `ungetc` method will not work for inherently unbuffered read operations (such as `sysread`).

Manipulating File Ownership and Permissions

The issue of file ownership and permissions is highly platform dependent. Typically, Unix provides a superset of the functionality; for other platforms many features may be unimplemented.

To determine the owner and group of a file (which are integers), `File::Stat` has a pair of instance methods, `uid` and `gid`, as shown here:

```
data = File.stat("somefile")
owner_id = data.uid
group_id = data.gid
```

Class `File::Stat` has the instance method `mode`, which will return the mode (or permissions) of the file:

```
perms = File.stat.mode("somefile")
```

`File` has class and instance methods named `chown` to change the owner and group IDs of a file. The class method will accept an arbitrary number of filenames. Where an ID is not to be changed, `nil` or `-1` can be used. Here's an example:

```
uid = 201
gid = 10
File.chown(uid, gid, "alpha", "beta")
f1 = File.new("delta")
f1.chown(uid, gid)
f2 = File.new("gamma")
f2.chown(nil, gid)       # Keep original owner id
```

Likewise, the permissions can be changed by `chmod` (also implemented both as class and instance methods). The permissions are traditionally represented in octal format, although they need not be:

```
File.chmod(0644, "epsilon", "theta")
f = File.new("eta")
f.chmod(0444)
```

A process always runs under the identity of some user (possibly root); as such, a user ID is associated with it. (Here we are talking about the *effective* user ID.) We frequently need to know whether that user has permission to read, write, or execute a given file. There are instance methods in `File::Stat` to make this determination, as shown here:

```
info = File.stat("/tmp/secrets")
rflag = info.readable?
wflag = info.writable?
xflag = info.executable?
```

Sometimes we need to distinguish between the effective user ID and the real user ID. The appropriate instance methods are `readable_real?`, `writable_real?`, and `executable_real?`. Here's an example:

```
info = File.stat("/tmp/secrets")
rflag2 = info.readable_real?
wflag2 = info.writable_real?
xflag2 = info.executable_real?
```

We can test the ownership of the file as compared with the effective user ID (and group ID) of the current process. The class `File::Stat` has instance methods `owned?` and `grpowned?` to accomplish this.

Note that many of these methods can also be found in the module `FileTest`:

```
rflag = FileTest::readable?("pentagon_files")
# Other methods are: writable? executable? readable_real? writable_real?
```

```
# executable_real? owned? grpowned?
# Not found here: uid gid mode
```

The "umask" associated with a process determines the initial permissions of new files created. The standard mode 0777 is logically ANDed with the negation of the umask so that the bits set in the umask are "masked" or cleared. If you prefer, you can think of this as a simple subtraction (without borrow). Therefore, a umask of 022 will result in files being created with a mode of 0755.

The umask can be retrieved or set with the class method umask of class File. If there is a parameter specified, the umask will be set to that value (and the previous value will be returned):

```
File.umask(0237)            # Set the umask
current_umask = File.umask  # 0237
```

Some file mode bits (such as the "sticky" bit) are not strictly related to permissions. For a discussion of these, see the section titled "Checking Special File Characteristics."

Retrieving and Setting Timestamp Information

Each disk file has multiple timestamps associated with it (although there are some variations between operating systems). The three timestamps that Ruby understands are the modification time (the last time the file contents were changed), the access time (the last time the file was read), and the change time (the last time the file's directory information was changed).

These three pieces of information can be accessed in three different ways. Each of these fortunately gives the same results.

The File class methods mtime, atime, and ctime will return the times without the file being opened or any File object being instantiated:

```
t1 = File.mtime("somefile")
# Thu Jan 04 09:03:10 GMT-6:00 2001
t2 = File.atime("somefile")
# Tue Jan 09 10:03:34 GMT-6:00 2001
t3 = File.ctime("somefile")
# Sun Nov 26 23:48:32 GMT-6:00 2000
```

If there happens to be a File instance already created, the instance method can be used:

```
myfile = File.new("somefile")
t1 = myfile.mtime
t2 = myfile.atime
t3 = myfile.ctime
```

And if there happens to be a File::Stat instance already created, it has instance methods to do the same thing:

```
myfile = File.new("somefile")
info = myfile.stat
t1 = info.mtime
t2 = info.atime
t3 = info.ctime
```

Note that a `File::Stat` is returned by `File`'s class (or instance) method `stat`. The class method `lstat` (or the instance method of the same name) is identical except that it reports on the status of the link itself instead of following the link to the actual file. In the case of links to links, all links are followed but the last one.

File access and modification times may be changed using the `utime` method. It will change the times on one or more files specified. The times may be given either as `Time` objects or as a number of seconds since the epoch. Here's an example:

```
today = Time.now
yesterday = today - 86400
File.utime(today, today, "alpha")
File.utime(today, yesterday, "beta", "gamma")
```

Because both times are changed together, if you want to leave one of them unchanged, you have to save it off first, as shown here:

```
mtime = File.mtime("delta")
File.utime(Time.now, mtime, "delta")
```

Checking File Existence and Size

One fundamental question we sometimes want to know about a file is whether the file of the given name exists. The `exist?` method in the `FileTest` module provides a way to find out:

```
flag = FileTest::exist?("LochNessMonster")
flag = FileTest::exists?("UFO")
# exists? is a synonym for exist?
```

Intuitively, such a method could not be a class instance of `File` because by the time the object is instantiated, the file has been opened; `File` conceivably could have a class method `exist?`, but in fact it does not.

Related to the question of a file's existence is the question of whether it has any contents. After all, a file may exist but have zero length (which is the next best thing to not existing).

If we are only interested in this yes/no question, `File::Stat` has two instance methods that are useful. The method `zero?` will return `true` if the file is zero length; otherwise, it will return `false`:

```
flag = File.new("somefile").stat.zero?
```

Conversely, the method `size?` will return either the size of the file in bytes, if it is nonzero length, or the value `nil`, if it is zero length. It may not be immediately obvious why `nil` is returned rather than `0`. The answer is that the method is primarily intended for use as a predicate, and `0` is "true" in Ruby, whereas `nil` tests as "false." Here's an example:

```
if File.new("myfile").stat.size?
  puts "The file has contents."
else
  puts "The file is empty."
end
```

The methods `zero?` and `size?` also appear in the `FileTest` module:

```
flag1 = FileTest::zero?("file1")
flag2 = FileTest::size?("file2")
```

This leads naturally to the question, how big is this file? We've already seen that in the case of a nonempty file, `size?` will return the length, but if we're not using it as a predicate, the `nil` value would confuse us.

The `File` class has a class method (but *not* an instance method) to give us this answer. The instance method of the same name is inherited from the `IO` class, and `File::Stat` has a corresponding instance method:

```
size1 = File.size("file1")
size2 = File.stat("file2").size
```

If we want the file size in blocks rather than bytes, we can use the instance method `blocks` in `File::Stat`. This is certainly dependent on the operating system. (The method `blksize` will also report on the operating system's idea of how big a block is.) Here's an example:

```
info = File.stat("somefile")
total_bytes = info.blocks * info.blksize
```

Checking Special File Characteristics

There are numerous aspects of a file that we can test. We summarize here the relevant built-in methods that we don't discuss elsewhere. Most, though not all, are predicates.

Bear in mind two facts throughout this section (and most of this chapter). First of all, because `File` mixes in `FileTest`, any test that can be done by invoking the method qualified with the module name may also be called as an instance method of any file object. Second, remember that there is a high degree of overlap between the `FileTest` module and the `File::Stat` object returned by `stat` (or `lstat`). In some cases, there will be three different ways to call what is essentially the same method. We won't necessarily show this every time.

Some operating systems have the concept of block-oriented devices as opposed to character-oriented devices. A file may refer to neither, but not both. The methods blockdev? and chardev? in the FileTest module will test for this:

```
flag1 = FileTest::chardev?("/dev/hdisk0")  # false
flag2 = FileTest::blockdev?("/dev/hdisk0") # true
```

Sometimes we want to know whether the stream is associated with a terminal. The IO class method tty? tests for this (as will the synonym isatty):

```
flag1 = STDIN.tty?                  # true
flag2 = File.new("diskfile").isatty # false
```

A stream can be a pipe or a socket. There are corresponding FileTest methods to test for these cases:

```
flag1 = FileTest::pipe?(myfile)
flag2 = FileTest::socket?(myfile)
```

Recall that a directory is really just a special case of a file. Therefore, we need to be able to distinguish between directories and ordinary files, which a pair of FileTest methods enable us to do. Here's an example:

```
file1 = File.new("/tmp")
file2 = File.new("/tmp/myfile")
test1 = file1.directory?        # true
test2 = file1.file?             # false
test3 = file2.directory?        # false
test4 = file2.file?             # true
```

Also, a File class method named ftype will tell us what kind of thing a stream is; it can also be found as an instance method in the File::Stat class. This method returns a string that has one of the following values: file, directory, blockSpecial, characterSpecial, fifo, link, or socket. (The string fifo refers to a pipe.) Here's an example:

```
this_kind = File.ftype("/dev/hdisk0")      # "blockSpecial"
that_kind = File.new("/tmp").stat.ftype    # "directory"
```

Certain special bits may be set or cleared in the permissions of a file. These are not strictly related to the other bits we discuss in the section "Manipulating File Ownership and Permissions." These are the set-group-id bit, the set-user-id bit, and the sticky bit. There are methods in FileTest for each of these, as shown here:

```
file = File.new("somefile")
info = file.stat
sticky_flag = info.sticky?
setgid_flag = info.setgid?
setuid_flag = info.setuid?
```

A disk file may have symbolic or hard links that refer to it (on operating systems supporting these features). To test whether a file is actually a symbolic link to some other file, use the `symlink?` method of `FileTest`. To count the number of hard links associated with a file, use the `nlink` method (found only in `File::Stat`). A hard link is virtually indistinguishable from an ordinary file; in fact, it *is* an ordinary file that happens to have multiple names and directory entries. Here's an example:

```
File.symlink("yourfile","myfile")        # Make a link
is_sym = FileTest::symlink?("myfile")    # true
hard_count = File.new("myfile").stat.nlink  # 0
```

Incidentally, note that in this example we use the `File` class method `symlink` to create a symbolic link.

In rare cases, you may want even lower-level information about a file. The `File::Stat` class has three more instance methods that give you the gory details. The method `dev` will give you an integer identifying the device on which the file resides; `rdev` will return an integer specifying the kind of device; and for disk files, `ino` will give you the starting "inode" number for the file:

```
file = File.new("diskfile")
info = file.stat
device = info.dev
devtype = info.rdev
inode = info.ino
```

Working with Pipes

Ruby provides various ways of reading and writing pipes. The class method `IO.popen` will open a pipe and hook the process's standard input and standard output into the `IO` object returned. Frequently we will have different threads handling each end of the pipe; here we just show a single thread writing and then reading:

```
check = IO.popen("spell","r+")
check.puts("'T was brillig, and the slithy toves")
check.puts("Did gyre and gimble in the wabe.")
check.close_write
list = check.readlines
list.collect! { |x| x.chomp }
# list is now %w[brillig gimble gyre slithy toves wabe]
```

Note that the `close_write` call is necessary. If it were not issued, we would not be able to reach end-of-file when we read the pipe.

There is also a block form:

```
File.popen("/usr/games/fortune") do |pipe|
  quote = pipe.gets
  puts quote
  # On a clean disk, you can seek forever. - Thomas Steel
end
```

If the string "-" is specified, a new Ruby instance is started. If a block is specified with this, the block is run as two separate processes rather like a fork; the child gets `nil` passed into the block, and the parent gets an `IO` object with the child's standard input and/or output connected to it, as shown here:

```
IO.popen("-") do |mypipe|
  if mypipe
    puts "I'm the parent: pid = #{Process.pid}"
    listen = mypipe.gets
    puts listen
  else
    puts "I'm the child: pid = #{Process.pid}"
  end
end


# Prints:
#   I'm the parent: pid = 10580
#   I'm the child: pid = 10582
```

Also, the `pipe` method returns a pair of pipe ends connected to each other. Here, we create a pair of threads and let one pass a message to the other (the first message that Samuel Morse sent over the telegraph):

```
pipe = IO.pipe
reader = pipe[0]
writer = pipe[1]

str = nil
thread1 = Thread.new(reader,writer) do |reader,writer|
  # writer.close_write
  str = reader.gets
  reader.close
end

thread2 = Thread.new(reader,writer) do |reader,writer|
  # reader.close_read
  writer.puts("What hath God wrought?")
  writer.close
end
```

```
thread1.join
thread2.join

puts str          # What hath God wrought?
```

Performing Special I/O Operations

It is possible to do lower-level I/O in Ruby. We will only mention the existence of these methods; if you need to use them, note that some of them will be highly machine specific (varying even between different versions of Unix).

The ioctl method ("I/O control") will accept two arguments. The first is an integer specifying the operation to be done. The second is either an integer or a string representing a binary number.

The fcntl method is also for low-level control of file-oriented streams in a system-dependent manner. It takes the same kinds of parameters as ioctl.

The select method (in the Kernel module) will accept up to four parameters; the first is the read-array, and the last three are optional (write-array, error-array, and the timeout value. When input is available from one or more devices in the read-array, or one or more devices in the write-array are ready, the call will return an array of three elements representing the respective arrays of devices that are ready for I/O.

The Kernel method syscall takes at least one integer parameter (and up to nine string or integer parameters in all). The first parameter specifies the I/O operation to be done.

The fileno method returns an old-fashioned file descriptor associated with an I/O stream. This is the least system dependent of all the methods mentioned. Here's an example:

```
desc = $stderr.fileno      # 2
```

Manipulating Pathnames

When manipulating pathnames, the first things to be aware of are the class methods File.dirname and File.basename; these work like the Unix commands of the same names and return the directory name and the filename, respectively. If an extension is specified as a second parameter to basename, that extension will be removed:

```
str = "/home/dave/podbay.rb"
dir = File.dirname(str)           # "/home/dave"
file1 = File.basename(str)        # "podbay.rb"
file2 = File.basename(str,".rb")  # "podbay"
```

Note that although these are methods of File, they are really simply doing string manipulation.

A comparable method is `File.split`, which returns these two components (directory and file-name) in a two-element array:

```
info = File.split(str)          # ["/home/dave","podbay.rb"]
```

The `expand_path` class method will expand a relative pathname, converting it to an absolute path. If the operating system understands such idioms as ~ and ~user, these will be expanded also. Here's an example:

```
Dir.chdir("/home/poole/personal/docs")
abs = File.expand_path("../../misc")    # "/home/poole/misc"
```

Given an open file, the `path` instance method will return the pathname used to open the file:

```
file = File.new("../../foobar")
name = file.path                        # "../../foobar"
```

The constant `File::Separator` gives the character used to separate pathname components (typically a backslash for Windows and a slash for Unix). An alias is `File::SEPARATOR`.

The class method `join` uses this separator to produce a path from a list of directory components:

```
path = File.join("usr","local","bin","someprog")
# path is "usr/local/bin/someprog"
# Note that it doesn't put a separator on the front!
```

Don't fall into the trap of thinking that `File.join` and `File.split` are somehow inverse operations. They're not.

Command-Level File Manipulation

Very often we need to manipulate files in a manner similar to the way we would at a command line. That is, we need to copy, delete, rename, and so on. Many of these capabilities are built-in methods; a few are added by the `ftools` library.

To delete a file, we can use `File.delete` or its synonym `File.unlink`, like so:

```
File.delete("history")
File.unlink("toast")
```

To rename a file, we can use `File.rename` as follows:

```
File.rename("Ceylon","SriLanka")
```

File links (hard and symbolic) can be created using `File.link` and `File.symlink`, respectively:

```
File.link("/etc/hosts","/etc/hostfile")    # hard link
File.symlink("/etc/hosts","/tmp/hosts")    # symbolic link
```

We can truncate a file to zero bytes (or any other specified number) by using the `truncate` instance method:

```
File.truncate("myfile",1000)    # Now at most 1000 bytes
```

Two files may be compared by means of the `compare` method (`cmp` is the alias):

```
require "ftools"

same = File.compare("alpha","beta")  # true
```

The method `syscopy` will efficiently copy a file to a new name or location. A similar method is `copy`, which has an optional flag parameter to write error messages to standard error (`cp` is the alias):

```
require "ftools"

File.syscopy("gamma","delta")      # Copies gamma to delta
File.syscopy("gamma","/tmp")       # Creates /tmp/gamma
# Copy epsilon to theta and log any errors.
File.copy("epsilon","theta", true)
```

A file may be moved with the `move` method (the alias is `mv`). Like `copy`, it also has an optional verbose-flag:

```
require "ftools"

File.move("/tmp/names","/etc")     # Move to new directory
File.move("colours","colors")      # Just a rename
```

The `safe_unlink` method will delete the specified file or files, first trying to make the files writable so as to avoid errors. If the last parameter is `true` or `false`, that value will be taken as the verbose-flag. Here's an example:

```
require "ftools"

File.safe_unlink("alpha","beta","gamma")
# Log errors on the next two files
File.safe_unlink("delta","epsilon",true)
```

Finally, the `install` method basically does a `syscopy`, except that it first checks that the file either does not exist or has different content:

```
require "ftools"

File.install("foo.so","/usr/lib")
# Existing foo.so will not be overwritten
# if it is the same as the new one.
```

Grabbing Characters from the Keyboard

We use the term "grabbing" here because we sometimes want to process a character as soon as it is pressed rather than buffer it and wait for a newline to be entered.

This can be done in both Unix variants and Windows variants. Unfortunately, the two methods are completely unrelated to each other.

The Unix version is straightforward. We use the well-known technique of putting the terminal in raw mode (and we usually turn off echoing at the same time):

```
system("stty raw -echo")   # Raw mode, no echo
char = STDIN.getc
system("stty -raw echo")   # Reset terminal mode
```

In the Windows world, we need to write a C extension for this. An alternative for now is to use a small feature of the Win32API library, shown here:

```
require 'Win32API'
char = Win32API.new("crtdll", "_getch", [], 'L').Call
```

This is obviously not pretty, but it works.

Reading an Entire File into Memory

To read an entire file into an array, you need not even open the file. The method IO.readlines will do this, opening and closing the file on its own:

```
arr = IO.readlines("myfile")
lines = arr.size
puts "myfile has #{lines} lines in it."

longest = arr.collect {|x| x.length}.max
puts "The longest line in it has #{longest} characters."
```

Iterating over a File by Line

To iterate over a file a line at a time, we can use the class method IO.foreach or the instance method each. In the former case, the file need not be opened in our code. Here's an example:

```
# Print all lines containing the word "target"
IO.foreach("somefile") do |line|
  puts line if line =~ /target/
end
```

```
# Another way...
file = File.new("somefile")
file.each do |line|
  puts line if line =~ /target/
end
```

Note that each_line is an alias for each.

Iterating over a File by Byte

To iterate a byte at a time, use the each_byte instance method. Remember that it feeds a character (that is, an integer) into the block; use the chr method if you need to convert to a "real" character. Here's an example:

```
file = File.new("myfile")
e_count = 0
file.each_byte do |byte|
  e_count += 1 if byte == ?e
end
```

Treating a String As a File

Sometimes people want to know how to treat a string as though it were a file. The answer depends on the exact meaning of the question.

An object is defined mostly in terms of its methods. The following code shows an iterator applied to an object called source; with each iteration, a line of output is produced. Can you tell the type of source by reading this fragment?

```
source.each do |line|
  puts line
end
```

Actually, source could be a file, or it could be a string containing embedded newlines. Therefore, in cases like these, a string can trivially be treated as a file.

This leads naturally to the idea of writing something like an IOString class. We could do that here, but the exact design of such a class would depend on what you want to do with it. Should we inherit from String or from IO, for instance? A third possibility would be to create a library that adds methods to the String class (just as ftools extends File).

We won't attempt any full implementation here. We'll only make a skeleton to show one approach (see Listing 4.1). Fleshing it out would involve an exhaustive set of methods and rigorous error checking; the example here is neither complete nor robust.

4

EXTERNAL DATA
MANIPULATION

LISTING 4.1   Outline of an *IOString* Class

```ruby
class IOString < String

  def initialize(str="")
    @fptr = 0
    self.replace(str)
  end

  def open
    @fptr = 0
  end

  def truncate
    self.replace("")
    @fptr = 0
  end

  def seek(n)
    @fptr = [n, self.size].min
  end

  def tell
    @fptr
  end

  def getc
    @fptr += 1
    self[@fptr-1].to_i
  end

  def ungetc(c)
    self[@fptr -= 1] = c.chr
  end

  def putc(c)
    self[@fptr] = c.chr
    @fptr += 1
  end

  def gets
    s = ""
    n = self.index("\n",@fptr)
    s = self[@fptr..n].dup
    @fptr += s.length
    s
  end
```

LISTING 4.1   Continued

```
  def puts(s)
    self[@fptr..@fptr+s.length-1] = s
    @fptr += s.length
  end

end


ios = IOString.new("abcdefghijkl\nABC\n123")

ios.seek(5)
ios.puts("xyz")

puts ios.tell       # 8

puts ios.dump       # "abcdexyzijkl\nABC\n123"

c = ios.getc
puts "c = #{c}"     # c = 105

ios.ungetc(?w)

puts ios.dump       # "abcdexyzwjkl\nABC\n123"

puts "Ptr = #{ios.tell}"

s1 = ios.gets       # "wjkl"
s2 = ios.gets       # "ABC"
```

Reading Data Embedded in a Program

When you were 12 years old and you learned BASIC by copying programs out of magazines, you may have used a DATA statement for convenience. The information was embedded in the program, but it could be read as if it originated outside.

Should you ever want to, you can do much the same thing in Ruby. The directive __END__ at the end of a Ruby program signals that embedded data follows. This can be read using the global constant DATA, which is an IO object like any other. (Note that the __END__ marker must be at the beginning of the line on which it appears.) Here's an example:

```
# Print each line backwards...
DATA.each_line do |line|
```

```
    puts line.reverse
  end
  __END__
A man, a plan, a canal... Panama!
Madam, I'm Adam.
,siht daer nac uoy fI
.drah oot gnikrow neeb ev'uoy
```

Reading Program Source

Suppose you want to access the source of your own program. This can be done using a variation on a trick we used elsewhere (see the section titled "Reading Data Embedded in a Program").

The global constant DATA is an IO object that refers to the data following the __END__ directive. However, if you perform a rewind operation, it will reset the file pointer to the beginning of the program source.

The following program will produce a listing of itself with line numbers (it is not particularly useful, but maybe you can find some other good use for this capability):

```
DATA.rewind
num = 1
DATA.each_line do |line|
  puts "#{'%03d' % num}  #{line}"
  num += 1
end
__END__
```

Note that the __END__ directive *is* necessary; without it, DATA cannot be accessed at all.

Performing Newline Conversion

One of the annoyances of dealing with different operating systems is that they may have different concepts of what an end-of-line character is. The "common sense" newline is a carriage return (CR) followed by a linefeed (LF); but in the earliest days of Unix, the decision was made to store only the linefeed, thus saving an entire byte per line of text. (This was when 512KB was a *lot* of memory.) Today we might expect that a text file is a text file, but in moving files between, say, a Unix machine and a Windows machine, we are bitten over and over by the newline problem.

Therefore, we offer a little solution here. The gets method will honor either kind of newline, and the puts method will always write in the native format. That means this same code will convert to native format on either kind of operating system. We show it here as a simple filter that reads standard input and writes to standard output:

```
while line = gets
  puts line
end
```

Another case might result from receiving an entire file in an unknown OS format. Whereas Unix variants use LF for their newline, and Windows versions use CR-LF, we have yet another possibility with Mac OS, which uses just CR. This very situation arises on the Web when a TEXTAREA is processed, among other times.

Here is one way to handle this situation, in which we wish to save the contents of a text area into a file on our Linux Web server:

```
tmp=cgi.params["mytextarea"].to_s
File.open("newfile","w") do |f|
  newstring = tmp.gsub!(/\r\n/m,"\n") or
               tmp.gsub!(/\r/m,"\n") or tmp
  newstring.each { |line| f.puts line }
end
```

The first gsub! looks for the CR-LF pair from a PC. If it finds none, it returns nil, meaning the or will allow the next gsub! to execute, which works on Mac OS–based files. If no carriage returns are found, the originally captured string is used. After conversion, the string is written line by line to a file.

Working with Temporary Files

In many circumstances we need to work with files that are all but anonymous. We don't want the trouble of naming them or making sure there is no name conflict, and we don't want to bother with deleting them.

All these issues are addressed in the Tempfile library. The new method (alias open) will take a base name as a "seed string" and will concatenate onto it the process ID and a unique sequence number. The optional second parameter is the directory to be used; it defaults to the value of environment variable TMPDIR, TMP, or TEMP, and finally the value "/tmp".

The resulting IO object may be opened and closed many times during the execution of the program. Upon termination of the program, the temporary file will be deleted.

The close method has an optional flag; if set to true, the file will be deleted immediately after it is closed (instead of waiting until program termination). The path method will return the actual pathname of the file, should you need it. Here's an example:

```
require "tempfile"

temp = Tempfile.new("stuff")
name = temp.path              # "/tmp/stuff17060.0"
```

```
temp.puts "Kilroy was here"
temp.close

# Later...
temp.open
str = temp.gets              # "Kilroy was here"
temp.close(true)             # Delete it NOW
```

Changing and Setting the Current Directory

The current directory may be determined by the use of Dir.pwd or its alias Dir.getwd; these abbreviations historically stand for *print working directory* and *get working directory*, respectively. In a Windows environment, the backslashes will probably show up as normal (forward) slashes.

The method Dir.chdir may be used to change the current directory. On Windows, the logged drive may appear at the front of the string. Here's an example:

```
Dir.chdir("/var/tmp")
puts Dir.pwd             # "/var/tmp"
puts Dir.getwd           # "/var/tmp"
```

Changing the Current Root

On most Unix variants, it is possible to change the current process's idea of where the root or "slash" is. This is typically done for security reasons (for example, when running unsafe or untested code). The chroot method will set the new root to the specified directory:

```
Dir.chdir("/home/guy/sandbox/tmp")
Dir.chroot("/home/guy/sandbox")
puts Dir.pwd                      # "/tmp"
```

Iterating over Directory Entries

The class method foreach is an iterator that will successively pass each directory entry into the block. The instance method each behaves the same way. Here's an example:

```
Dir.foreach("/tmp") { |entry| puts entry }

dir = Dir.new("/tmp")
dir.each  { |entry| puts entry }
```

Both of the preceding code fragments will print the same output (the names of all files and subdirectories in /tmp).

Getting a List of Directory Entries

The class method `Dir.entries` will return an array of all the entries in the specified directory:

```
list = Dir.entries("/tmp")  # %w[. .. alpha.txt beta.doc]
```

Creating a Chain of Directories

Sometimes we want to create a chain of directories where the intermediate directories themselves don't necessarily exist yet. At the Unix command line, we would use `mkdir -p` for this.

In Ruby code, we can do this by using the `makedirs` method, which the `ftools` library adds to `File`:

```
require "ftools"

File.makedirs("/tmp/these/dirs/need/not/exist")
```

Deleting a Directory Recursively

In the Unix world, we can type `rm -rf dir` at the command line and the entire subtree starting with `dir` will be deleted. Obviously, we should exercise caution in doing this.

If you need a piece of code to accomplish this, here it is:

```
def delete_all(dir)
  Dir.foreach(dir) do |e|
    # Don't bother with . and ..
    next if [".",".."].include? e
    fullname = dir + File::Separator + e
    if FileTest::directory?(fullname)
      delete_all(fullname)
    else
      File.delete(fullname)
    end
  end
  Dir.delete(dir)
end


delete_all("dir1")   # Remove dir1 and everything under it!
```

Finding Files and Directories

Here, we make use of the standard library `find.rb` to create a method that will find one or more files and return the list of files as an array. The first parameter is the starting directory; the second is either a filename (that is, a string) or a regular expression:

```ruby
require "find"

def findfiles(dir, name)
  list = []
  Find.find(dir) do |path|
    Find.prune if [".",".."].include? path
    case name
      when String
        list << path if File.basename(path) == name
      when Regexp
        list << path if File.basename(path) =~ name
    else
      raise ArgumentError
    end
  end
  list
end

findfiles "/home/hal", "toc.txt"
# ["/home/hal/docs/toc.txt", "/home/hal/misc/toc.txt"]

findfiles "/home", /^[a-z]+.doc/
# ["/home/hal/docs/alpha.doc", "/home/guy/guide.doc",
#  "/home/bill/help/readme.doc"]
```

Performing Higher-Level Data Access

Frequently we want to store and retrieve data in a more transparent manner. The `Marshal` module offers simple object persistence, and the `PStore` library builds on that functionality. Finally, the `dbm` library is used like a hash stored permanently on disk. It does not truly belong in this section, but it is rather too simple to put in the database section.

Simple Marshaling

In many cases, we would like to create an object and simply save it for use later. Ruby provides rudimentary support for such object persistence or *marshaling*. The `Marshal` module enables programs to *serialize* and *unserialize* Ruby objects in this way:

```ruby
# array of elements [composer, work, minutes]
works = [["Leonard Bernstein","Overture to Candide",11],
```

```
                ["Aaron Copland","Symphony No. 3",45],
                ["Jean Sibelius","Finlandia",20]]
# We want to keep this for later...
File.open("store","w") do |file|
  Marshal.dump(works,file)
end

# Much later...
File.open("store") do |file|
  works = Marshal.load(file)
end
```

This technique does have the shortcoming that not all objects can be dumped. If an object includes an object of a fairly low-level class, it cannot be marshaled; these include IO, Proc, and a few others. Singleton objects also cannot be serialized.

More Complex Marshaling

Sometimes we want to customize our marshaling to some extent. Creating _load and _dump methods will enable you to do this. These hooks are called when marshaling is done so that you are handling your own conversion to and from a string.

In this example, a person has been earning five percent interest on his beginning balance since he was born. We don't store the age and the current balance since they are a function of time:

```
class Person

  def initialize(name,birthdate,beginning)
    @name = name
    @birthdate = birthdate
    @beginning = beginning
    @age = (Time.now - @birthdate)/(365*86400)
    @balance = @beginning*(1.05**age)
  end

  def _dump(depth)
    # (We ignore depth here)
    @name + ":" + @birthdate + ":" + @beginning
  end

  def _load(str)
    a, b, c = str.split(":")
    Person.new(a,b,c)
  end
```

```
  # Other methods...

end
```

When an object of this type is saved, the age and current balance will not be stored; when the object is "reconstituted," they will be computed.

Performing Limited "Deep Copying" Using `Marshal`

Ruby has no "deep copy" operation. The methods `dup` and `clone` may not always work as you would initially expect. An object may contain nested object references that turn a copy operation into a game of Pick Up Sticks.

We offer here a way to handle a restricted deep copy (it is restricted because it is still based on `Marshal` and has the same inherent limitations):

```
def deep_copy(obj)
  Marshal.load(Marshal.dump(obj))
end


a = deep_copy(b)
```

Better Object Persistence with `PStore`

The `PStore` library provides file-based persistent storage of Ruby objects. A `PStore` object can hold a number of Ruby object hierarchies. Each hierarchy has a *root* identified by a key. Hierarchies are read from a disk file at the start of a transaction and written back at the end. Here's an example:

```
require "pstore"

# save
db = PStore.new("employee.dat")
db.transaction do
    db["params"] = {"name" => "Fred", "age" => 32,
                    "salary" => 48000 }
end


# retrieve
require "pstore"
db = PStore.new("employee.dat")
emp = nil
db.transaction { emp = db["params"] }
```

Typically, within a transaction block we use the PStore object passed in. We can also use the receiver directly, however.

This technique is transaction oriented; at the start of the block, data is retrieved from the disk file to be manipulated. Afterward, it is transparently written back out to disk.

In the middle of a transaction, we can interrupt with either commit or abort; the former will keep the changes we have made, whereas the latter will throw them away. Refer to the longer example in Listing 4.2.

LISTING 4.2   Using *PStore*

```
require "pstore"

store = PStore.new("objects")
store.transaction do |s|

  a = s["my_array"]
  h = s["my_hash"]

  # Imaginary code omitted, manipulating
  # a, h, etc.

  # Assume a variable named "condition" having
  # the value 1, 2, or 3...

  case condition
    when 1
      puts "Oops... aborting."
      s.abort   # Changes will be lost.
    when 2
      puts "Committing and jumping out."
      s.commit  # Changes will be saved.
    when 3
      # Do nothing...
  end

  puts "We finished the transaction to the end."
  # Changes will be saved.

end
```

Within a transaction, you can also use the method `roots` to return an array of roots (or `root?` to test membership). Also, the `delete` method is available to remove a root. Here' an example:

```
store.transaction do |s|
  list = s.roots            # ["my_array","my_hash"]
  if s.root?("my_tree")
    puts "Found my_tree."
  else
    puts "Didn't find # my_tree."
  end
  s.delete("my_hash")
  list2 = s.roots           # ["my_array"]
end
```

Using the dbm Library

The dbm library is a simple platform-independent, string-based hash, file-storage mechanism. It stores a key and some associated data, both of which must be strings. Ruby's dbm interface is built in to the standard installation.

To use this class, create a dbm object associated with a filename and work with the string-based hash however you want. When you have finished, you should close the file. Here's an example:

```
require 'dbm'

d = DBM.new("data")
d["123"] = "toodle-oo!"
puts d["123"]        # "toodle-oo!"
d.close

puts d["123"]        # RuntimeError: closed DBM file

e = DBM.open("data")
e["123"]             # "toodle-oo!"
w=e.to_hash          # {"123"=>"toodle-oo!"}
e.close

e["123"]             # RuntimeError: closed DBM file
w["123"]             # "toodle-oo!
```

Here, dbm is implemented as a single class that mixes in `Enumerable`. The two (aliased) class methods, `new` and `open`, are singletons, which means you may only have one dbm object per data file open at any given time:

```
q=DBM.new("data.dbm")    #
f=DBM.open("data.dbm")   # Errno::EWOULDBLOCK:
                         #   Try again - "data.dbm"
```

There are 34 instance methods, many of which are aliases or similar to the hash methods. Basically, if you are used to manipulating a real hash in a certain way, there is a good chance you can apply the same operation to a dbm object.

The method to_hash will make a copy of the hash file object in memory, and close will permanently close the link to the hash file. Most of the rest of the methods are analogous to hash methods, but there are no rehash, sort, default, and default= methods. The to_s method just returns a string representation of the object ID.

Connecting to External Databases

Ruby can interface to various databases, thanks to the development work of many different people. These range from monolithic systems such as Oracle down to the more petite MySQL. We have included the CSV (comma-separated values) format here for some measure of completeness.

The level of functionality provided by these packages will continually be changing. Be sure to refer to an online reference for the latest information. The Ruby Application Archive (RAA) is always a good starting point.

Interfacing to MySQL

Ruby's MySQL interface is the most stable and fully functional of its database interfaces. It is an extension and must be installed after both Ruby and MySQL are installed and running. If you upgrade Ruby, you will need to reinstall it. Installation itself is simple, using Ruby's make process.

There are three steps to using this module once you have it installed. First, load the module in your script; then connect to the database. Finally, work with your tables. Connecting requires the usual parameters for host, username, password, database, and so on, as shown here:

```
require 'mysql'

m = Mysql.new("localhost","ruby","secret","maillist")
r = m.query("SELECT * FROM people ORDER BY name")
r.each_hash do |f|
  print "#{f['name']} - #{f['email']}"
end
```

Partial output is shown here:

```
John Doe - jdoe@rubynewbie.com
Fred Smith - smithf@rubyexpert.com
Don Jackson - don@perl2.com
Jenny Williams - jwill27@miss-code.com
```

The class methods `Mysql.new` and `MysqlRes.each_hash` are very useful, along with the instance method `query`.

The module is composed of four classes: `Mysql`, `MysqlRes`, `MysqlField`, and `MysqlError`, as described in the README file. We summarize some useful methods here, but you can always find more information in the actual documentation.

The class method `Mysql.new` takes several string parameters, all defaulting to `nil`, and it returns a connection object. The parameters are `host`, `user`, `passwd`, `db`, `port`, `sock`, and `flag`. Aliases for `new` are `real_connect` and `connect`.

The methods `create_db`, `select_db`, and `drop_db` all take a database name as a parameter; they are used as shown here (note that the method `close` will close the connection to the server):

```
m=Mysql.new("localhost","ruby","secret")
m.create_db("rtest")     # Create a new database
m.select_db("rtest2")    # Select a different database
m.drop_db("rtest")       # Delete a database
m.close                  # Close the connection
```

The method `list_dbs` will return a list of available database names in an array:

```
dbs = m2.list_dbs        # ["people","places","things"]
```

The `query` takes a string parameter and returns a `MysqlRes` object by default. Depending on how `query_with_result` is set, it may return a `Mysql` object.

In the event of an error, the error number can be retrieved by `errno`; `error`, on the other hand, will return the actual error message. Here's an example:

```
begin
  r=m.query("create table rtable
    (
      id int not null auto_increment,
      name varchar(35) not null,
      desc varchar(128) not null,
      unique id(id)
    )")

# exception happens...

rescue
  puts m.error
  # Prints: You have an error in your SQL syntax
  # near 'desc varchar(128) not null ,
  #   unique id(id)
  # )' at line 5"
```

```
    puts m.errno
    # Prints 1064
    # ('desc' is reserved for descending order)
  end
```

A few useful instance methods of `MysqlRes` are summarized in the following list:

- `fetch_fields`—Returns an array of `MysqlField` objects from the next row.
- `fetch_row`—Returns an array of field values from the next row.
- `fetch_hash(with_table=false)`—Returns a hash containing the next row's field names and values.
- `num_rows`—Returns the number of rows in the result set.
- `each`—An iterator that sequentially returns an array of field values.
- `each_hash(with_table=false)`—An iterator that sequentially returns a hash of `{fieldname => fieldvalue}`. (Use `x['field name']` to get the field value.)

Here are some instance methods of `MysqlField`:

- `name`—Returns the name of the designated field
- `table`—Returns the name of table to which the designated field belongs
- `length`—Returns the defined length of the field
- `max_length`—Returns the length of the longest field from the result set
- `hash`—Returns a hash with a name and values for name, table, def, type, length, max_length, flags, and decimals

The material here is always superseded by online documentation. For more information, see the MySQL Web site (`www.mysql.com`) and the Ruby Application Archive.

Interfacing to PostgreSQL

An extension is available from the RAA that provides access to PostgreSQL (it works with PostgreSQL 6.5/7.0).

Assuming you already have PostgreSQL installed and set up (and you have a table named testdb), you merely need to follow essentially the same steps as used with other database interfaces in Ruby: Load the module, connect to the database, and then do your work with the tables. You'll probably want a way of executing queries, getting the results of a "select" operation back, and working with transactions. Here's an example:

```
require 'postgres'
conn = PGconn.connect("",5432, "", "", "testdb")
```

```
conn.exec("create table rtest ( number integer default 0 );")
conn.exec("insert into rtest values ( 99 )")
res = conn.query("select * from rtest")
# res id [["99"]]
```

The PGconn class contains the connect method, which takes the typical database connection parameters, such as host, port, database, username, and login, but it also takes options and tty parameters in positions three and four. We have connected in our example to the Unix socket via a privileged user, so we don't need a username and password. Also, the host, options, and tty parameters are left empty. The port must be an integer, whereas the others are strings. An alias for this is the new method.

The next thing of interest is working with our tables; this requires some means to perform queries. The instance methods PGconn#exec and PGconn#query are just what we need.

The exec method sends its string parameter as a SQL query request to PostgreSQL, and it returns a PGresult instance on success. On failure, it raises a PGError exception.

The query method also sends its string parameter as a SQL query request to PostgreSQL. However, it returns an array on success. The returned array is actually an array of tuples. On failure, it returns nil, and error details can be obtained by the error method call.

A special method, called insert_table, is available for inserting values into a specific table. Despite the name, insert_table actually means "insert into table." This method returns a PGconn object. Here's an example:

```
conn.insert_table("rtest",[[34]])
res = conn.query("select * from rtest")
# res is [["99"], ["34"]]
```

This inserts one row of values into the table rtest. For this simple example, there is only one column to begin with. Notice that the PGresult object res shows updated results with two tuples. We will discuss PGresult methods shortly.

Other potentially useful methods from the PGconn class include the following:

- db—Returns the connected database name.
- host—Returns the connected server name.
- user—Returns the authenticated username.
- error—Returns the error message about the connection.
- finish—Close the backend connection.
- loimport(file)—Imports a file to a large object; returns the PGlarge instance on success. On failure, this method raises the PGError exception.

- `loexport(oid, file)`—Saves a large object of `oid` to a file.
- `locreate([mode])`—Returns the `PGlarge` instance on success. On failure, it raises the `PGError` exception.
- `loopen(oid, [mode])`—Opens a large object of `oid`; returns the `PGlarge` instance on success. The mode argument specifies the mode for the opened large object, which is either `INV_READ` or `INV_WRITE` (if the mode is omitted, the default is `INV_READ`).
- `lounlink(oid)`—Unlinks (deletes) the `Postgres` large object of `oid`.

Notice that the last five methods of `PGconn` involve objects of the `PGlarge` class. The `PGlarge` class has specific methods for accessing and changing its own objects. (The objects are created as a result of the `PGconn` instance methods `loimport`, `locreate`, and `loopen` from the preceding list.)

Here is a list of `PGlarge` methods:

- `open([mode])`—Opens a large object. The mode argument specifies its mode (see `PGconn#loopen`).
- `close`—Closes a large object (also closed when it is garbage collected).
- `read([length])`—Attempts to read "length" bytes from a large object. If no length is given, all data is read.
- `write(str)`—Writes the string to the large object and returns the number of bytes written.
- `tell`—Returns the current position of the pointer.
- `seek(offset, whence)`—Moves the pointer to `offset`. The possible values for `whence` are `SEEK_SET`, `SEEK_CUR`, and `SEEK_END` (or 0, 1, and 2).
- `unlink`—Deletes a large object.
- `oid`—Returns the large object oid.
- `size`—Returns the size of a large object.
- `export(file)`—Saves a large object of `oid` to a file.

Of more interest to us are the instance methods of the `PGresult` class, which are created as the result of queries. Use `PGresult#clear` when finished with these objects to improve memory performance. Here's a list of these methods:

- `result`—Returns the query result tuple in the array.
- `each`—An iterator.
- `[]`—An accessor.
- `fields`—Returns the array of the fields of the query result.
- `num_tuples`—Returns the number of tuples of the query result.

4

- `fieldnum(name)`—Returns the index of the named field.
- `type(index)`—Returns an integer corresponding the type of the field.
- `size(index)`—Returns the size of the field in bytes. A value of `-1` indicates the field is variable length.
- `getvalue(tup_num, field_num)`—Returns the field value for the given parameters. `tup_num` is the same as row number.
- `getlength(tup_num, field_num)`—Returns the length of the field in bytes.
- `cmdstatus`—Returns the status string of the last query command.
- `clear`—Clears the `PGresult` object.

Working with CSV Data

The CSV format is something you may have had to deal with if you have ever worked with spreadsheets or databases. Fortunately, Hiroshi Nakamura has created a module for Ruby and has made it available in the Ruby Application Archive.

This is not a true database system. However, we felt that a discussion of it fits here better than anywhere else.

The CSV module (`csv.rb`) will parse or generate data in CSV format. The module author defines this format as follows:

```
Record separator: CR + LF
Field separator: comma (,)
Quote data with double quotes if it contains CR, LF, or comma
Quote double quote by prefixing it with another double quote (" -> "")
Empty field with quotes means null string (data,"",data)
Empty field without quotes means NULL (data,,data)
```

There are two ways to use this module: Parse/create single lines, and read/write through a file parsing/creating records sequentially. In the latter case, you will be dealing with arrays of column data objects instead of arrays of strings. The latter method requires the use of the record separator and the `isNull` flag of the column data object.

First, let's look at the handling of single, nonterminated lines. The method `CSV::parse` will parse the specified CSV-formatted string as a single line and return an array of strings; the method `CSV::create` will take the specified array of strings and create a single CSV-formatted line.

Suppose we have a data file `data.csv`, as shown here:

```
"name","age","salary"
"mark",29,34500
"joe",42,32000
```

```
"fred",22,22000
"jake",25,24000
"don",32,52000
```

We can process this file as follows:

```
require 'csv'
IO.foreach("data.csv") { |f| p CSV::parse(f.chomp) }
# Output:
# ["name", "age", "salary"]
# ["mark", "29", "34500"]
# ["joe", "42", "32000"]
# ["fred", "22", "22000"]
# ["jake", "25", "24000"]
# ["don", "32", "52000"]
```

We could also process each array and write it back to a file:

```
File.open("newdata.csv","w") do |file|
  IO.foreach("data.csv") do |line|
    a=CSV::parse line.chomp
    if a[1].to_i > 20
      s=a[2].to_i
      a[2]=s*1.1   # 10% raise
    end
    file.puts CSV::create(a)
  end
end
```

Now let's take a look at the multiline parsing commands. These commands handle data differently and do expect to see the record terminator CR-LF. The `parseLine` method populates an array with objects that contain the parsed field data and a flag for null data. Likewise, the `createLine` method uses such objects to generate CSV-formatted output.

To demonstrate, we can use the `data.csv` file again:

```
require 'csv'

file_str = File.open("data.csv").read
rec = []; pos=nil; i=-1
c,pos = CSV::parseLine(file_str,
                       pos.to_i,
                       rec[(i+=1)]=[]) until pos == 0
```

Note that if your data records are not separated by CR-LF, there will be a discrepancy. To ensure that your data records are separated by CR-LF, you might perform `#gsub!(/\n/,"\r\n")` on the file string beforehand.

You will still have to go through another step before you can use the information encapsulated inside the column data objects. However, this would be the only means available if you wish to detect null values. Otherwise, it would be better to use the simpler `CSV::parse` method because large files would have to be parsed line by line anyway.

Here is an example going the other way:

```
cd=[]
cd[0]=CSV::ColData.new
cd[0].data="joe"
cd[0].isNull=false
cd[1]=CSV::ColData.new
cd[1].data=27
cd[1].isNull=false
cd[2]=CSV::ColData.new
cd[2].data=32000
cd[2].isNull=false

csv_str=""
c = CSV::createLine(cd, 3, csv_str)
```

This will produce a CSV-formatted line including the CR-LF terminator. It seems like extra work, if you ask us.

Any material here is always superseded by online documentation. For more information, see the Ruby Application Archive.

Interfacing to Other Databases

Space does not permit us to delve into all the database interfaces available. Furthermore, at the time of this writing, these were of varying levels of maturity.

We'll just mention that there are several other libraries and tools in various stages of development. These will allow interfacing to Oracle, Interbase, mSql, LDAP, and others. There is also a usable ODBC driver. As always, refer to the Ruby Application Archive for the latest software and documentation.

Summary

That ends our look at files, I/O, and external data manipulation in Ruby. As always, more information can be found in any Ruby reference, and the latest versions of utilities and libraries can be found in the Ruby Application Archive.

The next chapter is a little more esoteric. In it, we discuss the dynamic features of Ruby and a number of techniques involving Ruby-specific object-oriented programming (OOP).

OOP and Dynamicity in Ruby

IN THIS CHAPTER

Just as the introduction of the irrational numbers... is a convenient myth [which] simplifies the laws of arithmetic... so physical objects are postulated entities which round out and simplify our account of the flux of existence.... The conceptional scheme of physical objects is [likewise] a convenient myth, simpler than the literal truth and yet containing that literal truth as a scattered part.

—Willard Van Orman Quine

This is an unusual chapter. Whereas most of the chapters in this book deal with a specific problem domain, this one doesn't. If the problem space is viewed as stretching out on one axis of a graph, this chapter extends out on the other axis, encompassing a slice of each of the problem domains. This is because object-oriented programming and dynamicity aren't problem domains themselves, but are paradigms that can be applied to any problem whether it be system administration, low-level networking, or Web development.

For this reason, much of this chapter's information should already be familiar to a programmer who knows Ruby. In fact, the rest of the book wouldn't make sense without some of the fundamental knowledge here. Any Ruby programmer knows how to create a subclass, for instance.

This raises the question of what to include and what to exclude. Does every Ruby programmer know about the `extend` method? What about the `instance_eval` method? What is obvious to one person might be big news to another.

We have decided to err on the side of completeness. We include in this chapter some of the more esoteric tasks you might want to do with dynamic OOP in Ruby, but we also include the more routine tasks in case anyone is unfamiliar with them. We go right down to the simplest level because people don't agree on where the middle level ends. And we have tried to offer a little extra information even on the most basic of topics to justify their inclusion here. On the other hand, topics that are fully covered elsewhere in the book are omitted here.

We'll also make two other comments. First of all, there is nothing magical about dynamic OOP. Ruby's object orientation and its dynamic nature do interact with each other, but they aren't inherently interrelated; we put them in a single chapter largely for convenience. Second, some language features might be mentioned here that aren't strictly related to either topic. Consider this to be cheating, if you will. We wanted to put them *somewhere*.

Everyday OOP Tasks

Of his quick objects hath the mind no part,
Nor his own vision holds what it doth catch....

—William Shakespeare, Sonnet 113

If you don't already understand OOP, you won't learn it here. And if you don't already understand OOP *in Ruby*, you probably won't learn it here, either. If you're rusty on those concepts, you can scan Chapter 1, "Ruby in Review," where we cover it rapidly (or you can look at another book).

On the other hand, much of this material is tutorial oriented and fairly elementary. So it will be of some value to the beginner and perhaps less value to the intermediate Ruby programmer. We maintain that a book is a random-access storage device so that you can easily skip the parts that don't interest you.

Using Multiple Constructors

There is no real constructor in Ruby as there is in C++ or Java. The concept is certainly there because objects have to be instantiated and initialized; but the behavior is somewhat different.

In Ruby, a class has a class method new, which is used to instantiate new objects. The new method calls the user-defined special method `initialize`, which then initializes the attributes of the object appropriately, and new returns a reference to the new object.

But what if we want to have multiple constructors for an object? How should we handle that?

Nothing prevents us from creating additional class methods that return new objects. Listing 5.1 shows a contrived example in which a rectangle can have two side lengths and three color values. We create additional class methods that assume certain defaults for some of the parameters. (For example, a square is a rectangle with all sides the same length.)

LISTING 5.1 Multiple Constructors

```
class ColoredRectangle

  def initialize(r, g, b, s1, s2)
    @r, @g, @b, @s1, @s2 = r, g, b, s1, s2
  end

  def ColoredRectangle.whiteRect(s1, s2)
    new(0xff, 0xff, 0xff, s1, s2)
  end

  def ColoredRectangle.grayRect(s1, s2)
    new(0x88, 0x88, 0x88, s1, s2)
  end

  def ColoredRectangle.coloredSquare(r, g, b, s)
    new(r, g, b, s, s)
  end
```

LISTING 5.1   Continued

```ruby
  def ColoredRectangle.redSquare(s)
    new(0xff, 0, 0, s, s)
  end

  def inspect
    "#@r #@g #@b #@s1 #@s2"
  end
end


a = ColoredRectangle.new(0x88, 0xaa, 0xff, 20, 30)
b = ColoredRectangle.whiteRect(15,25)
c = ColoredRectangle.redSquare(40)
```

So we can define any number of methods we want that create objects according to various specifications. Whether the term *constructor* is appropriate here is a question that we will leave to the language lawyers.

Creating Instance Attributes

An instance attribute in Ruby is always prefixed by an @ sign. It is like an ordinary variable in that it springs into existence when it is first assigned.

In OO languages, we frequently create methods that access attributes to avoid issues of data hiding. We want to have control over how the internals of an object are accessed from the outside. Typically we use setter and getter methods for this purpose (although in Ruby we don't typically use these terms). These are simply methods used to assign (set) a value or retrieve (get) a value, respectively.

Of course, it is possible to create these functions by hand, as shown here.

```ruby
  class Person

    def name
      @name
    end

    def name=(x)
      @name = x
    end
```

```ruby
    def age
      @age
    end

    # ...

  end
```

However, Ruby gives us a shorthand for creating these methods. The `attr` method takes a symbol as a parameter and creates the associated attribute. It also creates a getter of the same name. If the optional second parameter is `true`, it will create a setter as well.

```ruby
class Person
  attr :name, true  # Create @name, name, name=
  attr :age         # Create @age, age
end
```

The related methods `attr_reader`, `attr_writer`, and `attr_accessor` take any number of symbols as parameters. The first will only create `read` methods (to get the value of an attribute); the second will create only `write` methods (to set values); and the third will create both. For example,

```ruby
class SomeClass
  attr_reader :a1, :a2  # Creates @a1, a1, @a2, a2
  attr_writer :b1, :b2  # Creates @b1, a1=, @b2, b2=
  attr_reader :c1, :c2  # Creates @c1, c1, c1=, @c2, c2, c2=
  # ...
end
```

Recall that an assignment to a writer of this form can only be done with a receiver. So within a method, the receiver `self` must be used.

More Elaborate Constructors

As objects grow more complex, they accumulate more attributes that must be initialized when an object is created. The corresponding constructor can be long and cumbersome, forcing us to count parameters and wrap the line past the margin.

One good way to deal with this complexity is to pass in a *block* to the `initialize` method (see Listing 5.2). We can then evaluate the block in order to initialize the object. The trick is to use `instance_eval` instead of `eval` in order to evaluate the block *in the context of the object* rather than that of the caller.

LISTING 5.2   A Fancy Constructor

```ruby
class PersonalComputer

  attr_accessor :manufacturer,
    :model, :processor, :clock,
    :ram, :disk, :monitor,
    :colors, :vres, :hres, :net

  def initialize(&block)
    instance_eval &block;
  end

  # Other methods...

end

desktop = PersonalComputer.new do
  self.manufacturer = "Acme"
  self.model = "THX-1138"
  self.processor = "986"
  self.clock = 2.4          # GHz
  self.ram = 1024           # Mb
  self.disk = 800           # Gb
  self.monitor = 25         # inches
  self.colors = 16777216
  self.vres = 1280
  self.hres = 1600
  self.net = "T3"
end

p desktop
```

Several things should be noted here. First of all, we're using accessors for our attributes so that we can assign values to them in an intuitive way. Second, the reference to `self` is necessary because a setter method always takes an explicit receiver to distinguish the method call from an ordinary assignment to a local variable. Of course, rather than define accessors, we could use setter functions.

Obviously, we could perform any arbitrary logic we want inside the body of this block. For example, we could derive certain fields from others by computation.

Also, what if you didn't really want an object to have accessors for each of the attributes? If you prefer, you can use `undef` (at the bottom of the constructor block) to get rid of any or all of these. At the very least, this could prevent accidental assignment of an attribute from outside the object.

Creating Class-level Attributes and Methods

A method or attribute isn't always associated with a specific instance of a class; it can be associated with the class itself. The typical example of a *class method* is the new method; it is always invoked in this way because it is called in order to create a new instance (and thus can't belong to any particular instance).

We can define class methods of our own if we want. We have already seen this in "Using Multiple Constructors." But their functionality certainly isn't limited to constructors; they can be used for any general-purpose task that makes sense at the class level.

In this next highly incomplete fragment, we assume that we are creating a class to play sound files. The play method can reasonably be implemented as an instance method; we can instantiate many objects referring to many different sound files. But the detectHardware method has a larger context; depending on our implementation, it might not even make sense to create new objects if this method fails. Its context is that of the whole sound-playing environment rather than any particular sound file.

```
class SoundPlayer

  MAX_SAMPLE = 192

  def SoundPlayer.detectHardware
    # ...
  end

  def play
    # ...
  end

end
```

Let's note that there is another way to declare this class method. The following fragment is essentially the same:

```
class SoundPlayer

  MAX_SAMPLE = 192

  def play
    # ...
  end

end

def SoundPlayer.detectHardware
  # ...
end
```

The only difference relates to constants declared in the class. When the class method is declared *outside* of its class declaration, these constants aren't in scope. For example, detectHardware in the first fragment can refer directly to MAX_SAMPLE if it needs to; in the second fragment, the notation SoundPlayer::MAX_SAMPLE would have to be used instead.

Not surprisingly, there are class variables as well as class methods. These begin with a double @ sign, and their scope is the class rather than any instance of the class.

The traditional example of using class variables is counting instances of the class as they are created. But they can actually be used for any purpose in which the information is meaningful in the context of the class rather than the object. For a different example, see Listing 5.3.

LISTING 5.3   Class Variables and Methods

```ruby
class Metal

  @@current_temp = 70

  attr_accessor :atomic_number

  def Metal.current_temp=(x)
    @@current_temp = x
  end

  def Metal.current_temp
    @@current_temp
  end

  def liquid?
    @@current_temp >= @melting
  end

  def initialize(atnum, melt)
    @atomic_number = atnum
    @melting = melt
  end

end



aluminum = Metal.new(13, 1236)
copper = Metal.new(29, 1982)
gold = Metal.new(79, 1948)
```

LISTING 5.3   Continued

```
Metal.current_temp = 1600

puts aluminum.liquid?      # true
puts copper.liquid?        # false
puts gold.liquid?          # false

Metal.current_temp = 2100

puts aluminum.liquid?      # true
puts copper.liquid?        # true
puts gold.liquid?          # true
```

Note here that the class variable is initialized at the class level before it is used in a class method. Note also that we can access a class variable from an instance method, but we can't access an instance variable from a class method. After a moment of thought, this makes sense.

But what happens if you try? What if we try to print the attribute `@atomic_number` from within the `Metal.current_temp` method? We find that it seems to exist—it doesn't cause an error—but it has the value `nil`. What is happening here?

The answer is that we're not actually accessing the instance variable of class `Metal` at all. We're accessing an instance variable of class `Class` instead. (Remember that in Ruby, `Class` is a class!)

Such a beast is called a *class instance* variable. We would love to give you a creative example of how to use one, but we can't think of any use for it offhand. We summarize the situation in Listing 5.4.

LISTING 5.4   Class and Instance Data

```
class MyClass

  SOME_CONST = "alpha"     # A class-level constant

  @@var = "beta"           # A class variable
  @var = "gamma"           # A class instance variable

  def initialize
    @var = "delta"         # An instance variable
  end

  def mymethod
    puts SOME_CONST        # (the class constant)
    puts @@var             # (the class variable)
    puts @var              # (the instance variable)
```

LISTING 5.4   Continued

```
    end

    def MyClass.classmeth1
      puts SOME_CONST          # (the class constant)
      puts @@var               # (the class variable)
      puts @var                # (the class instance variable)
    end

  end

  def MyClass.classmeth2
    puts MyClass::SOME_CONST   # (the class constant)
    puts @@var                 # (the class variable)
    puts @var                  # (the class instance variable)
  end


  myobj = MyClass.new
  MyClass.classmeth1           # alpha, beta, gamma
  MyClass.classmeth2           # alpha, beta, gamma
  myobj.mymethod               # alpha, beta, delta
```

We should mention that a class method can be made private with the method
`private_class_method`. This works the same way `private` works at the instance level.

For additional information refer to "Automatically Defining Class-level Readers and Writers."

Inheriting from a Superclass

We can inherit from a class by using the < symbol:

```
class Boojum < Snark
  # ...
end
```

Given this declaration, we can say that the class Boojum is a *subclass* of the class Snark, or in
the same way, Snark is a *superclass* of Boojum. As we all know, every Boojum is a Snark, but
not every Snark is a Boojum.

The purpose of inheritance, of course, is to add or enhance functionality. We are going from
the more general to the more specific.

As an aside, many languages such as C++ implement *multiple inheritance*. Ruby (like Java and
some others) doesn't allow MI, but the mixin facility can compensate for this; see the section
"Working with Modules."

Let's look at a (slightly) more realistic example. Suppose that we have a `Person` class and want to create a `Student` class that derives from it. We'll define `Person` this way:

```ruby
class Person

  attr_accessor :name, :age, :sex

  def initialize(name, age, sex)
    @name, @age, @sex = name, age, sex
  end

  # ...

end
```

And we'll then define `Student` in this way:

```ruby
class Student < Person

  attr_accessor :idnum, :hours

  def initialize(name, age, sex, idnum, hours)
    super(name, age, sex)
    @idnum = idnum
    @hours = hours
  end

  # ...

end


# Create two objects
a = Person.new("Dave Bowman", 37, "m")
b = Student.new("Franklin Poole", 36, "m", "000-13-5031", 24)
```

Now let's look at what we've done here. What is this `super` that we see called from `Student`'s `initialize` method? It is simply *a call to the corresponding method in the parent class*. As such, we give it three parameters, whereas our own `initialize` method takes five.

It's not always necessary to use `super` in such a way, but it is often convenient. After all, the attributes of a class form a subset of the attributes of the parent class; so why not use the parent's constructor to initialize them?

Concerning what inheritance really means, it definitely represents the "is-a" relationship. A `Student` *is-a* `Person`, just as we expect. We'll make three other observations.

First, every attribute (and method) of the parent is reflected in the child. If `Person` had a `height` attribute, `Student` would inherit it; and if the parent had a method named `say_hello`, the child would inherit that, too.

Second, the child can have additional attributes and methods, as you have already seen. That is why the creation of a subclass is often referred to as *extending* a superclass.

Third, the child can *override* or redefine any of the attributes and methods of its parent. This brings up the question of how a method call is resolved. How do I know whether I'm calling the method of this particular class or its superclass?

The short answer is: You don't know, and you don't care. If we invoke a method on a `Student` object, the method for that class will be called *if it exists*. If it doesn't, the method in the superclass will be called, and so on. We say "and so on" because every class (except `Object`) has a superclass.

What if we specifically want to call a superclass method, but we don't happen to be in the corresponding method? We can always create an alias in the subclass before we do anything with it.

```ruby
class Student

  # Assuming Person has a say_hello method...

  alias :say_hi :say_hello

  def say_hello
    puts "Hi, there."
  end

  def formal_greeting
    # Say hello the way my superclass would.
    say_hi
  end

end
```

There are various subtleties relating to inheritance that we don't discuss here, but this is essentially how it works. Be sure to refer to the next section.

Testing Types or Classes of Objects

Frequently we will want to know: What kind of object is this, or how does it relate to this class? There are many ways of making a determination like this.

First of all, the `class` method (that is to say, the instance method named `class`) will always return the class of an object. A synonym is the `type` method.

```
s = "Hello"
n = 237
sc = s.class    # String
st = s.type     # String
nc = n.class    # Fixnum
```

Don't be misled into thinking that the thing returned by `class` or `type` is a string representing the class. It is an actual instance of the class `Class`. Thus if we wanted, we could call a `class` method of the target type as though it were an instance method of `Class` (which it is).

```
s2 = "some string"
var = s2.class              # String
my_str = var.new("Hi...")   # A new string
```

We could compare such a variable with a constant class name to see if they were equal; we could even use a variable as the superclass from which to define a subclass. Confused? Just remember that in Ruby, `Class` is an object and `Object` is a class.

Sometimes we want to compare an object with a class to see whether the object belongs to that class. The method `instance_of?` accomplishes this.

```
puts (5.instance_of? Fixnum)        # true
puts ("XYZZY".instance_of? Fixnum)  # false
puts ("PLUGH".instance_of? String)  # true
```

But what if we want to take inheritance relationships into account? The `kind_of?` method (similar to `instance_of?`) takes this issue into account. A synonym is `is_a?` naturally enough because we are describing the classic "is-a" relationship.

```
n = 9876543210
flag1 = n.instance_of? Bignum   # true
flag2 = n.kind_of? Bignum       # true
flag3 = n.is_a? Bignum          # true
flag3 = n.is_a? Integer         # true
flag4 = n.is_a? Numeric         # true
flag5 = n.is_a? Object          # true
flag6 = n.is_a? String          # false
flag7 = n.is_a? Array           # false
```

Obviously, `kind_of` or `is_a?` is more generalized than the `instance_of?` relationship. For an example from everyday life, every dog is a mammal, but not every mammal is a dog.

There is one surprise here for the Ruby neophyte. Any module that is mixed in by a class will maintain the "is-a" relationship with the instances. For example, the `Array` class mixes in `Enumerable`; this means that any array is a kind of enumerable entity.

```
x = [1, 2, 3]
flag8 = x.kind_of? Enumerable      # true
flag9 = x.is_a? Enumerable         # true
```

We can also use the numeric relational operators in a fairly intuitive way to compare one class to another. We say intuitive because the less-than operator is used to denote inheritance from a superclass.

```
flag1 = Integer < Numeric          # true
flag2 = Integer < Object           # true
flag3 = Object == Array            # false
flag4 = IO >= File                 # true
flag5 = Float < Integer            # false
```

Every class typically has a *relationship operator* === defined. The expression class === instance will be true if the instance belongs to the class. The relationship operator is also known as the *case equality* operator because it is used implicitly in a case statement. This is therefore a way to act on the type or class of an expression.

For additional information see the section "Testing Equality of Objects."

We should also mention the respond_to? method. This is used when we don't really care what the class is, but just want to know whether it implements a certain method. This, of course, is a rudimentary kind of type information. (In fact, we might say that this is the most important type information of all.) The method is passed a symbol and an optional flag (indicating whether to include private methods in the search).

```
# Search public methods
if wumpus.respond_to?(:bite)
  puts "It's got teeth!"
else
  puts "Go ahead and taunt it."
end

# Optional second parameter will search
# private methods also.

if woozle.respond_to?(:bite,true)
  puts "Woozles bite!"
else
  puts "Ah, the non-biting woozle."
end
```

Sometimes we want to know what class is the immediate parent of an object or class. The instance method superclass of class Class can be used for this.

```
array_parent = Array.superclass      # Object
```

```
fn_parent = 237.class.superclass    # Integer
obj_parent = Object.superclass      # nil
```

Every class except `Object` will have a superclass.

Testing Equality of Objects

All animals are equal, but some are more equal than others.

—George Orwell, *Animal Farm*

When you write classes, it's convenient if the semantics for common operations are the same as for Ruby's built-in classes. For example, if your classes implement objects that can be ranked, it makes sense to implement the method <=> and mix in the `Comparable` module. Doing so means that all the normal comparison operators work with objects of your class.

However, the picture is less clear when it comes to dealing with object equality. Ruby objects implement five different methods that test for equality. Your classes might end up implementing some of these, so let's look at each in turn.

The most basic comparison is the `equal?` method (that comes from `Object`), which returns `true` if its receiver and parameter have the same object ID. This is a fundamental part of the semantics of objects, and shouldn't be overridden in your classes.

The most common test for equality uses our old friend ==, which tests the values of its receiver with its argument. This is probably the most intuitive test for equality.

Next on the scale of abstraction is the method `eql?`, which is part of `Object`. (Actually, `eql?` is implemented in the `Kernel` module, which is mixed in to `Object`.) Like ==, `eql?` compares its receiver and its argument, but is slightly stricter. For example, different numeric objects will be coerced into a common type when compared using ==, but numbers of different types will never test equal using `eql?`.

```
flag1 = (1 == 1.0)      # true
flag2 = (1.eql?(1.0))   # false
```

The `eql?` method exists for one reason: It is used to compare the values of hash keys. If you want to override Ruby's default behavior when using your objects as hash keys, you'll need to override the methods `eql?` and `hash` for those objects.

Two more equality tests are implemented by every object. The === method is used to compare the target in a case statement against each of the selectors, using *selector===target*. Although apparently complex, this rule allows Ruby case statements to be very intuitive in practice. For example, you can switch based on the class of an object:

```
case an_object
  when String
    puts "It's a String."
  when Number
    puts "It's a Number."
  else
    puts "It's something else entirely."
end
```

This works because class `Module` implements `===` to test whether its parameter is an instance of its receiver or the receiver's parents. So, if `an_object` is the string `"cat"`, the expression `String === an_object` would be `true`, and the first clause in the case statement would fire.

Finally, Ruby implements the match operator `=~`. Conventionally, this is used by strings and regular expressions to implement pattern matching. However, if you find a use for it in some unrelated classes, you're free to overload it.

The equality tests `==` and `=~` also have negated forms, `!=` and `!~`, respectively. These are implemented internally by reversing the sense of the non-negated form. This means that if you implement (say) the method `==`, you also get the method `!=` for free.

Controlling Access to Methods

In Ruby, an object is pretty much defined by the interface it provides: the methods it makes available to others. However, when writing a class, you often need to write other, helper methods, used within your class but dangerous if available externally. That is where the `private` method of class `Module` comes in handy.

You can use `private` in two different ways. If you call `private` with no parameters in the body of a class or method definition, subsequent methods will be made private to that class or module. Alternatively, you can pass a list of method names (as symbols) to `private`, and these named methods will be made private. Listing 5.5 shows both forms.

LISTING 5.5   Private Methods

```
class Bank
  def openSafe
    # ...
  end
  def closeSafe
    # ...
  end

  private :openSafe, :closeSafe
```

LISTING 5.5 Continued

```ruby
  def makeWithdrawl(amount)
    if accessAllowed
      openSafe
      getCash(amount)
      closeSafe
    end
  end

  # make the rest private
  private

  def getCash
    # ...
  end
  def accessAllowed
    # ...
  end
end
```

Because the `attr` family of statements effectively just defines methods, attributes are affected by the access control statements such as `private`.

The implementation of `private` might seem strange, but is actually quite clever. Private methods cannot be called with an explicit receiver: They are always called with an implicit receiver of `self`. This means that you can never invoke a `private` method in another object: There is no way to specify that other object as the receiver of the method call. It also means that `private` methods are available to subclasses of the class that defines them, but again only in the same object.

The `protected` access modifier is less restrictive. Protected methods can only be accessed by instances of the defining class and its subclasses. You can specify a receiver with protected methods, so you can invoke those in different objects (as long as they are objects of the same class as the sender). A common use for protected methods is defining accessors to allow two objects of the same type to cooperate with each other. In the following example, objects of class `Person` can be compared based on the person's age, but that age isn't accessible outside the `Person` class.

```ruby
class Person

  def initialize(name, age)
    @name, @age = name, age
  end
```

```
    def <=>(other)
      age <=> other.age
    end

    attr_reader :name, :age

    protected   :age

  end

  p1 = Person.new("fred", 31)
  p2 = Person.new("agnes", 43)
  compare = (p1 <=> p2)        # -1
  x = p1.age                   # Error!
```

To complete the picture, the access modifier public is used to make methods public. This shouldn't be a surprise.

As a final twist, normal methods defined outside a class or module definition (that is, the methods defined at the top level) are made private by default. Because they are defined in class Object, they are globally available, but they cannot be called with a receiver.

Copying an Object

The Ruby built-in methods Object#clone and #dup produce copies of their receiver. They differ in the amount of context they copy. The dup method copies just the object's content, whereas clone also preserves things such as singleton classes associated with the object.

```
  s1 = "cat"

  def s1.upcase
    "CaT"
  end

  s1_dup   = s1.dup
  s1_clone = s1.clone
  s1                         #=> "cat"
  s1_dup.upcase              #=> "CAT"   (singleton method not copied)
  s1_clone.upcase            #=> "CaT"   (uses singleton method)
```

Both dup and clone are *shallow copies*: They copy the immediate contents of their receiver only. If the receiver contains references to other objects, those objects aren't in turn copied; the duplicate simply holds references to them. The following example illustrates this. The object arr2 is a copy of arr1, so changing entire elements, such as arr2[2] has no effect on arr1. However, both the original array and the duplicate contain a reference to the same String object, so changing its contents via arr2 also affects the value referenced by arr1.

```
arr1 = [ 1, "flipper", 3 ]
arr2 = arr1.dup

arr2[2] = 99
arr2[1][2] = 'a'

arr1                # [1, "flapper", 3]
arr2                # [1, "flapper", 99]
```

Sometimes, you want a *deep copy*, where the entire object tree rooted in one object is copied to create the second object. This way, there is guaranteed to be no interaction between the two. Ruby provides no built-in method to perform a deep copy, but there are a couple of techniques you can use to implement one.

The pure way to do it is to have your classes implement a deep_copy method. As part of its processing, this method calls deep_copy recursively on all the objects referenced by the receiver. You then add a deep_copy method to all the Ruby built-in classes that you use.

Fortunately, there's a quicker hack using the Marshal module. If you use marshaling to dump an object into a string and then load it back into a new object, that new object will be a deep copy of the original.

```
arr1 = [ 1, "flipper", 3 ]
arr2 = Marshal.load(Marshal.dump(arr1))

arr2[2] = 99
arr2[1][2] = 'a'

arr1                # [1, "flipper", 3]
arr2                # [1, "flapper", 99]
```

In this case, notice how changing the string via arr2 doesn't affect the string referenced by arr1.

Working with Modules

There are two basic reasons to use modules in Ruby. The first is simply namespace management; we'll have fewer name collisions if we store constants and methods in modules. A method stored in this way (a module method) is called with the module name; that is, without a real receiver. This is analogous to the way a class method is called. If we see calls such as File.ctime and FileTest.exist?, we can't tell just from context that File is a class and FileTest is a module.

The second reason is more interesting: We can use a module as a *mixin*. A mixin is similar to a specialized implementation of multiple inheritance in which only the interface portion is inherited.

5

OOP AND
DYNAMICITY IN
RUBY

We've talked about module methods, but what about instance methods? A module isn't a class, so it can't have instances; and an instance method can't be called without a receiver.

As it turns out, a module *can* have instance methods. These become part of whatever class does the `include` of the module.

```ruby
module MyMod

  def meth1
    puts "This is method 1"
  end

end


class MyClass

  include MyMod

  # ...
end


x = MyClass.new
a.meth1                    # This is method 1
```

Here `MyMod` is mixed into `MyClass`, and the instance method `meth1` is inherited. You have also seen an `include` done at the top level; in that case, the module is mixed into `Object` as you might expect.

But what happens to our module methods, if there are any? You might think they would be included as class methods, but for whatever reason, Ruby doesn't behave that way. The module methods aren't mixed in.

But we have a trick we can use if we want that behavior. There is a hook called `append_features` that we can override. It is called with a parameter that is the destination class or module (into which this module is being included). For an example of its use, see Listing 5.6.

LISTING 5.6 Including a Module with `append_features`

```ruby
module MyMod

  def MyMod.append_features(someClass)
    def someClass.modmeth
      puts "Module (class) method"
    end
```

LISTING 5.6   Continued

```
    super    # This call is necessary!
  end

  def meth1
    puts "Method 1"
  end

end


class MyClass

  include MyMod

  def MyClass.classmeth
    puts "Class method"
  end

  def meth2
    puts "Method 2"
  end

end


x = MyClass.new

                       # Output:
MyClass.classmeth      #    Class method
x.meth1                #    Method 1
MyClass.modmeth        #    Module (class) method
x.meth2                #    Method 2
```

This example is worth examining in detail. First of all, you should understand that append_features isn't *just* a hook that is called when an include happens; it actually does the work of the include operation. That's why the call to super is needed; without it, the rest of the module (in this case, meth1) wouldn't be included at all.

Also note that within the append_features call, there is a method definition. This looks unusual, but it works because the inner method definition is a singleton method (class-level or module-level). An attempt to define an instance method in the same way would result in a Nested method error.

Conceivably a module might want to determine the initiator of a mixin. The `append_features` method can also be used for this because the class is passed in as a parameter.

It is also possible to mix in the instance methods of a module as class methods. An example is shown in Listing 5.7.

LISTING 5.7   Module Instance Methods Becoming Class Methods

```ruby
class MyMod

  def meth3
    puts "Module instance method meth3"
    puts "can become a class method."
  end

end


class MyClass

  class << self    # Here, self is MyClass
    include MyMod
  end

end


MyClass.meth3

# Output:
#    Module instance method meth3
#    can become a class method.
```

We've been talking about methods. What about instance variables? Although it is certainly possible for modules to have their own instance data, it usually isn't done. However, if you find a need for this capability, nothing is stopping you from using it.

It is possible to mix a module into an object rather than a class (for example, with the `extend` method). See the section "Specializing an Individual Object."

It's important to understand one more fact about modules. It is possible to define methods in your class that will be called by the mixin. This is a very powerful technique that will seem familiar to those who have used Java interfaces.

The classic example (which we've seen elsewhere) is mixing in the `Comparable` module and defining a `<=>` method. Because the mixed-in methods can call the comparison method, we now have such operators as `<`, `>`, `<=`, and so on.

Another example is mixing in the `Enumerable` module and defining `<=>` and an iterator `each`. This will give us numerous useful methods such as `collect`, `sort`, `min`, `max`, and `select`.

You can also define modules of your own to be used in the same way. The principal limitation is the programmer's imagination.

Transforming or Converting Objects

Sometimes an object comes in exactly the right form at the right time, but sometimes we need to convert it to something else or pretend it's something it isn't. A good example is the well-known `to_s` method.

Every object can be converted to a string representation in some fashion. But not every object can successfully masquerade as a string. That in essence is the difference between the `to_s` and `to_str` methods. Let's elaborate on that.

Methods such as `puts` and contexts such as `#{...}` interpolation in strings expect to receive a `String` as a parameter. If they don't, they ask the object they *did* receive to convert itself to a `String` by sending it a `to_s` message. This is where you can specify how your object will appear when displayed; simply implement a `to_s` method in your class that returns an appropriate `String`.

```ruby
class Pet

  def initialize(name)
    @name = name
  end

  # ...

  def to_s
    "Pet: #@name"
  end

end
```

Other methods (such as the `String` concatenation operator `+`) are more picky; they expect you to pass in something that is really pretty close to a `String`. In this case, Matz decided not to have the interpreter call `to_s` to convert nonstring arguments because he felt this would lead to too many errors. Instead, the interpreter invokes a stricter method, to_str. Of the built-in classes, only String and Exception implement to_str, and only String, Regexp, and Marshal call it. Typically when you see the runtime error TypeError: Failed to convert xyz into String, you know that the interpreter tried to invoke to_str and failed.

You can implement to_str yourself. For example, you might want to allow numbers to be concatenated to strings:

```ruby
class Numeric

  def to_str
    to_s
  end

end

label = "Number " + 9     # "Number 9"
```

An analogous situation holds for arrays. The method to_a is called to convert an object to an array representation, and to_ary is called when an array is expected.

An example of when to_ary is called is with a multiple assignment. Suppose that we have a statement of this form:

```ruby
a, b, c = x
```

Assuming that x were an array of three elements, this would behave in the expected way. But if it isn't an array, the interpreter will try to call to_ary to convert it to one. For what it's worth, the method we define can be a singleton (belonging to a specific object). The conversion can be completely arbitrary; here we show an (unrealistic) example in which a string is converted to an array of strings:

```ruby
class String

  def to_ary
    return self.split("")
  end

end

str = "UFO"
a, b, c = str     # ["U", "F", "O"]
```

The inspect method implements another convention. Debuggers, utilities such as irb, and the debug print method p use the inspect method to convert an object to a printable representation. If you want classes to reveal internal details when being debugged, you should override inspect.

There is another situation in which we'd like to be able to do conversions of this sort under the hood. As a language user, you'd expect to be able to add a `Fixnum` to a `Float`, or divide a `Complex` number by a rational number. However, this is a problem for a language designer. If the `Fixnum` method + receives a `Float` as an argument, what can it do? It only knows how to add `Fixnum` values. Ruby implements the `coerce` mechanism to deal with this.

When (for example) + is passed an argument it doesn't understand, it tries to coerce the receiver and the argument to compatible types and then do the addition based on those types. The pattern for using `coerce` in a class you write is straightforward:

```
class MyNumberSystem

  def +(other)
    if other.kind_of?(MyNumberSystem)
      result = some_calculation_between_self_and_other
      MyNumberSystem.new(result)
    else
      n1, n2 = other.coerce(self)
      n1 + n2
    end
  end

end
```

The value returned by `coerce` is a two-element array containing its argument and its receiver converted to compatible types.

In this example, we're relying on the type of our argument to perform some kind of coercion for us. If we want to be good citizens, we also need to implement coercion in our class, allowing other types of numbers to work with us. To do this, we need to know the specific types that we can work with directly, and convert ourselves to those types when appropriate. When we can't do that, we fall back on asking our parent.

```
def coerce(other)
  if other.kind_of?(Float)
    return other, self.to_f
  elsif other.kind_of?(Integer)
    return other, self.to_i
  else
    super
  end
end
```

Of course, for this to work, our object must implement `to_i` and `to_f`.

You can use coerce as part of the solution for implementing a Perl-like auto-conversion of strings to numbers:

```
class String

  def coerce(n)
    if self['.']
      [n, Float(self)]
    else
      [n, Integer(self)]
    end
  end

end

x = 1 + "23"        # 24
y = 23 * "1.23"     # 29.29
```

We don't necessarily recommend this. But we do recommend that you implement a coerce method whenever you are creating some kind of numeric class.

Creating Data-only Classes (Structs)

Sometimes you need to group together a bunch of related data with no other associated processing. You could do this by defining a class:

```
class Address

  attr_accessor :street, :city, :state

  def initialize(street1, city, state)
    @street, @city, @state = street, city, state
  end

end

books = Address.new("411 Elm St", "Dallas", "TX")
```

This works, but it's tedious, with a fair amount of repetition. That's why the built-in class Struct comes in handy. In the same way that convenience methods such as attr_accessor define methods to access attributes, the class Struct defines classes that contain just attributes. These classes are *structure templates*.

```
Address = Struct.new("Address", :street, :city, :state)
books = Address.new("411 Elm St", "Dallas", "TX")
```

So, why do we pass the name of the structure to be created in as the first parameter of the constructor, and also assign the result to a constant (Address, in this case)?

When we create a new structure template by calling `Struct.new`, a new class is created within class `Struct` itself. This class is given the name passed in as the first parameter, and the attributes given as the rest of the parameters. This means that if we wanted, we could access this newly created class within the namespace of class `Struct`.

```
Struct.new("Address", :street, :city, :state)
books = Struct::Address.new("411 Elm St", "Dallas", "TX")
```

After you've created a structure template, you call its `new` method to create new instances of that particular structure. You don't have to assign values to all the attributes in the constructor: Those that you omit will be initialized to `nil`. Once created, you can access the structure's attributes using normal syntax or by indexing the structure object as if it were a `Hash`. For more information, look up class `Struct` in any reference.

By the way, we advise against the creation of a `Struct` named `Tms` because there is already a predefined `Struct::Tms` class.

Freezing Objects

Sometimes we want to prevent an object from being changed. The `freeze` method (in `Object`) will allow us to do this, effectively turning an object into a constant.

After we freeze an object, an attempt to modify it results in a `TypeError`. Listing 5.8 shows a pair of examples.

LISTING 5.8   Freezing an Object

```
str = "This is a test. "
str.freeze

begin
  str << " Don't be alarmed."   # Attempting to modify
rescue => err
  puts "#{err.class} #{err}"
end

 arr = [1, 2, 3]
 arr.freeze

begin
  arr << 4                       # Attempting to modify
rescue => err
  puts "#{err.class} #{err}"
end
```

LISTING 5.8   Continued

```
# Output:
#    TypeError: can't modify frozen string
#    TypeError: can't modify frozen array
```

However, bear in mind that `freeze` operates on an object reference, not on a variable! This means that any operation resulting in a new object will work. Sometimes this isn't intuitive.

```
str = "counter-"
str.freeze
str += "intuitive"        # "counter-intuitive"

arr = [8, 6, 7]
arr.freeze
arr += [5, 3, 0, 9]       # [8, 6, 7, 5, 3, 0, 9]
```

Why does this happen? A statement `a += x` is semantically equivalent to `a = a + x`. The expression `a + x` is evaluated to a new object, which is then assigned to a. The object isn't changed, but the variable now refers to a new object. All the reflexive assignment operators will exhibit this behavior, as will some other methods. Always ask yourself whether you are creating a new object or modifying an existing one; then `freeze` won't surprise you.

There is a method `frozen?`, which will tell you whether an object is frozen.

```
hash = { 1 => 1, 2 => 4, 3 => 9 }
hash.freeze
arr = hash.to_a
puts hash.frozen?                    # true
puts arr.frozen?                     # false
hash2 = hash
puts hash2.frozen?                   # true
```

As we see here (with `hash2`), it is the object, not the variable, that is frozen.

More Advanced Techniques

Not everything in Ruby OOP is straightforward. Some techniques are more complex than others, and some are rarely used. The dividing line will be different for each programmer. We've tried to put items in this part of the chapter that were slightly more involved or slightly more rare in terms of usage.

From time to time, you might ask yourself whether it's possible to do some task or other in Ruby. The short answer is that Ruby is a rich dynamic OOP language with a good set of reasonably orthogonal features; and if you want to do something that you're used to in another language, you can *probably* do it in Ruby.

As a matter of fact, all Turing-complete languages are pretty much the same from a theoretical standpoint. The whole field of language design is the search for a meaningful, convenient notation. Those of you who doubt the importance of a convenient notation should try writing a LISP interpreter in COBOL or doing long division with Roman numerals.

Of course, we won't say that *every* language task is elegant or natural in Ruby. Someone would quickly prove us wrong if we made that assertion.

This section also touches on the use of Ruby in various advanced programming styles such as functional programming and aspect-oriented programming. We don't claim expertise in these areas; we are only reporting what other people are saying. Take it all with a grain of salt.

Sending an Explicit Message to an Object

In a static language, you take it for granted that when you call a function, that function name is hard-coded into the program; it is part of the program source. In a dynamic language, we have more flexibility than that.

Every time you invoke a method, you're sending a message to an object. Most of the time, these messages are hard-coded as in a static language, but they need not always be. We can write code that determines at runtime which method to call. The send method will allow us to use a `Symbol` to represent a method name.

For an example, suppose that we had an array of objects we wanted to sort, and we wanted to be able to use different fields as sort keys. That's not a problem; we can easily write customized sort blocks. But suppose that we wanted to be a little more elegant and write only a single routine that could sort based on whatever key we specified. Listing 5.9 shows an example.

LISTING 5.9   Sorting by Any Key

```
class Person

  attr_reader :name,
    :age,
    :height

  def initialize(name, age, height)
    @name, @age, @height = name, age, height
  end

  def inspect
    "#@name #@age #@height"
  end
```

LISTING 5.9   Continued

```
  end

  class Array

    def sort_by(sym)
      self.sort {|x,y| x.send(sym) <=> y.send(sym) }
    end

  end


  people = []
  people << Person.new("Hansel", 35, 69)
  people << Person.new("Gretel", 32, 64)
  people << Person.new("Ted", 36, 68)
  people << Person.new("Alice", 33, 63)

  p1 = people.sort_by(:name)
  p2 = people.sort_by(:age)
  p3 = people.sort_by(:height)

  p p1    # [Alice 33 63, Gretel 32 64, Hansel 35 69, Ted 36 68]
  p p2    # [Gretel 32 64, Alice 33 63, Hansel 35 69, Ted 36 68]
  p p3    # [Alice 33 63, Gretel 32 64, Ted 36 68, Hansel 35 69]
```

Of course, if you really want efficient sorting, this example is incomplete. But it illustrates the
example of calling a method whose identity isn't known before runtime.

We'll also mention the alias __send__, which does exactly the same thing. It is given this
peculiar name, of course, because send is a name that might be used (purposely or accidentally)
as a user-defined method name.

Specializing an Individual Object

I'm a Solipsist, and I must say I'm surprised there aren't more of us.

> —Letter received by Bertrand Russell

In most object-oriented languages, all objects of a particular class share the same behavior. The
class acts as a template, producing an object with the same interface each time the constructor
is called.

Although Ruby acts the same way, that isn't the end of the story. When you have a Ruby object, you can change its behavior on-the-fly. Effectively, you're giving that object a private, anonymous subclass: All the methods of the original class are available, but you've added additional behavior for just that object. Because this behavior is private to the associated object, it can only occur once. A thing occurring only once is called a *singleton*, as in *singleton methods* and *singleton classes*.

The word singleton can be confusing because it is also used in a different sense as the name of a well-known design pattern for a class that can only be instantiated once. For this usage, refer to the `singleton.rb` library.

Here we see a pair of objects, both of which are strings. For the second one, we will add a method upcase that will override the existing method of that name.

```
a = "hello"
b = "goodbye"

def b.upcase       # create single method
  gsub(/(.)(.)/) { $1.upcase + $2 }
end

puts a.upcase    # HELLO
puts b.upcase    # GoOdBye
```

Adding a singleton method to an object creates a singleton class for that object if one doesn't already exist. This singleton class's parent will be the object's original class. (This could be considered an anonymous subclass of the original class.) If you want to add multiple methods to an object, you can create the singleton class directly.

```
b = "goodbye"

class << b

  def upcase       # create single method
    gsub(/(.)(.)/) { $1.upcase + $2 }
  end

  def upcase!
    gsub!(/(.)(.)/) { $1.upcase + $2 }
  end

end

puts b.upcase    # GoOdBye
puts b           # goodbye
b.upcase!
puts b           # GoOdBye
```

As an aside, we'll note that the more primitive objects (such as a `Fixnum`) cannot have singleton methods added. This is because an object of this nature is stored as an immediate value rather than as an object reference. However, we expect this functionality to be added in a future revision of Ruby.

If you read some of the library code, you're bound to come across an idiomatic use of singleton classes. Within class definitions, you might see something like this:

```ruby
class SomeClass

  # Stuff...

  class << self
    # more stuff...
  end

  # ... and so on.

end
```

Within the body of a class definition, `self` is the class you're defining, so creating a singleton based on it modifies the class's class. At the simplest level, this means that instance methods in the singleton class are class methods externally.

```ruby
class TheClass
  class << self
    def hello
      puts "hi"
    end
  end
end

# invoke a class method
TheClass.hello           # hi
```

Another common use of this technique is to define class-level helper functions, which we can then access in the rest of the class definition. As an example, we want to define several accessor functions that always convert their results to a string. We could do this by coding each individually. A neater way might be to define a class-level function `accessor_string` that generates these functions for us (as shown in Listing 5.10).

LISTING 5.10   A Class-level Method `accessor_string`

```ruby
class MyClass

  class << self
```

LISTING 5.10   Continued

```ruby
    def accessor_string(*names)
      names.each do |name|
        class_eval <<-EOD
          def #{name}
            @#{name}.to_s
          end
        EOD
      end
    end

    def initialize
      @a = [ 1, 2, 3 ]
      @b = Time.now
    end

    accessor_string :a, :b

  end


  o = MyClass.new
  puts o.a            # 123
  puts o.b            # Mon Apr 30 23:12:15 CDT 2001
```

More imaginative examples are left up to you.

The extend method will mix a module into an object. The instance methods from the module become instance methods for the object. Let's look at Listing 5.11.

LISTING 5.11   Using extend

```ruby
module Quantifier

  def any?
    self.each { |x| return true if yield x }
    false
  end

  def all?
    self.each { |x| return false if not yield x }
    true
  end
```

LISTING 5.11   Continued

```
end


list = [1, 2, 3, 4, 5]


list.extend(Quantifier)
flag1 = list.any? {|x| x > 5 }        # false
flag2 = list.any? {|x| x >= 5 }       # true
flag3 = list.all? {|x| x <= 10 }      # true
flag4 = list.all? {|x| x % 2 == 0 }   # false
```

In this example, the any? and all? methods are mixed into the list array.

Nesting Classes and Modules

We'll point out that it's possible to nest classes and modules arbitrarily. The programmer new to Ruby might not know this.

Mostly this is for namespace management. Note that the File class has a Stat class embedded inside it. This helps to encapsulate the Stat class inside a class of related functionality, and also allows for a future class named Stat, which won't conflict with that one (perhaps a statistics class, for instance).

The Struct::Tms class is a similar example. Any new Struct is placed in this namespace so as not to pollute the one above it, and Tms is really just another Struct.

It's also conceivable that you might want to create a nested class simply because the outside world doesn't need that class or shouldn't access it. In other words, you can create classes that are subject to the principle of data hiding just as the instance variables and methods are subject to the same principle at a lower level.

```
class BugTrackingSystem

  class Bug
    #...
  end

  #...

end

# Nothing out here knows about Bug.
```

You can nest a class within a module, a module within a class, and so on. If you find interesting and creative uses for this technique, let us all know about it.

Creating Parametric Classes

Learn the rules; then break them.

—Basho

Suppose that we wanted to create multiple classes that differed only in the initial values of the class-level variables. Recall that a class variable is typically initialized as a part of the class definition.

```
class Terran

  @@home_planet = "Earth"

  def Terran.home_planet
    @@home_planet
  end

  def Terran.home_planet=(x)
    @@home_planet = x
  end

  #...

end
```

That is all fine, but suppose that we had a number of similar classes to define? The novice will think, "Ah, I'll just define a superclass." (See Listing 5.12.)

LISTING 5.12   Parametric Classes #1

```
class IntelligentLife   # Wrong way to do this!

  @@home_planet = nil

  def IntelligentLife.home_planet
    @@home_planet
  end

  def IntelligentLife.home_planet=(x)
    @@home_planet = x
  end
```

LISTING 5.12   Continued

```
    #...

  end

  class Terran < IntelligentLife
    @@home_planet = "Earth"
    #...
  end

  class Martian < IntelligentLife
    @@home_planet = "Mars"
    #...
  end
```

But this won't work. If we call `Terran.home_planet`, we expect a result of `"Earth"`—but we get `"Mars"`!

Why would this happen? The answer is that class variables aren't *truly* class variables; they belong not to the class, but to the entire inheritance hierarchy. The class variables aren't copied from the parent class, but are shared with the parent (and thus with the sibling classes).

We could eliminate the definition of the class variable in the base class; but then the class methods we define would no longer work!

We *could* fix this by moving these definitions to the child classes, but now we've defeated our whole purpose. We're declaring separate classes without any parameterization.

We'll offer a different solution. We'll defer the evaluation of the class variable until runtime by using the `class_eval` method. Listing 5.13 shows a complete solution.

LISTING 5.13   Parametric Classes #2

```
  class IntelligentLife

    def IntelligentLife.home_planet
      class_eval("@@home_planet")
    end

    def IntelligentLife.home_planet=(x)
      class_eval("@@home_planet = #{x}")
    end

    #...
```

LISTING 5.13 Continued

```
    end

    class Terran < IntelligentLife
      @@home_planet = "Earth"
      #...
    end

    class Martian < IntelligentLife
      @@home_planet = "Mars"
      #...
    end


    puts Terran.home_planet          # Earth
    puts Martian.home_planet         # Mars
```

It goes without saying that inheritance still operates normally here. Any instance methods or instance variables defined within `IntelligentLife` will be inherited by `Terran` and `Martian` just as you would expect.

As a minor variation on this theme, we present a slightly different way of doing the same thing (see Listing 5.14). Here we have overridden the `Class.new` method to create a parametric class for us; we inherit from the specified base class and then do a `class_eval` of the block passed in.

LISTING 5.14 Parametric Classes #3

```
    class Class

      def initialize(klass, &block)
        block = Proc.new
        class_eval(&block)
      end

    end


    class IntelligentLife

      def IntelligentLife.home_planet
        class_eval("@@home_planet")
      end

      def IntelligentLife.home_planet=(x)
        class_eval("@@home_planet = #{x}")
```

LISTING 5.14   Continued

```
    end

    #...

  end

  Terran = Class.new(IntelligentLife) do
    @@home_planet = "Earth"
  end

  Martian = Class.new(IntelligentLife) do
    @@home_planet = "Mars"
  end
```

This technique resembles the fancy constructor of the section "More Elaborate Constructors." The principle is the same, but we are working at the class level rather than the instance level. (Of course, Class is an object, so we can still regard it as the instance level if we want.)

We should mention that there are other ways of doing this. Use your creativity.

Using Continuations to Implement a Generator

One of the more abstruse features of Ruby is the *continuation*. This is a structured way of handling a nonlocal jump and return; a continuation object stores a return address and an execution context. It is somewhat analogous to the setjmp/longjmp feature in C, but it stores more context.

The Kernel method callcc takes a block and returns an object of the Continuation class. The object returned is also passed into the block as a parameter, just to keep things confusing.

The only method of Continuation is call, which causes a nonlocal return to the end of the callcc block. The callcc can be terminated either by falling through the block or by calling the call method.

There is a known shortage of examples of how to use continuations. The best one we have seen comes from Jim Weirich, who implemented a generator as a result of his discussion with another Ruby programmer, Hugh Sasse.

A generator is made possible by suspend in Icon (also found in Prolog), which allows a function to resume execution just after the last place it returned a value. Hugh describes it as similar to an inside-out yield.

Listing 5.15, then, is Jim's implementation of a generator that generates Fibonacci numbers one after another. Continuations are used to preserve the call state from one invocation to the next.

LISTING 5.15   Fibonacci Generator

```ruby
class Generator

  def initialize
    do_generation
  end

  def next
    callcc { |here|
      @main_context = here;
        @generator_context.call
    }
  end

  private

  def do_generation
    callcc { |context|
      @generator_context = context;
      return
    }
    generating_loop
  end

  def generate(value)
    callcc { |context|
      @generator_context = context;
      @main_context.call(value)
    }
  end
end

# Subclass this and define a generating_loop

class FibGenerator < Generator
  def generating_loop
    generate(1)
    a, b = 1, 1
    loop do
      generate(b)
      a, b = b, a+b
    end
  end
end
```

LISTING 5.15   Continued

```
# Now instantiate the class...

fib = FibGenerator.new

puts fib.next          # 1
puts fib.next          # 1
puts fib.next          # 2
puts fib.next          # 3
puts fib.next          # 5
puts fib.next          # 8
puts fib.next          # 13

# And so on...
```

We can't help but feel that there are practical applications for this idea. If you think of some, share them with us all.

Storing Code as Objects

Not surprisingly, Ruby gives you several alternatives when it comes to storing a chunk of code in the form of an object. In this section, we'll take a look at Proc objects, Method objects, and UnboundMethod objects.

The built-in class Proc is used to wrap Ruby blocks in an object. Proc objects, like blocks, are closures, and therefore carry around the context in which they were defined.

```
p = Proc.new { |a| puts "Param is #{a}" }

p.call(99)          # Param is 99
```

Proc objects are also created automatically by Ruby when a method defined with a trailing & parameter is called with a block.

```
def take_block(a, &block)
  puts block.type
  a.times {|i| block[i, i*i] }
end

take_block(3) { |n,s| puts "#{n} squared is #{s}" }
```

This example also shows the use of braces ({}) as an alias for the call method. The output is shown here:

```
Proc
0 squared is 0
1 squared is 1
2 squared is 4
```

If you have a `Proc` object, you can pass it to a method that's expecting a block, preceding its name with an &, as shown here:

```
p = proc { |n| print n, "... " }
(1..3).each(&p)                    # 1... 2... 3...
```

Ruby also lets you turn a method into an object. Historically, this is done using `Object#method`, which creates a `Method` object as a closure in a particular object.

```
str = "cat"
meth = str.method(:length)

a = meth.call               #  3  (length of "cat")

str << "erpillar"

b = meth.call               # 11  (length of "caterpillar")

str = "dog"

# Note the next call! The variable str refers to a new object
# ("dog") now, but meth is still bound to the old object.

c = meth.call               # 11  (length of "caterpillar")
```

As of Ruby 1.6.2, you can also use `Module#instance_method` to create `UnboundMethod` objects. These represent a method that is associated with a class, rather than one particular object. Before calling an `UnboundMethod` object, you must first bind it to a particular object. This act of binding produces a `Method` object, which you call normally.

```
umeth = String.instance_method(:length)

m1 = umeth.bind("cat")
m1.call                     # 3

m2 = umeth.bind("caterpillar")
m2.call                     # 11
```

This explicit binding makes the `UnboundMethod` object a little more intuitive than `Method`.

Automatically Defining Class-level Readers and Writers

You have seen the methods `attr_reader`, `attr_writer`, and `attr_accessor`, which make it a little easier to define readers and writers (getters and setters) for instance attributes. But what about class-level attributes?

Ruby has no similar facility for creating these automatically. But we can make our own facility by adding to the class `Class`. In Listing 5.16 we name them similarly, only prefixing the names with a *c* for *class*.

LISTING 5.16   A Shorthand for Creating Class Attributes

```ruby
class Class

  def cattr_reader(*syms)
    syms.each do |sym|
      class_eval <<-EOS
        if ! defined? @@#{sym.id2name}
          @@#{sym.id2name} = nil
        end
        def self.#{sym.id2name}
          @@#{sym}
        end
      EOS
    end
  end

  def cattr_writer(*syms)
    syms.each do |sym|
      class_eval <<-EOS
        if ! defined? @@#{sym.id2name}
          @@#{sym.id2name} = nil
        end
        def self.#{sym.id2name}=(obj)
          @@#{sym.id2name} = obj
        end
      EOS
    end
  end

  def cattr_accessor(*syms)
    cattr_reader(*syms)
    cattr_writer(*syms)
  end

end
```

LISTING 5.16 Continued

```
class MyClass

  @@alpha = 123              # Initialize @@alpha

  cattr_reader :alpha        # MyClass.alpha()
  cattr_writer :beta         # MyClass.beta=()
  cattr_accessor :gamma      # MyClass.gamma() and
                             #   MyClass.gamma=()

  def MyClass.look
    puts "#@@alpha, #@@beta, #@@gamma"
  end

  #...

end


puts MyClass.alpha           # 123
MyClass.beta = 456
MyClass.gamma = 789
puts MyClass.gamma           # 789

MyClass.look                 # 123, 456, 789
```

Most classes are no good without instance level data. We've only omitted it from Listing 5.16 for clarity.

Working in Advanced Programming Disciplines

Brother, can you paradigm?

> —Graffiti seen at IBM Austin, 1989

Many philosophies of programming are popular in various circles. These are often difficult to characterize in relation to object-oriented or dynamic techniques; and some of these styles can be actually independent of whether a language is dynamic or object-oriented.

Because we are far from experts in these matters, we are relying mostly on hearsay. So take these next paragraphs with a grain of sodium chloride.

Some programmers prefer a flavor of OOP known as *prototype-based* OOP (or *classless* OOP). In this world, an object isn't described as a member of a class. It is built from the ground up, and other objects are created based on the prototype. Ruby has at least rudimentary support for this programming style because it allows singleton methods for individual objects, and the `clone` method will clone these singletons. Interested readers should also look at the simple `Ostruct` class for building Python-like objects; and you should also be aware of how `method_missing` works.

One or two limitations in Ruby hamper classless OOP. Certain objects such as `Fixnums` are stored not as references, but as immediate values so that they can't have singleton methods. This is supposed to change in the future; but at the time of this writing, it's impossible to project when it will happen.

In *functional programming* (*FP*), emphasis is placed on the evaluation of expressions rather than the execution of commands. An FP language is one that encourages and supports functional programming, and as such, there is a natural gray area. Nearly all would agree that Haskell is a *pure* functional language, whereas Ruby certainly is not.

But Ruby has at least some minimal support for FP; it has a fairly rich set of methods for operating on arrays (lists), and it has `Proc` objects so that code can be encapsulated and called over and over. Ruby allows the method chaining that is so common in FP; although it is easy to be bitten by the phenomenon of a bang method (such as `sort!` or `gsub!`) that returns `nil` when the receiver doesn't actually change.

There have been some initial efforts at a library that would serve as a kind of FP compatibility layer, borrowing certain ideas from Haskell. At the time of this writing, these efforts aren't complete.

The concept of *aspect-oriented programming (AOP)* is an interesting one. In AOP, we try to deal with programming issues that crosscut the modular structure of the program. In other words, some activities or features of a system will be scattered across the system in code fragments here and there, rather than being gathered into one tidy location. We are attempting to modularize things that in traditional OOP or procedural techniques are difficult to modularize. We are working at right angles to our usual way of thinking.

Ruby certainly wasn't created specifically with AOP in mind. But it was designed to be a very flexible and dynamic language, and it is conceivable that these techniques can be facilitated by a library. In fact, there is a library called `AspectR`, which is an early effort at implementing AOP; see the Ruby Application Archive for the most recent version.

The concept of *Design by Contract (DBC)* is well-known to Eiffel devotees, although it is certainly known outside those circles as well. The general idea is that a method or class implements a contract; certain pre-conditions must be true if it is going to do its job, and it guarantees that certain post-conditions are true afterward. The robustness of a system can be greatly enhanced by the ability to specify this contract explicitly and have it automatically checked at runtime. The usefulness of the technique is expanded by the inheritance of contract information as classes are extended.

The Eiffel language has DBC explicitly built in; Ruby doesn't. There are at least two usable implementations of DBC libraries, however, and we recommend that you choose one and learn it.

Design patterns have inspired much discussion over the last few years. These, of course, are highly language-independent and can be implemented well in many languages. But again, Ruby's unusual flexibility makes them perhaps more practical than in some other environments. Well-known examples of these are given elsewhere; the *Visitor* pattern is essentially implemented in Ruby's default iterator `each`, and other patterns are part of Ruby's standard distribution (see `delegator.rb` and `singleton.rb`).

The *Extreme Programming (XP)* discipline is gaining devotees daily. This methodology encourages (among other things) early testing and refactoring on-the-fly.

XP isn't language specific, although it might be easier in some languages than others. Certainly we maintain that Ruby makes refactoring easier than many languages would, although that is a highly subjective claim. But the existence of the `RubyUnit` library is what makes for a real blending of Ruby and XP. This library facilitates unit testing; it is powerful, easy to use, and it has proven useful in developing other Ruby software in current use. We highly recommend the XP practice of testing early and often, and we recommend `RubyUnit` for those who want to do this in Ruby.

We should also mention Lapidary, another unit-testing framework created by XP fan Nathaniel Talbott (coming from a Smalltalk perspective). It can be found in the Ruby Application Archive.

By the time you read this, many of the issues we talk about in this section will have been fleshed out more. As always, your two best resources for the latest information are the `comp.lang.ruby` newsgroup and the Ruby Application Archive.

Working with Dynamic Features

Skynet became self-aware at 2:14 a.m. EDT August 29, 1997.

> —Terminator 2: Judgment Day

Many of you will come from the background of a very static language such as C. To those readers, we will address this rhetorical question: Can you imagine writing a C function that will take a string, treat it as a variable name, and return the value of the variable?

No? Then can you imagine removing or replacing the definition of a function? Can you imagine trapping calls to nonexistent functions? Or determining the name of the calling function? Or automatically obtaining a list of user-defined program elements (such as a list of all your functions)?

Ruby makes this sort of thing possible. This runtime flexibility, the ability to examine and change program elements at runtime, makes many problems easier. A runtime tracing utility, a debugger, and a profiling utility are all easy to write *for* Ruby and *in* Ruby. The well-known programs irb and xmp both use dynamic features of Ruby in order to perform their magic.

These abilities take getting used to, and they are easy to abuse. But the concepts have been around for many years (they are at least as old as LISP) and are regarded as tried and true in the Scheme and Smalltalk communities as well. Even Java, which owes so much to C and C++, has some dynamic features; so we expect this way of thinking to increase in popularity as time goes by.

Evaluating Code Dynamically

The global function eval compiles and executes a string that contains a fragment of Ruby code. This is a powerful (if slightly dangerous) mechanism because it allows you to build up code to be executed at runtime. For example, the following code reads in lines of the form *name = expression*; it then evaluates each expression and stores the result in a hash indexed by the corresponding variable name.

```
parameters = {}

ARGF.each do |line|
   name, expr = line.split(/\s*=\s*/, 2)
   parameters[name] = eval expr
end
```

Suppose that the input contained these lines.

```
a = 1
b = 2 + 3
c = `date`
```

Then the hash parameters would end up with the value {"a"=>1, "b"=>5, "c"=>"Mon Apr 30 21:17:47 CDT 2001\n"}. This example also illustrates the danger of evaling strings when you don't control their contents; a malicious user could put d=`rm *` in the input and ruin your day.

Ruby has three other methods that evaluate code on-the-fly: class_eval, module_eval, and instance_eval. The first two are synonyms, and all three do effectively the same thing; they evaluate a string or a block, but while doing so, they change the value of self to their own receiver. Perhaps the most common use of `class_eval` allows you to add methods to a class when all you have is a reference to that class. We used this in the `hook_method` code in the `Trace` example in the section "Tracking Changes to a Class or Object Definition." You'll find other examples in the more dynamic library modules, such as `delegate.rb`.

The `eval` method also makes it possible to evaluate local variables in a context outside their scope. We don't advise doing this lightly, but it's nice to have the capability.

Ruby associates local variables with blocks, with high level definition constructs (class, module, and method definitions), and with the top-level of your program (the code outside any definition constructs). Associated with each of these scopes is the binding of variables, along with other housekeeping details. Probably the ultimate user of bindings is `irb`, the interactive Ruby shell, which uses bindings to keep the variables in the program that you type separate from its own.

You can encapsulate the current binding in an object using the method `Kernel#binding`. Having done that, you can pass the binding as the second parameter to `eval`, setting the execution context for the code being evaluated.

```
def aMethod
  a = "local variable"
  return binding
end

the_binding = aMethod
eval "a", the_binding   # "local variable"
```

Interestingly, the presence of a block associated with a method is stored as part of the binding, enabling tricks such as this:

```
def aMethod
  return binding
end

the_binding = aMethod { puts "hello" }
eval "yield", the_binding                # hello
```

Removing Definitions

The dynamic nature of Ruby means that pretty much anything that can be defined can also be undefined. One conceivable reason to do this is to decouple pieces of code that are in the same scope by getting rid of variables once they have been used; another reason might be to specifically disallow certain dangerous method calls. Whatever your reason for removing a definition, it should naturally be done with caution because it can conceivably lead to debugging problems.

The radical way to undefine something is with the `undef` keyword (not surprisingly, the opposite of `def`). You can `undef` methods, local variables, and constants at the top level. Although a classname is a constant, you *cannot* remove a class definition this way.

```
def asbestos
  puts "Now fireproof"
end

tax = 0.08

PI = 3

asbestos
puts "PI=#{PI}, tax=#{tax}"

undef asbestos
undef tax
undef PI

# Any reference to the above three
# would now give an error.
```

Within a class definition, a method or constant can be undefined in the same context in which it was defined. You can't `undef` within a method definition or `undef` an instance variable.

We also have the `remove_method` and `undef_method` methods available to us (defined in `Module`). The difference is slightly subtle: `remove_method` will remove the current (or nearest) definition of the method, whereas `undef_method` will literally cause the method to be undefined (removing it from superclasses as well). Listing 5.17 is an illustration of this.

LISTING 5.17   Removing and Undefining Methods

```
class Parent

  def alpha
    puts "parent alpha"
  end

  def beta
    puts "parent beta"
  end

end

class Child < Parent
```

LISTING 5.17 Continued

```
    def alpha
      puts "child alpha"
    end

    def beta
      puts "child beta"
    end

    remove_method :alpha    # Remove "this" alpha
    undef_method :beta       # Remove every beta

  end


  x = Child.new

  x.alpha          # parent alpha
  x.beta           # Error!
```

The `remove_const` method will remove a constant.

```
module Math

  remove_const :PI

end

# No PI anymore!
```

Note that it is possible to remove a class definition in this way (because a class identifier is simply a constant).

```
class BriefCandle
  #...
end

out_out = BriefCandle.new

class Object
  remove_const :BriefCandle
end

# Can't instantiate BriefCandle again!
# (Though out_out still exists...)
```

Note that methods such as `remove_const` and `remove_method` are (naturally enough) private methods. That is why we show them being called from inside a class or module definition rather than outside.

Obtaining Lists of Defined Entities

The reflection API of Ruby enables us to examine the classes and objects in our environment at runtime. We'll look at methods defined in `Module`, `Class`, and `Object`.

The `Module` module has a method named `constants` that returns an array of all the constants in the system (including class and module names). The `nesting` method returns an array of all the modules nested at the current location in the code.

The instance method `Module#ancestors` will return an array of all the ancestors of the specified class or module.

```
list = Array.ancestors
# [Array, Enumerable, Object, Kernel]
```

The `constants` method will list all the constants accessible in the specified module. Any ancestor modules are included.

```
list = Math.constants    # ["E", "PI"]
```

The `class_variables` method will return a list of all class variables in the given class and its superclasses. The `included_modules` method will list the modules included in a class.

```
class Parent
  @@var1 = nil
end

class Child < Parent
  @@var2 = nil
end

list1 = Parent.class_variables    # ["@@var1"]
list2 = Array.included_modules    # [Enumerable, Kernel]
```

The `Class` methods `instance_methods` and `public_instance_methods` are synonyms; they return a list of the public instance methods for a class. The methods `private_instance_methods` and `protected_instance_methods` behave as expected. Any of these can take a Boolean parameter, which defaults to `false`; if it is set to `true`, superclasses will be searched as well, resulting in a larger list.

```
n1 = Array.instance_methods.size            # 66
n2 = Array.public_instance_methods.size     # 66
n3 = Array.private_instance_methods.size    # 1
```

```
n4 = Array.protected_instance_methods.size      # 0
n5 = Array.public_instance_methods(true).size   # 106
```

The `Object` class has a number of similar methods that operate on instances (see Listing 5.18). `methods` and `public_methods` are synonyms that return a list of publicly accessible methods. The methods `private_methods`, `protected_methods`, and `singleton_methods` all behave as expected.

LISTING 5.18   Reflection and Instance Variables

```
class SomeClass

  def initialize
    @a = 1
    @b = 2
  end

  def mymeth
    #...
  end

  protected :mymeth

end


x = SomeClass.new

def x.newmeth
  # ...
end

iv = x.instance_variables      # ["@b", "@a"]

meth = x.methods.size            # 37
pub  = x.public_methods.size     # 37
pri  = x.private_methods.size    # 66
pro  = x.protected_methods.size  # 1
sm   = x.singleton_methods.size  # 1
```

Note that none of the preceding ever takes a parameter.

Examining the Call Stack

And you may ask yourself:
Well, how did I get here?

—Talking Heads, "Once in a Lifetime"

Sometimes we want to know who our caller was. This could be useful information if, for example, we had a fatal exception. The `caller` method, defined in `Kernel`, makes this possible. It returns an array of strings in which the first element represents the caller, the next element represents the caller's caller, and so on.

```
def func1
  puts caller[0]
end

def func2
  func1
end

func2                   # Prints: somefile.rb:6:in `func2'
```

The string is in the form *file;line* or *file:line: in method*, as shown previously.

Monitoring Execution of a Program

A Ruby program can *introspect* or examine its own execution. There are many applications for such an ability; the interested reader can refer to the sources `debug.rb`, `profile.rb`, and `tracer.rb`. It is even conceivable to use this facility in creating a *design-by-contract (DBC)* library—although the most popular one at the time of this writing doesn't use this technique.

The interesting thing is that this trick is implemented purely in Ruby. We use the Ruby method `set_trace_func`, which allows you to invoke a block whenever significant events happen in the execution of a program. A good reference will show the calling sequence for `set_trace_func`, so we'll just show a simple example here.

```
def meth(n)
  sum = 0
  for i in 1..n
    sum += i
  end
  sum
end

set_trace_func proc do |event, file, line,
                        id, binding, klass, *rest|
```

```
    printf "%8s %s:%d  %s/%s\n", event, file, line,
                            klass, id
  end

  meth(2)
```

This produces the output:

```
     line prog.rb:13  false/
     call prog.rb:1   Object/meth
     line prog.rb:2   Object/meth
     line prog.rb:3   Object/meth
   c-call prog.rb:3   Range/each
     line prog.rb:4   Object/meth
   c-call prog.rb:4   Fixnum/+
 c-return prog.rb:4   Fixnum/+
     line prog.rb:4   Object/meth
   c-call prog.rb:4   Fixnum/+
 c-return prog.rb:4   Fixnum/+
 c-return prog.rb:4   Range/each
     line prog.rb:6   Object/meth
   return prog.rb:6   Object/meth
```

Another related method is `Kernel#trace_var`, which invokes a block whenever a global variable is assigned a value.

Suppose that you want to trace the execution of a program from outside, strictly as an aid in debugging. The simplest way to see what a program is doing is to use the `tracer` library that we mentioned previously. Given a program `prog.rb`:

```
def meth(n)
  (1..n).each {|i| puts i}
end

meth(3)
```

You can simply load `tracer` from the command line:

```
% ruby -r tracer prog.rb
#0:prog.rb:1::-:      def meth(n)
#0:prog.rb:1:Module:>:    def meth(n)
#0:prog.rb:1:Module::    def meth(n)
#0:prog.rb:2:Object:-:     sum = 0
#0:prog.rb:3:Object:-:     for i in 1..n
#0:prog.rb:3:Range:>:     for i in 1..n
#0:prog.rb:4:Object:-:      sum += i
#0:prog.rb:4:Fixnum:>:      sum += i
#0:prog.rb:4:Fixnum::      sum += i
#0:prog.rb:4:Fixnum:
```

The lines output by `tracer` show the thread number, the filename and line number, the class being used, the event type, and the line from the source file being executed. The event types include `'-'` when a source line is executed, `'>'` for a call, `'<'` for a return, `'C'` for a class, and `'E'` for an end.

Traversing the Object Space

The Ruby runtime system needs to keep track of all known objects (if for no other reason than to be able to garbage-collect those no longer referenced). This information is made accessible via the `ObjectSpace.each_object` method.

```
ObjectSpace.each_object do |obj|
  printf "%20s: %s\n", obj.class, obj.inspect
end
```

If you specify a class or module as a parameter to `each_object`, only objects of that type will be returned.

The `ObjectSpace` module is also useful in defining object finalizers (see the section "Defining Finalizers for Objects").

Handling Calls to Nonexistent Methods

Sometimes it's useful to be able to write classes that respond to arbitrary method calls. For example, you might want to wrap calls to external programs in a class, providing access to each program as a method call. You can't know ahead of time the names of all these programs, so you can't create the methods as you write the class. Here comes `Object#method_missing` to the rescue. Whenever a Ruby object receives a message for a method that isn't implemented in the receiver, it invokes the `method_missing` method instead. You can use that to catch what would otherwise be an error, treating it as a normal method call. Let's implement the operating system `CommandWrapper` class:

```
class CommandWrapper

  def method_missing(method, *args)
    system(method.to_s, *args)
  end

end


cw = CommandWrapper.new
cw.date                    # Sat Apr 28 22:50:11 CDT 2001
cw.du '-s', '/tmp'         # 166749   /tmp
```

The first parameter to `method_missing` is the name of the method that was called (and that couldn't be found). Whatever was passed in that method call is then given as the remaining parameters.

If your `method_missing` handler decides that it doesn't want to handle a particular call, it should call `super`, rather than raising an exception. That allows `method_missing` handlers in superclasses to have a shot at dealing with the situation. Eventually, the `method_missing` method defined in class `Object` will be invoked, and that ends up raising an exception.

Tracking Changes to a Class or Object Definition

Perhaps we should start this by asking: Who cares? Why are we interested in tracking changes to classes?

One possible reason is that we're trying to keep track of the state of the Ruby program being run. Perhaps we're implementing some kind of GUI-based debugger, and we need to refresh a list of methods if our user adds one on-the-fly.

Another reason might be that we're doing clever things to other classes. For example, say that we wanted to write a module that could be included in any class definition. From then on, any call to a method in that class will be traced. We might use it something like this:

```
class MyClass

  def one
  end

  include Trace

  def two(x, y)
  end

end


m = MyClass.new
m.one                    # one called. Params =
m.two(1, 'cat')          # two called. Params = 1, cat
```

It will also work for any subclasses of the class we're tracing:

```
class Fred < MyClass

  def meth(*a)
  end
```

```
  end

  Fred.new.meth(2,3,4,5)    # meth called. Params = 2, 3, 4, 5
```

We could implement this module as shown in Listing 5.19.

LISTING 5.19   Trace Module

```
module Trace

  def Trace.append_features(into)
    into.instance_methods.each { |m| Trace.hook_method(into, m) }
    def into.method_added(method)
      unless @adding
        @adding = true
        Trace.hook_method(self, method)
        @adding = false
      end
    end
    super
  end

  def Trace.hook_method(klass, method)
    klass.class_eval <<-EOD
    alias :old_#{method}   :#{method}
    def #{method}(*args)
      puts "#{method} called. Params = #{args.join(', ')}"
      old_#{method}(*args)
    end
    EOD
  end

end
```

This code has two main methods. The first, append_features, is a callback invoked whenever a module is inserted into a class. Our version does two things. It calls hook_method for every method that's already been defined in the target class, and it inserts a definition for method_added into that class. This means that any subsequently added method will also be detected and hooked.

The hook itself is pretty straightforward: When a method is added, it is immediately aliased to the name old_*name*. The original method is then replaced by out tracing code, which dumps out the method name and parameters before invoking the original method.

To detect the addition of a new class method to a class or module, we can define a class method singleton_method_added within that class. (Recall that a singleton method in this sense is what we usually refer to as a class method because Class is an object.) This method comes from Kernel and by default does nothing, but we can make it behave as we prefer.

```ruby
class MyClass

  def MyClass.singleton_method_added(sym)
    puts "Added method #{sym.id2name} to class MyClass."
  end

  def MyClass.meth1
    puts "I'm meth1."
  end

end

def MyClass.meth2
  puts "And I'm meth2."
end
```

The output we get from this is as follows:

```
Added method singleton_method_added to class MyClass.
Added method meth1 to class MyClass.
Added method meth2 to class MyClass.
```

Note that there are actually three methods added here. Perhaps contrary to expectation, singleton_method_added is able to track its own addition to the class.

The inherited method (from Class) is used in much the same way. It is called whenever a class is subclassed by another.

```ruby
class MyClass

  def MyClass.inherited(subclass)
    puts "#{subclass} inherits from MyClass."
  end

  # ...

end


class OtherClass < MyClass

  # ...

end

# Output: OtherClass inherits from MyClass.
```

We can also track the addition of a module's instance methods to an object (done via the extend method). The method extend_object is called whenever an extend is done.

```
module MyMod

  def MyMod.extend_object(obj)
    puts "Extending object id #{obj.id}, type #{obj.type}"
    super
  end

  # ...

end


x = [1, 2, 3]
x.extend(MyMod)

# Output:
# Extending object id 36491192, type Array
```

Note that the call to super is needed in order for the real extend_object method to do its work. This is analogous to the behavior of append_features (see the section "Working with Modules"). This method can also be used to track the usage of modules.

Defining Finalizers for Objects

Ruby classes have constructors (the methods new and initialize) but don't have destructors (methods that delete objects). That's because Ruby uses mark-and-sweep garbage collection to remove unreferenced objects; a destructor would make no sense.

However, people coming to Ruby from languages such as C++ seem to miss the facility, and often ask how they can write code to handle the finalization of objects. The simple answer is that there is no real way to do it reliably. But you *can* arrange to have code called when an object is garbage-collected.

```
a = "hello"
puts "The string 'hello' has an object id #{a.id}"
ObjectSpace.define_finalizer(a) { |id| puts "Destroying #{id}" }
puts "Nothing to tidy"
GC.start
a = nil
puts "The original string is now a candidate for collection"
GC.start
```

This produces the following output:

```
The string 'hello' has an object id 537684890
Nothing to tidy
The original string is now a candidate for collection
Destroying 537684890
```

Note that by the time the finalizer is called, the object has basically been destroyed already. An attempt to convert the ID you receive back into an object reference using `ObjectSpace._id2ref` will raise a `RangeError`, complaining that you are attempting to use a recycled object.

However, all this might be moot. There's a style of programming in Ruby that uses blocks to encapsulate the use of a resource. At the end of the block, the resource is deleted and life carries on merrily, all without the use of finalizers. For example, consider the block form of `File.open`:

```
File.open("myfile.txt") do |aFile|
  l1 = aFile.read
  # ...
end
```

Here the `File` object is passed into the block. When the block exits, the file is closed, all under control of the open method. If you wanted to write a subset of `File.open` in Ruby (for efficiency, it's currently written in C as part of the runtime system), it might look something like this:

```
def File.open(name, mode = "r")
  f = os_file_open(name, mode)
  if block_given?
    begin
      yield f
    ensure
      f.close
    end
    return nil
  else
    return f
  end
end
```

The routine tests for the presence of a block. If found, it invokes that block, passing in the open file. It does this in the context of a `begin-end` block, ensuring that it will close the file after the block terminates, even if an exception is thrown.

Dynamically Instantiating a Class by Name

We have seen this question more than once. Given a string containing the name of a class, how can we create an instance of that class?

The answer is annoyingly simple. Use `eval` for the purpose.

```
classname = "Array"

classvar = eval(classname)
x = classvar.new(4, 1)        # [1, 1, 1, 1]
```

As always, make sure that the string you're evaluating is a safe one.

Summary

You've seen here a few of the more esoteric or advanced techniques in OOP, as well as some of the more everyday usages. We've also looked at Ruby's reflection API, some interesting consequences of Ruby's dynamic nature, and various neat tricks that can be done in a dynamic language.

It's time now to rejoin the real world. After all, OOP is not an end in itself, but a means to an end; the end is to write applications that are effective, bug free, and maintainable.

In modern computing, these applications frequently need a graphical interface. In Chapter 6, "Graphical Interfaces for Ruby," we discuss creating graphical interfaces in Ruby.

Graphical Interfaces for Ruby

IN THIS CHAPTER

Graphical excellence is often found in simplicity of design and complexity of data.

—Edward R. Tufte, *The Visual Display of Quantitative Information*

There is no denying that we are in the age of the GUI. For as far into the future as we can see, there is going to be some form of graphical interface as the preferred way to interact with a computer.

We don't see the command line going away in the next decade or so; it definitely has its place in the world. But even the old-time hackers (who would rather use `cp -R` than a drag-and-drop interface) still enjoy a GUI when it is appropriate.

However, there are significant difficulties with programming graphically. The first problem, of course, is designing a meaningful, usable "front end" for a program; in interface design, a picture is *not* always worth a thousand words. We can't address these issues here; we are not experts in ergonomics, aesthetics, or psychology.

The second obvious problem is that graphical programming is more complex. We have to worry about the sizes, shapes, locations, and behaviors of all the controls that can be displayed on the screen and manipulated with mouse and/or keyboard.

The third difficulty is that various computing subcultures have differing ideas of what a windowing system is and how it should be implemented. The disparity between these systems has to be experienced to be fully appreciated; many a programmer has attempted to produce a "cross-platform" tool only to find that the impedance mismatch between the GUIs was the hardest part to deal with.

We really can't help much with these problems. The most we can do is give a gentle introduction to a few popular GUI systems (as they relate to Ruby) and offer a few hints and observations.

The bulk of this chapter is devoted to Tk, GTK+, and FOX. Whatever your background is, there is a good chance you are asking, "Why wasn't (*insert name of favorite GUI*) included here?"

There could be several reasons for this. For one thing, we have limited space because this book is not primarily about graphical interfaces. For another, it's possible that your favorite system doesn't have a mature set of Ruby bindings as yet—in which case we encourage you to create them. Finally, not all GUI systems are created equal. We've tried to cover the ones that are most important and most mature; the rest we give at most a passing mention.

The Tk package is part of the standard Ruby installation. The other GUI packages mentioned here can be found in the Ruby Application Archive, which can be found on the official Ruby home page (`www.ruby-lang.org`).

Ruby/Tk

The roots of Tk go back as far as 1988, if you count prerelease versions. It has long been thought of as a companion of Tcl, but in recent years it has been used with several other languages, including Perl.

If Ruby had a "native" GUI, Tk would probably be it. It is the most mature of the GUI bindings at the time of this writing, and Ruby download versions are available that include Tk in a more or less turnkey fashion.

The preceding reference to Perl is not entirely gratuitous. The Tk bindings for Ruby and Perl are somewhat similar, enough so that any reference material for Perl/Tk should be mostly applicable to Ruby/Tk. One such reference is *Learning Perl/Tk*, by Nancy Walsh.

Overview

At the time of this writing, Tk is probably the most common GUI in use with Ruby. It was the first one made available, and it is part of the standard Ruby installation.

Some say that Tk is showing its age; for those who like clean, object-oriented interfaces, it may be something of a disappointment. However, it has the advantages of being well known, very portable, and very stable (at least insofar as the interface to Ruby is stable).

Any Ruby/Tk application must use `require` to load the `tk` extension. Following that, the application's interface is built up piecemeal starting with some kind of container and the controls that populate it. Finally, a call to `Tk.mainloop` is made; this method captures all the events, such as mouse movements and button presses, and acts on them accordingly:

```
require "tk"
# Setting up the app...
Tk.mainloop
```

As with most or all windowing systems, Tk graphical controls are called *widgets*; these widgets are typically grouped together in containers. The top-level container is called the *root*; it is not always necessary to specify an explicit root, but it is a good idea.

Every widget class is named according to its name in the Tk world (by appending `Tk` to the front). Therefore, the `Frame` widget corresponds to the `TkFrame` class.

Widgets are naturally instantiated using the `new` method. The first parameter specifies the container into which the widget is placed; if it is omitted, the root is assumed.

The options used to instantiate a widget may be specified in two ways. The first (Perl-like) way is to pass in a hash of attributes and values (recall that it is a quirk of Ruby syntax that a hash passed in as the last or only parameter may have its braces omitted):

```
my_widget = TkSomewidget.new( "borderwidth" => 2, "height" => 40 ,
                              "justify" => "center" )
```

The other way is to pass a block to the constructor that will be evaluated with `instance_eval`. Within this block, we can call methods to set the attributes of the widget (using methods that are named the same as the attributes). Bear in mind that the code block is evaluated in the context of the *object*, not the caller. This means, for instance, that the caller's instance variables cannot be referenced inside this block:

```
my_widget = TkSomewidget.new do
              borderwidth 2
              height 40
              justify "center"
            end
```

Three geometry managers are available with Tk; they all serve the purpose of controlling the relative size and placement of the widgets as they appear onscreen. The first (and most commonly used) is `pack`; the other two are `grid` and `place`. The `grid` manager is sophisticated but somewhat prone to bugs; the `place` manager is the most simpleminded of all because it requires absolute values for the positioning of widgets. We will only use `pack` in our examples.

A Trivial Windowed Application

In this section we'll demonstrate the simplest possible application—a calendar app that displays the current date.

Because it's good form, we'll begin by explicitly creating a `root` and placing a `Label` widget inside it:

```
require "tk"

root = TkRoot.new() { title "Today's Date" }
str = Time.now.strftime("Today is \n%B %d, %Y")
lab = TkLabel.new(root) do
        text str
        pack("padx" => 15, "pady" => 10,
             "side" => "top")
      end
Tk.mainloop
```

Here, we create the root, set the date string, and create a label. In creating the label, we set the text to be the value of `str`, and we call `pack` to arrange everything neatly. We tell `pack` to use a padding of 15 pixels horizontally and 10 pixels vertically, and we ask that the text be centered on the label. Figure 6.1 shows what this looks like.

FIGURE 6.1

A trivial Tk application.

As mentioned, the creation of the label could also be done in this way:

```
lab = TkLabel.new(root) do
      text str
      pack("padx" => 15, "pady" => 10,
           "side" => "top")
    end
```

The units for screen measurement (as used in this example for padx and pady) are in pixels by default. We can also work in another unit by appending a suffix onto the number; the value now becomes a string, of course, but because Ruby/Tk doesn't care about that, we don't care, either). The available units are centimeters (c), millimeters (m), inches (i), and points (p). All of these are valid padx calls:

```
pack("padx" => "80m")
pack("padx" => "8c")
pack("padx" => "3i")
pack("padx" => "12p")
```

The side attribute doesn't actually contribute anything in this case because we have set it to its default. If you resize the application window, you will notice that the text "sticks" to the top part of the area in which it lives. Other possible values are right, left, and bottom, as you might expect.

The pack method has other options that govern the placement of widgets onscreen. We'll look at just a few.

The fill option specifies whether a widget fills its allocation rectangle (in the horizontal and/or vertical directions). Possible values are x, y, both, and none (the default being none).

The anchor option anchors the widget inside its allocation rectangle using a "compass point" notation; the default is center, and the other possible values are n, s, e, w, ne, nw, se, and sw.

The in option will pack the widget with respect to some container other than its parent. The default, of course, is the parent.

The `before` and `after` options can be used to change the packing order of the widgets in any way desired. This is useful because widgets may not be created in any particular order as compared to their locations onscreen.

All in all, Tk is fairly flexible about placing widgets onscreen. Search the documentation and try things out.

Working with Buttons

One of the most common widgets in any GUI is the pushbutton (or simply *button*). As you would expect, the `TkButton` class enables the use of buttons in Ruby/Tk applications.

In any nontrivial application, we usually create frames in order to contain the various widgets we'll be placing onscreen. Button widgets can be placed in these containers.

A button will ordinarily have at least three attributes set:

- The text of the button
- The command associated with the button (to be executed when it is clicked)
- The packing of the button within its container

Here is a little example of a button:

```
btnOK = TkButton.new do
  text "OK"
  command proc { puts "The user says OK." }
  pack("side" => "left")
end
```

Here, we create a new button and assign the new object to the `btnOK` variable; we pass in a block to the constructor, although we could use a hash instead. In this case, we use the "multi-line" form (which we prefer), although in practice you can cram as much code onto a single line as you want. Recall, by the way, that the block is executed using `instance_eval` so that it is evaluated in the context of the object (in this case, the new `TkButton` object).

The text specified as a parameter to the `text` method will simply be placed on the button. It can be multiple words or even multiple lines.

The `pack` method you have already seen. It is nothing interesting, although it is essential if the widget is going to be visible at all.

The interesting part here is the `command` method, which takes a `Proc` object and associates it with the button. Frequently, as we do here, we will use the `Kernel` method `proc`, which will convert a block to a `Proc` object.

The action we're performing here is rather silly. When the user clicks the button, a (nongraphical) puts will be done; the output will go to the command-line window from which the program was started or perhaps an auxiliary console window.

We now offer a better example. This is a fake thermostat application that will increment and decrement the displayed temperature (giving us at least the illusion that we are controlling the heating or cooling and making ourselves more comfortable). The code for this application is shown in Listing 6.1, and an explanation follows.

LISTING 6.1   A Thermostat Simulation in Tk

```ruby
require "tk"

# Common packing options...
$top    = { 'side' => 'top',    'padx'=>5, 'pady'=>5 }
$left   = { 'side' => 'left',   'padx'=>5, 'pady'=>5 }
$bottom = { 'side' => 'bottom', 'padx'=>5, 'pady'=>5 }


$temp = 74   # Starting temperature...


root = TkRoot.new { title "Thermostat" }


top = TkFrame.new(root) { background "#606060" }
bottom = TkFrame.new(root)


$tlab = TkLabel.new(top) do
  text $temp.to_s
  font "{Arial} 54 {bold}"
  foreground "green"
  background "#606060"
  pack $left
end


TkLabel.new(top) do            # the "degree" symbol
  text "o"
  font "{Arial} 14 {bold}"
  foreground "green"
  background "#606060"
  # Add anchor-north to the hash (make a superscript)
  pack $left.update({ 'anchor' => 'n' })
end


TkButton.new(bottom) do
  text " Up "
```

LISTING 6.1   Continued

```
      command proc { $tlab.configure("text"=>($temp+=1).to_s) }
      pack $left
    end

    TkButton.new(bottom) do
      text "Down"
      command proc { $tlab.configure("text"=>($temp-=1).to_s) }
      pack $left
    end

    top.pack $top
    bottom.pack $bottom

    Tk.mainloop
```

We create two frames here. The upper one holds only a display. We display the temperature in Fahrenheit in a large font for realism. We use a small, strategically placed letter "o" for a degree mark.

Notice that we are using some new attributes for the TkLabel object. The font method speci-fies the typeface and size of the text in the label. The string value is platform dependent; the one shown here is valid on a Windows system. On a Unix system, it would typically be a full X-style font name, long and ugly, something like -Adobe-Helvetica-Bold-R-Normal—*-120-*-*-*-*-*-*-*.

The foreground method sets the color of the text itself. Here, we pass in the string "green" (which has a predefined meaning in the internals of Tk). If you're wondering whether a color is predefined in Tk, an easy way to find out is simply to try it.

Likewise, the background method sets the color of the background against which the text appears. In this case, we pass it a different kind of string as a parameter, a color in typical red-green-blue hex format as you would see in HTML or in various other situations. (The string "#606060" represents a nice gray color.)

You'll notice we haven't added any kind of "exit" button here (to avoid cluttering a nice, sim-ple design). As always, you can close the app by clicking the close icon at the upper-right cor-ner of the window frame.

You might wonder why we've used these ugly global variables in this program. Chiefly, we've done it to simplify the example. For instance, the variables $tlab and $temp have to be used inside the blocks passed to various constructors; this implies they can't be local variables.

Also note that the `configure` method is used in the commands for the buttons; this changes the text of the top label as it increments or decrements the current temperature. As mentioned earlier, basically any attribute can be changed at runtime in this way, and the change will be reflected onscreen immediately.

We'll mention two other little tricks that you can do with text buttons. The `justify` method will accept a parameter (`"left"`, `"right"`, or `"center"`) to specify how the text will be placed on the button (`"center` is the default). We already mentioned that multiple lines could be displayed; the `wraplength` method will specify the column at which word wrapping should occur.

The button's style may be changed with the `relief` method, giving it a slight three-dimensional appearance. The parameter to this method must be one of these strings: `"flat"`, `"groove"`, `"raised"`, `"ridge"` (the default), `"sunken"`, or `"solid"`. The `width` and `height` methods will control the size of the button explicitly, and other methods, such as `borderwidth`, are also available. For other options (which are numerous), consult a reference.

Figure 6.2 provides an additional example of a button with an image on it.

FIGURE 6.2

Tk thermostat simulation (with graphical buttons).

We created a pair of GIF images of an upward-pointing arrow and a downward-pointing one. We can use the `TkPhotoImage` class to get references to each of these. Then we can use these references when we instantiate the buttons, as shown here:

```
upImg = TkPhotoImage.new("file"=>"up.gif")
downImg = TkPhotoImage.new("file"=>"down.gif")

TkButton.new(bottom) do
  image upImg
  command proc { $tlab.configure("text"=>($temp+=1).to_s) }
  pack $left
```

```
end

TkButton.new(bottom) do
  image downImg
  command proc { $tlab.configure("text"=>($temp-=1).to_s) }
  pack $left
end
```

This button code simply replaces the corresponding lines in our first thermostat example. Except for the appearance of the buttons, the behavior is the same.

Working with Text Fields

A text entry field can be displayed and manipulated using the TkEntry widget. As you would expect, there are numerous options governing the size, color, and behavior of this widget; we will offer one sizeable example that illustrates a few of these.

An entry field is only useful if there is some way to retrieve the value typed into it. Typically, the field will be bound to a variable (actually a TkVariable as you'll see), although the get method can also be used.

For our code fragment, let's assume that we're writing a Telnet client that accepts four pieces of information: the host machine, the port number (defaulting to 23), the user ID, and the password. We'll add a couple of buttons, just for looks, for the "sign on" and "cancel" operations. Figure 6.3 shows what this client looks like.

FIGURE 6.3

The simulated Telnet client.

As we've written it, this code fragment also does some little tricks with frames to make things line up and look better. It's not written in a truly portable way, and a real Tk guru would disdain this approach. However, just for your information, we've documented this "quick and dirty" approach to screen layout. The code for this client is provided in Listing 6.2.

LISTING 6.2   Tk Telnet

```ruby
require "tk"

def packing(padx, pady, side, anchor=nil)
  side = :left if not side
  anchor = :n if anchor == nil
  { "padx" => padx, "pady" => pady,
    "side" => side.to_s, "anchor" => anchor.to_s  }
end

root = TkRoot.new() { title "Telnet session" }
top = TkFrame.new(root)
fr1   = TkFrame.new(top)
fr1a  = TkFrame.new(fr1)
fr1b  = TkFrame.new(fr1)
fr2   = TkFrame.new(top)
fr3   = TkFrame.new(top)
fr4   = TkFrame.new(top)

$labelPack  = packing(5, 5, :top, :w)
$entryPack  = packing(5, 2, :top)
$buttonPack = packing(15, 5, :left, :center)
framePack   = packing(2, 2, :top)
frame1Pack  = packing(2, 2, :left)

$varHost = TkVariable.new
$varPort = TkVariable.new
$varUser = TkVariable.new
$varPass = TkVariable.new

labHost = TkLabel.new(fr1a) do
  text "Host name"
  pack $labelPack
end
entHost = TkEntry.new(fr1a) do
  textvariable $varHost
  font "{Arial} 10"
  pack $entryPack
end

labPort = TkLabel.new(fr1b) do
  text "Port"
  pack $labelPack
end
entPort = TkEntry.new(fr1b) do
```

LISTING 6.2 Continued

```ruby
  width 4
    textvariable $varPort
    font "{Arial} 10"
    pack $entryPack
  end

  labUser = TkLabel.new(fr2) do
    text "User name"
    pack $labelPack
  end
  entUser = TkEntry.new(fr2) do
    width 21
    font "{Arial} 12"
    textvariable $varUser
    pack $entryPack
  end

  labPass = TkLabel.new(fr3) do
    text "Password"
    pack $labelPack
  end
  entPass = TkEntry.new(fr3) do
    width 21
    show "*"
    textvariable $varPass
    font "{Arial} 12"
    pack $entryPack
  end

  btnSignon = TkButton.new(fr4) do
    text "Sign on"
    command proc {}          # Does nothing!
    pack $buttonPack
  end
  btnCancel = TkButton.new(fr4) do
    text "Cancel"
    command proc { exit }   # Just exits
    pack $buttonPack
  end

  top.pack framePack
  fr1.pack framePack
  fr2.pack framePack
  fr3.pack framePack
```

LISTING 6.2   Continued

```
fr4.pack framePack
fr1a.pack frame1Pack
fr1b.pack frame1Pack

$varHost.value = "samspublishing.com"
$varUser.value = "william"
$varPort.value = 23

entPass.focus

foo = entUser.font

Tk.mainloop
```

Let's get the layout issues out of the way. First of all, note that we begin by creating some frames that will stack vertically from top to bottom. The topmost frame will have two smaller ones inside it, placed onscreen from left to right.

We have also created a method called `packing` that exists only to make the code a tiny bit cleaner. It returns a hash with the specified values set for the `padx`, `pady`, `side`, and `anchor` options.

We use the `TkVariable` objects just to associate the entry fields with variables. A `TkVariable` has a `value` accessor that will allow these values to be set and retrieved.

When we create a `TkEntry` such as `entHost`, we use the `textvariable` option to associate it with its corresponding `TkVariable` object. In some cases, we use `width` to set the horizontal width of the field; if it is omitted, a reasonable default will be picked, usually based on the width of the current value stored in the field. We confess to picking these widths by trial and error.

Fonts work for entry fields as they do for labels (as do colors, which we don't play with in this example). If a font is proportional, then two fields that are given the same width may not appear equal-sized onscreen.

As always, `pack` must be called. We've simplified these calls a little with our global variables.

The password field has a call to the `show` method because it is the one field whose value is kept secret from people reading over our shoulders. The character specified as a parameter to `show` (in this case, an asterisk) will be displayed in place of each of the user's keystrokes.

As we said, the buttons are used mainly for show. The "sign on" button does nothing at all; the "cancel" button does exit the program, however.

Other options exist for manipulating entry fields. For example, we can change the value under program control rather than having the user change it, specify the font and the foreground/background colors, change the characteristics of the insertion cursor and move it where we wish, and much more. For all the details, consult a reference.

Because the topic is entering text, it's appropriate to mention the related Text widget. It is related to the entry widget in the way the space shuttle is related to a two-seater plane. It is specifically designed to handle large pieces of multiline text and, in effect, forms the basis for a full-fledged editor.

We won't cover it here because of its complexity. However, you can again consult a reference to find out about the numerous features of this widget.

Working with Other Widgets

Many other widgets are available for Tk. We'll mention a few here.

A checkbox is commonly used for a toggled value—a simple true/false or on/off field. The Tk terminology is *checkbutton*, and TkCheckButton is the class name for the widget.

Listing 6.3 shows a little example. This is a completely bare-bones code fragment because it does not even have any buttons. It displays checkboxes for three areas in which you might take coursework (computer science, music, and literature). It prints a message to the console when you select (or deselect) one of them.

LISTING 6.3   Tk Checkboxes

```
require "tk"

root = TkRoot.new() { title "Checkbutton demo" }
top = TkFrame.new(root)

$packopts  = { "side" => "top", "anchor" => "w" }

$cb1var = TkVariable.new
$cb2var = TkVariable.new
$cb3var = TkVariable.new

cb1 = TkCheckButton.new(top) do
  variable $cb1var
  text "Computer science"
  command { puts "Button 1 = #{$cb1var.value}" }
  pack $packopts
end
```

LISTING 6.3   Continued

```
cb2 = TkCheckButton.new(top) do
  variable $cb2var
  text "Music"
  command { puts "Button 2 = #{$cb2var.value}" }
  pack $packopts
end

cb3 = TkCheckButton.new(top) do
  variable $cb3var
  text "Literature"
  command { puts "Button 3 = #{$cb3var.value}" }
  pack $packopts
end

top.pack $packopts

Tk.mainloop
```

Note that the variable associated with a checkbox receives the value 1 when the box is selected and 0 when it is deselected. These default values can be changed with the onvalue and off-value methods. Furthermore, the variable can be set prior to the creation of the checkbox to establish its initial on/off status.

If for some reason we want a checkbox to be "grayed out," we can use the state method to set its state to disabled. The other states are active and normal; the latter is the default.

Let's alter this little example. Suppose we are representing not just areas of potential study but actual university majors. Ignore double majors for now; it's not appropriate for more than one option to be selected at a time. In this case, of course, we need *radio buttons* (implemented by the TkRadioButton class).

The example we show in Listing 6.4 is nearly the same as the previous one. Obviously, the class name is different. Another critical difference is that the radio buttons all share the same variable. In fact, this is how Tk knows that these buttons all belong to the same group. It is possible to have more than one group of radio buttons, but each group must share one variable among its buttons.

LISTING 6.4   Tk Radio Buttons

```
require "tk"

root = TkRoot.new() { title "Radiobutton demo" }
top = TkFrame.new(root)
```

LISTING 6.4   Continued

```ruby
$packopts  = { "side" => "top", "anchor" => "w" }

$major = TkVariable.new

b1 = TkRadioButton.new(top) do
  variable $major
  text "Computer science"
  value 1
  command { puts "Major = #{$major.value}" }
  pack $packopts
end

b2 = TkRadioButton.new(top) do
  variable $major
  text "Music"
  value 2
  command { puts "Major = #{$major.value}" }
  pack $packopts
end

b3 = TkRadioButton.new(top) do
  variable $major
  text "Literature"
  value 3
  command { puts "Major = #{$major.value}" }
  pack $packopts
end

top.pack $packopts

Tk.mainloop
```

The `value` method is used here to associate a specific value with each of the buttons. It's important to realize that *any* value can be used here (strings, for example). We didn't use strings simply because we wanted to emphasize that there is no direct relationship between the text of the widget and the value that is returned.

Numerous options are available to customize the appearance and behavior of both checkboxes and radio button groups. The `image` method, for example, allows you to display an image rather than a text string. Most of the "usual" options for formatting and displaying widgets also apply here; consult a reference for complete details.

If this book (or even this chapter) were fully devoted to Tk, we would have more to say, but it's not possible to cover it all. The remaining widgets are not discussed here in detail; we mention them only to make you aware of their existence.

The list box (TkListBox) widget allows you to specify a list of values in a "pull-down" format so that the user can select from them. The selection mode (governed by the selectmode method) makes it possible to select these values in single, extended, or browse mode. The first two modes simply determine whether the user can select only one or more than one item at a time. Browse mode is like single mode except that the selection can be moved around as the mouse button is held down. List boxes can be made fully scrollable and can hold an arbitrary number of items.

Tk has advanced menuing capabilities, including pull-down menus, tear-off menus, cascading submenus, keyboard shortcut facilities, radio button menu items, and much more. For more information, investigate the classes TkMenu, TkMenubar, and TkMenuButton.

Perhaps the "sexiest" of the widgets is TkCanvas, which enables the programmer to manipulate images more or less at the pixel level. It has facilities for drawing lines and shapes, manipulating colors, and loading images in various graphics formats. If your application involves advanced graphics or user-controlled drawing, this widget will be of interest to you.

The scrollbar widget handles customized scrolling, both horizontal and vertical (for example, synchronized scrolling of two separate windows). The scale widget is basically a slider that represents a numeric value; it can be placed horizontally or vertically and can be used as input or output. For any others, consult advanced documentation.

Other Notes

The future of Tk is uncertain (as is true of any software system), but it is not going away in the foreseeable future. Ruby/Tk is based on Tk 8.3 at the time of this writing, although it is probably not complete and definitely has a few bugs. We're unable to predict when updates might happen.

We should also say a few words about operating systems. In theory, Tk is platform independent, and the practice is close to the theory. Some users, however, have reported that the Windows version is not as stable as the Unix version. Although this is a bit of a generalization, it is probably correct. For the record, all the examples here have been tested on Windows platforms and are known to work as expected.

Before we close, we should at least mention SpecRuby, the one existing Tk-based application builder for Ruby. This is based on the original SpecTcl (presumably pronounced *spectacle*, a pun that was lost as soon as it was ported from Tcl to other languages such as Perl, Java, and

Ruby). While not necessarily a true RAD (rapid application development) tool, it is still useful and convenient, especially if you are developing a large or complex GUI application. SpecRuby can be found in the Ruby Application Archive.

Ruby/GTK

The GTK+ library is a byproduct of the GIMP (the *GNU Image Manipulation Program*); the name actually means the *GIMP Toolkit*. Like BSD and LSD, GTK+ comes to us from the University of California at Berkeley.

For those familiar with X/Motif, GTK+ has a similar look and feel but is more lightweight. GTK+ originates in the Unix world and forms the underlying basis for GNOME (increasingly familiar to Linux users), but it is relatively cross-platform. There is an ongoing port to the Windows family of operating systems, although at the time of this writing it is not completely stable.

Because GTK+ is relatively new technology, it is arguably easier to use than some older, less object-oriented systems. It also offers a reasonably intuitive paradigm for programming and a comfortable rich set of widgets. However, these assessments are highly subjective, and we'll leave the final judgment to you, the reader.

Overview

Ruby/GTK is a library that allows Ruby applications to use the GTK+ library. GTK+ is open source and is released under the GNU LGPL license, so it may be used freely in commercial applications.

Like most GUI toolkits, GTK+ has such concepts as frames, windows, dialog boxes, and layout managers. It has a rich set of widgets and includes all the most basic ones, such as labels, buttons, and text edit boxes, as well as advanced widgets, such as tree controls and multicolumn lists.

Although GTK+ was written in C, it was designed with a strong object-oriented flavor. Ruby/GTK thus presents a very clean, object-oriented API, while also staying very close to the underlying C language. This enables Ruby/GTK developers to take advantage of the large number of "native C" GTK+ tutorials and reference documents available.

GTK+ is actually built on top of a library named GDK. In Ruby/GTK, this means that some of the lower-level graphical objects are in the Gdk module, rather than the Gtk module. The native GTK+ documentation makes it clear which objects are in each library. Native GTK+ also includes a library named GLIB, which contains an assortment of nongraphical classes that handle items such as strings and lists. Because Ruby already has nice string and list classes, Ruby/GTK programs do not have to deal with GLIB concepts much.

At the time of this writing, Ruby/GTK is at version 0.25 and is compatible with the current
stable versions of Ruby and GTK+ (1.2). However, Ruby/GTK is not yet at version 1 and is
described by the author as "usable, but not completed." Furthermore, the MS Windows port of
GTK+ is "not really targeted at end-users yet." So although simple Ruby/GTK applications
seem to work fine under MS Windows, it's probably not the best choice for projects that
require Windows compatibility.

GTK+ is very object oriented and has a logical widget hierarchy. The concepts of `Bin` and
`Container` are powerful, and the combination of `Box` and `Table` layout managers is simple yet
flexible. The Ruby/GTK mechanism for setting up signal handlers is extremely convenient.

Some of the GTK+ widgets include menus, toolbars, tooltips, trees, progress bars, sliders, and
calendars. However, one current weakness of GTK+ is that it does not yet provide a good
selection of standard dialog boxes, and it is difficult to set them up modally. In addition, the
standard multiline text editor widget has some weaknesses.

A Trivial Windowed Application

Any program using Ruby/GTK must do a `require` of the GTK library. Ruby/GTK provides its
functionality through the `Gtk` and `Gdk` modules, meaning that GTK+ classes are typically prefixed with `Gtk::` (or `Gdk::`).

Normally we create a top-level window and a handler for the `destroy` signal (which results
when a window is closed by the user). A call to `show_all` makes the window (and its children)
visible, and a call to `Gtk.Main` initiates the event loop.

We'll expand on this a little after looking at an example. Here is a code fragment similar to the
one for Tk that displays the current date:

```
require "gtk"

mainWindow = Gtk::Window.new
mainWindow.signal_connect("destroy") { Gtk::main_quit }
str = Time.now.strftime("Today is \n%B %d, %Y")
mainWindow.add(Gtk::Label.new(str))
mainWindow.set_default_size(200, 100)
mainWindow.show_all
Gtk::main
```

The main window (of type `Gtk::Window`) is created as a "top-level" window. Top-level windows have a standard title bar and generally behave as you would expect the main window of
an application to behave.

Next, a handler is created for the destroy signal, which is generated after the main window is closed. This handler (here, a single block) simply exits the main event loop. The GTK+ documentation lists all the signals that each widget might receive. (Be sure to look at superclasses, too). These are typically triggered by mouse or keyboard input, timers, changes in window state, and so on.

The next line of code adds a text label widget directly to the main window. The default size of the label will be calculated automatically based on the size of the text.

By default, GTK+ parent widgets are automatically sized according to the sizes of their children. In this case, the size of the string in the default font will determine the size of the label widget, and the main window would become just large enough to hold the label. That's pretty small, so set_default_size is used to indicate that the initial size of the main window is 200 pixels wide and 100 pixels tall.

After that, show_all is used to make the main window and all its children visible. By default, the main window is hidden, so it is necessary to invoke this method for the main window of most applications.

The call to Gtk::main starts the GTK+ event loop. This method will not return until GTK+ is terminated. In this application, the destroy event handler will cause Gtk::main to exit, at which point the app will terminate.

Working with Buttons

To create a pushbutton in Ruby/GTK, we define it using the Button class. In the simple case, we set up a handler for the clicked event that is generated when a user clicks the button.

This code fragment shown in Listing 6.5 will accept a simple line of text in a text-entry field and (when the button is clicked) will convert the string to uppercase. Figure 6.4 shows a screenshot of this example.

LISTING 6.5 GTK Buttons

```
require "gtk"

  class SampleWindow < Gtk::Window

    def initialize
      super
      set_title("Ruby/GTK Sample")
      signal_connect("destroy") { Gtk::main_quit }

      entry = Gtk::Entry.new
```

LISTING 6.5   Continued

```
      button = Gtk::Button.new("All Caps!")
      button.signal_connect("clicked") { cmdAllCaps(entry) }

      box = Gtk::HBox.new
      box.add(Gtk::Label.new("Text:"))
      box.add(entry)
      box.add(button)

      add(box)
      show_all
    end

    def cmdAllCaps(textField)
      textField.set_text(textField.get_text.upcase)
    end
  end

  SampleWindow.new
  Gtk::main
```

FIGURE 6.4

A simple GTK pushbutton example.

In this example, a SampleWindow class is defined; this is a cleaner approach because it allows the class to control its own look and behavior (rather than requiring the caller to configure the window). This main window is derived from Gtk::Window.

The call to set_title configures the text that will appear in the title bar of the application. As with the first example, a signal handler for destroy exits the GTK+ event loop when the main window is closed.

This class creates a single-line text-entry field using the Entry class, and it creates a button with the text label All Caps!. The signal handler for the button's clicked event calls the cmdUpperCase method, which is defined afterward. (The clicked event is generated after the user presses *and releases* the button.)

The Gtk::Window class is a Bin, so it can only contain a single child widget. In order to put our two child widgets in the window, we place those widgets in a box and add the box to the main window. As widgets are added to an HBox, they are positioned at the right edge of the box (by default). There is a corresponding Gtk::VBox widget that can stack multiple widgets vertically.

As with the earlier example, show_all is necessary to make the main window (and all its children) visible.

The cmdAllCaps method is invoked by the button's signal handler whenever the button is clicked. It gets the current text out of the entry field, converts it to uppercase, and sets it back into the entry field.

The actual application code is below the SampleWindow class definition. It simply creates the main window and runs the GTK+ event loop.

Working with Text Fields

GTK+ provides the Entry class for single-line input, as shown in the previous example. It also has the Text class, which is a multiline editor that we will describe here. Both Entry and Text are derived from the base class Editable, so they have several text-manipulation methods in common.

The code fragment shown in Listing 6.6 creates a multiline edit box and inserts some text into it. As the contents change, the current length of the text is reflected in a label at the bottom of the window.

LISTING 6.6   GTK Text Editor

```
require "gtk"

class TextWindow < Gtk::Window

  def initialize
    super
    set_title("Ruby/GTK Text Sample")
    signal_connect("destroy") { Gtk::main_quit }

    @text = Gtk::Text.new
    @text.signal_connect("changed") { onChanged }
    @text.set_word_wrap(true)
    @text.set_editable(true)

    font = Gdk::Font::font_load("times")
    style = @text.get_style
    style.set_font(font)
```

LISTING 6.6   GTK Text Editor

```
    @status = Gtk::Label.new("")

    scroller = Gtk::ScrolledWindow.new
    scroller.set_policy(Gtk::POLICY_NEVER,
        Gtk::POLICY_AUTOMATIC)
    scroller.add(@text)

    box = Gtk::VBox.new
    box.add(scroller)
    box.add(@status)
    add(box)

    @text.insert_text("This is an editor", 0)
    @text.insert_text("really ", 5)

    show_all
  end

  def onChanged
    text = "Length: " + @text.get_length.to_s
    @status.set_text(text)
  end

end

TextWindow.new
Gtk::main
```

The code in Listing 6.6 gives us a simple text editor. Figure 6.5 shows a screenshot of this application.

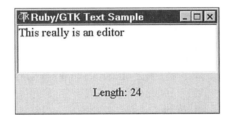

FIGURE 6.5
A small GTK text editor.

The basic structure of the code is very similar to the buttons example: A window class is defined, with an event handler to terminate the app cleanly. At the end of `initialize`, `show_all` is used to make the window visible. The last two lines actually create the window and run the GTK+ event loop.

We create an editor widget named `@text` and set up a signal handler for the `changed` event. Any time text is inserted, deleted, or modified, this signal will fire, and we will execute the `onChanged` method. Word wrapping is enabled (the default is to wrap lines regardless of word breaks), and `set_editable` allows the user to change the contents (by default it is read-only).

Next, we want to configure the `@text` widget to display its text in a different font. Unfortunately, this is difficult to do in a way that works on all platforms.

GTK+ actually discourages programmers from configuring specific fonts and colors in most cases. Instead, it is often better to allow the users to customize their own system using *themes*. If you do wish to override the defaults, however, you must do so through the `Style` class.

In this case, we attempt to load a font from the "Times" family, which on a Windows platform is likely to bring up some variant of Times Roman. On a Linux/Unix platform, the parameter would be a standard X Window System font string. The system will return whatever font is the closest match available.

Each widget has a `Style` object, which you can access using the `get_style` method. In this case, we update the font for that style using `set_font`. You could also configure the text color of this style.

The `@status` label is initially empty. We will change its text later.

GTK+ provides two ways to add scrollbars to an application. You can directly create `ScrollBar` objects and use signals to synchronize them with the content widget(s). However, in most cases, it is simpler to use the `ScrolledWindow` widget instead.

The `ScrolledWindow` widget is a `Bin`, meaning it can only contain a single child widget. Of course, that child widget could be a `Box` or other container that allows multiple children. Several GTK+ widgets, including `Text`, automatically interact with a `ScrolledWindow` widget, requiring almost no additional code.

In this example, we create a `ScrolledWindow` widget named `scroller` and configure it using `set_policy`. We choose never to display a horizontal scrollbar and to automatically display a vertical scrollbar only when the editor has more lines than can be seen at once. We add the text editor directly to `scroller`.

We now set up a `Vbox` that will stack our widgets vertically. The scrolling window that contains the text field is added first, so it will appear at the top of the main window. The `@status` text will appear at the bottom. The box is then added to our main window.

The next two lines insert text into the text editor. The first line inserts a string at offset 0 (at the beginning of the text). Because there was no text, 0 is the only reasonable place to insert. We then insert some additional text at offset 5. The result is a text editor containing the string This really is an editor.

Because we already configured the handler for the changed event, it will be triggered by our calls to insert_text. This means the status will already display correctly, even before the user makes any changes to the text.

The onChanged method handles the changed event. It uses get_length to determine the length of the text currently in the text editor and creates a message string. That message is displayed by calling @status.set_text(text).

Working with Other Widgets

Even a relatively simple GUI may need more than text fields and buttons. Often we find a need for radio buttons, checkboxes, and similar widgets. This next example illustrates a few of these.

Here, we assume the user is making an airline reservation. The Gtk::CList class (representing a multicolumn list) is used for the destination city. A checkbox (actually called a *checkbutton*) determines whether the ticket is roundtrip, and a set of radio buttons (class RadioButton) is used for the seating. A Purchase button completes the interface.

The code is shown in Listing 6.7. A screenshot of the application can be seen in Figure 6.6.

LISTING 6.7   GTK Buttons

```ruby
require "gtk"

class TicketWindow < Gtk::Window

  def initialize
    super
    set_title("Purchase Ticket")
    signal_connect("destroy") { Gtk::main_quit }

    @destination = Gtk::CList.new(["Destination", "Country"])
    @destination.append(["Cairo", "Egypt"]);
    @destination.append(["New York", "USA"]);
    @destination.append(["Tokyo", "Japan"]);
    @destination.signal_connect("select_row") do
      |list,row,col,event|
      @city = @destination.get_text(row, 0)
    end
    @destination.select_row(0, 0)
```

LISTING 6.7   continued

```ruby
    @roundTrip = Gtk::CheckButton.new("Round Trip")

    purchase = Gtk::Button.new("Purchase")
    purchase.signal_connect("clicked") { cmdPurchase }

    @result = Gtk::Label.new("")

    @coach = Gtk::RadioButton.new(nil, "Coach class")
    @business = Gtk::RadioButton.new(@coach, "Business class")
    @first = Gtk::RadioButton.new(@business, "First class")

    flightBox = Gtk::VBox.new
    flightBox.add(@destination)
    flightBox.add(@roundTrip)

    seatBox = Gtk::VBox.new
    seatBox.add(@coach)
    seatBox.add(@business)
    seatBox.add(@first)

    topBox = Gtk::HBox.new
    topBox.add(flightBox)
    topBox.add(seatBox)

    mainBox = Gtk::VBox.new
    mainBox.add(topBox)
    mainBox.add(purchase)
    mainBox.add(@result)

    add(mainBox)
    show_all
  end

  def cmdPurchase
    text = @city
    if(@first.active?)
      text += ": first class"
    elsif(@business.active?)
      text += ": business class"
    elsif(@coach.active?)
      text += ": coach"
    end
    if(@roundTrip.active?) then text += ", round trip " end
    @result.set_text(text)
```

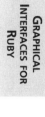

LISTING 6.7   continued

```
    end

  end

  TicketWindow.new
  Gtk::main
```

FIGURE 6.6

A sample app illustrating various GTK widgets.

This application creates a main window with a signal handler, as before. Next, a multicolumn list box (`Gtk::CList`) widget is created with two columns. Three rows of data are added to the list, and a signal handler is created for the `"select_row"` event. This will be invoked whenever the user selects a different row. The handler will update the `@city` member variable to contain the text from the first column (column number 0) of the newly selected row.

A simple checkbox (`Gtk::CheckButton`) and pushbutton (`Gtk::Button`) are created. The signal handler for the pushbutton will execute the `cmdPurchase` method whenever the button is clicked. The label named `@result` is initially blank, but later will be set to a string indicating what type of ticket was purchased.

Three radio buttons are created as a group, meaning that only one of them can be selected at a time. When the user clicks any of these radio buttons, any previously selected button will automatically be deselected. The first parameter to the radio button constructor is the previous radio button within the same group. Therefore, the first radio button in a group passes `nil`, and the rest of the buttons pass the earlier button.

The widgets need to be arranged in a way that will make sense to the user, so a combination of `HBox` and `VBox` widgets is used. The list box will appear above the checkbox. The three radio buttons will appear in a vertical stack to the right of the list box. Finally, the Purchase pushbutton will appear below all the other widgets.

The `cmdPurchase` method is straightforward: It builds a string that reflects all the current widget states when the Purchase button is clicked. Radio buttons and checkboxes have a method named `active?` that returns `true` if the button is selected. The text is then placed in the `@result` label so it will appear on the screen.

Most applications use menus as a key part of their user interface. This next example demonstrates how to set up menus using Ruby/GTK. It also shows how easy it is to add tooltips—a nice touch for any program.

The code in Listing 6.8 creates a main window that has a File menu, along with two other dummy items on the menu bar. The File menu contains an Exit item that exits the application. Both the File and Exit items have tooltips. Figure 6.7 shows a screenshot of this example.

LISTING 6.8   GTK Menu

```ruby
require "gtk"

class MenuWindow < Gtk::Window

  def initialize
    super
    set_title("Ruby/GTK Menu Sample")
    signal_connect("destroy") { Gtk::main_quit }

    fileExitItem = Gtk::MenuItem.new("Exit")
    fileExitItem.signal_connect("activate") { Gtk::main_quit }

    fileMenu = Gtk::Menu.new
    fileMenu.add(fileExitItem)

    fileMenuItem = Gtk::MenuItem.new("File")
    fileMenuItem.set_submenu(fileMenu)

    menuBar = Gtk::MenuBar.new
    menuBar.append(fileMenuItem)
    menuBar.append(Gtk::MenuItem.new("Nothing"))
    menuBar.append(Gtk::MenuItem.new("Useless"))

    tooltips = Gtk::Tooltips.new
    tooltips.set_tip(fileMenuItem, "File Menu", "")
    tooltips.set_tip(fileExitItem, "Exit the app", "")

    box = Gtk::VBox.new
    box.pack_start(menuBar, false, false, 0)
    box.add(Gtk::Label.new("Try the menu and tooltips!"))
```

LISTING 6.8   Continued

```
      add(box)
      set_default_size(300, 100)
      show_all
    end

  end

  MenuWindow.new
  Gtk::main
```

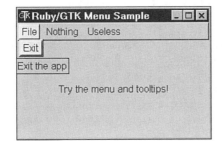

FIGURE 6.7
A GTK menu with tooltips.

Again, the basic structure is like the other examples. In this case, we create a `MenuItem` widget named `Exit` and a signal handler so it will actually exit the program. The signal is `activate`, and it will be generated when a user actually invokes this item on the menu.

The File menu is created, and the Exit item is added to it. This is all that is required to create a pop-up menu. Next, the File menu item is created—this is what will actually appear on the menu bar. We call `set_submenu` to connect the File menu item with the File menu itself.

We create the menu bar and add its three items: File, Nothing, and Useless. Only the first item is actually functional—the other two are just for show.

A single `Tooltips` object manages all the actual tooltips. To create a tooltip for any widget, such as a menu item, call `set_tip`, passing the widget, the tooltip text, and another string that contains additional "private" text. This private text is not shown as part of the tooltip; it could be used by a help system, for example.

A `Vbox` is used to place the menu bar at the top of the main window, above any other widgets. In this case, instead of using `add` to place the menu bar in the box, we use `pack_start` to gain more control over the exact look and placement of the widget.

The first parameter to `pack_start` is the widget we are placing. The second parameter is a Boolean indicating whether this widget should take up all the available space. Note that it won't make the widget actually grow; instead, it will typically center the widget. In this case, we want the menu bar at the very top of the screen, so we pass `false`.

The third parameter is a Boolean for whether this widget should grow to fill all the available space. Because we just want a small menu bar, we pass `false` for this as well. The last parameter to `pack_start` is for padding. This would be used to create additional space all around the widget. We don't want any, so we pass zero.

A text label will take up most of the main window. Finally, we force the initial size of the window to be 300 pixels wide by 100 pixels tall.

Other Notes

We should mention GNOME at least briefly. This is a higher-level package that depends on GTK+, and some GNOME-Ruby bindings are available. However, it is not part of the core GTK+ functionality and is not available for MS Windows.

At the time of this writing, we are anticipating the next major release of GTK+, which will be version 2.0. A preview release (known as "unstable version 1.3") shipped in September 2000, and the official release is expected soon. We should note that existing GTK+ 1.2 applications will likely not be compatible with the newer version.

Among the improvements expected in GTK+ 2.0 are the following:

- Stronger support for internationalization
- Better font support (via a new library named Pango)
- New and improved widgets and dialog boxes
- Built-in portability to the MS Windows, BeOS, and Mac platforms
- A simplified API with unneeded methods removed

The official Ruby/GTK home page is at `http://www.ruby-lang.org/gtk/en/`, and the official GTK+ home page, including a comprehensive API reference, is at `www.gtk.org`.

FX/Ruby (FOX)

The FOX system is also relatively new technology; its emphasis is on speed and consistency among platforms. Its extreme consistency is achieved in part by its self-reliance; it is not a wrapper for a native GUI, as some other systems are implemented.

At its heart, it is based on C++, although bindings can be created for essentially any language (as they have been for Ruby). Because its internals are object oriented from the start, it interfaces well with Ruby and is fairly naturally extensible.

Although it is not extremely widespread at this time, FOX is growing in popularity. We believe it has a future, and we want to present it to you for that reason.

Overview

FX/Ruby is a Ruby binding to the FOX C++ library; it has a large number of classes for developing full-featured GUI applications. Although FOX stands for *Free Objects for X*, it has been ported to a variety of platforms, including MS Windows. Lyle Johnson created the Ruby binding to FOX as well as much of the Windows port of the FOX C++ toolkit itself. FOX was created by Jeroen van der Zijp with the support of CFD Research Corporation.

FOX widgets provide a modern look and feel. The widget choices rival native GUI interfaces, including MS Windows, and the toolkit also has features beyond many other widget libraries.

The FOX class library is clean and powerful, and it can be learned easily by programmers familiar with most other GUI toolkits. Platform dependencies are not apparent in the API. Because FOX itself is implemented in C++, some aspects of the FXRuby API are still influenced by the static nature and programming conventions of C++—for example, enumerations and bit operations as well as message maps based on enumerations.

A central simplifying mechanism in FOX is the message/target paradigm. A FOX object is an instance of FXObject or one of its subclasses. User-defined FOX objects must inherit from one of these classes. Every instance of FXObject is able to send and receive messages; a message is associated with a specific target at runtime, when the message is sent. A message in FOX is an integer unique to a class and its super classes. Many of the FOX classes use a common set of message definitions to allow widgets to interoperate.

An application-specific instance of an FXRuby class should initialize a message map from FOX messages (integers) to message handlers (Ruby methods). A message handler should return 1 to indicate that the message has been handled or 0 to indicate it has not. FOX does not implicitly forward unhandled messages to other widgets. The return value is used by FOX to determine whether the GUI requires updating. An FXRuby application could use the return value to forward unhandled messages itself and thus implement the *Chain of Responsibility* pattern (refer to the book *Design Patterns* by the "Gang of Four").

Another simplifying mechanism in FOX is the automatic update paradigm. The implicit FOX event loop includes an update phase where instances of FOX objects can handle update messages. An update handler is typically used to change the look and feel of a widget based on the new state of some application data. An example of this later in this chapter is a button that updates its active/inactive status based on an application variable.

A Trivial Windowed Application

Here is a minimal FXRuby application, the equivalent of the others you saw for Tk and GTK+ earlier:

```
require "fox"

include Fox

application = FXApp.new("Today", "Sample programs")
application.init(ARGV)
main = FXMainWindow.new(application, "Hello")
str = Time.now.strftime("&Today is %B %d, %Y")
FXButton.new(main, str, nil, application,
             FXApp::ID_QUIT)
application.create
main.show(PLACEMENT_SCREEN)
application.run
```

This application is enough to illustrate two fundamental classes of FXRuby: FXApp and FXMainWindow. Each application must have one instance of FXApp created and initialized before anything is done with the other FOX classes. FXMainWindow is a subclass of FXTopWindow; every widget in FOX is a kind of "window." FXTopWindow is a window that appears directly on the screen. A more complex FXRuby application will create a subclass of FXMainWindow and create its widgets during initialization.

The FXApp constructor is given an application name and a vendor key as arguments. The vendor key is a unique string for your applications using the FOX registry mechanism, which we describe later.

The FXMainWindow constructor requires an instance of FXApp as its first argument. The second argument is the window title. An instance of FXMainWindow will be placed in the center of the screen with all the window decorations of FXTopWindow. Therefore, it will be resizable, show its title bar, and include minimize, maximize, and close buttons in the title bar.

The decoration argument in the constructor can explicitly name each decoration to be included. For example, it is possible to prevent a window from being resized:

```
main = FXMainWindow.new(application, "Hello", nil, nil,
                        DECOR_TITLE | DECOR_CLOSE)
```

The two `nil` arguments in this example are placeholders for icons to be used on the desktop by the window manager. The decoration options are bitwise ORed together in true C++ fashion. The result is a window that has a title and just a close button in the title bar.

This simple application has one widget in its main window—an instance of `FXButton` displaying the text `Hello, world!`:

```
FXButton.new(main, "&Hello, world!", nil,
             application, FXApp::ID_QUIT)
```

The first argument is the parent window that contains the widget. In this example, it is the main window. The second argument is the button's text. The ampersand defines a *hot key* equated with a button click. The `nil` argument is a placeholder for a button icon.

The final two arguments in the button constructor illustrate the message/target paradigm of FOX. The application argument can be any instance of `FXObject`. It is the target of the message `FXApp::ID_QUIT` that the button will send when clicked. In this example, the instance of `FXApp` will respond by stopping event processing and closing the instance of `FXMainWindow`.

The remaining lines of the application illustrate the common "mating ritual" of `FXApp` and `FXMainWindow` instances:

```
application.create()
main.show(PLACEMENT_SCREEN)
application.run()
```

All FXRuby applications should include lines like these to create the application, show the `FXMainWindow` object, and run the `FXApp` event loop for processing GUI events. The `PLACEMENT_SCREEN` argument to the `show` procedure determines where the main window will appear on the screen. Interesting alternative arguments are `PLACEMENT_CURSOR` (to place it under the cursor location), `PLACEMENT_OWNER` (to place it centered on its owner), and `PLACEMENT_MAXIMIZED` (to place it maximized to the screen size).

These simple examples illustrate the use of messages and targets rather than callbacks in FXRuby. In that example, the target is an object implemented in the FOX library. The application shown in Listing 6.9 illustrates how to implement a simple message handler in a Ruby code. The application will appear similar to the previous ones except that when the button is clicked, Ruby code will print text to the console.

LISTING 6.9   FOX Messages and Targets

```
require "fox"
require "responder"

include Fox
```

LISTING 6.9   Continued

```ruby
class SimpleMessageHandlerWindow < FXMainWindow

  include Responder

  # Message identifiers for this class
  ID_HELLO_WORLD = FXMainWindow::ID_LAST

  def initialize(app)
    # Invoke base class initialize first
    super(app, "Simple Message Handler", nil, nil,
          DECOR_TITLE | DECOR_CLOSE)

    # Define the message map for the class
    FXMAPFUNC(SEL_COMMAND, ID_HELLO_WORLD,
              "onCmdHelloWorld")

    # The button
    FXButton.new(self, "&Hello, World", nil, self,
                 ID_HELLO_WORLD)
  end

  def onCmdHelloWorld(sender, sel, ptr)
    puts "Hello, World"
  end

end

def run
  application = FXApp.new("SimpleButton",
                          "Sample programs")
  application.init(ARGV)
  main = SimpleMessageHandlerWindow.new(application)
  application.create
  main.show(PLACEMENT_SCREEN)
  application.run
end

run
```

This application creates a subclass of FXMainWindow. The purpose of this subclass is to define an application-specific message handler. Again, any FXObject instance can handle messages, so the use of FXMainWindow as the superclass is simply a useful convention.

`Responder` is a module that is in the `examples` directory of the FXRuby distribution. It is included to provide convenience methods for creating the message map that associates an ID with a handler method. This example defines one association—from `ID_HELLO_WORLD` to the handler method `onCmdHelloWorld`.

Evidence of FOX's native C++ code betrays itself again in the use of integer IDs. An ID value has to be unique within an `FXObject` and its superclasses. The convention is to define `ID_LAST` as the last ID in a superclass. This ID also serves as the first ID in each subclass. The class in this example will not be used as a superclass, so it does not define its own `ID_LAST`.

The `FXMAPFUNC` method is a convenience method in the `Responder` module. The flavor used in this example adds to the sample window's message map the association from `ID_HELLO_WORLD` to `onCmdHelloWorld`. Every message has a message type and a message ID. `SEL_COMMAND` is the type, and `ID_HELLO_WORLD` the ID in this example. Buttons can send two types of messages: `SEL_COMMAND` and `SEL_UPDATE`. An example of an update message is provided later.

Working with Buttons

You have already seen simple button handling in FXRuby. Now let's look a little deeper.

A button can display more than a short text string. The following example illustrates the use of an image and multiple lines of text in a button:

```
text = "&Hello, World\nDo you see the image?\n" +
       "Do you see multiple lines of text?"
gif = File.open("icons/ruby_button.gif", "rb").read()
image = FXGIFIcon.new(app, gif)
FXButton.new(self, text, image, self, ID_HELLO_WORLD)
```

The example shown in Listing 6.10 illustrates the mechanism the FOX toolkit provides for updating the GUI state.

LISTING 6.10   FOX State-Update Example

```
require "fox"
require "responder"

include Fox

class TwoButtonUpdateWindow < FXMainWindow

   include Responder

   # Message identifiers for this class
   ID_TOGGLE_BUTTON = FXMainWindow::ID_LAST
```

LISTING 6.10   Continued

```ruby
def initialize(app)
  # Invoke base class initialize first
  super(app, "Update Example", nil, nil,
        DECOR_TITLE | DECOR_CLOSE)

  # Define the message map for the class
  FXMAPFUNC(SEL_COMMAND, ID_TOGGLE_BUTTON,
            "onCommand")
  FXMAPFUNC(SEL_UPDATE,  ID_TOGGLE_BUTTON,
            "onUpdate")

  # First button
  @button_one = FXButton.new(self, "Enable Button 2",
                             nil, self,
                             ID_TOGGLE_BUTTON)
  @button_one_enabled = true

  # Second button
  @button_two = FXButton.new(self, "Enable Button 1",
                             nil, self,
                             ID_TOGGLE_BUTTON)
  @button_two.disable
  @button_two_enabled = false
end

def onCommand(sender, sel, ptr)
  # Update the application state
  @button_one_enabled = !@button_one_enabled
  @button_two_enabled = !@button_two_enabled
end

def onUpdate(sender, sel, ptr)
  # Update the buttons based on the application state
  @button_one_enabled ?
    @button_one.enable : @button_one.disable
  @button_two_enabled ?
    @button_two.enable : @button_two.disable
end

end

def run
  application = FXApp.new("UpdateExample",
                          "Sample programs")
```

LISTING 6.10 Continued

```
    application.init(ARGV)
    main = TwoButtonUpdateWindow.new(application)
    application.create
    main.show(PLACEMENT_SCREEN)
    application.run
  end

run
```

This example creates a message map with two associations. The same ID is used
(ID_TOGGLE_BUTTON), and two message types are used (SEL_COMMAND and SEL_UPDATE).

Two buttons are added to the main window. The same message ID (ID_TOGGLE_BUTTON) is sent
from each button. Two types of messages are sent from each button. The SEL_COMMAND type is
sent when a button is clicked. The SEL_UPDATE type is sent when a button is updated. Updates
occur when there are no higher-priority events being processed by the GUI toolkit. An application's update methods should be "short and sweet" to maintain an interactive feel for the user.

The use of the SEL_UPDATE message type allows for the independence of GUI widgets from
each other and the application code. This example illustrates that the two buttons are unaware
of each other. One updates the state of the other by sending messages to handlers that maintain
their state.

The class FXButton is a subclass of FXLabel. A window can display static text and/or an image
very simply using a label. The next example illustrates how to change the font as well.

Working with Text Fields

FOX has some useful features for text entry. The following example illustrates the use of
FXTextField for editing single lines of text. The options are used to constrain the format of the
text. TEXTFIELD_PASSWD is used for disguising the text when it is a password, TEXTFIELD_REAL
constrains the text to the syntax for numbers in scientific notation, and TEXTFIELD_INTEGER
constrains the text to the syntax for integers:

```
simple = FXTextField.new(main, 20, nil, 0,
                         JUSTIFY_RIGHT|FRAME_SUNKEN|
                         FRAME_THICK|LAYOUT_SIDE_TOP)
simple.setText("Simple Text Field")
passwd = FXTextField.new(main, 20, nil, 0,
                         JUSTIFY_RIGHT|TEXTFIELD_PASSWD|
                         FRAME_SUNKEN|FRAME_THICK|
                         LAYOUT_SIDE_TOP)
```

```
    passwd.setText("Password")
    real = FXTextField.new(main, 20, nil, 0,
                          TEXTFIELD_REAL|FRAME_SUNKEN|
                          FRAME_THICK|LAYOUT_SIDE_TOP|
                          LAYOUT_FIX_HEIGHT, 0, 0, 0, 30)
    real.setText("1.0E+3")
    int = FXTextField.new(main, 20, nil, 0, TEXTFIELD_INTEGER|
                          FRAME_SUNKEN|FRAME_THICK|
                          LAYOUT_SIDE_TOP|LAYOUT_FIX_HEIGHT,
                          0, 0, 0, 30)
    int.setText("1000")
```

The following example illustrates a simple way to enter text using a dialog box. Again, the text can be constrained to an integer or scientific number, based on the method used:

```
    puts FXInputDialog.getString("initial text",
                                 self, "Text Entry Dialog",
                                 "Enter some text:", nil)
    puts FXInputDialog.getInteger(1200, self,
                                  "Integer Entry Dialog",
                                  "Enter an integer:", nil)
    puts FXInputDialog.getReal(1.03e7, self,
                               "Scientific Entry Dialog",
                               "Enter a real number:", nil)
```

To save space, we don't show the full application here. But, of course, the FOX toolkit requires initialization before displaying a dialog window.

Working with Other Widgets

The next example illustrates the use of menus and menu bars in FXRuby applications. Instances of FXMenuCommand follow the FOX message/target paradigm. In this example, the message once again is FXApp::ID_QUIT and the target is the FXApp itself, so there is no need to implement a new message handler method:

```
    require "fox"

    include Fox

    application = FXApp.new("SimpleMenu", "Sample programs")
    application.init(ARGV)
    main = FXMainWindow.new(application, "Simple Menu")
    menubar = FXMenubar.new(main, LAYOUT_SIDE_TOP |
                            LAYOUT_FILL_X)
    filemenu = FXMenuPane.new(main)
    FXMenuCommand.new(filemenu, "&Quit\tCtl-Q", nil,
                      application, FXApp::ID_QUIT)
```

```
FXMenuTitle.new(menubar, "&File", nil, filemenu)
application.create
main.show(PLACEMENT_SCREEN)
application.run
```

Both `FXMenubar` and `FXMenuPane` appear directly on the `FXMainWindow` object in this example. The options `LAYOUT_SIDE_TOP` and `LAYOUT_FILL_X` place the menu bar at the top of the parent window and stretch it across the width of the window. The text of the menu command, `"&Quit\tCtl-Q"`, defines the Alt+Q keystroke as a keyboard hotkey equivalent and Ctrl+Q as a keyboard shortcut. Typing Alt+F then Alt+Q is equivalent to clicking the File menu and then the Quit menu command. Typing Ctrl+Q is a shortcut equivalent for the entire sequence.

Another message, this one understood by `FXTopWindow`, can be sent from an `FXMenuCommand` object to iconify the main window. The following line adds that command to the File menu:

```
FXMenuCommand.new(filemenu, "&Icon\tCtl-I", nil,
                  main, FXTopWindow::ID_ICONIFY)
```

Note also that menu items can be cascaded through the use of the class `FXMenuCascade`.

The example shown in Listing 6.11 illustrates the use of radio buttons. The example also uses the FOX toolkit's message-passing mechanism explicitly. The radio buttons determine the target and the message dynamically.

LISTING 6.11   FOX Radio Buttons

```
require "fox"
require "responder"

include Fox

class RadioButtonHandlerWindow < FXMainWindow

  include Responder

  # Message identifiers for this class
  ID_EXECUTE_CHOICE,
  ID_CHOOSE_QUIT,
  ID_CHOOSE_ICON = enum(FXMainWindow::ID_LAST, 3)

  def initialize(app)
    # Invoke base class initialize first
    super(app, "Radio Button Handler", nil, nil,
          DECOR_TITLE | DECOR_CLOSE)

    # Define the message map for the class
```

LISTING 6.11   Continued

```
            FXMAPFUNC(SEL_COMMAND, ID_EXECUTE_CHOICE,
                     "onCmdExecuteChoice")
            FXMAPFUNC(SEL_COMMAND, ID_CHOOSE_QUIT,
                     "onCmdChooseQuit")
            FXMAPFUNC(SEL_COMMAND, ID_CHOOSE_ICON,
                     "onCmdChooseIcon")

            group = FXGroupBox.new(self, "Radio Test Group",
                                   LAYOUT_SIDE_TOP |
                                   FRAME_GROOVE |
                                   LAYOUT_FILL_X)
            FXRadioButton.new(group, "&Quit the application",
                              self, ID_CHOOSE_QUIT,
                              ICON_BEFORE_TEXT |
                              LAYOUT_SIDE_TOP)
            FXRadioButton.new(group, "&Iconify the window",
                              self, ID_CHOOSE_ICON,
                              ICON_BEFORE_TEXT |
                              LAYOUT_SIDE_TOP)
            FXButton.new(self, "&Do it now!", nil, self,
                         ID_EXECUTE_CHOICE)

        @target = app
        @choice = FXApp::ID_QUIT
      end

      def onCmdChooseQuit(sender, sel, ptr)
        @target = getApp()
        @choice = FXApp::ID_QUIT
      end

      def onCmdChooseIcon(sender, sel, ptr)
        @target = self
        @choice = FXTopWindow::ID_ICONIFY
      end

      def onCmdExecuteChoice(sender, sel, ptr)
        @target.handle(self, MKUINT(@choice, SEL_COMMAND),
                       nil)
      end
    end

    def run
      application = FXApp.new("RadioButton", "Sample programs")
      application.init(ARGV)
```

LISTING 6.11   Continued

```
    main = RadioButtonHandlerWindow.new(application)
    application.create
    main.show(PLACEMENT_SCREEN)
    application.run
  end

  run
```

Several application-specific messages are used in this example. The `responder.rb` module has a convenience method for defining multiple FOX identifiers. The enum method returns an array of sequential integers. The first argument is the first integer of the array. The second argument is the length of the array. This example returns an array of three integers, from `FXMainWindow::ID_LAST` through `FXMainWindow::ID_LAST + 3`. The Ruby assignment operator converts the integers into three "rvalues" and assigns those values to the three "lvalues":

```
ID_EXECUTE_CHOICE,
ID_CHOOSE_QUIT,
ID_CHOOSE_ICON = enum(FXMainWindow::ID_LAST, 3)
```

Instances of `FXRadioButton` work together as a group of buttons when they are added to the same parent. This example adds an instance of `FXGroupBox` to the main window and then adds the radio buttons to the group box:

```
group = FXGroupBox.new(self, "Radio Test Group",
                       LAYOUT_SIDE_TOP | FRAME_GROOVE |
                       LAYOUT_FILL_X)
FXRadioButton.new(group, "&Quit the application", self,
                  ID_CHOOSE_QUIT, ICON_BEFORE_TEXT |
                  LAYOUT_SIDE_TOP)
FXRadioButton.new(group, "&Iconify the window", self,
                  ID_CHOOSE_ICON, ICON_BEFORE_TEXT |
                  LAYOUT_SIDE_TOP)
```

The radio buttons are mapped to methods in the application's `RadioButtonHandlerWindow` class. The pushbutton is mapped to a method that send the message in `@choice` to the target in `@target`. The `MKUINT` method is used to create the message to be sent. A *message* is a combination of an identifier such as `FXApp::ID_QUIT` and a message type such as `SEL_COMMAND`. In this way, the same identifier can be used for multiple types of messages:

```
def onCmdChooseQuit(sender, sel, ptr)
  @target = getApp()
  @choice = FXApp::ID_QUIT
end
```

```ruby
def onCmdChooseIcon(sender, sel, ptr)
  @target = self
  @choice = FXTopWindow::ID_ICONIFY
end

def onCmdExecuteChoice(sender, sel, ptr)
  @target.handle(self, MKUINT(@choice, SEL_COMMAND),
                 nil)
end
```

The `FXCheckButton` class, as well as the `FXRadioButton` class, has `getCheck` and `setCheck` methods for programmatically inspecting and modifying the widgets. A checkbutton can be added in just a couple of lines to the previous example. This new button, when checked, will cause the pushbutton command to be ignored (see Figure 6.8):

```ruby
@ignore = FXCheckButton.new(self, "Ig&nore", nil, 0,
                            ICON_BEFORE_TEXT |
                            LAYOUT_SIDE_TOP)
```

FIGURE 6.8
Radio buttons and checkboxes in FOX.

The constructor for the checkbutton initializes the target to `nil` and the message ID to `0`. In this example, the checkbutton will not have to send a message to have an effect on the application. The redefinition of the `onCmdExecuteChoice` method inspects the state of the check button to decide what to do:

```ruby
def onCmdExecuteChoice(sender, sel, ptr)
  unless @ignore.getCheck then
    @target.handle(self, MKUINT(@choice, SEL_COMMAND),
                   nil)
  end
end
```

The complete example is shown in Listing 6.12. Figure 6.8 shows a screenshot of this example.

LISTING 6.12   Radio Buttons and Checkboxes in FOX

```ruby
require "fox"
require "responder"

include Fox

class RadioButtonHandlerWindow < FXMainWindow

  include Responder

  # Message identifiers for this class
  ID_EXECUTE_CHOICE,
  ID_CHOOSE_QUIT,
  ID_CHOOSE_ICON = enum(FXMainWindow::ID_LAST, 3)

  def initialize(app)
    # Invoke base class initialize first
    super(app, "Radio Button Handler", nil, nil,
          DECOR_TITLE | DECOR_CLOSE)

    # Define the message map for the class
    FXMAPFUNC(SEL_COMMAND, ID_EXECUTE_CHOICE,
              "onCmdExecuteChoice")
    FXMAPFUNC(SEL_COMMAND, ID_CHOOSE_QUIT,
              "onCmdChooseQuit")
    FXMAPFUNC(SEL_COMMAND, ID_CHOOSE_ICON,
              "onCmdChooseIcon")

    group = FXGroupBox.new(self, "Radio Test Group",
                           LAYOUT_SIDE_TOP |
                           FRAME_GROOVE |
                           LAYOUT_FILL_X)
    FXRadioButton.new(group, "&Quit the application",
                      self, ID_CHOOSE_QUIT,
                      ICON_BEFORE_TEXT |
                      LAYOUT_SIDE_TOP)
    FXRadioButton.new(group, "&Iconify the window",
                      self, ID_CHOOSE_ICON,
                      ICON_BEFORE_TEXT |
                      LAYOUT_SIDE_TOP)
    FXButton.new(self, "&Do it now!", nil, self,
                 ID_EXECUTE_CHOICE)

    @ignore = FXCheckButton.new(self, "Ig&nore", nil, 0,
                                ICON_BEFORE_TEXT |
                                LAYOUT_SIDE_TOP)
```

LISTING 6.12   Continued

```
      @target = app
      @choice = FXApp::ID_QUIT
  end

  def onCmdChooseQuit(sender, sel, ptr)
    @target = getApp()
    @choice = FXApp::ID_QUIT
  end

  def onCmdChooseIcon(sender, sel, ptr)
    @target = self
    @choice = FXTopWindow::ID_ICONIFY
  end

  def onCmdExecuteChoice(sender, sel, ptr)
    unless @ignore.getCheck then
      @target.handle(self, MKUINT(@choice, SEL_COMMAND),
                     nil)
    end
  end
end

def run
  application = FXApp.new("RadioButton",
                          "Sample programs")
  application.init(ARGV)
  main = RadioButtonHandlerWindow.new(application)
  application.create
  main.show(PLACEMENT_SCREEN)
  application.run
end

run
```

A list widget, FXList, can also be added to a window and populated in just a few lines. The LIST_BROWSESELECT option enforces one item being selected at all times. The first item is selected initially. Replacing this option with LIST_SINGLESELECT allows zero or one item to be selected. With this option, zero items are initially selected:

```
@list = FXList.new(self, 5, self, ID_SELECT,
                   LIST_BROWSESELECT |
                   LAYOUT_FILL_X)
@names = ["Chuck", "Sally", "Franklin", "Schroeder",
          "Woodstock", "Matz", "Lucy"]
@names.each {|each| @list.appendItem(each) }
```

The entire example is shown in Listing 6.13. The message is handled in the main window by displaying the item that was clicked. If the LIST_SINGLESELECT option were used as discussed previously, it would be important to distinguish a click that selects an item from a click that deselects an item.

LISTING 6.13 FOX List

```ruby
require "fox"
require "responder"

include Fox

class ListHandlerWindow < FXMainWindow

  include Responder

  # Message identifiers for this class
  ID_SELECT = FXMainWindow::ID_LAST

  def initialize(app)
    # Invoke base class initialize first
    super(app, "List Handler", nil, nil,
          DECOR_TITLE | DECOR_CLOSE)

    # Define the message map for the class
    FXMAPFUNC(SEL_COMMAND, ID_SELECT,
              "onCmdSelect")

    @list = FXList.new(self, 5, self, ID_SELECT,
                       LIST_BROWSESELECT |
                       LAYOUT_FILL_X)
    @names = ["Chuck", "Sally", "Franklin",
              "Schroeder", "Woodstock",
              "Matz", "Lucy"]
    @names.each {|each| @list.appendItem(each) }
  end

  def onCmdSelect(sender, sel, i)
    puts i.to_s + " => " + @names[i]
  end
end

def run
  application = FXApp.new("List",
                          "Sample programs")
```

LISTING 6.13   continued

```
    application.init(ARGV)
    main = ListHandlerWindow.new(application)
    application.create
    main.show(PLACEMENT_SCREEN)
    application.run
  end

  run
```

Changing the `LIST_BROWSESELECT` option to `LIST_EXTENDEDSELECT` allows the list to have more than one item selected at once:

```
@list = FXList.new(self, 5, self, ID_SELECT,
                   LIST_EXTENDEDSELECT | LAYOUT_FILL_X)
```

The message handler can be redefined to display all the selected items. All items in the list have to be enumerated to find those that are selected:

```
def onCmdSelect(sender, sel, pos)
  puts "Clicked on " + pos.to_s + " => " +
      @names[pos]
  puts "Currently selected:"
  for i in 0 .. @names.size-1
    if @list.isItemSelected(i)
      puts "      " + @names[i]
    end
  end
end
```

The second argument of the `FXList` constructor controls how many items are visible in the widget. Another widget, `FXListBox`, can be used to display just the current selection. The `FXListBox` interface is similar to `FXList`, with a few exceptions. The arguments to the constructor are the same, as shown here (note that `FXListBox` can only be used to select a single item, so options such as `LIST_EXTENDEDSELECT` are ignored):

```
@list = FXListBox.new(self, 5, self, ID_SELECT,
                      LIST_BROWSESELECT |
                      LAYOUT_FILL_X)
@names = ["Chuck", "Sally", "Franklin", "Schroeder",
          "Woodstock", "Matz", "Lucy"]
@names.each {|each| @list.appendItem(each) }
```

The message handler has to change for `FXListBox`. The third argument is no longer the position of the selected item in the list. The selected item must be inspected directly from the list box:

```
def onCmdSelect(sender, sel, ptr)
  puts @list.getCurrentItem
end
```

A dialog box can be defined once as a subclass of FXDialogBox. That class can then be used to create modal or nonmodal dialog boxes. However, modal dialog boxes interact with their owners differently from their nonmodal counterparts.

By *modal*, we mean that a window or dialog box prevents access to other parts of the application until it is serviced; that is, the software is in a "mode" that requires this dialog to be given attention. A nonmodal entity, on the other hand, will allow focus to change from itself to other entities.

The following example defines a modal and a nonmodal dialog class. The modal class uses the predefined messages ID_CANCEL and ID_ACCEPT. The nonmodal class uses the predefined message ID_HIDE.

The nonmodal dialog box is displayed using the familiar FXTopWindow.show method. The modal dialog box is displayed in its own event loop, which preempts the application's event loop. This is accomplished with the FXDialogBox.execute method. The method returns 1 if the ID_ACCEPT message is sent to close the dialog box or 0 if the ID_CANCEL message is sent. Here's the example:

```
def onCmdModalDialog(sender, sel, ptr)
  dialog = ModalDialogBox.new(self)
  if dialog.execute(PLACEMENT_OWNER) == 1
    puts dialog.getText
  end
  return 1
end
```

The nonmodal dialog box runs continuously alongside the other windows of an application. The application should query the dialog box for interesting values as they are needed. One mechanism to announce the availability of new values would be an "Apply" button on the dialog box sending an application-specific message to the main window. The following example uses another interesting feature of FXRuby: a timer. When the timer goes off, a message is sent to the main window. The handler for that message, listed here, queries the dialog box for a new value and then reestablishes the timer for another second:

```
def onCmdTimer(sender, sel, ptr)
  text = @non_modal_dialog.getText
  unless text == @previous
    @previous = text
    puts @previous
  end
```

```
        @timer = getApp().addTimeout(1000, self, ID_TIMER);
    end
```

The complete example for the modal and nonmodal dialog boxes is shown in Listing 6.14.

LISTING 6.14   FOX Dialog Boxes

```
require "fox"
require "responder"

include Fox

class NonModalDialogBox < FXDialogBox

  def initialize(owner)
    # Invoke base class initialize function first
    super(owner, "Test of Dialog Box",
          DECOR_TITLE|DECOR_BORDER)

    text_options = JUSTIFY_RIGHT | FRAME_SUNKEN |
                   FRAME_THICK | LAYOUT_SIDE_TOP
    @text_field = FXTextField.new(self, 20, nil, 0,
                   text_options)
    @text_field.setText("")

    layout_options = LAYOUT_SIDE_TOP | FRAME_NONE |
                     LAYOUT_FILL_X | LAYOUT_FILL_Y |
                     PACK_UNIFORM_WIDTH
    layout = FXHorizontalFrame.new(self, layout_options)

    options = FRAME_RAISED | FRAME_THICK |
              LAYOUT_RIGHT | LAYOUT_CENTER_Y
    FXButton.new(layout, "&Hide", nil, self, ID_HIDE,
                 options)
  end

  def onCmdCancel
    @text_field.setText("")
    super
  end

  def getText
    @text_field.getText
  end
end

class ModalDialogBox < FXDialogBox
```

LISTING 6.14   Continued

```ruby
  def initialize(owner)
    # Invoke base class initialize function first
    super(owner, "Test of Dialog Box",
          DECOR_TITLE|DECOR_BORDER)

    text_options = JUSTIFY_RIGHT | FRAME_SUNKEN |
                   FRAME_THICK | LAYOUT_SIDE_TOP
    @text_field = FXTextField.new(self, 20, nil, 0,
                  text_options)
    @text_field.setText("")

    layout_options = LAYOUT_SIDE_TOP | FRAME_NONE |
                     LAYOUT_FILL_X | LAYOUT_FILL_Y |
                     PACK_UNIFORM_WIDTH
    layout = FXHorizontalFrame.new(self, layout_options)

    options = FRAME_RAISED | FRAME_THICK |
              LAYOUT_RIGHT | LAYOUT_CENTER_Y
    FXButton.new(layout, "&Cancel", nil, self,
                 ID_CANCEL, options)
    FXButton.new(layout, "&Accept", nil, self,
                 ID_ACCEPT, options)
  end

  def onCmdCancel
    @text_field.setText("")
    super
  end

  def getText
    @text_field.getText
  end
end

class DialogTestWindow < FXMainWindow

  include Responder

  # Message identifiers
  ID_NON_MODAL,
  ID_MODAL,
  ID_TIMER = enum(FXMainWindow::ID_LAST, 3)

  def initialize(app)
```

LISTING 6.14   Continued

```ruby
      # Invoke base class initialize first
      super(app, "Dialog Test", nil, nil,
            DECOR_ALL, 0, 0, 400, 200)

      # Set up the message map for this window
      FXMAPFUNC(SEL_COMMAND, ID_NON_MODAL,
               "onCmdNonModelDialog")
      FXMAPFUNC(SEL_COMMAND, ID_MODAL,
               "onCmdModalDialog")
      FXMAPFUNC(SEL_TIMEOUT, ID_TIMER,
               "onCmdTimer")

      layout_options = LAYOUT_SIDE_TOP | FRAME_NONE |
                       LAYOUT_FILL_X | LAYOUT_FILL_Y |
                       PACK_UNIFORM_WIDTH
      layout = FXHorizontalFrame.new(self, layout_options)

      button_options = FRAME_RAISED | FRAME_THICK |
                       LAYOUT_CENTER_X | LAYOUT_CENTER_Y
      FXButton.new(layout, "&Non-Modal Dialog...", nil,
                   self, ID_NON_MODAL, button_options)
      FXButton.new(layout, "&Modal Dialog...",     nil,
                   self, ID_MODAL, button_options)

      @timer = getApp().addTimeout(1000, self, ID_TIMER);
      @non_modal_dialog = NonModalDialogBox.new(self)
    end

    def onCmdNonModelDialog(sender, sel, ptr)
      @non_modal_dialog.show(PLACEMENT_OWNER)
    end

    def onCmdModalDialog(sender, sel, ptr)
      dialog = ModalDialogBox.new(self)
      if dialog.execute(PLACEMENT_OWNER) == 1
        puts dialog.getText
      end
      return 1
    end

    def onCmdTimer(sender, sel, ptr)
      text = @non_modal_dialog.getText
      unless text == @previous
        @previous = text
        puts @previous
```

LISTING 6.14 Continued

```
      end
      @timer = getApp().addTimeout(1000, self,
                               ID_TIMER);
   end

  def create
     super
     show(PLACEMENT_SCREEN)
  end
end

def run
  application = FXApp.new("DialogTest",
                          "Sample programs")
  application.init(ARGV)
  DialogTestWindow.new(application)
  application.create
  application.run
end

run
```

Long computations in FXRuby should change the current cursor to a wait cursor and then restore the original cursor afterward. The FXApp application class has two convenient methods for making the change without having to remember the original cursor. These methods are beginWaitCursor and endWaitCursor. Ruby's begin/ensure form and yield statement make cursor management even more convenient:

```
def busy
  begin
    getApp().beginWaitCursor
    yield
  ensure
    getApp().endWaitCursor
  end
end
```

The busy example method shown here can be used to change to a wait cursor for the duration of any block of code passed to it.

Other Notes

Many other widgets and features are available using the FOX toolkit. Examples include tree widgets, dockable toolbars, tooltips, status lines, and tabbed pages. More advanced GUI features include drag-and-drop operations between applications and data targets for ease of connecting application data to widgets. FOX also includes non-graphical features that support cross-platform programming (for example, `FXFile` and `FXRegistry`).

Messages can be used to connect an application with its environment using signal and input-based messages. Operating system signals, as well as input and output, will cause messages to be sent to FOX objects.

The FOX toolkit has widgets that support most common image formats as well as the OpenGL 3D API. This appears not to be just lip service to 3D capability. The FOX C++ toolkit has been used in many engineering applications. FXRuby has been used with OpenGL as well but was not ready for general release at the time of this writing.

Because the FOX toolkit is written in C++, there are methods that rely on the C++ overloading syntax. This syntax is incompatible with Ruby, a dynamically typed language. The current documentation is lacking in explanation of what mappings to FOX are still missing. Other language features overlap successfully; for example, both C++ and Ruby have optional arguments, and the FOX toolkit and the FXRuby binding take advantage of this feature.

The FOX toolkit was started in 1997. The FXRuby binding dates from early 2001. FXRuby is stable for its age and is more than usable; some core architectural issues are currently being worked out by its creator. The most recent release appears to cooperate with the Ruby garbage collector. Future work is planned for tackling interaction with Ruby threads as well as other Ruby extensions.

Other GUIs

As already mentioned, your favorite GUI may not be covered in this chapter. However, we'll use the remaining space in this chapter just to mention some other alternatives.

Many of these alternatives are not fully mature, and one (wxWindows) is completely unavailable to Ruby programmers at this time. However, we expect this list to grow and the supported bindings to become more stable as time goes on.

The (Nongraphical) Curses Environment

In a chapter on graphical interfaces, the venerable curses library might seem to have no place at all. However, there is still a place for curses even today (especially where Telnet is used). It can give you some of the convenience of a graphical interface even in a purely text-based environment—a convenience at least comparable to that of a smart terminal of the late 1970s.

We don't discuss the usage of the curses extension here, but we do want you to be aware of it. It is a part of the standard Ruby distribution for Unix and should run fine on any Unix variant.

Microsoft Windows is another matter. There are probably curses and ncurses sources available for MS Windows also, in the event anyone wants to run a curses app on such a platform. However, at this time, this would be a more-or-less "roll your own" solution.

Ruby and X

The X Window System is colloquially (although not correctly) referred to as *X Windows*. It is perhaps not the grandfather of all GUI systems, but it is certainly the ancestor of many of them.

Unix users of all breeds have long been familiar with X (as users, even if not as developers). Frequently the Motif window manager is run on top of X.

The advantages of X are that it is widely known, very portable, and has a rich feature set. The disadvantages are that it is rather complex and difficult to use.

Not surprisingly, libraries are available for using X with Ruby. We don't document them here because of complexity and lack of space.

We refer you instead to the Ruby Application Archive, where you can find Xlib by Kazuhiro Yoshida (also known as *moriq*) and Ruby/X11 by Mathieu Bouchard (also known as *matju*). Either can be used to create X client applications.

Ruby and Qt

The Qt system is well known to many C++ programmers (as well as others). It is a modern graphical system—full featured and stable. However, in the Windows world, it is currently a commercial product, which has affected its acceptance as a cross-platform solution.

A Ruby/Qt package is available (as of midsummer 2001) in the Ruby Application Archive; it is the work of Nobuyuki Horie. At the present time, it is not yet mature.

Ruby and wxWindows

The wxWindows system is also full featured and stable; it is widely used in the Python world, and there has been some talk of making it the standard or "native" GUI for that language.

As is so often the case, it is more mature on the Unix platforms than in its Windows version. This is expected to change.

At this time, there is no library for writing wxWindows applications in Ruby. There has been talk of creating one (probably with the help of SWIG), but it is sheer vaporware currently. We mention it only for some measure of completeness.

Apollo (Ruby and Delphi)

The true hacker knows that standard Pascal is all but useless. However, there have been many attempts over the years to improve it so that it is a language worth the effort of using. One of the most successful of these is Borland's Object Pascal, used in its RAD tool called *Delphi*.

The popularity of Delphi is not due to the Pascal language extensions, although these are a contributing factor, but to the development environment itself and the richness of the graphical interface. Delphi has a rich set of widgets for creating stable, attractive GUI applications on MS Windows.

The Apollo library is a marriage of Ruby and Delphi; it is the brainchild of Kazuhiro Yoshida, although others are also working on it. The advantage of Apollo, of course, is that it makes a giant set of stable, usable widgets available; the biggest disadvantage is that it currently requires a slightly "tweaked" version of Ruby. See the Ruby Application Archive for details.

We'll mention one other thing here. Borland (Inprise) has recently released the Kylix development environment for Linux, which is essentially a Linux-based version of Delphi. The plans for Apollo are to interoperate as fully as possible so that applications using it will have basically the same "look and feel" on Linux as on the Microsoft platforms.

Ruby and the Windows API

In Chapter 8, "Scripting and System Administration," we describe a sort of "poor man's GUI" in which we use the WIN32OLE library to get access to the features of Internet Explorer and other such things. Refer to those examples for more details. If you need something quick and dirty, this might be acceptable.

If you are a real glutton for punishment, you could access the Windows API directly. The WIN32API library (also discussed in Chapter 8) makes this kind of coding possible. We don't necessarily recommend the practice, but we want you to be aware of this capability.

Summary

That ends our overview of graphical programming in Ruby. We now turn to an area more concerned with program internals than with human interface. The next chapter deals with Ruby threads.

Ruby Threads

IN THIS CHAPTER

He draweth out the thread of his verbosity
finer than the staple of his argument.

—William Shakespeare,
Love's Labours Lost, act 5, scene 1

Threads are sometimes called *lightweight processes*. They are nothing more than a way to achieve concurrency without all the overhead of switching tasks at the operating system level. (Of course, the computing community isn't in perfect agreement about the definition of threads; but we won't go into that.)

Ruby threads are *user-level* threads and are operating system independent. They will work on DOS as well as on Unix. There will definitely be a performance hit, however, which will also vary by operating system.

Threads are useful in circumstances where, for instance, there are separate pieces of code that naturally function independently of each other. They are also used when an application spends much of its time waiting for an event. Often, while a thread is waiting, another one can be doing useful processing.

On the other hand, there are some potential disadvantages in the use of threads. The decrease in speed has to be weighed against the benefits. Also, there are cases in which access to a resource is inherently serialized, so threading doesn't help. Finally, there are times when the overhead of synchronizing access to global resources exceeds the saving due to multithreading.

For these and other reasons, some authorities claim that threaded programming is to be avoided. Indeed, concurrent code can be complex, error-prone, and difficult to debug. But we will leave it to you when it is appropriate to use these techniques.

The difficulties associated with unsynchronized threads are well-known. Global data can be corrupted by threads attempting simultaneous access to those data. Race conditions can occur wherein one thread makes some assumption about what another has done already; these commonly result in "non-deterministic" code that might run differently with each execution. Finally, there is the danger of deadlock, wherein no thread can continue because it is waiting for a resource held by some other thread that is also blocked. Code written to avoid these problems is referred to as *thread-safe* code.

Not all of Ruby is thread-safe, but synchronization methods are available that will enable you to control access to variables and resources, protect critical sections of code, and avoid deadlock. We will deal with these techniques in this chapter and give code fragments to illustrate them.

Creating and Manipulating Threads

The most basic operations on threads include creating a thread, passing information in and out, stopping a thread, and so on. We can also obtain lists of threads, check the state of a thread, and check various other information. We present an overview of these basic operations here.

Creating Threads

Creating a thread is easy. We call the `new` method and attach a block that will be the body of the thread.

```ruby
thread = Thread.new do
  # Statements comprising
  #   the thread...
end
```

The value returned is obviously an object of type `Thread`, which is used by the main thread to control the thread it has created.

What if we want to pass parameters into a thread? We can do this by passing parameters into `Thread.new`, which in turn will pass them into the block.

```ruby
a = 4
b = 5
c = 6
thread2 = Thread.new(a,b,c) do |a, x, y|
  # Manipulate a, x, and y as needed.
end

# Note that if a is changed in the new thread, it will
#   change suddenly and without warning in the main
#   thread.
```

Similar to any other block parameters, any of these that correspond to existing variables will be effectively identical to those variables. The variable a in the previous fragment is a "dangerous" variable in this sense, as the comment points out.

Threads might also access variables from the scope in which they were created. Obviously, without synchronization, this can be problematic. The main thread and one or more other threads might modify the variable independently of each other, and the results can be unpredictable.

```ruby
x = 1
y = 2
thread3 = Thread.new do
  # This thread can manipulate x and y from the outer scope,
  #   but this is not always safe.
```

```
    sleep(rand(0))  # Sleep a random fraction of a second.
    x = 3
  end

  sleep(rand(0))
  puts x
  # Running this code repeatedly, x may be 1 or 3 when it
  #   is printed here!
```

The method fork is an alias for new; this name is derived from the well-known Unix system call of the same name.

Accessing Thread-local Variables

We know that it can be dangerous for a thread to use variables from outside its scope; we know also that a thread can have local data of its own. But what if a thread wants to "make public" some of the data that it owns?

A special mechanism exists for this purpose. If a thread object is treated as a hash, thread-local data can be accessed from anywhere within the scope of that thread object. We don't mean that actual local variables can be accessed in this way, but only that we have access to named data on a per-thread basis.

There is also a method called key? that will tell us whether a given name is in use for this thread.

Within the thread, we must refer to the data in the same hash-like way. Using Thread.current will make this a little less unwieldy.

```
  thread = Thread.new do
    t = Thread.current
    t[:var1] = "This is a string"
    t[:var2] = 365
  end

  # Access the thread-local data from outside...

  x = thread[:var1]              # "This is a string"
  y = thread[:var2]              # 365

  has_var2 = thread.key?("var2") # true
  has_var3 = thread.key?("var3") # false
```

Note that these data are accessible from other threads even after the thread that owned them is dead (as in this case).

Besides a symbol (as you just saw), we can also use a string to identify the thread-local variable.

```
thread = Thread.new do
  t = Thread.current
  t["var3"] = 25
  t[:var4] = "foobar"
end

a = thread[:var3] = 25
b = thread["var4"] = "foobar"
```

Don't confuse these special names with actual local variables.

```
thread = Thread.new do
  t = Thread.current
  t["var3"] = 25
  t[:var4] = "foobar"
  var3 = 99             # True local variables (not
  var4 = "zorch"        # accessible from outside)
end

a = thread[:var3]      # 25
b = thread["var4"]     # "foobar"
```

Finally, note that an object reference to a true local variable can be used as a sort of shorthand within the thread. This is true as long as you carefully preserve the same object reference rather than creating a new one.

```
thread = Thread.new do
  t = Thread.current
  x = "nXxeQPdMdxiBAxh"
  t[:my_message] = x
  x.reverse!
  x.delete! "x"
  x.gsub!(/[A-Z]/,"")
  # On the other hand, assignment would create a new
  # object and make this shorthand useless...
end

a = thread[:my_message]   # "hidden"
```

Also, this shortcut obviously won't work when you are dealing with values such as Fixnums, which are stored as immediate values rather than object references.

Querying and Changing Thread Status

The Thread class has several class methods that serve various purposes. The list method returns an array of all living threads, the main method returns a reference to the main thread that spawns the others, and the current method that allows a thread to find its own identity.

```
t1 = Thread.new { sleep 100 }
t2 = Thread.new do
  if Thread.current == Thread.main
    puts "This is the main thread."    # Does NOT print
  end
  1.upto(1000)
    sleep 0.1
  end
end

count = Thread.list.size               # 3
if Thread.list.include?(Thread.main)
  puts "Main thread is alive."         # Always prints!
end
if Thread.current == Thread.main
  puts "I'm the main thread."          # Prints here...
end
```

The exit, pass, start, stop, and kill methods are used to control the execution of threads (often from inside or outside).

```
# In the main thread...
Thread.kill(t1)          # Kill this thread now
Thread.pass(t2)          # Pass execution to t2 now
t3 = Thread.new do
  sleep 20
  Thread.exit            # Exit the thread
  puts "Can't happen!"   # Never reached
end
Thread.kill(t2)          # Now kill t2
# Now exit the main thread (killing any others)
Thread.exit
```

Note that there is no instance method stop, so a thread can stop itself but not another thread.

Various methods exist for checking the state of a thread. The instance method alive? will tell whether the thread is still "living" (not exited), and stop? will tell whether the thread is in a stopped state.

```
count = 0
t1 = Thread.new { loop { count += 1 } }
t2 = Thread.new { Thread.stop }
```

```
sleep 1
flags = [t1.alive?,    # true
         t1.stop?,     # false
         t2.alive?,    # true
         t2.stop?]     # true
```

The status of a thread can be determined using the `status` method. The value returned will be `"run"` if the thread is currently running; `sleep` if it is stopped, sleeping, or waiting on I/O; `false` if it terminated normally, and `nil` if it terminated with an exception.

```
t1 = Thread.new { loop {} }
t2 = Thread.new { sleep 5 }
t3 = Thread.new { Thread.stop }
t4 = Thread.new { Thread.exit }
t5 = Thread.new { raise "exception" }
s1 = t1.status    # "run"
s2 = t2.status    # "sleep"
s3 = t3.status    # "sleep"
s4 = t4.status    # false
s5 = t5.status    # nil
```

The global variable `$SAFE` can be set differently in different threads. In this sense, it isn't truly a global variable at all; but we shouldn't complain because this allows us to have threads run with different levels of safety. The `safe_level` method will tell us at what level a thread is running.

```
t1 = Thread.new { $SAFE = 1; sleep 5 }
t2 = Thread.new { $SAFE = 3; sleep 5 }
sleep 1
lev0 = Thread.main.safe_level    # 0
lev1 = t1.safe_level             # 1
lev2 = t2.safe_level             # 3
```

The priority of a thread can be examined and changed using the `priority` accessor.

```
t1 = Thread.new { loop { sleep 1 } }
t2 = Thread.new { loop { sleep 1 } }
t2.priority = 3    # Set t2 at priority 3
p1 = t1.priority   # 0
p2 = t2.priority   # 3
```

A thread with higher (numerically greater) priority will be scheduled more often.

The special method `pass` is used when a thread wants to yield control to the scheduler. The thread merely yields its current timeslice; it doesn't actually stop or go to sleep.

```
t1 = Thread.new do
  puts "alpha"
```

```
      Thread.pass
      puts "beta"
   end
   t2 = Thread.new do
     puts "gamma"
     puts "delta"
   end

   t1.join
   t2.join
```

In this contrived example, we get output in the order `alpha gamma delta beta` when `Thread.pass` is called as shown. Without it, we get `alpha beta gamma delta` as the order. Of course, this feature shouldn't be used for synchronization, but only for the "thrifty" allocation of timeslices.

A thread that is stopped can be awakened by using the `run` or `wakeup` methods:

```
   t1 = Thread.new do
     Thread.stop
     puts "There is an emerald here."
   end
   t2 = Thread.new do
     Thread.stop
     puts "You're at Y2."
   end

   sleep 1
   t1.wakeup
   t2.run
```

The difference in these is somewhat subtle. The `wakeup` call changes the state of the thread so that it is runnable, but won't schedule it to be run; on the other hand, `run` wakes up the thread and schedules it for immediate running.

In this particular case, the result is that `t1` wakes up *before* `t2`, but `t2` gets scheduled first, producing the following output:

```
   You're at Y2.
   There is an emerald here.
```

Of course, it would be unwise to attempt true synchronization by depending on this subtlety.

The `raise` instance method raises an exception in the thread specified as the receiver. (The call doesn't have to originate within the thread.)

```
   factorial1000 = Thread.new do
     begin
```

```
      prod = 1
      1.upto(1000) {|n| prod *= n }
      puts "1000! = #{prod}"
    rescue
      # Do nothing...
    end
  end

  sleep 0.01              # Your mileage may vary.
  if factorial1000.alive?
    factorial1000.raise("Stop!")
    puts "Calculation was interrupted!"
  else
    puts "Calculation was successful."
  end
```

The thread spawned previously tries to calculate the factorial of 1000; if it doesn't succeed within a hundredth of a second, the main thread will kill it. Thus, on a relatively slow machine, this code fragment will print the message Calculation was interrupted!. Concerning the rescue clause inside the thread, obviously we could have put any code there that we wanted, as with any other such clause.

Achieving a Rendezvous (and Capturing a Return Value)

Sometimes the main thread wants to wait for another thread to finish. The instance method join will accomplish this.

```
  t1 = Thread.new { do_something_long() }

  do_something_brief()
  t1.join                # Wait for t1
```

Note that a join is necessary if the main thread is to wait on another thread. Otherwise, when the main thread exits, a thread is killed. For example, this code fragment would never give us its final answer without the join at the end:

```
  meaning_of_life = Thread.new do
    puts "The answer is..."
    sleep 10
    puts 42
  end

  sleep 9
  meaning_of_life.join
```

Here is a useful little idiom. It will call join on every living thread except the main one. (It is an error for any thread, even the main thread, to call join on itself.)

```
Thread.list.each { |t| t.join if t != Thread.main }
```

It is, of course, possible for one thread to do a `join` on another when neither is the main thread. If the main thread and another attempt to join each other, a deadlock results; the interpreter will detect this case and exit the program.

```
thr = Thread.new { sleep 1; Thread.main.join }

thr.join          # Deadlock results!
```

A thread has an associated block, and a block can have a return value. This implies that a thread can return a value. The `value` method will implicitly do a `join` operation and wait for the thread to complete; then it will return the value of the last evaluated expression in the thread.

```
max = 10000
thr = Thread.new do
  sum = 0
  1.upto(max) { |i| sum += i }
  sum
end

guess = (max*(max+1))/2
print "Formula is "
if guess == thr.value
  puts "right."
else
  puts "right."
end
```

Dealing with Exceptions

What happens if an exception occurs within a thread? As it turns out, the behavior is configurable.

A flag called `abort_on_exception` operates both at the class and instance levels. This is implemented as an accessor at both levels (that is, it is readable and writable).

In short, if `abort_on_exception` is true for a thread, an exception in that thread will terminate all the other threads also.

```
Thread.abort_on_exception = true

t1 = Thread.new do
  puts "Hello"
  sleep 2
  raise "some exception"
```

```
  puts "Goodbye"
end

t2 = Thread.new { sleep 100 }

sleep 2
puts "The End"
```

In the preceding code, the systemwide abort_on_exception is set to true (overriding the default). Thus, when t1 gets an exception, t1 and the main thread are also killed. The word Hello is the only output generated.

In this next example, the effect is the same:

```
t1 = Thread.new do
  puts "Hello"
  sleep 2
  raise "some exception"
  puts "Goodbye"
end

t1.abort_on_exception = true

t2 = Thread.new { sleep 100 }

sleep 2
puts "The End"
```

In the final example, the default of false is assumed, and we finally get to see the output The End from the main thread. (We never see Goodbye because t1 is always terminated when the exception is raised.)

```
t1 = Thread.new do
  puts "Hello"
  sleep 2
  raise "some exception"
  puts "Goodbye"
end

t2 = Thread.new { sleep 100 }

sleep 2
puts "The End"
```

Output:

```
Hello
The End
```

Using a Thread Group

A *thread group* is a way of managing threads that are logically related to each other. Normally, all threads belong to the Default thread group (which is a class constant). But if a new thread group is created, new threads can be added to it.

A thread can only be in one thread group at a time. When a thread is added to a thread group, it is automatically removed from whatever group it was in previously.

The ThreadGroup.new class method creates a new thread group, and the add instance method adds a thread to the group:

```ruby
f1thread = Thread.new("file1") { |file| waitfor(file) }
f2thread = Thread.new("file2") { |file| waitfor(file) }

file_threads = ThreadGroup.new
file_threads.add f1
file_threads.add f2
```

The instance method list returns an array of all the threads in the thread group:

```ruby
# Count living threads in this_group
count = 0
this_group.list.each {|x| count += 1 if x.alive? }
if count < this_group.list.size
  puts "Some threads in this_group are not living."
else
  puts "All threads in this_group are alive."
end
```

There is plenty of room for useful methods to be added to ThreadGroup. Here we show methods to wake up every thread in a group, to wait for all threads to catch up (via join), and to kill all threads in a group:

```ruby
class ThreadGroup

  def wakeup
    list.each { |t| t.wakeup }
  end

  def join
    list.each { |t| t.join if t != Thread.current }
  end

  def kill
    list.each { |t| t.kill }
  end

end
```

Synchronizing Threads

Why is synchronization necessary? It is because the "interleaving" of operations causes variables and other entities to be accessed in ways that aren't obvious from reading the code of the individual threads. Two or more threads accessing the same variable might interact with each other in ways that are unforeseen and difficult to debug.

Let's take this simple piece of code as an example:

```
x = 0
t1 = Thread.new do
  1.upto(1000) do
    x = x + 1
  end
end

t2 = Thread.new do
  1.upto(1000) do
    x = x + 1
  end
end

t1.join
t2.join
puts x
```

The variable x starts at 0. Each thread increments it a thousand times. Logic tells us that x must be 2000 when it is printed out.

But what have we here? On one particular system, it prints 1044 as the result. What has gone wrong?

Our code assumes that the incrementing of an integer is an *atomic* (or indivisible) operation. But it isn't. Consider the following logic flow. We put thread t1 on the left side and t2 on the right. Each separate timeslice is on a separate line, and we assume that when we enter this piece of logic, x has the value 123.

t1	t2
Retrieve value of x (123)	
	Retrieve value of x (123)
Add one to value (124)	
	Add one to value (124)
Store result back in x	
	Store result back in x

It's obvious that each thread is doing a simple increment from its own point of view. In this case, also obvious is that x is only 124 after having been incremented by both threads.

This is only the simplest of synchronization problems. The worst ones become truly difficult to manage and also become genuine objects of study by computer scientists and mathematicians.

Performing Simple Synchronization with Critical Sections

The simplest form of synchronization is to use a *critical section*. When a thread enters a critical section of code, this technique guarantees that no other thread will run until the first thread has left its critical section.

The Thread.critical accessor, when set to true, will prevent other threads from being scheduled. Here we look at the example we just mentioned and use this technique to fix it.

```
x = 0
t1 = Thread.new do
  1.upto(1000) do
    Thread.critical = true
    x = x + 1
    Thread.critical = false
  end
end

t2 = Thread.new do
  1.upto(1000) do
    Thread.critical = true
    x = x + 1
    Thread.critical = false
  end
end

t1.join
t2.join
puts x
```

Now the logic flow is forced to resemble the following. (Of course, outside of the incrementing part, the threads are free to interleave operations more or less randomly.)

```
t1                                t2
_____            _____


Retrieve value of x (123)
Add one to value (124)
Store result back in x
                                  Retrieve value of x (124)
                                  Add one to value (125)
                                  Store result back in x
```

It is possible to perform combinations of thread manipulation operations that cause a thread to be scheduled even if another thread is in a critical section. In the simplest case, a thread that is *newly created* will be run immediately regardless of whether another thread is in a critical section. For this reason, this technique should be used only in the simplest of circumstances.

Synchronizing Access to Resources (mutex.rb)

Let's take a Web indexing application as an example. We retrieve words from multiple sources over the Net and store them in a hash. The word itself will be the key and the value will be a string that identifies the document and the line number within the document.

This is a very crude example. But we will make it even more crude with these simplifying assumptions:

- We will represent the remote documents as simple strings.
- We will limit it to three such strings (simple hard-coded data).
- We will simulate the variability of Net access with random sleeps.

So let's look at Listing 7.1. It doesn't even print out the data it collects, but only a (non-unique) count of the number of words found. Note that every time the hash is examined or changed, we call the `hesitate` method to sleep for a random interval. This will cause the program to run in a less deterministic and more realistic way.

LISTING 7.1   Flawed Indexing Example (with a Race Condition)

```
$list = []
$list[0]="shoes ships\nsealing-wax"
$list[1]="cabbages kings"
$list[2]="quarks\nships\ncabbages"

def hesitate
  sleep rand(0)
end

$hash = {}

def process_list(listnum)
  lnum = 0
  $list[listnum].each do |line|
    words = line.chomp.split
    words.each do |w|
      hesitate
      if $hash[w]
        hesitate
```

7

RUBY THREADS

LISTING 7.1   Continued

```
          $hash[w] += ["#{listnum}:#{lnum}"]
        else
          hesitate
          $hash[w] = ["#{listnum{:#{lnum}"]
        end
      end
      lnum += 1
    end
  end


t1 = Thread.new(0) { |list| process_list(list) }
t2 = Thread.new(1) { |list| process_list(list) }
t3 = Thread.new(2) { |list| process_list(list) }

t1.join
t2.join
t3.join

count = 0
$hash.values.each do |v|
  count += v.size
end

puts "Total: #{count} words"      # May print 7 or 8!
```

But there is a problem. If your system behaves as ours has, there are two possible numbers this program can output! In our tests, it prints the answers 7 and 8 with approximately equal likelihood. In a situation with more words and more lists, there would be even more variation.

Let's try to fix this with a *mutex* that controls access to a shared resource. (The term is derived, of course, from the words *mutual exclusion*.) The Mutex library will allow us to create and manipulate a mutex. We can lock it when we are about to access the hash and unlock it when we have finished with it (see Listing 7.2).

LISTING 7.2   Mutex Protected Indexing Example

```
require "thread.rb"

$list = []
$list[0]="shoes ships\nsealing-wax"
$list[1]="cabbages kings"
$list[2]="quarks\nships\ncabbages"
```

LISTING 7.2 Continued

```ruby
def hesitate
  sleep rand(0)
end

$hash = {}

$mutex = Mutex.new

def process_list(listnum)
  lnum = 0
  $list[listnum].each do |line|
    words = line.chomp.split
    words.each do |w|
      hesitate
      $mutex.lock
        if $hash[w]
          hesitate
          $hash[w] += ["#{listnum}:#{lnum}"]
        else
          hesitate
          $hash[w] = ["#{listnum{:#{lnum}"]
        end
      $mutex.unlock
    end
    lnum += 1
  end
end

t1 = Thread.new(0) { |list| process_list(list) }
t2 = Thread.new(1) { |list| process_list(list) }
t3 = Thread.new(2) { |list| process_list(list) }

t1.join
t2.join
t3.join

count = 0
$hash.values.each do |v|
  count += v.size
end

puts "Total: #{count} words"     # Always prints 8!
```

We should mention that in addition to `lock`, the `Mutex` class also has a `try_lock` method. It behaves the same as `lock` except that if another thread already has the lock, it will return `false` immediately rather than waiting.

```
$mutex = Mutex.new
t1 = Thread.new { $mutex.lock; sleep 30 }

sleep 1

t2 = Thread.new do
  if $mutex.try_lock
    puts "Locked it"
  else
    puts "Could not lock"   # Prints immediately
  end
end

sleep 2
```

This feature is useful any time a thread doesn't want to be blocked.

Using the Predefined Synchronized Queue Classes

The thread library `thread.rb` has a couple of classes that will be useful from time to time. The class `Queue` is a thread-aware queue that synchronizes access to the ends of the queue; that is, different threads can use the same queue without fear of problems. The class `SizedQueue` is essentially the same, except that it allows a limit to be placed on the size of the queue (the number of elements it can contain).

These have much the same set of methods available because `SizedQueue` actually inherits from `Queue`. The descendant also has the accessor `max`—used to get or set the maximum size of the queue.

```
buff = SizedQueue.new(25)
upper1 = buff.max         # 25
# Now raise it...
buff.max = 50
upper2 = buff.max         # 50
```

Listing 7.3 shows a simple producer-consumer illustration. The consumer is delayed slightly longer on the average (through a longer sleep) so that the items will pile up a little.

LISTING 7.3   The Producer-Consumer Problem

```
require "thread"

buffer = SizedQueue.new(2)
```

LISTING 7.3   Continued

```ruby
producer = Thread.new do
  item = 0
  loop do
    sleep rand 0
    puts "Producer makes #{item}"
    buffer.enq item
    item += 1
  end
end

consumer = Thread.new do
  loop do
    sleep (rand 0)+0.9
    item = buffer.deq
    puts "Consumer retrieves #{item}"
    puts "  waiting = #{buffer.num_waiting}"
  end
end

sleep 60   # Run a minute, then die and kill threads
```

The methods enq and deq are the recommended way to get items into and out of the queue. We can also use push to add to the queue and pop or shift to remove items, but these names have somewhat less mnemonic value when we are explicitly using a queue.

The method empty? tests for an empty queue, and clear causes a queue to be empty. The method size (or its alias length) returns the actual number of items in the queue.

```ruby
# Assume no other threads interfering...

buff = Queue.new
buff.enq "one"
buff.enq "two"
buff.enq "three"
n1 = buff.size        # 3
flag1 = buff.empty?   # false
buff.clear
n2 = buff.size        # 0
flag2 = buff.empty?   # true
```

The num_waiting method is the number of threads waiting to access the queue. In the non-sized queue, this is the number of threads waiting to remove elements; in the sized queue, this is also the threads waiting to add elements to the queue.

An optional parameter `non_block` defaults to `false` for the `deq` method in the `Queue` class. If it is `true`, an empty queue will give a `ThreadError` rather than blocking the thread.

Using Condition Variables

And he called for his fiddlers three.

—"Old King Cole" (traditional folk tune)

A *condition variable* is really just a queue of threads. It is used in conjunction with a mutex to provide a higher level of control when synchronizing threads.

A condition variable is always associated with a specific mutex; it is used to relinquish control of the mutex *until a certain condition has been met.* Imagine a situation in which a thread has a mutex locked but cannot continue because the circumstances aren't right. It can sleep on the condition variable and wait to be awakened when the condition is met.

It is important to understand that while a thread is waiting on a condition variable, the mutex is released so that other threads can gain access. It is also important to realize that when another thread does a signal operation (to awaken the waiting thread), the waiting thread *reacquires* the lock on the mutex.

Here, we present a very contrived example in the tradition of the dining philosophers. Imagine a table in which three violinists are seated, all of whom want to take turns playing. However, there are only two violins and only one bow. Obviously, a violinist can play only if she has one of the violins *and* the lone bow at the same time.

We keep a count of the violins and bows available. When a player wants a violin or a bow, she must wait for it. In our code, we protect the test with a mutex and do separate waits for the violin and the bow—both associated with that mutex. If a violin or a bow isn't available, the thread sleeps. It loses the mutex until it is awakened by another thread signaling that the resource is available, whereupon the original thread wakes up and once again owns the lock on the mutex.

Let's take a look at Listing 7.4.

LISTING 7.4   The Three Violinists

```
require "thread"

$music  = Mutex.new
$violin = ConditionVariable.new
$bow    = ConditionVariable.new

$violinsFree = 2
$bowsFree    = 1
```

LISTING 7.4   Continued

```ruby
def musician(n)
  loop do
    sleep rand 0
    $music.synchronize do
      $violin.wait($music) while $violinsFree == 0
      $violinsFree -= 1
      puts "#{n} has a violin"
      puts "violins #$violinsFree, bows #$bowsFree"

      $bow.wait($music) while $bowsFree == 0
      $bowsFree -= 1
      puts "#{n} has a bow"
      puts "violins #$violinsFree, bows #$bowsFree"
    end

    sleep rand 0
    puts "#{n}:  (...playing...)"
    sleep rand 0
    puts "#{n}: Now I've finished."

    $music.synchronize do
      $violinsFree += 1
      $violin.signal if $violinsFree == 1
      $bowsFree += 1
      $bow.signal if $bowsFree == 1
    end
  end
end

threads = []
3.times do |i|
  threads << Thread.new { musician(i) }
end

threads.each {|t| t.join }
```

We believe that this solution will never deadlock, although we've found it difficult to prove. But it is interesting to note that this algorithm isn't a *fair* one. In our tests, the first player always got to play more often than the other two, and the second more often than the third. The cause and cure for this behavior are left as an interesting exercise.

Using Other Synchronization Techniques

Yet another synchronization mechanism is the *monitor*, implemented in Ruby in the form of the monitor.rb library. This technique is somewhat more advanced than the mutex; notably, a mutex lock cannot be nested, but a monitor lock can.

The trivial case of this would never occur. That is, no one would ever write the following:

```
$mutex = Mutex.new

$mutex.synchronize do
  $mutex.synchronize do
    #...
  end
end
```

But it might happen this way (or through a recursive method call). The result is a deadlock in any of these situations. Avoiding deadlock in this circumstance is one of the advantages of the Monitor mixin.

```
$mutex = Mutex.new

def some_method
  $mutex.synchronize do
    #...
    some_other_method    # Deadlock!
  end
end

def some_other_method
  $mutex.synchronize do
    #...
  end
end
```

The Monitor mixin is typically used to extend any object. The new_cond method can then be used to instantiate a condition variable.

The class ConditionVariable in monitor.rb is enhanced from the definition in the thread library. It has methods wait_until and wait_while, which block a thread based on a condition. It also allows a timeout while waiting because the wait method has a timeout parameter that is a number of seconds (defaulting to nil).

Because we are rapidly running out of thread examples, we present to you a rewrite of the Queue and SizedQueue classes using the monitor technique in Listing 7.5. The code is by Shugo Maeda, used with permission.

Listing 7.5   Implementing a Queue with a Monitor

```
# Author:  Shugo Maeda

require "monitor"

class Queue
  def initialize
    @que = []
    @monitor = Monitor.new
    @empty_cond = @monitor.new_cond
  end

  def enq(obj)
    @monitor.synchronize do
      @que.push(obj)
      @empty_cond.signal
    end
  end

  def deq
    @monitor.synchronize do
      while @que.empty?
        @empty_cond.wait
      end
      return @que.shift
    end
  end
end

class SizedQueue < Queue
  attr :max

  def initialize(max)
    super()
    @max = max
    @full_cond = @monitor.new_cond
  end

  def enq(obj)
    @monitor.synchronize do
      while @que.length >= @max
        @full_cond.wait
      end
      super(obj)
    end
  end
```

LISTING 7.5   Continued

```
      def deq
        @monitor.synchronize do
          obj = super
          if @que.length < @max
            @full_cond.signal
          end
          return obj
        end
      end

      def max=(max)
        @monitor.synchronize do
          @max = max
          @full_cond.broadcast
        end
      end
    end
```

The sync.rb library is one more way of performing thread synchronization. For those who know and care about such things, it implements a two-phase lock with a counter. At the time of this writing, the only documentation is inside the library itself.

Allowing Timeout of an Operation

There are many situations in which we want to allow a maximum length of time for an action to be performed. This avoids infinite loops and allows an additional level of control over processing. A feature such as this is useful in the environment of the Net, where we might or might not get a response from a distant server, and in other circumstances.

The timeout.rb library is a thread-based solution to this problem. The timeout method executes the block associated with the method call; when the specified number of seconds has elapsed, it throws a TimeoutError that can be caught with a rescue clause (see Listing 7.6).

LISTING 7.6   A Timeout Example

```
require "timeout.rb"

flag = false
answer = nil

begin
  timeout(5) do
    puts "I want a cookie!"
```

LISTING 7.6   Continued

```
      answer = gets.chomp
      flag = true
    end
  rescue TimeoutError
    flag = false
  end

  if flag
    if answer == "cookie"
      puts "Thank you! Chomp, chomp, ..."
    else
      puts "That's not a cookie!"
      exit
    end
  else
    puts "Hey, too slow!"
    exit
  end

  puts "Bye now..."
```

Waiting for an Event

There are many situations in which we might want to have one or more threads monitoring the outside world while other threads are doing other things. The examples here are all rather contrived, but they illustrate the general principle.

Here, we see three threads doing the work of an application. Another thread simply wakes up every five seconds, checks the global variable $flag, and wakes up three other threads when it sees the flag set. This saves the three worker threads from interacting directly with the two other threads and possibly making multiple attempts to awaken them.

```
$job = false
work1 = Thread.new { job1() }
work2 = Thread.new { job2() }
work3 = Thread.new { job3() }

thread5 = Thread.new { Thread.stop; job4() }
thread6 = Thread.new { Thread.stop; job5() }

watcher = Thread.new do
  loop do
    sleep 5
```

```
      if $flag
        thread5.wakeup
        thread6.wakeup
        Thread.exit
      end
    end
  end
```

If at any point during the execution of the job methods the variable $flag becomes true, thread5 and thread6 are guaranteed to start within five seconds. After that, the watcher thread terminates.

In this next example, we are waiting for a file to be created. We check every 30 seconds for it, and start another thread if we see it; meanwhile, other threads can be doing anything at all. Actually, we are watching for three separate files here.

```
def waitfor(filename)
  loop do
    if File.exist? filename
      file_processor = Thread.new do
        process_file(filename)
      end
      Thread.exit
    else
      sleep 30
    end
  end
end

waiter1 = Thread.new { waitfor("Godot") }
sleep 10
waiter2 = Thread.new { waitfor("Guffman") }
sleep 10
headwaiter = Thread.new { waitfor("head") }

# Main thread goes off to do other things...
```

There are many other situations in which a thread might wait for an outside event, such as a networked application where the server at the other end of a socket is slow or unreliable.

Continuing Processing During I/O

Frequently, an application might have one or more I/O operations that are lengthy or time-consuming. This is especially true in the case of user input because a user typing at a keyboard is slower even than any disk operation. We can make use of this time by using threads.

Consider the case of a chess program that must wait for the human player to make her move. Of course, we present here only the barest outline of this concept.

We assume that the iterator predictMove will repeatedly generate likely moves that the person might make (and then determine the program's own responses to those moves). Then when the person moves, it is possible that the move has already been anticipated.

```ruby
scenario = {}     # move-response hash
humans_turn = true
thinking_ahead = Thread.new(board) do
  predictMove do |m|
    scenario[m] = myResponse(board,m)
    Thread.exit if humans_turn == false
  end
end

human_move = getHumanMove(board)
humans_turn = false    # Stop the thread gracefully

# Now we can access scenario which may contain the
# move the person just made...
```

We have to make the disclaimer that real chess programs don't usually work this way. The concern is usually to search quickly and thoroughly to a certain depth; in real life, a better solution would be to store partial state information obtained during the thinking thread, and then continue in the same vein until the program finds a good response or time runs out for its turn.

Implementing Parallel Iterators

Imagine that you wanted to iterate in parallel over more than one object. That is, for each of *n* objects, you want the first item of each of them, the second item of each, the third, and so on.

To make this a little more concrete, look at the following example. Here we assume that compose is the name of the magic method that provides a composition of iterators. We also assume that every object specified has a default iterator each that will be used, and that each object contributes one item at a time.

```ruby
arr1 = [1, 2, 3, 4]
arr2 = [5, 10, 15, 20]
compose(arr1, arr2) do |a,b|
  puts "#{a} and #{b}"
end

# Should output:
# 1 and 5
# 2 and 10
```

```
# 3 and 15
# 4 and 20
```

We could take the most simple-minded approach and iterate over the objects to completion, one after another, storing the results. But if we want a more elegant solution, one that doesn't actually store all the items, threads are the only easy solution. Our solution is shown in Listing 7.7.

LISTING 7.7   Iterating in Parallel

```ruby
def compose(*objects)

  threads = []
  for obj in objects do
    threads << Thread.new(obj) do |myobj|
      me = Thread.current
      me[:queue] = []
      myobj.each do |element|
        me[:queue].push element
      end
    end
  end

  list = [0]                        # Dummy non-nil value
  while list.nitems > 0 do          # Still some non-nils
    list = []
    for thr in threads
      list << thr[:queue].shift     # Remove one from each
    end
    yield list if list.nitems > 0   # Don't yield all nils
  end

end

x = [1, 2, 3, 4, 5, 6, 7, 8]
y = " first\n second\n  third\n fourth\n  fifth\n"
z = %w[a b c d e f]


compose(x, y, z) do |a,b,c|
  p [a, b, c]
end

# Output:
#
# [1, " first\n", "a"]
```

LISTING 7.7 Continued

```
# [2, " second\n", "b"]
# [3, "  third\n", "c"]
# [4, " fourth\n", "d"]
# [5, "  fifth\n", "e"]
# [6, nil, "f"]
# [7, nil, nil]
# [8, nil, nil]
```

Notice that we do *not* assume that the objects all have the same number of items over which to iterate. If an iterator "runs out" before the others, it will generate nil values until the longest-running iterator has exhausted itself.

Of course, it is possible to write a more general method that will grab more than one value from each iteration. (After all, not all iterators return just one value at a time.) We could let the first parameter specify the number of values per iterator.

It would also be possible to use arbitrary iterators (rather than the default each). We might pass in their names as strings and use send to invoke them. Doubtless there are other tricks that could be performed.

However, we think that the example given here is adequate for most circumstances. We will leave the other variations as an exercise for you.

Recursive Deletion in Parallel

Just for fun, let's take an example from Chapter 4, "External Data Manipulation," and "parallelize" it. (No, we don't mean *parallel* in the sense of using multiple processors.) The recursive deletion routine appears here in a threaded form. When we find that a directory entry is itself a directory, we start a new thread to traverse that directory and delete its contents.

As we go along, we keep track of the threads we've created in an array called threads; because this is a local variable, each thread will have its own copy of the array. It can be accessed by only one thread at a time, and there is no need to synchronize access to it.

Note also that we pass fullname into the thread block so that we don't have to worry about the thread accessing a changing value. The thread uses fn as a local copy of the same variable.

When we have traversed an entire directory, we want to wait on the threads we have created before deleting the directory we've just finished working on.

```
def delete_all(dir)
  threads = []
  Dir.foreach(dir) do |e|
    # Don't bother with . and ..
    next if [".",".."].include? e
```

```
      fullname = dir + File::Separator + e
      if FileTest::directory?(fullname)
        threads << Thread.new(fullname) do |fn|
          delete_all(fn)
        end
      else
        File.delete(fullname)
      end
    end
    threads.each { |t| t.join }
    Dir.delete(dir)
  end

  delete_all("/tmp/stuff")
```

Is this actually faster than the non-threaded version? We've found that the answer isn't consistent. It probably depends on your operating system as well as on the actual directory structure being deleted, that is, its depth, size of files, and so on.

Summary

Threads can be a useful technique in many circumstances, but they can be somewhat problematic to code and debug. This is particularly true when we use sophisticated synchronization methods to achieve correct results.

In the next chapter, we move away from a discussion of the programming technique back to a task-oriented topic. We'll discuss the use of Ruby for everyday scripting and system administration tasks.

Scripting and System Administration

IN THIS CHAPTER

Thus spake the master programmer: "Though a program be but three lines long, someday it will have to be maintained."

　　—Geoffrey James, *The Tao of Programming*

As programmers, we often need to glue programs together with little scripts that are able to talk to the operating system at a fairly high level and run external programs. This is especially true in the UNIX world, where shell scripts are relied on daily for countless tasks.

Ruby isn't always a convenient glue language because it is more general-purpose than that. But in the long run, anything that can be done in ksh, bash, or the others can also be done in Ruby.

In many cases, you might just as well use one of the more traditional languages for this purpose. The advantage that Ruby has, of course, is that it really is a general-purpose language, full-featured and truly object-oriented. On the theory that people might want to use Ruby to talk to the OS at this level, we present here a few tricks that might prove useful.

We've found this chapter a little hard to organize because much of the functionality could logically be grouped in different ways. If you don't find what you are looking for in the expected place, scan the rest of the chapter also.

In addition, much of what *could* be covered here is actually dealt with in other chapters entirely. Refer in particular to Chapter 4, "External Data Manipulation," which covers file I/O and attributes of files. These features are frequently used in the kind of scripts we will discuss in this chapter.

Running External Programs

A language can't be a glue language unless it can run external programs. Ruby offers more than one way to do this.

We can't resist mentioning here that if you are going to run an external program, you should be certain you know what that program is doing. We're thinking about viruses and other potentially destructive programs here. Don't just run any old command string, especially if it came from a source outside the program. This is true regardless of whether the application is Web-based.

Using `system` and `exec`

The `system` method (in `Kernel`) is equivalent to the C call of the same name. It will execute the given command in a subshell.

```
system("/usr/games/fortune")
# Output goes to stdout as usual...
```

Note that the second parameter, if present, will be used as list of arguments; in most cases, the arguments can also be specified as part of the command string with the same effect. The only difference is that filename expansion is done on the first string but not on the others.

```
system("rm", "/tmp/file1")
system("rm /tmp/file2")
# Both the above work fine.

# However, below, there's a difference...
system("echo *")     # Print list of all files
system("echo","*")   # Print an asterisk (no filename
                     # expansion done)

# More complex command lines also work.
system("ls -l | head -n 1")
```

Let's look at how this works on the Windows family of operating systems. For a simple executable, the behavior should be the same. Depending on your exact variant of Ruby, invoking a shell `builtin` might require a reference to `cmd.exe`, the Windows command processor (which might be `command.com` on some versions). Both cases, executable and `builtin`, are shown here:

```
system("notepad.exe ","myfile.txt")  # No problem...
system("cmd /c dir","somefile")      # 'dir' is a builtin!
```

Another solution to this is to use the `Win32API` library and define your own version of the `system` method.

```
require "Win32API"

def system(cmd)
  sys = Win32API.new("crtdll", "system", ['P'], 'L')
  sys.Call(cmd)
end

system("dir")  # cmd /c not needed!
```

So the behavior of `system` can be made relatively OS-independent. But, getting back to the big picture, if you want to capture the output (for example, in a variable), `system` of course isn't the right way (see the next section).

We'll also mention `exec` here. The `exec` method behaves much the same as `system`, except that the new process actually overlays or replaces the current one. Thus any code following the `exec` won't be executed.

```
puts "Here's a directory listing:"
exec("ls", "-l")

puts "This line is never reached!"
```

Command Output Substitution

The simplest way to capture command output is to use the *backtick* (also called *backquote* or *grave accent*) to delimit the command. Here are a couple of examples:

```
listing = `ls -l`   # Multiple lines in one string
now = `date`        # "Mon Mar 12 16:50:11 CST 2001"
```

The generalized delimiter %x calls the backquote operator (which is really a `Kernel` method). It works essentially the same way:

```
listing = %x(ls -l)
now = %x(date)
```

The %x form is often useful when the string to be executed contains characters such as single and double quotes.

Because the backquote method really is a method (in some sense), it is possible to override it. Here we change the functionality so that we return an array of lines rather than a single string. Of course, we have to save an alias to the old method so that we can call it.

```
alias old_execute `

def `(cmd)
  out = old_execute(cmd)  # Call the old backtick method
  out.split("\n")         # Return an array of strings!
end

entries = `ls -l /tmp`
num = entries.size                      # 95

first3lines = %x(ls -l | head -n 3)
how_many = first3lines.size             # 3
```

Note that, as we show here, the functionality of %x is affected when we perform this redefinition.

Here is another example. Here we append a "shellism" to the end of the command to ensure that standard error is mixed with standard output:

```
alias old_execute `

def `(cmd)
  old_execute(cmd + " 2>&1")
end

entries = `ls -l /tmp/foobar`
# "/tmp/foobar: No such file or directory\n"
```

There are many other ways we could change the default behavior of the backquote.

Manipulating Processes

We mention process manipulation in this section even though a new process might or might not involve calling an external program. The principal way to create a new process is with the `fork` method. This takes its name from Unix tradition, from the idea of a fork in the path of execution, like a fork in the road.

The `fork` method in `Kernel` (also found in the `Process` module) shouldn't be confused with the `Thread` instance method of the same name.

There are two ways of invoking the `fork` method. The first is the more Unix-like way; we simply call it and test its return value. If that value is `nil`, we are in the child process; otherwise we execute the parent code. The value returned to the parent is actually the *process ID* (or *pid*) of the child.

```
pid = fork
if (pid == nil)
  puts "Ah, I must be the child."
  puts "I guess I'll speak as a child."
else
  puts "I'm the parent."
  puts "Time to put away childish things."
end
```

In this unrealistic example, the output might be interleaved or the parent's output might appear first. For purposes of this example, it's irrelevant.

We should also note that the child process might outlive the parent. We've seen that this isn't the case with Ruby threads, but system-level processes are entirely different.

The second form of `fork` takes a block. The code in the block comprises the child process. Our previous example could thus be rewritten in this simpler way:

```
fork do
  puts "Ah, I must be the child."
  puts "I guess I'll speak as a child."
end

puts "I'm the parent."
puts "Time to put away childish things."
```

The pid is still returned, of course. We just don't show it here.

When we want to wait for a process to finish, we can call the `wait` method in the `Process` module. It waits for any child to exit and returns the process ID of that child. The `wait2` method will behave similarly except that it returns a two-value array consisting of the pid and a left-shifted exit status.

```
pid1 = fork { sleep 5; exit 3 }
pid2 = fork { sleep 2; exit 3 }

Process.wait     # Returns pid2
Process.wait2    # Returns [pid1,768]
```

To wait for a specific child, use `waitpid` and `waitpid2`, respectively.

```
pid3 = fork { sleep 5; exit 3 }
pid4 = fork { sleep 2; exit 3 }

Process.waitpid(pid4,Process::WNOHANG)     # Returns pid4
Process.waitpid2(pid3,Process:WNOHANG)     # Returns [pid3,768]
```

If the second parameter is unspecified, the call might block (if no such child exists). It might be ORed logically with `Process::WUNTRACED` to catch child processes that have been stopped. This second parameter is rather OS sensitive; experiment before relying on its behavior.

The `exit!` method will exit immediately from a process (bypassing any exit handlers). The integer value, if specified, will be returned as a return code; -1 (not 0) is the default.

```
pid1 = fork { exit! }      # Return -1 exit code
pid2 = fork { exit! 0 }    # Return 0 exit code
```

The `pid` and `ppid` methods will return the process ID of the current process and the parent process, respectively.

```
proc1 = Process.pid
fork do
  if Process.ppid == proc1
    puts "proc1 is my parent"  # Prints this message
  else
    puts "What's going on?"
  end
end
```

The `kill` method can be used to send a Unix-style signal to a process. The first parameter can be an integer, a POSIX signal name including the `SIG` prefix, or a non-prefixed signal name. The second parameter represents a pid; if it is zero, it refers to the current process.

```
Process.kill(1,pid1)          # Send signal 1 to process pid1
Process.kill("HUP",pid2)      # Send SIGHUP to pid2
Process.kill("SIGHUP",pid2)   # Send SIGHUP to pid3
Process.kill("SIGHUP",0)      # Send SIGHUP to self
```

The `Kernel.trap` method can be used to handle such signals. It typically takes a signal number or name and a block to be executed.

```
trap(1) { puts "Caught signal 1" }
sleep 2
Process.kill(1,0)  # Send to self
```

For advanced uses of `trap`, consult Ruby and Unix references.

The `Process` module also has methods for examining and setting such attributes as user ID, effective user ID, priority, and others. Consult any Ruby reference for details.

Manipulating Standard Input/Output

We've shown how `IO.popen` and `IO.pipe` work in Chapter 4. But there is a library we haven't mentioned that can prove handy at times.

The `Open3.rb` library contains a method `popen3`, which will return an array of three `IO` objects. These objects correspond to the standard input, standard output, and standard error for the process kicked off by the `popen3` call. Here's an example:

```
require "open3"

filenames = %w[ file1 file2 this that another one_more ]

inp, out, err = Open3.popen3("xargs", "ls", "-l")

filenames.each { |f| inp.puts f }   # Write to the process's stdin
inp.close                           # Close is necessary!

output = out.readlines              # Read from its stdout
errout = err.readlines              # Also read from its stderr

puts "Sent #{filenames.size} lines of input."
puts "Got back #{output.size} lines from stdout"
puts "and #{errout.size} lines from stderr."
```

This contrived little example does an `ls -l` on each of the specified filenames and captures the standard output and standard error separately. Note that the `close` is needed so that the sub-process will be aware that end of file has been reached.

For additional information refer to the section "The Shell Library."

Command-Line Options and Arguments

Rumors of the death of the command line are greatly exaggerated. Although we live in the age of the GUI, every day thousands of us retreat to the older text-based interfaces for one reason or another.

8

SCRIPTING AND
SYSTEM
ADMINISTRATION

Ruby has many of its roots in Unix, as we've said. Yet even in the Windows world, there is such a thing as a command line; and frankly, we don't see it going away any time soon.

When operating at this level, parameters and switches are used to communicate with the program at the time of its invocation. We show here how to deal with these parameters (or arguments) and switches (or options).

Parsing Command-Line Options

The `getoptlong` library is probably the most commonly used command-line parser. (The `getopts.rb` library is considered obsolete because it has more limited functionality.) It can accept both single-letter and longer option names, and it recognizes the double hyphen (—) as meaning the end of all the options. Its behavior is essentially the same as its GNU counterpart, for those who are familiar with that code.

The `GetoptLong` class must be instantiated, giving a parser object. This object can then be set up with the allowed command-line options and used to retrieve them one at a time.

The parser object has a `set_options` method that takes a list of arrays. Each array contains one or more options (as strings) and one argument flag, which tells whether an argument is allowed for that option. The options in each array are considered synonyms; the first one mentioned is the canonical name of the option, as returned by a `get` operation.

As an example, suppose that we have a tool with these options: `-h` or `—help` will print help information, `-f` or `—file` will specify a filename argument, and `-l` or `—lines` will truncate the output after the specified number of lines (defaulting to 100).

We could begin in this way:

```
require "getoptlong"

parser = GetoptLong.new
parser.set_options(
        ["-h", "—help", GetoptLong::NO_ARGUMENT],
        ["-f", "—file", GetoptLong::REQUIRED_ARGUMENT],
        ["-l", "—lines", GetoptLong::OPTIONAL_ARGUMENT])
```

Now we can use a loop to call `get` repeatedly (see Listing 8.1); we can fake a post-test loop because we are using `begin` and `end` anyway. A synonym for `get` is `get_option`; there are also iterators named `each` and `each_option`, which are identical.

LISTING 8.1   Getting Command-Line Options

```
filename = nil
lines = 0                    # Default means no truncating
```

LISTING 8.1 Continued

```
loop do
  begin
    opt, arg = parser.get
    break if not opt
    # Only for debugging purposes...
    puts (opt + " => " + arg)

      case opt
        when "-h"
          puts "Usage: ..."
          break             # Stop processing if -h
        when "-f"
          filename = arg   # Save the file argument
        when "-l"
          if arg != ""
            lines = arg     # Save lines arg (if given)
          else
            lines = 100    # Default for truncating
          end
      end

    rescue => err
      puts err
      break
  end
end

puts "filename = #{filename}"
puts "lines    = #{lines}"
```

Note that `get` returns `nil` for a nonexistent option but a null string for a nonexistent argument. This could be a bug.

Note also that we are catching errors here. Four possible exceptions that could be raised are summarized here:

AmbiguousOption	A long option name seems to have been abbreviated, but it isn't unique.
InvalidOption	The option is unknown.
MissingArgument	The option is missing its argument.

NeedlessArgument   The option has an argument when it isn't expected to
                          take an argument.

Errors are normally reported to `stderr` when they occur, but the `quiet=` accessor can be set to `true` to override this.

There are other features of `getoptlong`, which we haven't discussed here. See the documentation for further details.

There are also other possibilities out there, such as `OptionParser`, which offer somewhat different functionality and usage. Refer to the Ruby Application Archive for more information.

Working with ARGF

The special global constant `ARGF` represents the pseudo-file resulting from a concatenation of every file named on the command line. It behaves similar to an `IO` object in most ways.

When you have a bare input method (without a receiver), you are typically using a method mixed in from the `Kernel` module. (Examples are `gets` and `readlines`.) The actual source of input will default to `STDIN` if no files are on the command line. If there are files, however, input will be taken from them. End of file will be reached only at the end of the last file.

If you prefer, you can access `ARGF` explicitly.

```
# Copy all files to stdout
puts ARGF.readlines
```

Perhaps contrary to most people's expectations, end of file is set after each file. The previous code fragment will output all the files. This one will output only the first:

```
until ARGF.eof?
  puts ARGF.gets
end
```

Whether this is a bug or a feature, we will leave it up to you to decide. Of course, there are other unexpected surprises that might actually be pleasant. The input isn't simply a stream of bytes flowing through our program; we can actually perform operations such as `seek` and `rewind` on `ARGF` as though it were a real file.

There is a `file` method associated with `ARGF`; it returns an `IO` object corresponding to the file that is currently being processed. As such, the value it returns will change as the files on the command line are processed in sequence.

What if we don't want command-line arguments to be interpreted as files? The solution is to not use the bare (receiverless) call of the input methods. If you want to read standard input, you can use `STDIN` as the receiver, and all will work as expected.

Working with ARGV

The global constant ARGV represents the list of arguments passed to the Ruby program via the command line. This is essentially an array.

```
n = ARGV.size
argstr = '"' + ARGV*"," + '"'
puts "I was given #{n} arguments..."
puts "They are: #{argstr}"
puts "Note that ARGV[0] = #{ARGV[0]}"
```

Assume that we invoke this little program with the arguments red green blue on the command line. It then produces this output:

```
I was given 3 arguments.
They are: "red,green,blue"
Note that ARGV[0] = red
```

Obviously there is no need for an argument count as in the old days; that information is part of the array.

Another thing that might trip up old-timers is the assignment of the zeroth argument to an actual argument (rather than, for example, the script name). The arguments themselves are zero-based rather than one-based, as in C and the various shell languages.

The Shell Library

Ruby isn't necessarily convenient to use as a scripting language in every situation. For example, a Kornshell script can execute external programs simply by naming them, with no extraneous syntax.

The power and flexibility of Ruby has given it a more complex syntax than the average shell language. Additionally its functionality is segmented into different classes, modules, and libraries.

This situation motivated the creation of the Shell library. This library makes it easier to do things, such as connecting commands with pipes and redirecting output to files. It also consolidates functionality from several different sources so that they are transparently accessible from a Shell object.

Using Shell for I/O Redirection

The Shell class has two methods, new and cd, for instantiating a new object. The former creates a shell object associated with the current directory; the latter creates a shell object whose working directory will be the one specified.

```
require "shell"

sh1 = Shell.new              # Work in the current directory
sh2 = Shell.cd("/tmp/hal")   # Work in /tmp/hal
```

The `Shell` library defines a few built-in commands as methods, such as `echo`, `cat`, and `tee`. These always return objects of class `Filter` (as do the user-defined commands that we'll look at shortly).

The nice thing about a `Filter` is that it understands I/O redirection. The methods (or operators) <, >, and | are defined so that they behave more or less as we expect from long experience with shell scripts.

If a redirection method has a string as a parameter, that string is taken to be the name of a file. If it has an `IO` object as a parameter, that object is used for the input or output operation. Here are some small examples:

```
sh = Shell.new

# Print the motd file to stdout
sh.cat("/etc/motd") > STDOUT

# Print it again
(sh.cat < "/etc/motd") > STDOUT
(sh.echo "This is a test") > "myfile.txt"

# Append a line to /etc/motd
sh.echo("Hello, world!") >> "/etc/motd"

# Cat two files to stdout, tee-ing to a third
(sh.cat "file1" "file2") | (tee "file3") > STDOUT
```

Note that the > binds tightly. The parentheses that you see in the preceding code are necessary in most cases. Here are two correct usages and one incorrect one:

```
# Ruby parser understands this...
sh.cat("myfile.txt") > STDOUT

# ...and this also.
(sh.cat "myfile.txt") > STDOUT

# TypeError! (a precedence problem)
sh.cat "myfile.txt" > STDOUT
```

Note that it's also possible to install system commands of your own choosing. The method `def_system_command` will accomplish this. For example, here we define two methods `ls` and `ll`, which will list files in the current directory (short and long listings, respectively).

```
# Method name is identical to command...
# only one parameter necessary
Shell.def_system_command "ls"

# Two parameters needed here
Shell.def_system_command "ll", "ls -l"

sh = Shell.new
sh.ls > STDOUT    # Short listing
sh.ll > STDOUT    # Long listing
```

You will notice that in many cases we explicitly send output to STDOUT. This is because output from a Shell command doesn't automatically go anywhere. It's simply associated with the Filter object until that object is connected to a file or an IO object.

Other Notes on `shell.rb`

The transact method will execute a block using the receiver for its context. Thus we can use this shorthand:

```
sh = Shell.new
sh.transact do
  echo("A line of data") > "somefile.txt"
  cat("somefile.txt","otherfile.txt") > "thirdfile"
  cat("thirdfile") | tee("file4") > STDOUT
end
```

There is an iterator foreach that will take either a file or a directory as a parameter. If it is a file, it will iterate over the lines of that file; if it is a directory, it will iterate over the filenames in that directory.

```
sh = Shell.new

# List all lines in /tmp/foo
sh.foreach("/tmp/foo") {|l| puts l }

# List all files in /tmp
sh.foreach("/tmp") {|f| puts f }
```

There are pushdir and popdir methods that will save and restore the current directory, respectively. Aliases are pushd and popd. The method pwd will determine the current working directory; aliases are getwd, cwd, and dir.

```
sh = Shell.cd "/home"

puts sh.pwd      # /home
sh.pushd "/tmp"
```

```
puts sh.pwd        # /tmp

sh.popd
puts sh.pwd        # /home
```

For convenience, numerous methods are imported into `Shell` from various sources, including the `File` class, the `FileTest` module, and the `ftools.rb` library. This saves the trouble of doing requires and includes, creating objects, qualifying method calls, and so on.

```
sh = Shell.new
flag1 = sh.exist? "myfile"        # Test file existence
sh.delete "somefile"              # Delete a file
sh.move "/tmp/foo", "/tmp/bar"    # Move a file
```

There are other features of the `Shell` library we don't cover here. See the associated documentation for more details.

Accessing Environment Variables

Occasionally we need to access *environment variables* as a link between our program and the outer world. An environment variable is essentially a label referring to a piece of text (typically a small piece); they can be used to store configuration information such as paths, usernames, and so on.

The notion of an environment variable is very common in the Unix world. The Windows world has borrowed it from Unix (by way of MS-DOS), so the code we show here should run on variants of both Windows and Unix.

Getting and Setting Environment Variables

The global constant `ENV` can be used as a hash both for purposes of retrieving and assigning values. Here we retrieve the value of an environment variable:

```
mypath = ENV["PATH"]
# Let's get an array now...
dirs = mypath.split(":")
```

Here's an example of setting a variable. We take the trouble to fork another process to illustrate two facts. First of all, a child process inherits the environment variables that its parent knows. Second, an environment variable set by a child is *not* propagated back up to the parent.

```
ENV["alpha"] = "123"
ENV["beta"]  = "456"
puts "Parent: alpha = #{ENV['alpha']}"
puts "Parent: beta  = #{ENV['beta']}"
fork do   # Child code...
```

```
    x = ENV["alpha"]
    ENV["beta"] = "789"
    y = ENV["beta"]
    puts " Child: alpha = #{x}"
    puts " Child: beta  = #{y}"
  end
  Process.wait
  a = ENV["alpha"]
  b = ENV["beta"]
  puts "Parent: alpha = #{a}"
  puts "Parent: beta  = #{b}"
```

The output here would be the following:

```
Parent: alpha = 123
Parent: beta  = 456
 Child: alpha = 123
 Child: beta  = 789
Parent: alpha = 123
Parent: beta  = 456
```

There is a consequence of the fact that parent processes don't know about their children's variables. Because a Ruby program is typically run in a subshell, any variables changed during execution will *not* be reflected in the current shell after execution has terminated.

Storing Environment Variables as an Array or Hash

It's important to realize that ENV isn't really a hash; it just looks like one. For example, we can't call the invert method on it; it gives us a NameError because there is no such method. The reason for this implementation is the close tie between the ENV object and the underlying operating system; setting a value has an actual impact on the OS, a behavior that a mere hash can't mimic.

However, we can call the to_hash method to give us a real live hash:

```
envhash = ENV.to_hash
val2var = envhash.invert
```

Of course, once we have a hash, we can convert it to any other form we prefer (for example, an array):

```
envarr = ENV.to_hash.to_a
```

It's not possible to directly reassign a hash to ENV; but we can fake it easily if we need to:

```
envhash = ENV.to_hash
# Manipulate as needed... then assign back.
envhash.each {|k,v| ENV[k] = v }
```

Importing Environment Variables as Globals

A small library called `importenv.rb` will run through all the environment variables and import them into the program as global variables. It is used in this way:

```
require "importenv"

# Now our environment variables are all globals...
# E.g., $PWD and $LOGNAME

where = $PWD
who = $LOGNAME
puts "In directory #{where}, logged in as #{who}"
```

Note that because the `importenv` uses `trace_var`, the reflection is actually two-way: We can set one of these global variables in our program and the real environment variable will be set in the same way.

```
require "importenv"

puts "My path is #$PATH"
# Prints: /usr/local/bin:/usr/bin:/usr/ucb:/etc:.
$PATH = "/ruby-1.8.0:" + $PATH

puts "My actual $PATH variable is now #{ENV['PATH']}"
# Prints: /ruby-1.8.0:/usr/local/bin:/usr/bin:/usr/ucb:/etc:.
```

Again, we point out that a change in an environment variable within a Ruby program doesn't affect the environment external to the program.

Scripting in Microsoft Windows

Like the ski resort full of girls hunting for husbands and husbands hunting for girls, the situation is not as symmetrical as it might seem.

—Alan Lindsay Mackay

It has been said that Ruby has a Unix bias. In a sense, this is true; it was conceived in a Unix environment and works best there. Yet there are other ports out there at the time of this writing, including DOS and Amiga; and there are others ports in progress, such as Macintosh and Palm OS. But if Unix is the primary platform for Ruby, the secondary platform is Windows.

Windows users certainly aren't left out in the cold. Windows-based tools and libraries are in existence, and more are being created. Much of Ruby is platform-independent anyhow, even the threading capabilities; most of the platform difficulties occur in the areas of I/O, process management, and other similar low-level operations.

One problem for Windows users is that different *variants* of Ruby exist for the Windows platforms. These have little to do with differing versions of Ruby or differing versions of Windows; rather they have to do with how the interpreter was built. It might have been built with gcc or Visual C; it might or might not depend on the Cygwin DLL, and so on.

The environment is changing too rapidly to document at this point. But we will mention a few of the high points in Windows scripting and automation. These techniques and utilities should work for anyone, and if there are problems, the online support community is very helpful with such things.

Using Win32API

The Win32API is exceptionally powerful if you want to code at a fairly low level. Essentially it allows access to any Windows API function in any DLL, making it callable from Ruby code.

The specified function is instantiated as an object, with relevant parameters precisely describing the function being passed into the new method. The first parameter, a string, identifies the DLL containing the function (such as crtdll). The second parameter is the name of the function itself. The third parameter is an array of strings identifying the types of the function parameters (the import array); and the fourth is a string specifying the function's return type.

The import array can contain these (not case sensitive) values:

```
I    Integer
L    Number
N    Number
P    Pointer to a string
```

The export string can also contain any one of these. Additionally it can take the value V, meaning void.

After we have created this object, we can invoke its call method to call the Windows function. Note that Call is an alias.

Here we call the Windows function GetCursorPos, which returns a pointer to a POINT structure. This structure consists of two long fields; we can use unpack to examine these fields and retrieve their values.

```
result = "0"*8   # Eight bytes (enough for two longs)
getCursorXY = Win32API.new("user32","GetCursorPos",["P"],"V")
getCursorXY.call(result)
x, y = result.unpack("LL")   # Two longs
```

Sometimes we need to pass in complex binary data, whereas in this case it was passed back to us. In that case, we could obviously use pack to pack the data into a string.

There are obviously many possible applications for this technique. Two other code fragments can be seen in the section "Grabbing a Character from the Keyboard," from Chapter 4 and the section "Using `system` and `exec`" in this chapter.

Using Win32OLE

The Win32OLE extension library (actually spelled in lowercase, `win32ole`) provides an interface to Windows OLE automation. Your Ruby code can act as a client for any OLE automation server such as Microsoft Word, Outlook, Internet Explorer, and many third-party software products.

To interact with an external application, we first create a new object of the `WIN32OLE` class. This object is used to access all the exposed properties and methods of the specified application.

In this example, we associate an object with the Microsoft Word application. We set the `visible` attribute to `true`, and eventually we `quit`, exiting the application.

```
require "win32ole"

word = WIN32OLE.new "Word.Application"

word.visible = true

# ...

word.quit
```

Every property of the automation server is reflected as an attribute of the object. These can be set or examined at will.

An alternate notation uses a hash-like construct to access these properties.

```
player["FileName"] = "file.wav"
name = player["FileName"]
# Equivalent to these statements:
# player.FileName = "file.wav"
# name = player.FileName
```

One advantage of this is that it can easily handle the more programmatic situations as shown in this contrived example:

```
puts "Enter the property name"
prop = gets
puts "Enter the new value"
```

```
val = gets
old = obj[prop]
obj[prop] = val
puts "#{prop} was #{old}... now is #{obj[prop]}"
```

But let's look at some more concrete examples. Here is a code fragment that takes a filename from the command line, passes it into Microsoft Word, and prints the file:

```
require "win32ole"

print "Enter the filename to print: "
docfile = gets

word = WIN32OLE.new "Word.Application"
word.visible = true
word.documents.open docfile
word.options.printBackground = false

# We could also set printBackground to true, but we
# would have to sleep until the file all got sent to
# the printer buffer before we quit...

word.activeDocument.printOut
word.quit
```

Here is an example of playing a WAV file. It has the disadvantage of an arbitrary sleep at the end rather than waiting for the output to finish. Fixing this is left as an exercise.

```
require "win32ole"

sound = WIN32OLE.new("MCI.MMcontrol")

wav = "c:\\windows\\media\\The Microsoft Sound.wav"
sound.fileName = wav

sound.autoEnable = true

sound.command = "Open"
sound.command = "Play"

sleep 7
```

In Listing 8.2, we use Internet Explorer to generate a text input box for us.

LISTING 8.2   Browser Text Input Box

```ruby
require "win32ole"

def ieInputBox( msg, default )
  ie = WIN32OLE.new("InternetExplorer.Application");
  ie.visible  = false
  sleep 0.01 while (ie.busy)

  script = ie.Document.Script;
  result = script.prompt(msg,default);
   ie.quit

   result
end


# Main...

result = ieInputBox( "Please enter your name",
                     "Dave Bowman")

if result
  puts result
else
  puts "User pressed Cancel"
end
```

In Listing 8.3, we open a small IE window and write HTML to it.

LISTING 8.3   Writing to a Browser Window

```ruby
require "win32ole"

html = <<EOF
<html>
<body>
<h3>And now for something</h3>
<h2>completely</h2>
<h1>different...</h1>
</body>
 </html>
 EOF

 ie = WIN32OLE.new("InternetExplorer.Application");
```

LISTING 8.3 Continued

```
ie.left      = 150
ie.top       = 150
ie.height    = 200
ie.width     = 300
ie.menubar   = 0
ie.toolbar   = 0
ie.navigate "about:blank"
ie.visible=TRUE;

ie.document.open
ie.document.write html
ie.document.close
sleep 5
ie.quit
```

Here we open a file dialog box and allow the user to select a file from a list:

```
require "win32ole"

cd = WIN32OLE.new("MSComDlg.CommonDialog")

# Set file filter
cd.filter = "All Files(*.*)|*.*" +
            "|Ruby Files(*.rb)|*.rb"
cd.filterIndex = 2

cd.maxFileSize = 128    # Set MaxFileSize

cd.showOpen()

file = cd.fileName      # Retrieve file, path

if not file or file==""
   puts "No filename entered."
else
   puts "The user selected: #{file}\n"
end
```

And finally, here is a little fragment that will discover the IP address of the local machine:

```
require "win32ole"

ws = WIN32OLE.new "MSWinsock.Winsock"

# Retrieve LocalIP property
```

```
    ipAddress = ws.localIP

    puts "The local IP is : #{ipAddress}"
```

As you can see, the possibilities are limitless. Have fun, and don't forget to share your code with others.

Using ActiveScriptRuby

You have probably used Internet Explorer at some point to view a Web page that contained embedded JavaScript or VBScript code. (We'll ignore the differences between JScript and JavaScript here.)

You can do the same thing with ActiveScriptRuby, which is like a bridge between COM and Ruby. For example, we can embed Ruby in an HTML page (as seen in Listing 8.4).

LISTING 8.4   Ruby Embedded in HTML

```
<html>

<script language="RubyScript">
  # This is Ruby code...
  def helloMethod
    @window.alert "Running Ruby Inside!"
  end
</script>

 <body>

 Here is an input button...
 <input id=Hello type=button onclick="helloMethod"
        language="RubyScript">

 </body>
 </html>
```

Using this technique of embedding Ruby, we can call Ruby code from any native Windows application that supports the IActiveScript interface, such as Internet Explorer or WScript (the WSH executable).

Working with Files, Directories, and Trees

A broad area of everyday scripting is to work with files and directories, including entire sub-trees of files. Much of the relevant material has already been covered in Chapter 4, but we will hit a few high points here.

Because I/O is a fairly system-dependent thing, many tricks will vary from one operating system to another. If you are in doubt, you should either consult a reference or resort to experimentation.

A Few Words on Text Filters

Many tools that we use every day (both vendor-supplied and home-grown) are simply *text filters*; that is, they accept textual input, process or transform it in some way, and output it again. Classic examples of text filters in the Unix world are `sed` and `tr`, among others.

Sometimes a file is small enough to be read into memory. This allows processing that might otherwise be difficult.

```
file = File.open(filename)
lines = file.readlines
# Manipulate as needed...
lines.each { |x| puts x }
```

Sometimes we'll need to process it a line at a time.

```
IO.foreach(filename) do |line|
  # Manipulate as needed...
  puts line
end
```

Finally, don't forget that any filenames on the command line are automatically gathered into `ARGF`, representing a concatenation of all input. (See the section "Working with ARGF.") In this case, we can use calls such as `ARGF.readlines` just as if `ARGF` were an `IO` object. All output would go to standard output as usual.

Copying a Directory Tree (with Symlinks)

Suppose that you wanted to copy an entire directory structure to a new location. There are various ways of doing this operation. But what if the tree has internal symbolic links? This becomes a little more difficult.

Listing 8.5 shows a recursive solution with a little user-friendliness added in. It is smart enough to check the most basic error conditions and also print a usage message.

LISTING 8.5   Copy Tree

```
require "ftools"

def recurse(src, dst)
  Dir.mkdir(dst)
  Dir.foreach(src) do |e|
```

LISTING 8.5   Continued

```ruby
      # Don't bother with . and ..
      next if [".",".."].include? e
      fullname = src + "/" + e
      newname = fullname.sub(Regexp.new(Regexp.escape(src)),dst)
       if FileTest::directory?(fullname)
         recurse(fullname,newname)
       elsif FileTest::symlink?(fullname)
         linkname = `ls -l #{fullname}`.sub(/.* -> /,"").chomp
         newlink = linkname.dup
         n = newlink.index($oldname)
         next if n == nil
         n2 = n + $oldname.length - 1
         newlink[n..n2] = $newname
         newlink.sub!(/\/\///,"/")
         # newlink = linkname.sub(Regexp.new(Regexp.escape(src)),dst)
           File.symlink(newlink, newname)
       elsif FileTest::file?(fullname)
         File.copy(fullname, newname)
       else
         puts "??? :  #{fullname}"
       end
    end
end


# "Main"

if ARGV.size != 2
  puts "Usage: copytree oldname newname"
  exit
end


oldname = ARGV[0]
newname = ARGV[1]

if ! FileTest::directory?(oldname)
  puts "Error: First parameter must be an existing directory."
  exit
end

if FileTest::exist?(newname)
  puts "Error: #{newname} already exists."
  exit
end
```

LISTING 8.5   Continued

```
oldname = File.expand_path(oldname)
newname = File.expand_path(newname)

$oldname=oldname
$newname=newname

recurse(oldname, newname)
```

Probably there are Unix variants in which there is a `cp -R` option that will preserve symlinks—but not any that we're using. Listing 8.5 was actually written to address that need in a real-life situation.

Deleting Files by Age or Other Criteria

Imagine that you want to scan through a directory and delete the oldest files. This directory might be some kind of repository for temporary files, log files, browser cache files, or similar data.

Here we present a little code fragment that will remove all the files older than a certain timestamp (passed in as a `Time` object):

```
def delete_older(dir, time)
  save = Dir.getwd
  Dir.chdir(dir)
  Dir.foreach(".") do |entry|
    # We're not handling directories here
    next if File.stat(entry).directory?
    # Use the modification time
    if File.mtime(entry) < time
      File.unlink(entry)
    end
  end
  Dir.chdir(save)
end

delete_older("/tmp",Time.local(2001,3,29,18,38,0))
```

This is nice, but let's generalize it. Let's make a similar method called `delete_if` that takes a block which will evaluate to `true` or `false`. Let's then delete the file only if it fits the given criteria.

```
def delete_if(dir)
  save = Dir.getwd
  Dir.chdir(dir)
```

```
Dir.foreach(".") do |entry|
  # We're not handling directories here
  next if File.stat(entry).directory?
  if yield entry
    File.unlink(entry)
  end
end
Dir.chdir(save)
end

# Delete all files over 3000 bytes
delete_if("/tmp") { |f| File.size(f) > 3000 }

# Delete all LOG and BAK files
delete_if("/tmp") { |f| f =~ /(log|bak)$/i }
```

Determining Free Space on a Disk

Suppose that you want to know how many bytes are free on a certain device. We present here a very crude way of doing this, by running a system utility:

```
def freespace(device=".")
  lines = %x(df -k #{device}).split("\n")
  n = lines.last.split[1].to_i * 1024
end

puts freespace("/tmp")    # 16772204544
```

Better ways of doing this might exist. Sometimes the better they are, the more system-dependent they are.

So that Windows users won't feel left out, we offer an equally ugly solution for them.

```
def freespace(device=".")
  lines = %x(cmd /c dir #{device}).split("\n")
  n = lines.last.split[2].delete(",").to_i
end

puts freespace "C:"      # 5340389376
```

This code fragment assumes that the free space reported by dir is given in bytes (which isn't true for all variants of Windows).

Miscellaneous Scripting Tasks

We have a few tidbits left over. We have decided to classify these as miscellaneous.

Piping into the Ruby Interpreter

Because the Ruby interpreter is a single-pass translator, it is possible to pipe code into it and have it executed. One conceivable purpose for this is to use Ruby for more complex tasks when you are required by circumstance to work in a traditional scripting language like Kornshell.

In Listing 8.6, for example, is a Kornshell script that uses Ruby (via a here document) to calculate the elapsed time in seconds between two dates. The Ruby program prints a single value to standard output, which is then captured by the ksh script.

LISTING 8.6   Kornshell Script Invoking Ruby

```
#!/usr/bin/ksh

# Let ksh find the difference in seconds
# between two dates using Ruby...

export time1="2001-04-02 15:56:12"
export time2="2001-12-08 12:03:19"

cat <<EOF | ruby | read elapsed
require "parsedate"

time1 = ENV["time1"]
time2 = ENV["time2"]

args1 = ParseDate.parsedate(time1)
args2 = ParseDate.parsedate(time2)

args1 = args1[0..5]
args2 = args2[0..5]

t1 = Time.local(*args1)
t2 = Time.local(*args2)

diff = t2 - t1
puts diff
EOF

echo "Elapsed seconds = " $elapsed
```

Note that the two input values in this case are passed as environment variables (which must be exported). The two lines that retrieve these values could also be coded in this way:

```
time1="$time1"  # Embed the ksh variable directly
time2="$time2"  #   into a string...
```

However, the difficulties are obvious. It could get very confusing whether a certain string represents a ksh variable or a Ruby global variable, and there could be a host of problems with quoting and escaping.

It's also possible to use a Ruby one-liner with the -e option. Here's a little ksh script that reverses a string using Ruby:

```
#!/usr/bin/ksh

string="Francis Bacon"

ruby -e "puts '$string'.reverse" | read reversed

#  $reversed now has value "nocaB sicnarF"
```

Unix geeks will note that awk has been used in a similar way since time immemorial.

Getting and Setting Exit Codes

The exit method will raise a SystemExit exception and ultimately return the specified exit code to the operating system (or to the calling entity). This is a Kernel method. There is also a method exit! that differs in two ways: It doesn't run the exit handlers before quitting, and the default return value is -1.

```
# ...
if (allOK)
  exit      # Normally (0)
else
  exit!     # In a hurry (-1)
end
```

When a Ruby return code is retrieved by the operating system (for example, by doing echo $?), it is seen as the same integer specified in the code. When a subprocess exits and we use wait2 (or waitpid2) to examine the return code, we will find it left-shifted by eight bits. This is a POSIX quirk that Ruby has inherited.

```
child = fork { sleep 1; exit 3 }

pid, code = Process.wait2      # [12554,768]
status = code << 8            # 3
```

Testing Whether a Program Is Running Interactively

A good way to determine whether a program is interactive is to test its standard input. The method isatty? (which historically means "is a teletype") will tell us whether the device is an interactive one as opposed to a disk file or socket.

```
if STDIN.isatty?
  puts "Hi! I see you're typing at"
  puts "the keyboard..."
end
```

Determining the Current Platform or Operating System

If a program wants to know what operating system it's running on, it can access the global constant RUBY_PLATFORM. This will return a cryptic string (usually something similar to i386-cygwin or sparc-solaris2.7), telling the platform on which the Ruby interpreter was built.

Because we primarily use Unix variants (Solaris, AIX, Linux) and Windows variants (98, NT, 2000), we've found the following crude piece of code to be useful. It will distinguish between the Unix family and the Windows family of operating systems (unceremoniously lumping all others into other).

```
def os_family
  case RUBY_PLATFORM
    when /ix/i, /ux/i, /gnu/i,
         /sysv/i, /solaris/i,
         /sunos/i, /bsd/i
      "unix"
    when /win/i, /ming/i
      "windows"
    else
      "other"
  end
end
```

This little set of regular expressions will correctly classify the vast majority of platforms. Of course, this is only a very clumsy way of determining how to handle OS dependencies. Even if you correctly determine the OS family, that might not always imply the availability (or absence) of any specific feature.

Using the Etc Module

The Etc module retrieves useful information from the /etc/passwd and /etc/group files. Obviously, this is only useful in a Unix environment.

The getlogin method will return the login name of the user. If it fails, getpwuid might work (taking an optional parameter, which is the uid).

```
myself = getlogin             # hal9000
myname = getpwuid(2001).name  # hal9000

# Without a parameter, getpwuid calls
# getuid internally...
me2 = getpwuid.name           # hal9000
```

The `getpwnam` method returns a `passwd` struct, which contains relevant entries such as `name`, `dir` (home directory), `shell` (login shell), and others.

```
rootshell = getpwnam("root").shell   # /sbin/sh
```

At the group level, `getgrgid` or `getgrnam` behave similarly. They will return a `group` struct consisting of group name, group `passwd`, and so on.

The iterator `passwd` will iterate over all entries in the `/etc/passwd` file. Each entry passed into the block is a `passwd` struct.

```
all_users = []
passwd { |entry| all_users << entry.name }
```

There is an analogous iterator `group` for group entries.

Libraries and Utilities You Should Know About

Several other items are worth a brief mention. As always, see the Ruby Application Archive for the latest and greatest tools.

For Tcl fans, the standard Ruby distribution has a library called `expect.rb`, which acts similar to Tcl's `expect` extension. See the README for limited documentation.

For those needing to do error logging from Ruby, there is a `syslog` extension. It is a wrapper for the Unix function of the same name.

Minero Aoki has created several tools, notably `setup.rb` (which aids in installing Ruby scripts and libraries) and `TMail`, which aids in handling mail messages (including some MIME support). Another mail library is Michael Neumann's `mbox`, which reads and writes the Unix mailbox format.

Summary

That ends our discussion of Ruby scripting for everyday automation tasks. Because much of this material is operating system dependent, we urge you to experiment on your own. There are differences between Windows and Unix, and there are even differences in behavior within those families. In particular, we can't predict the behavior of all these scripts on Windows XP, which isn't even released as of this writing.

In a sense, a network is a great equalizer; over a remote connection, it is frequently irrelevant what operating system is at the other end. It's appropriate that we move from the narrow viewpoint of this chapter into the wider world of Chapter 9, "Network and Web Programming," where we discuss network clients and servers, distributed Ruby, and Web development.

Network and Web Programming

IN THIS CHAPTER

Never underestimate the bandwidth of a station wagon full of tapes hurtling down the highway.

—Andrew S. Tanenbaum

This book strives for compactness. As such, we've put networking and Web development in the same chapter (and even squeezed in some XML examples). In a broad sense, these topics belong together. Without the lower-level networking in place, it would be impossible for a browser to communicate with a Web server sending and receiving information. Of course, separate chapters could be devoted to these areas; in fact, separate books could be devoted to them. But we've decided to do what we could in a limited space.

When a marketing type says *networking*, he probably means that he wants to give you his business card. But when a programmer says it, he's talking about electronic communication between physically separated machines—whether across the room, across the city, or across the world.

In the authors' world, networking usually implies TCP/IP, the native tongue in which millions of machines whisper back and forth across the Internet. We'll say a few words about this before diving into some concrete examples.

Network communication is conceptualized at different levels (or layers) of abstraction. The lowest level is the *data link layer*, or actual hardware-level communication, which we need not discuss here. Immediately above this is the *network layer*, which is concerned with the actual moving around of packets; this is the realm of IP (Internet Protocol). At a still higher level of abstraction is the *transport layer*, where we find TCP (Transmission Control Protocol) and UDP (User Datagram Protocol). At the level above this, we find the *application layer*; at this point we finally enter the world of telnet, FTP, e-mail protocols, and much more.

It's possible to communicate directly in IP, but normally you wouldn't do such a thing. Most of the time, we are concerned with TCP or UDP.

TCP provides reliable communication between two hosts; it is concerned with the blocking and deblocking of packet data, acknowledgement of receipt, handling timeouts, reassembling the packets in the proper order, and so on. Because it is a reliable protocol, the application using it need not worry about a packet in the middle of a message not arriving; packets are re-sent as needed.

UDP is much simpler, merely sending packets (datagrams) to the remote host, like binary postcards. There is no guarantee that these will be received, nor that the ones received will be in order, so the protocol is unreliable (and thus the application has some extra details to worry about.) It's logical to use UDP when you have a simple, short message that will fit in a single packet, and it is convenient to handle a timeout manually. In such a case, TCP might be overkill.

Ruby supports low-level networking (chiefly in TCP and UDP), as well as coding at higher levels. These higher levels include applications for remote login, file transfer, e-mail, and others (for example, telnet, FTP, and SMTP).

Figure 9.1 is a class hierarchy showing the highlights of Ruby's networking support. We include HTTP and certain other high-level items here; some others are omitted for clarity.

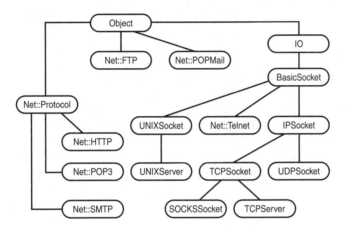

FIGURE 9.1
Partial Inheritance hierarchy for networking support in Ruby.

Note that the bulk of these classes derive from the IO class. This means that we can use the methods of IO that are so familiar to us.

We'd like to document all the features of all these classes. Unfortunately, that task would exceed our space requirements. We only present a task-oriented approach to all this and offer a little explanation. For a comprehensive list of available methods, consult a reference.

A few significant areas are not covered here at all, so we'll mention these up front. The Net::Telnet class is covered only in connection with NTP servers in the section "Contacting an Official Timeserver;" this class is not just for implementing your own telnet client, but is potentially useful for automating anything that has a telnet interface.

The Net::FTP library is also not covered here. In general, FTP is very easy to automate in its everyday form, so there is less motivation to use this class than there might be for some others.

The Net::Protocol class is the parent of HTTP, POP3, and SMTP. It would probably prove useful in the development of other customized networking protocols, but time and space prevent us from delving into something of that nature.

That ends our broad overview. Let's look at some code.

Network Servers

A *server* spends its lifetime waiting for messages and answering them. It might have to do some serious processing in order to construct those answers, such as accessing a database, but from a networking point of view, it simply receives requests and sends responses.

Having said that, there is still more than one way to accomplish this. A server might respond to only one request at a time, or it might thread its responses. The former is easier to code, but the latter is better if there are many clients trying to connect simultaneously.

It's also conceivable that a server might be used to facilitate communication in some way between the clients. The classic examples are chat servers, game servers, and peer-to-peer file sharing.

A Simple Serialized Server: Time of Day

Let's look at the simplest server we can think of, which might require a little suspension of disbelief. Let's suppose that we have a server whose clock is so accurate that we use it as a standard. There are such servers, of course, but they don't communicate with the simple protocol we show here.

We use the term *port* frequently in this chapter. A port is simply an "address" on a client or server used to identify the process with which we are communicating. The combination of IP address and port are enough to uniquely specify one end of a connection. Often port numbers are arbitrary, even randomly generated; but there are certain *well-known* ports that are universally agreed upon (such as port 80 for HTTP).

In our example, a single-threaded server handles requests in line. When the client makes a request of us, we return a string with the time of day. Here's the server code.

```ruby
require "socket"

PORT = 12321
HOST = ARGV[0] || 'localhost'

server = UDPSocket.open         # Using UDP here...
server.bind(nil, PORT)

loop do
  text, sender = server.recvfrom(1)
  server.send(Time.new.to_s + "\n", 0, sender[3], sender[1])
end
```

And here is the client code:

```
require "socket"
require "timeout"

PORT = 12321

HOST = ARGV[0] || 'localhost'

socket = UDPSocket.new
socket.connect(HOST, PORT)

socket.send("", 0)
timeout(10) do
  time = socket.gets
  puts time
end
```

Note that the client makes its request simply by sending a null packet. The server has no knowledge of the client until the client makes contact, after which the server knows the client's identity (IP address). Because UDP is unreliable, we time out after a reasonable length of time.

Here is a similar server implemented with TCP. It listens on port 12321 and can actually be used by telnetting into that port (or by using the client code we show afterward).

```
require "socket"

PORT = 12321

server = TCPServer.new(PORT)

while (session = server.accept)
  session.puts Time.new
  session.close
end
```

Note the straightforward use of the TCPServer class. Here is the TCP version of the client code:

```
require "socket"

PORT = 12321
HOST = ARGV[0] || "localhost"
```

```
session = TCPSocket.new(HOST, PORT)
time = session.gets
session.close
puts time
```

Implementing a Threaded Server

Some servers get heavy traffic. It can be efficient to handle each request in a separate thread.

Here is a re-implementation of the time-of-day server in the previous example. It uses TCP and threads all the client requests.

```
require "socket"

PORT = 12321

server = TCPServer.new(PORT)

while (session = server.accept)
  Thread.new(session) do |my_session|
    my_session.puts Time.new
    my_session.close
  end
end
```

Because it uses threads and spawns a new one with every client request, greater parallelism is achieved. No join is done because the loop is essentially infinite, running until the server is interrupted manually.

Note how the session variable is passed into the thread, which then refers to it by the name my_session instead. For more information on this or other aspects of threading, refer to Chapter 7, "Ruby Threads."

The client code is, of course, unchanged. From the point of view of the client, the server's behavior is unchanged (except that it might appear more reliable).

Case Study: A Peer-to-Peer Chess Server

> *But helpless Pieces of the Game He plays*
> *Upon this Chequer-board of Nights and Days;*
> *Hither and thither moves, and checks, and slays,*
> *And one by one back in the Closet lays.*
> —The Rubaiyat, Omar Khayyam (trans. Fitzgerald)

It isn't always the server that we're ultimately concerned about communicating with. Sometimes the server is more of a directory service to put clients in touch with each other. An example is a peer-to-peer file sharing service such as Napster; other examples are various game servers or chat programs (including some sophisticated ones such as NetMeeting).

Let's create a skeletal implementation of a chess server. Here we don't mean a server that will play chess with a client, but simply one that will point clients to each other so that they can then play without the server's involvement.

We'll warn you that for the sake of simplicity, the code really knows nothing about chess. All the game logic is simulated (stubbed out) so that we can focus on the networking issues.

First of all, let's use TCP for the initial communication between each client and the server. We could use UDP, but it isn't reliable; we would have to use timeouts as we saw in an earlier example.

We'll let each client provide two pieces of information—his own name (like a username), and the name of the desired opponent. We'll introduce a notation user:hostname to fully identify the opponent; we'll use a colon instead of the more intuitive @ so that it won't resemble an e-mail address, which it isn't.

When a client contacts the server, the server stores the client's information in a list. When *both* clients have contacted the server, then a message is sent back to each of them; each client is given enough information to contact his opponent.

Then there's the small issue of white and black. Somehow the roles have to be assigned in such a way that both players agree on what color they are playing. For simplicity, we're letting the server assign it. The first client contacting the server will get to play white (and thus move first); the other player will play the black pieces.

Don't get confused here. Once the server has introduced them, the clients talk to each other, so that effectively one of them is really a server by this point. This is a semantic distinction that we won't bother with.

Because the clients will be talking to each other in alternation, and there is more than just a single brief exchange, we'll use TCP for their communication. This means that the client which is "really" a server will instantiate a TCPServer and the other will instantiate a TCPSocket at the other end. We're assuming a mutually agreed-on port for peer-to-peer communication as we did with the initial client-server handshaking. (The two ports are different, of course.)

What we're really describing here is a simple application-level protocol. It could be made more sophisticated, of course.

Let's look first at the server (see Listing 9.1). For the convenience of running it at a command line, we start a thread that terminates the server when a carriage return is pressed. The main server logic is threaded; we can handle multiple clients connecting at once. For safety's sake, we use a mutex to protect access to the user data. In theory there could be multiple threads trying to add users to the list at one time.

LISTING 9.1   The Chess Server

```ruby
require "thread"
require "socket"

ChessServer     = "127.0.0.1"  # Replace this IP address!
ChessServerPort = 12000

# Exit if user presses Enter at server end
waiter = Thread.new do
  puts "Press Enter to exit the server."
  gets
  exit
end

$mutex = Mutex.new
$list = {}

Player = Struct.new("Player", :opponent, :address,
                    :port, :ipname, :session,
                    :short, :long, :id)

def match?(p1, p2)
  $list[p1] and $list[p2] and
    $list[p1][0] == p2 and $list[p2][0] == p1
end

def handle_client(sess, msg, addr, port, ipname)
  $mutex.synchronize do
    cmd, p1short, p2long = msg.split
    if cmd != "login"
      puts "Protocol error: client msg was #{msg}"
      return
    end

    p1long = p1short.dup + ":#{addr}"
    p2short, host2 = p2long.split(":")
    host2 = ipname if host2 == nil
    p2long = p2short + ":" + IPSocket.getaddress(host2)
```

LISTING 9.1   Continued

```ruby
    p1 = Struct::Player.new(p2long, addr, port, ipname,
                            sess, p1short, p1long)
    p2 = Struct::Player.new

    # Note: We get user:hostname on the command line,
    # but we store it in the form user:address

    $list[p1long] = p1

    if match?(p1long, p2long)
      # Note these names are "backwards" now: player 2
      # logged in first, if we got here.
      p1, p2 = $list[p1long], $list[p2long]
      # Player ID = name:ipname:color
      # Color: 0=white, 1=black
      p1.id = "#{p1short}:#{p1.ipname}:1"
      p2.id = "#{p2short}:#{p2.ipname}:0"
      sess1, sess2 = [p1.session, p2.session]
      sess1.puts "#{p2.id}"
      sess1.close
      sess2.puts "#{p1.id}"
      sess2.close
    end
  end
end

text = nil

$server = TCPServer.new(ChessServer, ChessServerPort)
while session = $server.accept do
  Thread.new(session) do |sess|
    text = sess.gets
    puts "Received: #{text}"  # So we know server gets it
    domain, port, ipname, ipaddr = sess.peeraddr
    handle_client sess, text, ipaddr, port, ipname
    sleep 1
  end
end

waiter.join    # Exit if user presses Enter (this is only
               # for convenience in running this example)
```

The `handle_client` method stores information for the client. If the corresponding client is already stored, each client is sent a message with the whereabouts of the other client. As we've defined this simple problem, the server's responsibility ends at this point.

The client code (see Listing 9.2) is naturally written so that there is only a single program; the first invocation will become the TCP server, and the second will become the TCP client. To be fair, we should point out that our choice to make the server white and the client black is arbitrary. There's no particular reason we couldn't implement the application so that the color issue was independent of such considerations.

LISTING 9.2   The Chess Client

```ruby
require "socket"
require "timeout"

ChessServer     = '127.0.0.1'  # Replace this IP address
ChessServerPort = 12000
PeerPort        = 12001

WHITE, BLACK = 0, 1
Colors = %w[White Black]

def drawBoard(board)
  puts <<-EOF
+ — — — — — — — — — — — — — — +
| Stub! Drawing the board here...  |
+ — — — — — — — — — — — — — — +
  EOF
end

def analyzeMove(who, move, num, board)
  # Stub - black always wins on 4th move
  if who == BLACK and num == 4
    move << "  Checkmate!"
  end
  true  # Stub again - always say it's legal.
end

def ended?(myColor, whoseMove,
          whiteName, blackName, move)
  opponent = (myColor==WHITE ? blackName : whiteName)
  case move
    when /resign/i    # Player explicitly resigns
      if myColor == whoseMove
        puts "You've resigned. #{opponent} wins."
      else
        puts "#{opponent} resigns. You win!"
      end
      return true
```

LISTING 9.2   Continued

```ruby
      when /Checkmate/   # analyzeMove detects mate
        if myColor == whoseMove
          puts "You have checkmated #{opponent}."
        else
          puts "#{opponent} has checkmated you."
        end
        return true
    end
    return false
  end

  def myMove(who, lastmove, num, board, sock)
    # lastmove not actually used in dummy example
    ok = false
    until ok do
      print "\nYour move: "
      move = STDIN.gets.chomp
      ok = analyzeMove(who, move, num, board)
      puts "Illegal move" if not ok
    end
    sock.puts move
    drawBoard(board)
    move
  end

  def otherMove(who, lastmove, num, board, sock)
    # lastmove not actually used in dummy example
    move = sock.gets.chomp
    puts "\nOpponent: #{move}"
    drawBoard(board)
    move
  end

  def setupWhite(opponent)
    puts "\nWaiting for a connection..."
    server = TCPServer.new(PeerPort)
    session = server.accept
    str = nil
    begin
      timeout(30) do
        str = session.gets.chomp
        if str != "ready"
          raise "Protocol error: ready-message was #{str}"
        end
      end
```

LISTING 9.2   Continued

```ruby
    rescue TimeoutError
      raise "Did not get ready-message from opponent."
    end
    puts "Playing #{opponent}... you are white.\n"
    session                 # Return connection
  end

  def setupBlack(opponent, ipname)
    # Asymmetrical because we assume black is the client
    puts "\nConnecting..."
    socket = TCPSocket.new(ipname, PeerPort)
    socket.puts "ready"
    puts "Playing #{opponent}... you are black.\n"
    socket                  # Return connection
  end


  # "Main"...

  if ARGV.size != 2
    puts "Parameters required: myname opponent[:hostname]"
    exit
  end

  myself, opponentID = ARGV
  opponent = opponentID.split(":")[0]    # Remove hostname

  # Contact the chess server

  print "Connecting to the chess server... "
  STDOUT.flush

  socket = TCPSocket.new(ChessServer, ChessServerPort)

  socket.puts "login #{myself} #{opponentID}"
  response = socket.gets.chomp

  puts "got response.\n"

  name, ipname, oppColor = response.split ":"
  oppColor = oppColor.to_i
  myColor = if oppColor == WHITE then BLACK else WHITE end

  move = nil
  board = nil      # Not really used in this dummy example
  num = 0
```

LISTING 9.2   Continued

```
if myColor == WHITE         # We're white
  who, opp = WHITE, BLACK
  session = setupWhite(opponent)
  drawBoard(board)
  loop do
    num += 1
    move = myMove(who, move, num, board, session)
    break if ended?(who, who, myself, opponent, move)
    move = otherMove(who, move, num, board, session)
    break if ended?(who, opp, myself, opponent, move)
  end
else                        # We're black
  who, opp = BLACK, WHITE
  socket = setupBlack(opponent, ipname)
  drawBoard(board)
  loop do
    num += 1
    move = otherMove(who, move, num, board, socket)
    break if ended?(who, opp, opponent, myself, move)
    move = myMove(who, move, num, board, socket)
    break if ended?(who, who, opponent, myself, move)
  end
  socket.close
end
```

We've defined our little protocol so that the black client sends a "ready" message to the white client to let it know it's prepared to begin the game. The white player then moves first. The move is sent to the black client so that it can draw its own board in sync with the other player's board.

As we said, there's no real knowledge of chess built into this application. There's a stub in place to check the validity of each player's move; this check is done on the local side in each case. But this is only a stub that always says that the move is legal. At the same time, it does a bit of hocus-pocus; we want this simulated game to end after only a few moves, so we fix the game so that black always wins on the fourth move. This win is indicated by appending the string "Checkmate!" to the move; this prints on the opponent's screen and also serves to terminate the loop.

A move, by the way, is simply a string. Two notations are in common use, but our code is stubbed so heavily that it doesn't even know which one we're using.

The drawing of the board is also a stub. Those wanting to do so can easily design some bad ASCII art to output here.

The myMove method always refers to the local side; likewise, otherMove refers to the remote side.

We show some sample output in Listing 9.3. The client executions are displayed side by side in this listing.

LISTING 9.3   Sample Chess Client Execution

```
% ruby chess.rb Hal Capablanca:        % ruby chess.rb Capablanca
deepthought.org                        Hal:deepdoodoo.org

Connecting...                          Connecting...
Playing Capablanca... you are white.   Playing Hal... you are black.
+— — — — — — — — — — — — — —+          +— — — — — — — — — — — — — —+
| Stub! Drawing the board here... |    | Stub! Drawing the board here... |
+— — — — — — — — — — — — — —+          +— — — — — — — — — — — — — —+

Your move: N-QB3                       Opponent: N-QB3
+— — — — — — — — — — — — — —+          +— — — — — — — — — — — — — —+
| Stub! Drawing the board here... |    | Stub! Drawing the board here... |
+— — — — — — — — — — — — — —+          +— — — — — — — — — — — — — —+

Opponent: P-K4                         Your move: P-K4
+— — — — — — — — — — — — — —+          +— — — — — — — — — — — — — —+
| Stub! Drawing the board here... |    | Stub! Drawing the board here... |
+— — — — — — — — — — — — — —+          +— — — — — — — — — — — — — —+

Your move: P-K4                        Opponent: P-K4
+— — — — — — — — — — — — — —+          +— — — — — — — — — — — — — —+
| Stub! Drawing the board here... |    | Stub! Drawing the board here... |
+— — — — — — — — — — — — — —+          +— — — — — — — — — — — — — —+

Opponent: B-QB4                        Your move: B-QB4
+— — — — — — — — — — — — — —+          +— — — — — — — — — — — — — —+
| Stub! Drawing the board here... |    | Stub! Drawing the board here... |
+— — — — — — — — — — — — — —+          +— — — — — — — — — — — — — —+

Your move: B-QB4                       Opponent: B-QB4
+— — — — — — — — — — — — — —+          +— — — — — — — — — — — — — —+
| Stub! Drawing the board here... |    | Stub! Drawing the board here... |
+— — — — — — — — — — — — — —+          +— — — — — — — — — — — — — —+

Opponent: Q-KR5                        Your move: Q-KR5
+— — — — — — — — — — — — — —+          +— — — — — — — — — — — — — —+
| Stub! Drawing the board here... |    | Stub! Drawing the board here... |
+— — — — — — — — — — — — — —+          +— — — — — — — — — — — — — —+
```

LISTING 9.3   Continued

```
Your move: N-KB3                    Opponent: N-KB3
+— — — — — — — — — — — — — —+       +— — — — — — — — — — — — — — —+
| Stub! Drawing the board here... | | Stub! Drawing the board here... |
+— — — — — — — — — — — — — —+       +— — — — — — — — — — — — — — —+


Opponent: QxP   Checkmate!          Your move: QxP
+— — — — — — — — — — — — — —+       +— — — — — — — — — — — — — — —+
| Stub! Drawing the board here... | | Stub! Drawing the board here... |
+— — — — — — — — — — — — — —+       +— — — — — — — — — — — — — — —+


Capablanca has checkmated you.      You have checkmated Hal!
```

This little example could serve as the beginning of a genuine application. We'd have to add knowledge of chess, add security, improve reliability, add a graphical interface, and so on. The possibilities are endless. If you do anything with this idea, let us know about it.

Network Clients

Sometimes the server is a well-known entity or is using a well-established protocol. In this case, we need simply to design a client that will talk to this server in the way it expects.

This can be done with TCP or UDP, as you saw previously. However, it's common to use other higher-level protocols such as HTTP or SNMP. We'll give just a few examples here.

Retrieving Truly Random Numbers from the Web

> *Anyone who attempts to generate random numbers by deterministic means is, of course, living in a state of sin.*
>
> —John von Neumann

There is a rand function in Kernel to return a random number; but there is a fundamental problem with it. It isn't really random. If you are a mathematician, cryptographer, or other nit-picker, you will refer to this as a *pseudorandom* number generator, because it uses algebraic methods to generate numbers in a deterministic fashion. These numbers "look" random to the casual observer, and may even have the correct statistical properties; but the sequences *do* repeat eventually, and we can even repeat a sequence purposely (or accidentally) by using the same seed.

But processes in nature are considered to be truly random. That is why in state lotteries, winners of millions of dollars are picked based on the chaotic motions of little white balls. Other sources of randomness are radioactive emissions or atmospheric noise.

There are sources of random numbers on the Web. One of these is www.random.org, which we use in this example.

The sample code in Listing 9.4 simulates the throwing of five ordinary (six-sided) dice. Of course, gaming fans could extend it to ten-sided or twenty-sided, but the ASCII art would get tedious.

LISTING 9.4   Casting Dice at Random

```ruby
HOST = "www.random.org"
RAND_URL = "/cgi-bin/randnum?col=5&"

def get_random_numbers(count=1, min=0, max=99)
  path = RAND_URL + "num=#{count}&min=#{min}&max=#{max}"
  connection = Net::HTTP.new(HOST)
  response, data = connection.get(path)
  if response.code == "200"
    data.split.collect { |num| num.to_i }
  else
    []
  end
end


DICE_LINES = [
  "+ — —.+ +— — .+ +— —.+ +— —.+ +— —.+ +— —.+ ",
  "|    | | *  | | *   | | * *  | | * *  | | * *  | ",
  "|  *  | |    | | *  | |     | | *  | | * *  | ",
  "|    | | *  | |   *  | | * *  | | * *  | | * *  | ",
  "+— —.+ +— — .+ +— —.+ +— —.+ +— —.+ +— —.+ "
]

DIE_WIDTH = DICE_LINES[0].length/6

def draw_dice(values)
  DICE_LINES.each do |line|
    for v in values
      print line[(v-1)*DIE_WIDTH, DIE_WIDTH]
      print " "
    end
    puts
  end
end

draw_dice(get_random_numbers(5, 1, 6))
```

Here we're using the `Net::HTTP` class to communicate directly with a Web server. Think of it as a highly specialized, all-purpose Web browser. We form the URL and try to connect; when we make a connection, we get a response and a piece of data. If the response indicates that all is well, we can parse the data that we received. Exceptions are assumed to be handled by the caller.

Here's a variation on the same basic idea. What if we really wanted to use these random numbers in an application? Because the CGI at the server end asks us to specify how many numbers we want returned, it's logical to buffer them. It's a fact of life that there is usually a delay involved when accessing a remote site. We want to fill a buffer so that we are not making frequent Web accesses and incurring delays.

We've decided to go ahead and get a little fancy here (see Listing 9.5). The buffer is filled by a separate thread, and it is shared among all the instances of the class. The buffer size and the "low water mark" (`@slack`) are both tunable; appropriate real-world values for them would be dependent on the reachability (ping-time) of the server and on how often the application requested a random number from the buffer.

Though we haven't shown it here, it would probably be logical to make this a singleton (in the sense of the *singleton* design pattern). That way, all the code could share a single pool of random numbers and a single interface to the Web page. Refer to the `singleton.rb` library.

LISTING 9.5   A Buffered Random Number Generator

```
class TrueRandom

      require "net/http"
      require "thread"

      def initialize(min=0,max=1,buff=1000,slack=300)
        @site = "www.random.org"
        @min, @max = min, max
        @bufsize, @slack = buff, slack
        @buffer = Queue.new
        @url  = "/cgi-bin/randnum?num=nnn&min=#@min&max=#@max&col=1"
        @thread = Thread.new { fillbuffer }
      end

      def fillbuffer
        h = Net::HTTP.new(@site, 80)
        true_url = @url.sub(/nnn/,"#{@bufsize-@slack}")
        resp, data = h.get(true_url, nil)
        data.split.each {|x| @buffer.enq x }
      end
```

LISTING 9.5   Continued

```ruby
    def rand
      if @buffer.size < @slack
        if ! @thread.alive?
          @thread = Thread.new { fillbuffer }
        end
      end
      num = nil
      num = @buffer.deq until num!=nil
      num.to_i
    end

end


t = TrueRandom.new(1,6,1000,300)

count = {1=>0, 2=>0, 3=>0, 4=>0, 5=>0, 6=>0}

10000.times do |n|
  x = t.rand
  count[x] += 1
end

p count

# In one run:
# {4=>1692, 5=>1677, 1=>1678, 6=>1635, 2=>1626, 3=>1692}
```

Contacting an Official Timeserver

As we promised, here's a bit of code to contact an NTP (Network Time Protocol) server on the Net. We do this by means of a telnet client. This example is adapted from the one in *Programming Ruby* (Dave Thomas and Andy Hunt, Addison-Wesley, 2000).

```ruby
    require "net/telnet"
    timeserver = "www.fakedomain.org"

    tn = Net::Telnet.new("Host"       => timeserver,
                         "Port"       => "time",
                         "Timeout"    => 60,
                         "Telnetmode" => false)
    local = Time.now.strftime("%H:%M:%S")
```

```
msg = tn.recv(4).unpack('N')[0]
# Convert to epoch
remote = Time.at(msg - 2208988800).strftime("%H:%M:%S")

puts "Local : #{local}"
puts "Remote: #{remote}"
```

When we call `Telnet.new`, we pass in a set of options as a hash. Note that the port is given here as a string; most or all of the well-known ports can be specified by name rather than number in this way (not just in the context of `Telnet`, but in other classes as well). Note also that we set the `Telnetmode` flag to false because we are using a telnet client to talk with a non-telnet server.

We establish a connection and grab four bytes. These represent a 32-bit quantity in network byte order (big endian); we convert this number to something we can digest and then convert from the epoch to a `Time` object.

Note that we didn't use a real timeserver name. This is because the usefulness of such a server frequently is dependent on your geographic location. Furthermore, many of these have access restrictions, and may require permission, or at least notification, before they are used. A Web search should turn up an open-access NTP server less than a thousand miles from you.

Interacting with a POP Server

The *Post Office Protocol* (*POP*) is very commonly used by mail servers. Ruby's `POP3` class enables you to examine the headers and bodies of all messages waiting on a server and process them as you see fit. After processing, you can easily delete one or all of them.

The `Net::POP3` class must be instantiated with the name or IP address of the server; the port number defaults to 110. No connection is established until the method `start` is invoked (with the appropriate user name and password).

Invoking the method `mails` on this object will return an array of objects of class `POPMail`. (There is also an iterator `each` that will run through these one at a time.)

A `POPMail` object corresponds to a single e-mail message. The `header` method will retrieve the message's headers; the method `all` will retrieve the header and the body. (There are also other usages of `all` as we'll see shortly.)

A code fragment is worth a thousand words. Here's a little example that will log on to the server and print the subject line for each e-mail.

```
require "net/pop"
```

```
pop = Net::POP3.new("pop.fakedomain.org")
pop.start("gandalf", "mellon")      # user, password
pop.mails.each do |msg|
  puts msg.header.grep /^Subject: /
end
```

The delete method will delete a message from the server. (Some servers require that finish be called, to close the POP connection, before such an operation becomes final.) Here is the world's most trivial spam filter.

```
require "net/pop"

pop = Net::POP3.new("pop.fakedomain.org")
pop.start("gandalf", "mellon")       # user, password
pop.mails.each do |msg|
  if msg.all =~ /make money fast/i
    msg.delete
  end
end
pop.finish
```

We'll mention that start can be called with a block. By analogy with File.open, it opens the connection, executes the block, and closes the connection.

The all method can also be called with a block. This will simply iterate over the lines in the e-mail message; it is equivalent to calling each on the string resulting from all.

```
# Print each line backwards... how useful!
msg.all { |line| print line.reverse }
# Same thing...
msg.all.each { |line| print line.reverse }
```

We can also pass an object into the all method. In this case, it will call the append operator (<<) repeatedly for each line in the string. Because this operator is defined differently for different objects, the behavior may be radically different, as shown here:

```
arr = []          # Empty array
str = "Mail: "     # String
out = $stdout      # IO object

msg.all(arr)       # Build an array of lines
msg.all(str)       # Concatenate onto str
msg.all(out)       # Write to standard output
```

Finally, we'll give you a way to return only the body of the message, ignoring all headers.

```ruby
module Net

  class POPMail

    def body
      # Skip header bytes
      self.all[self.header.size..-1]
    end

  end

end
```

This method doesn't have all the properties that `all` has; for example, it does not take a block. It can easily be extended, however.

The IMAP protocol is somewhat less common than POP3. But for those who need it, there is an `imap.rb` library for that purpose.

Sending Mail with SMTP

A child of five could understand this. Fetch me a child of five.

—Groucho Marx

The Simple Mail Transfer Protocol (SMTP) might seem like a misnomer. If it is "simple," it is only by comparison with more complex protocols.

Of course, the `smtp.rb` library shields the programmer from most of the details of the protocol. However, we have found that the design of this library is not entirely intuitive and perhaps overly complex (and we hope it will change in the future). In this section, we'll present a few examples to you in easy-to-digested pieces.

The `Net::SMTP` class has two class methods, `new` and `start`. The `new` method takes two parameters—the name of the server (defaulting to `localhost`) and the port number (defaulting to the well-known port 25).

The `start` method takes these parameters:

- *server* is the IP name of the SMTP server (defaulting to `"localhost"`).
- *port* is the port number, defaulting to `25`.
- *domain* is the domain of the mail sender (defaulting to `ENV["HOSTNAME"]`).
- *account* is the username (default is `nil`).

- *password* is the user password, defaulting to `nil`.
- *authtype* is the authorization type, defaulting to `:cram_md5`.

Many or most of these parameters can be omitted under normal circumstances.

If `start` is called normally (without a block), it returns an object of class `SMTP`. If it is called with a block, that object is passed into the block as a convenience.

An `SMTP` object has an instance method called `sendmail` that will typically be used to do the work of mailing a message. It takes three parameters:

- *source* is a string or array (or anything with an `each` iterator returning one string at a time).
- *sender* is a string that will appear in the From field of the e-mail.
- *recipients* is a string or an array of strings representing the addressee(s).

Here is an example of using the class methods to send an e-mail:

```
require 'net/smtp'

msg = <<EOF
Subject: Many things
"The time has come," the Walrus said,
"To talk of many things —
Of shoes, and ships, and sealing wax,
Of cabbages and kings;
And why the sea is boiling hot,
And whether pigs have wings."
EOF

Net::SMTP.start("smtp-server.fake.com") do |smtp|
  smtp.sendmail(msg, 'walrus@fake1.com', 'alice@fake2.com')
end
```

Because the string `Subject:` was specified at the beginning of the string, `Many things` will appear as the subject line when the message is received.

There is also an instance method named `start` that behaves much the same as the class method. Because `new` specifies the server, `start` doesn't have to specify it. This parameter is omitted, and the other parameters are the same as for the class method. This gives us a similar example using an `SMTP` object:

```
require 'net/smtp'
```

```
msg = <<EOF
Subject: Logic
"Contrariwise," continued Tweedledee,
"if it was so, it might be, and if it
were so, it would be; but as it isn't,
it ain't. That's logic."
EOF

smtp = Net::SMTP.new("smtp-server.fake.com")
smtp.start
smtp.sendmail(msg, 'tweedledee@fake1.com', 'alice@fake2.com')
```

In case you are not confused yet, the instance method can also take a block:

```
require 'net/smtp'

msg = <<EOF
Subject: Moby-Dick
Call me Ishmael.
EOF

addressees = ['reader1@fake2.com', 'reader2@fake3.com']

smtp = Net::SMTP.new("smtp-server.fake.com")
smtp.start do |obj|
  obj.sendmail msg, 'narrator@fake1.com', addressees
end
```

As the example shows, the object passed into the block (`obj`) certainly need not be named the same as the receiver (`smtp`). We also take this opportunity to emphasize that the recipient can be an array of strings.

There is also an oddly-named instance method called `ready`. This is much the same as `send-mail`, with some crucial differences. Only the sender and recipients are specified; the body of the message is constructed using an *adapter*—an object of class `Net::NetPrivate::WriteAdapter` that has a `write` method as well as an append method. This adapter is passed into the block and can be written to in an arbitrary way:

```
require "net/smtp"

smtp = Net::SMTP.new("smtp-server.fake1.com")

smtp.start
```

```
smtp.ready("t.s.eliot@fake1.com", "reader@fake2.com") do |obj|
  obj.write "Let us go then, you and I,\r\n"
  obj.write "When the evening is spread out against the sky\r\n"
  obj.write "Like a patient etherised upon a table...\r\n"
end
```

Note here that the carriage-return linefeed pairs are necessary (if we actually want line breaks in the message). Those who are familiar with the actual details of the protocol should note that the message is "finalized" (with "dot" and "QUIT") without any action on our part.

We can append instead of calling `write` if we prefer:

```
smtp.ready("t.s.eliot@fake1.com", "reader@fake2.com") do |obj|
  obj << "In the room the women come and go\r\n"
  obj << "Talking of Michelangelo.\r\n"
end
```

Finally, we offer a minor improvement by adding a `puts` method that will tack on the newline for us:

```
module Net
  module NetPrivate
    class WriteAdapter
      def puts(args)
        self.write(*(args+["\r\n"]))
      end
    end
  end
end
```

This new method enables us to write this way:

```
smtp.ready("t.s.eliot@fake1.com", "reader@fake2.com") do |obj|
  obj.puts "We have lingered in the chambers of the sea"
  obj.puts "By sea-girls wreathed with seaweed red and brown"
  obj.puts "Till human voices wake us, and we drown."
end
```

If your needs are more specific than what we've detailed here, we suggest you do your own experimentation; different environments may differ in their handling of authentication and such things. And if you decide to write a new interface for SMTP, feel free to do so.

Retrieving a Web Page from a Specified URL

Here's a simple code fragment. Let's suppose that, for whatever reason, we want to retrieve an HTML document from where it lives on the Web. Maybe our intent is to do a checksum and find out whether it has changed so that our software can inform us of this automatically. Maybe our intent is to write our own Web browser; this would be the proverbial first step on a journey of a thousand miles.

```
require "net/http"

begin
  h = Net::HTTP.new("www.ruby-lang.org", 80)
  resp, data = h.get("/en/index.html", nil)
rescue => err
  puts "Error: #{err}"
  exit
end

puts "Retrieved #{data.split.size} lines, #{data.size} bytes"
# Process as desired...
```

We begin by instantiating an HTTP object with the appropriate domain name and port. (The port, of course, is usually 80.) We then do a get operation, which returns an HTTP response and a string full of data. Here we don't actually test the response, but if there is any kind of error, we'll catch it and exit.

If we skip the rescue clause as we normally would, we can expect to have an entire Web page stored in the data string. We can then process it however we want.

What could go wrong here—what kind of errors do we catch? Actually, there are several. The domain name could be nonexistent or unreachable; there could be a redirect to another page (which we don't handle here); or we might get the dreaded 404 error (meaning that the document was not found). We'll leave this kind of error handling to you.

Case Study: A Mail-News Gateway

Online communities keep in touch with each other in many ways. Two of the most traditional ways are mailing lists and newsgroups.

Not everyone wants to be on a mailing list that might generate dozens of messages per day; some would rather read a newsgroup and pick through the information at random intervals. On the other hand, some people are impatient with Usenet and want to get the messages before the electrons have time to cool off.

So we get situations in which a fairly small, fairly private mailing list deals with the same subject matter as an unmoderated newsgroup open to the whole world. Eventually someone gets the idea for a mirror—a gateway between the two.

Such a gateway isn't appropriate in every situation, but in the case of the Ruby mailing list, it was and is. The newsgroup messages needed to be copied to the list, and the list e-mails needed to be posted on the newsgroup.

This need was addressed by Dave Thomas (in Ruby, of course), and we present the code here with his kind permission.

But let's look at a little background first. We've taken a quick look at how e-mail is sent and received; but how do we deal with Usenet? As it turns out, we can access the newsgroups via a protocol called *NNTP* (*Network News Transfer Protocol*). This, incidentally, was the work of Larry Wall, who later on gave us Perl.

Ruby doesn't have a "standard" library to handle NNTP. However, a Japanese developer (known to us only as *greentea*) has written a very nice library for this purpose.

The `nntp.rb` library defines a module `NNTP` containing a class called `NNTPIO`; it has the instance methods `connect`, `get_head`, `get_body`, and `post` (among others). To retrieve messages, you connect to the server and call `get_head` and `get_body` repeatedly. (We're over-simplifying this.) Likewise, to post a message, you basically construct the headers, connect to the server, and call the `post` method.

These programs use the `smtp` library that we've looked at previously. The original code also does some logging in order to track progress and record errors; we've removed this logging for greater simplicity.

The file `params.rb` is used by both programs. This file contains the parameters that drive the whole mirroring process—the names of the servers, account names, and so on. Here is a sample file that you will need to reconfigure for your own purposes. (The following domain names, which all contain the word *fake*, are obviously intended to be fictitious.)

```
# These are various parameters used by the mail-news gateway

module Params
  NEWS_SERVER = "usenet.fake1.org"      # name of the news server
  NEWSGROUP   = "comp.lang.ruby"        # mirrored newsgroup
  LOOP_FLAG   = "X-rubymirror: yes"     # line added to avoid loops
  LAST_NEWS_FILE = "/tmp/m2n/last_news" # Records last msg num read
  SMTP_SERVER = "localhost"             # host for outgoing mail

  MAIL_SENDER = "myself@fake2.org"      # Name used to send mail
  # (On a subscription-based list, this
  # name must be a list member.)

  MAILING_LIST = "list@fake3.org"       # Mailing list address
end
```

The module Params merely contains constants that are accessed by the two programs. Most are self-explanatory; we'll only point out a couple of items here. First, the LAST_NEWS_FILE constant identifies a file where the most recent newsgroup message ID is stored; this is "state information" so that work is not duplicated or lost.

Perhaps even more important, the LOOP_FLAG constant defines a string that marks a message as having already passed through the gateway. This avoids an infinite regress and prevents the programmer from being mobbed by hordes of angry netizens who have received thousands of copies of the same message.

You might be wondering: How do we actually get the mail into the mail2news program? After all, it appears to read standard input. The author recommends a setup like this: The sendmail program's .forward file first forwards all incoming mail to procmail. The .procmail file is set up to scan for messages from the mailing list and pipe them into the mail2news program. For the exact details of this, see the documentation associated with RubyMirror (found in the Ruby Application Archive). Of course, if you are on a non-Unix system, you will likely have to come up with your own scheme for handling this situation.

With this overview, the rest of the code is easy to understand. Refer to Listings 9.6 and 9.7.

LISTING 9.6   Mail-to-News

```
# mail2news: Take a mail message and post it
# as a news article

require "nntp"
include NNTP

require "params"

# Read in the message, splitting it into a
# heading and a body. Only allow certain
# headers through in the heading

HEADERS = %w{From Subject References Message-ID
            Content-Type Content-Transfer-Encoding Date}

allowed_headers = Regexp.new(%{^(#{HEADERS.join("|")}):},
                            Regexp::IGNORECASE)

# Read in the header. Only allow certain
# ones. Add a newsgroups line and an
# X-rubymirror line.
```

LISTING 9.6   Continued

```ruby
head = "Newsgroups: #{Params::NEWSGROUP}\n"
subject = "unknown"

valid_header = false
msg_id = "unknown"

while line = gets
  exit if line =~ /^#{Params::LOOP_FLAG}/o # shouldn't happen
  break if line =~ /^\s*$/


  # allow continuation lines only after valid headers
  if line =~ /^\s/
    head << line if valid_header
    next
  end

  msg_id = $1 if line =~ /Message-Id:\s+(.*)/i

  valid_header = (line =~ allowed_headers)
  next unless valid_header

  if line =~ /^Subject:\s*(.*)/
    # The following strips off the special ruby-talk number
    # from the front of mailing list messages before
    # forwarding them on to the news server.

    line.sub!(/\[ruby-talk:(\d+)\]\s*/, '')
    head << "X-ruby-talk: #$1\n"
  end
  head << line
end

head << "X-ruby-talk: #{msg_id}\n"

head << "#{Params::LOOP_FLAG}\n"

body = ""
while line = gets
  body << line
end

msg = head + "\n" + body
msg.gsub!(/\r?\n/, "\r\n")
```

LISTING 9.6   Continued

```
nntp = NNTPIO.new(Params::NEWS_SERVER)
raise "Failed to connect" unless nntp.connect
nntp.post(msg)
```

LISTING 9.7   News-to-Mail

```
##
# Simple script to help mirror the comp.lang.ruby
# traffic on to the ruby-talk mailing list.
#
# We are called periodically (say once every 20 minutes).
# We look on the news server for any articles that have a
# higher message ID than the last message we'd sent
# previously. If we find any, we read those articles,
# send them on to the mailing list, and record the
# new hightest message id.

require 'nntp'
require 'net/smtp'
require 'params'

include NNTP

##
# Send mail to the mailing-list. The mail must be
# from a list participant, although the From: line
# can contain any valid address
#

def send_mail(head, body)
  smtp = Net::SMTP.new
  smtp.start(Params::SMTP_SERVER)
  smtp.ready(Params::MAIL_SENDER, Params::MAILING_LIST) do |a|
    a.write head
    a.write "#{Params::LOOP_FLAG}\r\n"
    a.write "\r\n"
    a.write body
  end
end

##
# We store the mssage ID of the last news we received.
```

LISTING 9.7   Continued

```
begin
  last_news = File.open(Params::LAST_NEWS_FILE) {|f| f.read} .to_i
rescue
  last_news = nil
end


##
# Connect to the news server, and get the current
# message numbers for the comp.lang.ruby group
#
nntp = NNTPIO.new(Params::NEWS_SERVER)
raise "Failed to connect" unless nntp.connect
count, first, last = nntp.set_group(Params::NEWSGROUP)


##
# If we didn't previously have a number for the highest
# message number, we do now

if not last_news
  last_news = last
end


##
# Go to the last one read last time, and then try to get more.
# This may raise an exception if the number is for a
# nonexistent article, but we don't care.

begin
  nntp.set_stat(last_news)
rescue
end

##
# Finally read articles until there aren't any more,
# sending each to the mailing list.

new_last = last_news

begin
  loop do
    nntp.set_next
    head = ""
    body = ""
    new_last, = nntp.get_head do |line|
```

LISTING 9.7 Continued

```
      head << line
    end

    # Don't sent on articles that the mail2news program has
    # previously forwarded to the newsgroup (or we'd loop)
    next if head =~ %r{^X-rubymirror:}

    nntp.get_body do |line|
      body << line
    end

    send_mail(head, body)
  end
rescue
end

##
# And record the new high water mark

File.open(Params::LAST_NEWS_FILE, "w") do |f|
  f.puts  new_last
end  unless new_last == last_news
```

Ruby and the Web Server

Oh, what a tangled web we weave...!

—Sir Walter Scott

Various tools and libraries are available for the Ruby Web developer; standalone Web servers, tools that process and/or generate HTML and XML, and server add-ons and CGI libraries. Most of these are written in pure Ruby, although some have been written as extensions, usually for the sake of speed.

We can't cover everything here. However, we will present a good overview of Ruby and Web development.

Self-Contained Web Servers

Some developers in the Ruby community have implemented Web servers in Ruby. Of course, a fair question would be: Why would we be concerned with writing a new Web server? Aren't there plenty of good ones in existence, such as Apache?

There are several situations in which you might actually want your own proprietary Web server. The first is to handle Web pages in a specialized way, such as sacrificing functionality for speed.

Second, you might also want to experiment with the behavior of the server and its interaction with external code such as CGIs. You might want to play with your own ideas for creating an application server or a server-side development environment. We all know that Ruby is a fun language for software experimentation.

Third, you might want to embed a Web server inside another application. This possibility is sometimes exploited by developers who want to expose the functionality of a software system to the outside world; the HTTP protocol is well-defined and simple, and Web browsers that serve as clients are everywhere. This trick can even be used as a remote debugging tool, assuming that the system updates its internal state frequently and makes it available to the embedded server.

With these ideas in mind, let's look at what is available in the Ruby arena as far as Web servers are concerned. The Ruby Application Archive has at least four such entries.

The first is `httpd` by Michel van de Ven. This is a basic server that supports CGI; it is a good introduction to the functionality of a Web server. It is also an illustration of the power of Ruby because the entire piece of code is barely 250 lines. The license is GPL, so you can not only learn from the code, but you can actually re-use it, subject to certain restrictions.

Another server is Michael Neumann's `httpserv`. This is a multi-threaded server that can handle CGI and is known to work under both Unix and Windows. This server also integrates with the IOWA package (see the RAA), and includes a slightly modified `iowa.cgi` file.

Another interesting piece of code is `wwwd`, by Kengo Nakajima. This is billed by the author as "the fastest Web server in the world." It takes an interesting approach to achieve this speed. First, all the files are stored in memory, making disk accesses unnecessary. Second, because the overhead of threading and forking would become significant, it doesn't do any forking or use threads. A downside is that it doesn't support CGI (although you can get a similar effect by using Ruby scripts). Overall, it is designed for Web sites that are very small but heavily accessed.

There is also `wwwsrv` by Yoshinori Toki. This is a new package at the time of this writing, and has no English documentation. But it does already have usable CGI and SSI features, and it looks promising in general.

Using Embedded Ruby

First of all, let's dispel any confusion over terminology. We're not talking about embedding a Ruby interpreter in an electronic device like a TV or a toaster. We're talking about embedding Ruby code inside text.

Second of all, we'll note that there is more than one scheme for embedding Ruby code in text files. Here we only discuss the most common tool, which is eruby (created by Shugo Maeda).

Why do we mention such a tool in connection with the Web? Obviously, it's because the most common form of text in which we'll embed Ruby code is HTML (or XML).

Having said that, it's conceivable that there might be other uses for eruby. Perhaps it could be used in an old-fashioned text-based adventure game; or in some kind of mail-merge utility; or as part of a cron job to create a customized message-of-the-day file (/etc/motd) every night at midnight. Don't let your creativity be constrained by our lack of imagination. Feel free to dig up new and interesting uses for eruby, and share them with the rest of us. Most of the examples we give here are very generic (and thus are very contrived); they don't have much to do with HTML specifically.

The eruby utility is simply a filter or preprocessor. A special notation is used to delimit Ruby code, expressions, and comments; all other text is simply passed through "as is."

The symbols are used to mark the pieces of text that will be treated specially. There are three forms of this notation, varying in the first character inside the "tag."

If it is an equal sign (=), the tag is treated as a Ruby expression that is evaluated; the resulting value is inserted at the current location in the text file. Here is a sample text file:

```
This is <%= "ylno".reverse %> a test.
Do <%= "NOT".downcase %> be alarmed.
```

Assuming that the file for this example is called myfile.txt, we can filter it in this way:

```
eruby myfile.txt
```

The output, by default written to standard output, will look like this:

```
This is only a test.
Do not be alarmed.
```

We can also use the character # to indicate a comment:

```
Life <%# so we've heard %> is but a dream.
```

As you'd expect, the comment is ignored. The preceding line will produce this line of output:

```
Life  is but a dream.
```

Any other character following the percent sign will be taken as the first character of a piece of Ruby code, and its *output* (not its evaluated value) will be placed into the text stream. For readability, we recommend using a blank space here, though eruby does not demand it.

In this example, the tag in the first line of text does *not* insert any text (because it doesn't produce any output). The second line works as expected.

```
The answer is <% "42" %>.
Or rather, the answer is <% puts "42" %>.
```

So the output would be:

```
The answer is .
Or rather, the answer is 42.
```

The effect of the Ruby code is cumulative. For example, a variable defined in one tag can be used in a subsequent tag.

```
<% x=3; y=4; z=5 %>
Given a triangle of sides <%=x%>, <%=y%>, and <%=z%>,
we know it is a right triangle because
<%= x*x %> + <%= y*y %> = <%= z*z %>.
```

The spaces we used inside the tags in the last line are not necessary, but they do increase readability. The output will be

```
Given a triangle of sides 3, 4, and 5,
we know it is a right triangle because
9 + 16 = 25.
```

Try putting a syntax error inside a tag. You'll find that eruby has very verbose reporting; it actually prints out the generated Ruby code and tells us as precisely as it can where the error is.

What if we want to include one of the "magic" strings as a literal part of our text? You might be tempted to try a backslash to escape the characters, but this won't work. We recommend a technique like the following:

```
There is a less-than-percent <%="<%"%> on this line
and a percent-greater-than <%="%"+">"%> on this one.
Here we see <%="<%="%> and <%="<%#"%> as well.
```

The output then will be

```
There is a less-than-percent <% on this line
and a percent-greater-than %> on this one.
Here we see <%= and <%# as well.
```

Note that it's a little easier to embed an opening symbol than a closing one. This is because they can't be nested, and eruby is not smart enough to ignore a closing symbol inside a string.

Of course, eruby does have certain features that are tailored to HTML. The flag -M can be used to specify a mode of operation; the valid modes are f, c, and n, respectively.

The f mode (filter) is the default, which is why all our previous examples worked without the -Mf on the command line. The -Mc option means CGI mode; it prints all errors as HTML. The -Mn option means NPH-CGI mode ("no-parse-headers"); it outputs extra HTML headers automatically. Both CGI and NPH-CGI modes set $SAFE to be 1 for security reasons (assuming that the application is a CGI and thus may be invoked by a hostile user). The -n flag (or the equivalent —noheader) will suppress CGI header output.

It's possible to set up the Apache Web server to recognize embedded Ruby pages. You do this by associating the type application/x-httpd-eruby with some extension (.rhtml being a logical choice) and defining an action that associates this type with the eruby executable. For more information, consult the Apache documentation.

Using mod_ruby

Typically when a CGI script is written in an interpreted language, an instance of the interpreter is launched with every invocation of the CGI. This can be expensive in terms of server utilization and execution time.

The Apache server solves this problem by allowing loadable modules that in effect attach themselves to the server and become part of it. Such a module is loaded dynamically as needed, and is shared by all the scripts that depend on it.

The mod_ruby package (available from the Ruby Application Archive) is such a module. Support for Apache 2.0 is not yet available, but it is in the works.

The mod_ruby package implements several Apache directives. At the present time, these are as follows:

- RubyRequire—Specifies one or more libraries needed.
- RubyHandler—Specifies a handler for *ruby-object*.
- RubyPassEnv—Specifies names of environment variables to pass to scripts.
- RubySetEnv—Sets environment variables.

- RubyTimeOut—Specifies a timeout value for Ruby scripts.
- RubySafeLevel—Sets the $SAFE level.
- RubyKanjiCode—Sets the Ruby character encoding.

The software also provides Ruby classes and modules for interacting with Apache. The Apache module (using *module* here in the Ruby sense) has a few module functions as server_version and unescape_url; it also contains the Request and Table classes.

Apache::Request is a wrapper for the request_rec data type, defining methods such as request_method, content_type, readlines, and more. The Apache::Table class is a wrapper for the table data type, defining methods such as get, add, and each.

Extensive instructions are available for compiling and installing the mod_ruby package. Refer to its accompanying documentation (or the equivalent information on the Web).

We'll also mention that there is an alternative, FastCGI, that is not tied so closely to the Web server. Refer to the section "Using FastCGI" for a discussion of the pros and cons.

Ruby and CGI Programming

Anyone familiar with Web programming has at least heard of CGI (Common Gateway Interface). CGI was created in the early days of the Web to enable programmatically implemented sites and to allow for more interaction between the end user and the Web server. Although countless replacement technologies have been introduced since its inception, CGI is still alive and well in the world of Web programming. Much of CGI's success and longevity can be attributed to its simplicity. Because of this simplicity, it is quite easy to implement CGI programs in any language. The CGI standard specifies how a Web server process will pass data between itself and its children. Most of this interaction occurs through standard environment variables and streams in the implementation operating system.

CGI programming, and HTTP for that matter, are based around a "stateless" request and response mechanism. Generally, a single TCP connection is made, and the client (usually a Web browser) initiates conversation with a single HTTP command. The two most commonly used commands in the protocol are GET and POST. (We'll get to the meaning of these shortly.) After issuing the command, the Web server responds and closes its output stream.

The following code sample, only slightly more advanced than the standard "Hello world," shows how to do input and output via CGI.

```ruby
def parse_query_string
  inputs = Hash.new
  raw = ENV['QUERY_STRING']
```

```
    raw.split("&").each do |pair|
      name,value = pair.split("=")
      inputs[name] = value
    end
    inputs
  end

  inputs = parse_query_string
  print "Content-type: text/html\r\n\r\n"
  print "<HTML><BODY>"
  print "<B><I>Hello</I>, #{inputs['name']}!</B>"
  print "</BODY></HTML>"
```

Accessing the URL (for example) `http://mywebserver/cgi-bin/hello.cgi?name=Dali` would produce the output `"Hello, Dali!"` in your Web browser.

As we previously mentioned, there are two main ways to access a URL: the HTTP GET and POST methods. For the sake of brevity, we offer extremely simple explanations of these methods, rather than rigorous definitions. The GET method is usually called when clicking a link or directly referencing a URL (as in the preceding example). Any parameters are passed via the URL query string, which is made accessible to CGI programs via the QUERY_STRING environment variable. The POST method is usually used in HTML form processing. The parameters sent in a POST are included in the message body, and are not visible via the URL. They are delivered to CGI programs via the standard input stream.

Though the previous example was very simple, anything less trivial could quickly become messy. Programs needing to deal with multiple HTTP methods, file uploads, cookies, "stateful" sessions, and other complexities are best suited by a general purpose library for working with the CGI environment. Thankfully, Ruby provides a full-featured set of classes that automate much of the mundane work one would otherwise have to do manually.

We should mention that recently there has been much discussion of a "next generation" CGI library for Ruby—one with enhanced capabilities, a better interface, and separation of real CGI issues from mere HTML generation. We hope that great things come from this; but as we go to press, it is sheer vaporware. We can only document what already exists; and though it might be imperfect, it certainly is stable and usable.

Overview: Using the CGI Library

The CGI library is in the file `cgi.rb` in the standard Ruby distribution. Most of its functionality is implemented around a central class, aptly named CGI. One of the first things you'll want to do when using the library, then, is to create an instance of CGI.

```
require "cgi"
cgi = CGI.new("html4")
```

The initializer for the CGI class takes a single parameter, which specifies the level of HTML that should be supported by the HTML generation methods in the CGI package. These methods keep the programmer from having to embed a truckload of escaped HTML into otherwise pristine Ruby code:

```
cgi.out do
  cgi.html do
    cgi.body do
      cgi.h1 { "Hello Again, " } +
      cgi.b { cgi['name']}
    end
  end
end
```

Here, we've used the CGI libraries to almost exactly reproduce the functionality of the previous program. As you can see, the CGI class takes care of parsing any input, and stores the resulting values internally as a hash-like structure. So if you specified the URL as some_program.cgi?age=4, the value could be accessed via cgi['age'].

Note in the previous code fragment that it's really only the return value of a block that is used; the HTML is built up gradually and stored, rather than being output immediately. This means that the string concatenation we see here is absolutely necessary; without it, only the last string evaluated would appear.

The CGI class also provides some convenience mechanisms for dealing with URL-encoded strings and escaped HTML or XML. URL encoding is the process of translating strings with unsafe characters to a format that is representable in a URL string. The result is all those weird-looking % strings you see in some URLs while you browse the Web. These strings are actually the numeric ASCII codes represented in hexadecimal with % prepended.

```
require "cgi"
s = "This| is^(aT$test"
s2 = CGI.escape(s)          # "This%7C+is%5E%28aT%24test"
puts CGI.unescape(s2)       # Prints "This| is^(aT$test"
```

Similarly, the CGI class can be used to escape HTML or XML text that should be displayed verbatim in a browser. For example, the string *<some_stuff>* would not display properly in a browser. If there is a need to display HTML or XML literally in a browser—in an HTML tutorial, for example—the CGI class offers support for translating special characters to their appropriate entities:

```
require "cgi"
some_text = "<B>This is how you make text bold</B>"
translated = CGI.escapeHTML(some_text)
# "&lt;B&gt;This is how you make text bold&lt;/B&gt;"
puts CGI.unescapeHTML(translated)
# Prints "<B>This is how you make text bold</B>"
```

Displaying and Processing Forms

The most common way of interacting with CGI programs is through HTML forms. HTML forms are created by using specific tags that will be translated to input widgets in a browser. A full discussion or reference is beyond the scope of this text, but there are numerous references available, both in books and on the Web.

The CGI class offers generation methods for all the HTML form elements. The following example shows how to both display and process an HTML form:

```
require "cgi"

def reverse_ramblings(ramblings)
  if ramblings[0] == nil then return "" end
  chunks = ramblings[0].split(/\s+/)
  chunks.reverse.join(" ")
end

cgi = CGI.new("html4")
cgi.out do
  cgi.html do
    cgi.body do
      cgi.h1 { "sdrawkcaB txeT" } +
      cgi.b { reverse_ramblings(cgi['ramblings'])} +
      cgi.form("action" => "/cgi-bin/rb/form.cgi") do
        cgi.textarea("ramblings") { cgi['ramblings'] } + cgi.submit
      end
    end
  end
end
```

This example displays a text area, the contents of which will be tokenized into words and reversed. For example, typing **This is a test** into the text area would yield test a is This after processing. The form method of the CGI class can accept a method parameter, which will set the HTTP method (GET, POST, and so on) to be used on form submittal. The default, used in this example, is POST.

This example contains only a small sample of the form elements available in an HTML page. For a complete list, go to any HTML reference.

Working with Cookies

HTTP is, as mentioned previously, a stateless protocol. This means that after a browser finishes a request to a Web site, the Web server has no way to distinguish its next request from any other arbitrary browser on the Web. This is where HTTP cookies come into the picture. Cookies offer a way, albeit somewhat crude, to maintain state between requests from the same browser.

The cookie mechanism works by way of the Web server issuing a command to the browser, via an HTTP response header, asking the browser to store a name/value pair. The data can be stored either in memory or on disk. For every successive request to the cookie's specified domain, the browser will send the cookie data in an HTTP request header.

Of course, you could read and write all these cookies manually, but you've probably already guessed that you're not going to need to. Ruby's CGI libraries provide a `Cookie` class that conveniently handles these chores.

```ruby
require "cgi"
lastacc = CGI::Cookie.new("kabhi",
                          "lastaccess=#{Time.now.to_s}")
cgi = CGI.new("html3")
if cgi.cookies.size < 1
  cgi.out("cookie" => lastacc) do
    "Hit refresh for a lovely cookie"
  end
else
  cgi.out("cookie" => lastacc) do
    cgi.html do
      "Hi, you were last here at: " +
      "#{cgi.cookies['kabhi'].join.split('=')[1]}"
    end
  end
end
```

Here, a cookie called `kabhi` is created, with the key `lastaccess` set to the current time. Then, if the browser has a previous value stored for this cookie, it is displayed. The cookies are represented as an instance variable on the `CGI` class and stored as a `Hash`. Each cookie can store multiple key/value pairs, so when you access a cookie by name, you will receive an array.

Working with User Sessions

Cookies are fine if you want to store simple data, and you don't mind the browser being responsible for persistence. But, in many cases, data persistence needs are a bit more complex. What if you've got a lot of data you want to maintain persistently, and you don't want to have to send it back and forth from the client and server with each request? What if there is sensitive data you need associated with a session, and you don't trust the browser with it?

For more advanced persistence in Web applications, use the CGI::Session class. Working with this class is similar to working with the CGI::Cookie class, in that values are stored and retrieved via a hash-like structure.

```ruby
require "cgi"
require "cgi/session"

cgi = CGI.new("html4")

sess = CGI::Session.new( cgi, "session_key" => "a_test",
                              "prefix" => "rubysess.")
lastaccess = sess["lastaccess"].to_s
sess["lastaccess"] = Time.now
if cgi['bgcolor'][0] =~ /[a-z]/
  sess["bgcolor"] = cgi['bgcolor']
end

cgi.out do
  cgi.html do
    cgi.body ("bgcolor" => sess["bgcolor"]) do
      "The background of this page"   +
      "changes based on the 'bgcolor'" +
      "each user has in session."      +
      "Last access time: #{lastaccess}"
    end
  end
end
```

Accessing /thatscript.cgi?bgcolor=red would turn the page red for a single user for each successive hit until a new bgcolor was specified via the URL. CGI::Session is instantiated with a CGI object and a set of options in a Hash. The optional session_key parameter specifies the key that will be used by the browser to identify itself on each request. Session data is stored in a temporary file for each session, and the prefix parameter assigns a string to be prepended to the filename, making your sessions easy to identify on the filesystem of the server.

There are still many features that CGI::Session is lacking, such as the ability to store objects other than Strings, session storage across multiple servers, and other "nice-to-have" capabilities. Fortunately, a pluggable database_manager mechanism is already in place, and would make some of these features quite easy to add. If you do anything exciting with CGI::Session, be sure to let us know.

9

Using FastCGI

The most criticized shortcoming of CGI is that it requires a new process to be created for every invocation. The effect on performance is significant. The lack of a capability to leave objects in memory between requests can also have a negative impact on design. The combination of these difficulties has led to the creation of something called FastCGI.

FastCGI is basically nothing more than a protocol definition, a design, and a set of software implementing that protocol. Usually implemented as a Web server plug-in, such as an Apache module, it enables an in-process helper to intercept HTTP requests and route them via socket to a long running backend process. This has a very positive effect on speed compared to the traditional forking approach. It also gives the programmer the freedom to put things in memory and still find them there on the next request.

A fair question would be: How do mod_ruby and FastCGI compare? There are definite trade-offs involved.

Because Apache is a forking Web server, resources are allocated and freed without the full knowledge of the application, making it problematic to store session information. In FastCGI, all requests are handled by a single process, making it easy to cache data, keep database connections open, and store session data in memory (where arguably it should be).

FastCGI offers no access to Apache's internals. If you really need that kind of access, mod_ruby is a better choice.

FastCGI also works with other Web servers such as Zeus and Netscape. Potentially any server can be supported by using the CGI-to-FastCGI adapter, which is a tiny CGI script that handles CGI connections for you. It is not as efficient as a plug-in like mod_fastcgi, but does still eliminate the overhead of (for example) reconnecting to a database and reloading config files every time a CGI executes.

Conveniently, servers for FastCGI have been implemented in a number of languages, including Ruby. Eli Green created a module (available via the RAA) entirely in Ruby, which implements the FastCGI protocol and eases the development of FastCGI programs.

We present a sample application in Listing 9.8. As you can see, this code fragment mirrors the functionality of the earlier example.

LISTING 9.8   A FastCGI Example

```
require "fastcgi"
require "cgi"
```

LISTING 9.8   Continued

```ruby
last_time = ""

def get_ramblings(instream)
  # Unbeautifully retrieve the value of the first name/value pair
  # CGI would have done this for us.
  data = ""
  if instream != nil
    data = instream.split("&")[0].split("=")[1] || ""
  end
  return CGI.unescape(data)
end

def reverse_ramblings(ramblings)
  if ramblings == nil then return "" end
  chunks = ramblings.split(/\s+/)
  chunks.reverse.join(" ")
end

server = FastCGI::TCP.new('localhost', 9000)
begin
  server.each_request do |request|
  stuff = request.in.read
  out = request.out
  out << "Content-type: text/html\r\n\r\n"
  out << "<html>"
  out << "<head><title>Text Backwardizer</title></head>"
  out << "<h1>sdrawkcaB txeT</h1>"
  out << "<i>You previously said: #{last_time}</i><BR>"
  out << "<b>#{reverse_ramblings(get_ramblings(stuff))}</b>"
  out << "<form method=\"POST\" action=\"/fast/serv.rb\">"
  out << "<textarea name=\"ramblings\">"
  out << "</textarea>"
  out << "<input type=\"submit\" name=\"submit\""
  out << "</form>"
  out << "</body></html>"
  last_time = get_ramblings(stuff)
  request.finish
  end
ensure
  server.close
end
```

The first thing that strikes you about this code (if you've read the previous section) is the couple of things that you have to do manually in FastCGI that you wouldn't have had to do with the CGI library. One is the messy hard-coding of escaped HTML. The other is the get_ramblings method, which manually parses the input and returns only the relevant value. This code, by the way, only works with the HTTP POST method—another convenience lost when not using the CGI library.

That being said, FastCGI is by no means without its advantages. We didn't run any benchmarks on this example, but—it's in the name—FastCGI is *faster* than normal CGI. The overhead of starting up a new process is avoided in favor of making a local network connection to port 9000 (FastCGI::TCP.new('localhost', 9000)). Also, the last_time variable in this example is used to maintain a piece of state in memory in between requests—something impossible with traditional CGI. Of course, the actual speed increase will depend on a number of complex factors, such as the choice of OS and Web server, the nature of the CGI, the amount of Web traffic, and so on.

We'll also point out that it's possible to a limited extent to mix and match these libraries. The helper functions from cgi.rb can be used on their own (without actually using this library to drive the application). For example, CGI.escapeHTML can be used in isolation from the rest of the library. This would make the previous example a little more readable.

Case Study: A Message Board

One of the most exciting things about the Web today is its ability to create a sense of virtual *community*. With the Internet, you have the potential to communicate in real-time with people from around the world. People who have never actually met in person can share common interests and even strike up friendships.

There are many ways by which this type of communication can happen via the Internet. The oldest and most firmly established way is the bulletin board metaphor. Since the advent of Usenet or the good old days of BBSs (Bulletin Board Systems), online communities have prospered around this asynchronous form of communication. The new breed of this age-old species is the Web-based message board application. From cheesy online matchmaking services to geek sites like userfriendly.org, the bulletin board metaphor is alive and well on the Web.

If you've ever wondered how to write your own bulletin board, we're here to help you. What follows is a treatise on our own lean, not-so-mean bulletin board system RuBoard.

Although RuBoard works, it certainly isn't good for much more than a starting point in the ways of the bulletin board. It is not the most robust or secure application ever written for the Web, but it should illustrate some concepts that will put you well on your way to making something deployable. During the discussion, we will point out some areas of potential improvement and leave them as the proverbial exercise for the reader.

This is the most lengthy example in the book, consisting of several files. For the sake of completeness, we've included them all in print. The following is a list of the files and their purposes:

- `board.cgi`—The main piece of code or "driver" for the entire CGI, through which all requests must pass.
- `mainlist.rb`—The main or default screen that displays the entire list of messages previously posted (see Figure 9.2).
- `message.rb`—The `Message` and `MessageStore` classes that handle the loading and storing of messages.
- `savepost.rb`—The code for the save-post page (saving a post or reply).
- `viewmessage.rb`—The code for the view-message page, displaying a single message with all the relevant fields.
- `post.rb`—The code for the post-page, enabling the creation of a new post (message).
- `reply.rb`—The code for the reply-page, displayed when replying to a previous post.
- `authenticate.rb`—The code for authenticating a user (rudimentary in this example). Redirects to whatever page the user was originally trying to reference.

One thing will probably stand out after you've read some of the previous examples. Despite its relative complexity, RuBoard has only one actual CGI program. It consists of several screens (or pages), but there's only one CGI program controlling them all. In past examples, with simplicity in mind, we have always demonstrated CGI programs that served only one distinct page. In this case study, you'll see a central program `board.cgi` acting as a *controller* for all the bulletin board's logic and presentation-related activities. Refer to Listing 9.9 for the `board.cgi` source.

LISTING 9.9 Message Board CGI (`board.cgi`)

```
#!/usr/local/bin/ruby
require "cgi"
require "cgi/session"
$session = nil

def header(cgi)
  "<B>Welcome, #{get_session(cgi)['user']}!</B> - " +
  "<i><a href=\"/cgi-bin/rb/board.cgi?cmd=post\">" +
  "post a message</a></i> - <i>" +
  "<a href=\"/cgi-bin/rb/board.cgi?cmd=mainlist\">home</a>." +
  <BR><HR>"
end
```

LISTING 9.9   Continued

```ruby
def do_oops_page(cgi, err)
  cgi.out do
    cgi.html do
      cgi.body do
        "It appears that you have invoked the" +
        " message board incorrectly. Oops.<BR>|#{err}|"
      end
    end
  end
end

def do_login_page(cgi)
  cgi.out do
    cgi.html do
      cgi.body do
        cgi.h1 { "Welcome to Ruby Board" } +
        cgi.b { "Please Login:" } +
        cgi.form("METHOD" => "get",
                 "action" => "/cgi-bin/rb/board.cgi") do
          cgi.text_field({ "name" => "user" })  +
          cgi.submit("Login") +
          cgi.input({"name" => "cmd",
                     "value" => "authenticate",
                     "type" => "hidden"}) +
          cgi.input({"name" => "page",
                     "value" => "#{cgi['cmd'][0]}",
                     "type" => "hidden"})
        end
      end
    end
  end
end

def run_command(cgi)
  command = cgi['cmd'][0]
  if command == "" || command == nil
    command = "mainlist"
  end
  if command_safe?(command)
    methname = "do_#{command}_page"
  else
    do_oops_page(cgi, "Command \"#{command}\"" +
                      " inappropriately formatted.")
  end
```

LISTING 9.9 Continued

```ruby
    begin
      eval "#{methname}(cgi)"
    rescue NameError
      begin
        require "#{command}.rb"
      rescue LoadError
        do_oops_page(cgi, "Error loading #{command}")
      end
    end
    eval "#{methname}(cgi)"
    exit

  end

  def command_safe?(command)
    if command =~ (/^[a-zA-Z0-9]+$/) then
      return true
    end
    false
  end

  def get_session(cgi)
    if $session == nil then
      $session = CGI::Session.new( cgi, "session_key" => "a_test",
                                        "prefix" => "rubysess.")
    end
    return $session
  end

  def validate_session(cgi)
    session = get_session(cgi)
    if cgi["user"][0] =~ /[a-zA-Z0-9]/
      return
    end
    if session["user"] !~ /[a-zA-Z0-9]/
      do_login_page(cgi)
    end
  end

  if __FILE__ == $0 then
    cgi = CGI.new("html4")
    validate_session(cgi)
    err = run_command(cgi)
  end
```

This is a vague hint of the Model View Controller (MVC) design pattern, referenced in *Design Patterns,* published by Addison-Wesley and authored by the so-called "Gang of Four" (Gamma, Helm, Johnson, and Vlissides). The main advantage of our trimmed down, almost-MVC architecture is that application-wide changes can be implemented in a single place. For example, if we wanted to add a central logging facility, we could easily add it to `board.cgi`, and every page request would invoke the new utility.

The first thing a user must do when attempting to use the bulletin board is log in. As a function of our centralized CGI design, authentication is handled in one place. (Refer to the `validate_session` method in `board.cgi`.) This code won't enable unauthenticated requests through to any page other than the login page.

As you can see, the authentication scheme used ("we'll believe that you are whoever you say you are") isn't all that secure. But it suffices as a more-than-stub example of how you might force authentication in your own application. The basic flow is that a user comes to the application requesting a page, and `validate_session` first checks to make sure that the user is either already logged in or trying to log in. If the user hasn't logged in and isn't passing in a `userid` with which to attempt to authenticate himself, the login page will be displayed to prompt for a username. Because the central `board.cgi` handles all authentication in the application, it would be trivial to replace `validate_session` with a more robust security implementation.

You might have noticed the `get_session` call in `board.cgi`, which gets a handle to the current user's session; this is an implementation of the singleton design pattern (not a rigorous implementation). Here we've used a global variable; this is OK because CGI programs are forked as separate processes, giving each invocation its own memory space. If we were making, for example, a FastCGI program, we would need to devise a different strategy to keep users' sessions from clobbering each other. For this reason, we've hidden the session retrieval logic behind a method, as opposed to directly referencing the global variable from any code that needs access to the session. Again, we could change this method alone if we needed to move our program to an environment that was less friendly to global variables.

The next important piece of RuBoard's design emerges in the calls to the `do_login_page` and `run_command` methods. Each page in our humble framework can be referenced internally by a call to do_*PAGENAME*_page. So, for example, the login page is called via the `do_login_page` method. The `run_command`, also in `board.cgi`, is responsible for determining which page the user is trying to reach and dynamically invoking the necessary code to fulfill the request.

This code is both a little tricky and a little dangerous. It determines which method to run by looking at the value of the `cmd` key, passed in as a `QUERY_STRING` parameter from the Web browser. So, for example, invoking `/board.cgi?cmd=hello` would attempt to run a method called do_hello_page. If the method is not defined, a NameError will be raised, and the program will attempt to require a separate library containing the requested page. There are two red flags here, both involving the use of the cmd key. With the call to eval, we are executing arbitrary code, passed in from an anonymous Internet user, and with the call to require, we are reading arbitrary files from the server's hard disk. The command_safe? method's job is to allay these fears. Of course, this specific implementation leaves much to be desired. The code provided here is a simple starting point for a more robust set of checks.

After having successfully logged in, run_command defaults to an invocation of do_mainlist_page (see Listing 9.10), which creates the page called *mainlist*. This page gets the current list of messages on the bulletin board, and displays them to the user in a list. The user can then choose to read one of the messages, or to post a new message.

LISTING 9.10   Message Board CGI (mainlist.rb)

```ruby
require "message"

def do_mainlist_page(cgi)
  messages = get_messages
  user = get_session(cgi)['user']
  template = get_template
  messagerows = get_message_rows(template, messages)
  template.gsub!(/%%LISTROW%%/, messagerows)
  template.gsub!(/%%USER%%/, user)
  template.gsub!(/%%HEADER%%/, header(cgi))
  cgi.out{ template }
end

def get_message_rows(template, messages)
  rows = ""
  messages.each do |message|
    rows << "<TR><TD><a href=\"/cgi-bin/rb/board.cgi?" +
            "cmd=viewmessage&id=#{message.id}\">" +
            "#{message.id}</a></TD><TD>#{message.title}" +
            "</TD><TD>#{message.sender}</TD><TD>" +
            "#{message.date}</TD></TR>"
  end
  rows
end

def get_template
  "<HTML><HEAD>
    <TITLE>RuBoard!</TITLE>
    </HEAD>
```

LISTING 9.10   Continued

```
        <BODY>
        %%HEADER%%
        <B>Message List</B><BR>
        <TABLE border=1>
          <TR>
          <TD>ID</TD>
          <TD>Title</TD>
          <TD>Sender</TD>
          <TD>Time</TD>
          </TR>
          %%LISTROW%%
        </TABLE>
      </BODY></HTML>"
    end
```

For a screenshot of a simple mainlist page, refer to Figure 9.2. This figure shows a list with only two messages in it.

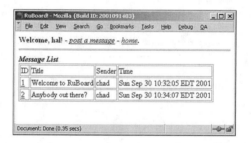

FIGURE 9.2
RuBoard MainList page.

The most interesting thing about this listing is the generation of the HTML. We have created our own scaled-down templating system. For a feature-filled, robust templating solution, see eruby or ERb in the Ruby Application Archive. (Also see the section "Using Embedded Ruby.") To keep our examples simple, we're sticking to a basic text replacement here. The advantage of these sorts of templating methods is that they enable the programmer to deal with HTML in a very familiar way—as simple HTML source code. This can sometimes be easier to visualize than the built-in "elements-as-methods" approach of the Ruby CGI library.

When this page is called, run_command will either find cmd=mainlist in the input parameters for the CGI program, or it will default to the mainlist page. It will then load mainlist.rb and execute the do_mainlist_page method. This method uses the Message and MessageStore classes (described later in this section) to retrieve the list of all messages currently on the bulletin board. It then makes a call to `get_template` and replaces the specially labeled keys, arbitrarily marked with surrounding double percent markers (`%%`), with dynamically generated text. After we've created a `String` with the desired presentation, we simply spit it into the `cgi` object's output stream and the program then exits.

So, where do these messages come from? How are they stored? Let's have a look at Listing 9.11.

LISTING 9.11   Message Board CGI (`message.rb`)

```ruby
$filepath = "/tmp/messagestore.dat"

class Message
  attr_accessor :id, :title, :sender, :replies, :date, :body
  def initialize(title, sender)
    @title = title
    @sender = sender
    @date = Time.now
    @replies = Array.new
  end
  def add_reply(message)
    @replies.push message
  end
end


class MessageStore
  attr_accessor :messages, :filepath, :id, :message_table

  def MessageStore.load(filepath)
    if !FileTest.exist?(filepath)
      welcomemsg = Message.new("Welcome to RuBoard", "chad")
      welcomemsg.body = "Please enjoy your stay!"
  mstore = MessageStore.new
      mstore.add_message(welcomemsg)
      f = File.new(filepath, "w")
      Marshal.dump(mstore, f)
      f.close
    end
    file = File.open(filepath, "r")
    Marshal.load(file)
  end

  def save(filepath)
    File.delete(filepath)
```

LISTING 9.11   Continued

```ruby
      Marshal.dump(self, File.new(filepath, "w"))
    end

    def initialize
      @message_table = Hash.new
      @id = 0
      @messages = Array.new
    end

    def add_message(message)
      message.id = next_id
      @message_table[message.id] = message
      @messages.push message
    end

    def get_message(num)
      @message_table[num]
    end

    private
    def next_id
      @id += 1
    end

  end


  # Auxiliary methods...

  def get_message_view(message)
    template = "<i>Message %%NUM%%</i><BR>
    <i>From: %%SENDER%%</i><BR>
    <i>Date: %%DATE%%</i><BR>
    <i>Title: %%TITLE%%</i><BR>
    <HR>
    %%BODY%%
    <HR>"
    template.gsub!(/%%NUM%%/, message.id.to_s)
    template.gsub!(/%%SENDER%%/, message.sender)
    template.gsub!(/%%DATE%%/, message.date.to_s)
    template.gsub!(/%%TITLE%%/, message.title)
    template.gsub!(/%%BODY%%/, message.body)
    template
  end
```

LISTING 9.11 Continued

```ruby
def get_messages
  mstore = get_message_store
  mstore.messages
end

def get_message_store
MessageStore.load($filepath)
end
```

The two most important items here are the Message class, providing a simple object-oriented view of a message, and the MessageStore class, which handles the storage and retrieval of messages. MessageStore is where most of the message-related work actually takes place. This also happens to be one of those areas of potential improvement that we alluded to earlier.

Looking at MessageStore.load and MessageStore.save, you'll notice that the entire set of bulletin board messages is stored in a single file of marshalled Ruby objects on the server system. Although this design is simple, there are some problems with it. The worst of the problems is that the system can't handle concurrent users correctly. If two users were to attempt to update the message board at the same time, the result would certainly include failure and data loss. A better approach would be to use an RDBMS, such as MySQL or PostgreSQL, as the storage mechanism for bulletin board items. The internals of MessageStore could easily be replaced with database access or some other more suitable solution, because its interface doesn't fully expose the underlying storage strategy. Refer to Chapter 4, "External Data Manipulation," for more ideas about data storage in Ruby, including examples of how to interface with MySQL, a very popular database for Web application programming.

The four methods at the end of message.rb are convenience methods to avoid duplication in the various pages of the message board that require access to this data. Because each Web page is a separate, viewable entity, CGI applications can quickly degrade into an unmaintainable mound of copies and pastes. For this reason, it's important to be especially careful to look for chances to generalize and remove duplication when making CGI programs.

Five other files help comprise RuBoard. We've added these others to a single listing (Listing 9.12) because they are fairly short. These files get required by the run_command method as they are needed; they are kept separate for maintainability.

LISTING 9.12 Message Board CGI (Other Files)

```ruby
#
# File: authenticate.rb
```

9

NETWORK AND
WEB
PROGRAMMING

LISTING 9.12   Continued

```
#

require "message"

def do_authenticate_page(cgi)
  session = get_session(cgi)
  session['user'] = cgi['user'][0]
  page = cgi['page'][0]
  if page == nil || page == ""
    cgi.out do
      '<HTML><HEAD><META HTTP-EQUIV="REFRESH"' +
      ' CONTENT="1;URL=/cgi-bin/rb/board.cgi?cmd=mainlist">' +
      '</HEAD><BODY></BODY></HTML>'
    end
  else
    cgi['cmd'][0] = page
    run_command(cgi)
  end
end


#
# File: post.rb
#

require "message"

def do_post_page(cgi)
  mstore = get_message_store
  user = get_session(cgi)['user']
  num = cgi['id'][0]
  message = mstore.get_message(num.to_i)

  template = get_template
  template.gsub!(/%%HEADER%%/, header(cgi))
  template.gsub!(/%%USER%%/, user)
  cgi.out{ template }
end

def get_template
  "<HTML><BODY>
  %%HEADER%%
  <FORM ACTION=\"/cgi-bin/rb/board.cgi\" METHOD=\"GET\">
  <INPUT TYPE=HIDDEN NAME=cmd VALUE=savepost>
  <INPUT TYPE=HIDDEN NAME=SENDER VALUE=%%USER%%>
```

LISTING 9.12   Continued

```
    <TABLE BORDER=0>
    <TR>
    <TD>Title:</TD><TD><INPUT TYPE=TEXT NAME=TITLE></TD>
    </TR>
    <TR>
    <TD>Message Body:</TD>
    <TD> <TEXTAREA rows=25 cols=80 NAME=BODY> </TEXTAREA></TD>
    <TR><TD><INPUT TYPE=SUBMIT NAME=SUBMIT></TD><TD></TD></TR>
    </TR>
    </TABLE>
    </FORM>
    </BODY></HTML>"
end

#
# File: reply.rb
#

require "message"

def do_reply_page(cgi)
  mstore = get_message_store
  user = get_session(cgi)['user']
  num = cgi['id'][0]
  message = mstore.get_message(num.to_i)

  template = get_template(message)
  template.gsub!(/%%HEADER%%/, header(cgi))
  template.gsub!(/%%USER%%/, user)
  template.gsub!(/%%NUM%%/, num)
  cgi.out{ template }
end

def get_template(message)
"<HTML><BODY>
%%HEADER%%
#{get_message_view(message)}
<FORM ACTION=\"/cgi-bin/rb/board.cgi\" METHOD=\"GET\">
<INPUT TYPE=HIDDEN NAME=SENDER VALUE=%%USER%%>
<INPUT TYPE=HIDDEN NAME=cmd VALUE=savepost>
<INPUT TYPE=HIDDEN NAME=id VALUE=%%NUM%%>
<TABLE BORDER=0>
<TR>
<TD>Title:</TD><TD><INPUT TYPE=TEXT NAME=TITLE></TD>
</TR>
```

9

LISTING 9.12   Continued

```
<TR>
<TD>Message Body:</TD>
<TD> <TEXTAREA rows=25 cols=80 NAME=BODY> </TEXTAREA></TD>
</TR>
<TR><TD><INPUT TYPE=SUBMIT NAME=SUBMIT></TD><TD></TD></TR>
</TABLE>
</FORM>
</BODY></HTML>"
end


#
# File: savepost.rb
#

require "message"
require "viewmessage"

def do_savepost_page(cgi)
  user = get_session(cgi)['user']
  mstore = get_message_store
  newmsg = Message.new(cgi['TITLE'][0], user)
  newmsg.body = cgi['BODY'][0]
  mstore.add_message(newmsg)
  viewid = do_reply(mstore, newmsg, cgi)
  if !viewid
    viewid = newmsg.id
  end
  mstore.save($filepath)
  cgi.out { "<HTML><HEAD><META HTTP-EQUIV=\"REFRESH\"" +
            " CONTENT=\"1;URL=/cgi-bin/rb/board.cgi?" +
            "cmd=viewmessage&id=#{viewid}\"></HEAD>"  +
            "<BODY></BODY></HTML>" }
end

def do_reply(mstore, newmsg, cgi)
  id = cgi['id'][0]
  if id != nil && id != ""
    orig = mstore.get_message(cgi['id'][0].to_i)
    orig.add_reply(newmsg)
    return id
  end
end

#
```

LISTING 9.12 Continued

```ruby
# File: viewmessage.rb
#

require "message"

def do_viewmessage_page(cgi)
  mstore = get_message_store
  user = get_session(cgi)['user']
  num = cgi['id'][0]
  message = mstore.get_message(num.to_i)

  template = get_template(message)
  template.gsub!(/%%USER%%/, user)
  template.gsub!(/%%HEADER%%/, header(cgi))
  template.gsub!(/%%NUM%%/,num)
  template.gsub!(/%%RESPONSES%%/,
                  get_message_rows(message.replies))
  cgi.out{ template }
end


def get_message_rows(messages)
  if messages.size < 1
    return ""
  end
  rows = String.new("<TABLE border=1>")
  messages.each do |message|
    rows << "<TR><TD><a href=\"/cgi-bin/rb/board.cgi?" +
            "cmd=viewmessage&id=#{message.id}\">" +
            "#{message.id}</a></TD><TD>#{message.title}" +
            "</TD><TD>#{message.sender}</TD><TD>" +
            "#{message.date}</TD></TR>"
  end
  rows << "</TABLE>"
  rows
end

def get_template(message)
  "<HTML><BODY>
    %%HEADER%%
    #{get_message_view(message)}
    <a href=\"/cgi-bin/rb/board.cgi?cmd=reply&id=%%NUM%%\">reply
  to this message.</a>
    <HR>
```

LISTING 9.12   continued

```
        <B>Previous Reponses:</B>
        <BR>
        %%RESPONSES%%
    </BODY></HTML>"
  end
```

We hope this case study has given you a good feeling for what it's like to program a real CGI-based Web application. As with all the examples of significant size, an online copy of the full source code is available at the Web site for this book, which is referenced in Appendix D, "Resources on the Web (and Elsewhere)."

Distributed Ruby

Less is more.

—Robert Browning, "Andrea del Sarto"

There are a plethora of technologies today that enable distributed computing. These include various flavors of RPC, as well as such things as COM, CORBA, DCE, and Java's RMI.

These all vary in complexity, but they all do essentially the same thing. They provide relatively transparent communication between objects in a networking context so that remote objects can be used as though they were local.

Why should we want to do something like this in the first place? There might be many reasons. One excellent reason is to share the burden of a computing problem between many processors at once. An example would be the SETI@home program, which uses your PC to process small data sets in the search for extraterrestrial intelligence. (SETI@home is not a project of the SETI Institute, by the way.) Another example would be the grassroots effort to decode the RSA129 encryption challenge (which succeeded a few years ago). There are countless other areas where it is possible to split a problem into individual parts for a distributed solution.

It's also conceivable that you might want to expose an interface to a service without making the code itself available. This is frequently done via a Web application, but the inherently stateless nature of the Web makes this a little unwieldy (in addition to other disadvantages). A distributed programming mechanism makes this kind of thing possible in a more direct way.

Ruby's answer to this challenge is drb, or *distributed Ruby* by Masatoshi Seki. (The name is also written DRb.) It doesn't have such advanced facilities as CORBA's naming service, but it is a simple and usable library with all the most basic functionality you would need.

An Overview: Using drb

A drb application has two basic components—a server and a client. A rough breakdown of their responsibilities is given here.

The server:

- Starts a TCPServer and listens on a port.
- Binds an object to the drb server instance.
- Accepts connections from clients and responds to their messages.
- May optionally provide access control (security).

The client:

- Establishes a connection to the server process.
- Binds a local object to the remote server object.
- Sends messages to the server object and gets responses.

The class method start_service takes care of starting a TCP server that listens on a specified port; it takes two parameters. The first is a *URI* (*Universal Resource Identifier*) specifying a port. (If it is nil, a port will be chosen dynamically.) The second is an object to which we want to bind. This object will be remotely accessible by the client, invoking its methods as though it were local.

```
require "drb"

myobj = MyServer.new
DRb.start_service("druby://:1234", myobj)    # Port 1234

# ...
```

If the port is chosen dynamically, the class method uri can be used to retrieve the full URI, including the port number.

```
DRb.start_service(nil, myobj)
myURI = DRb.uri                    # "druby://hal9000:2001"
```

Because drb is threaded, any server application will need to do a join on the server thread (to prevent the application from exiting prematurely and killing the thread).

```
# Prevent premature exit
DRb.thread.join
```

On the client side, we can invoke `start_service` with no parameters, and use `DRbObject` to create a local object that corresponds to the remote one. We typically use `nil` as the first parameter in creating a new `DRbObject`.

```
require "drb"

DRb.start_service
obj = DRbObject.new(nil, "druby://hal9000:2001")

# Messages passed to obj will get forwarded to the
# remote object on the server side...
```

We should point out that on the server side, when we bind to an object, we really are binding to a *single object* which will answer all requests that it receives. If there is more than one client, we will have to make our code *thread-safe* to avoid that object somehow getting into an inconsistent state. (For really simple or specialized applications, this might not be necessary.)

We can't go into great detail here. Just be aware that if a client both reads and writes the internal state of the remote object, two or more clients have the potential to interfere with each other. To avoid this, we recommend a straightforward solution using some kind of synchronization mechanism like a `Mutex`. (Refer to Chapter 7 for more on threads and synchronization issues.)

We will say at least a few words about security. After all, you may not want just any old client to connect to your server. You can't prevent them from trying, but you can prevent their succeeding.

Distributed Ruby has the concept of an *access control list*, or *ACL* (often pronounced to rhyme with "crackle"). These are simply lists of clients (or categories of clients) that are specifically allowed (or not allowed) to connect.

Here is a little example. We use the `ACL` class to create a new ACL, passing in one or two parameters.

The second (optional) parameter to `ACL.new` answers the question, "Do we *deny* all clients except certain ones, or *allow* all clients except certain ones?" The default is `DENY_ALLOW`, represented by a `0`; `ALLOW_DENY` is represented by a `1`.

The first parameter for `ACL.new` is simply an array of strings; these strings are taken in pairs, where the first in the pair is `deny` or `allow`, and the second represents a client or category of clients (by name or address). Here is an example:

```
acl = ACL.new( %w[ deny all
                   allow 192.168.0.*
                   allow 210.251.121.214
                   allow localhost] )
```

The first entry `deny all` is somewhat redundant, but it does make the meaning more explicit.

Now how do we use an ACL? The `install_acl` method will put an ACL into effect for us. Note that this has to be done *before* the call to the `start_service` method, or it will have no effect.

```
# Continuing the above example...

DRb.install_acl(acl)

DRb.start_service(nil, some_object)

# ...
```

When the service then starts, any unauthorized client connection will result in a `RuntimeError` being thrown on the server side (with the message `"Forbidden"`).

There is somewhat more to `drb` than we cover here. But this is enough for an overview.

We'll also mention that `drb` comes with a module (`rinda.rb`) that does much the same as Sun's Javaspaces, the basis of Jini. (The name is a pun based on *Linda*, the technology underlying Javaspaces.)

For those who are more interested in CORBA, there are efforts by another Japanese developer to produce a complete Ruby-CORBA mapping. At present, there is already an interface definition, an IDL compiler called `Ridl`, and `Ruby-ORBit`, which provides a wrapper for ORBit. We are far out of our depth here; but if this appeals to you, you can refer to the `Rinn` project in the Ruby Application Archive.

Case Study: A Stock Ticker Simulation

This example is taken from the Pragmatic Programmers' Ruby course (used by permission). Here we're assuming that we have a server application that is making stock prices available to the network. Any client wanting to check the value of his thousand shares of Gizmonic Institute can contact this server.

There is a small twist to this, however. We don't just want to watch every little fluctuation in the stock price. We've implemented an `Observer` module that will let us subscribe to the stock feed; the client then watches the feed and warns us only when the price goes above or below a certain value.

First let's look at the DrbObservable module. This is a straightforward implementation of the *Observer* pattern, another design pattern from the "Gang of Four's" *Design Patterns*. This is also known as the *Publish-Subscribe* pattern.

This module is actually an adaptation of the standard observer.rb library. It has been changed so that it does not abort on an error.

Listing 9.13 defines an *observer* as an object that responds to the update method call. Observers are added (by the server) at their own request, and are sent information via the notify_observers call.

LISTING 9.13   The drb Observer Module

```ruby
module DRbObservable

  def add_observer(observer)
    @observer_peers ||= []
    unless observer.respond_to? :update
      raise NameError, "observer needs to respond to `update'"
    end
    @observer_peers.push observer
  end

  def delete_observer(observer)
    @observer_peers.delete observer if defined? @observer_peers
  end

  def notify_observers(*arg)
    return unless defined? @observer_peers
    for i in @observer_peers.dup
      begin
        i.update(*arg)
      rescue
        delete_observer(i)
      end
    end
  end

end
```

The server (or feed) in Listing 9.14 simulates the stock price by a sequence of pseudorandom numbers. (This is as good a simulation of the market as we have ever seen, if you will pardon the irony.) The stock symbol identifying the company is only used for cosmetics in the simulation, and has no actual purpose in the code. Every time the price changes, the observers are all notified.

LISTING 9.14   The drb Stock Price Feed (Server)

```ruby
require "drb"
require "drb_observer"

# Generate random prices
class MockPrice

  MIN = 75
  RANGE = 50

  def initialize(symbol)
    @price = RANGE / 2
  end

  def price
    @price += (rand() - 0.5)*RANGE
    if @price < 0
      @price = -@price
    elsif @price >= RANGE
      @price = 2*RANGE - @price
    end
    MIN + @price
  end
end

class Ticker # Periodically fetch a stock price
  include DRbObservable

  def initialize(price_feed)
    @feed = price_feed
    Thread.new { run }
  end

  def run
    lastPrice = nil
    loop do
      price = @feed.price
      print "Current price: #{price}\n"
      if price != lastPrice
        lastPrice = price
        notify_observers(Time.now, price)
      end
```

9

LISTING 9.14   Continued

```
      sleep 1
    end
  end
end

ticker = Ticker.new(MockPrice.new("MSFT"))

DRb.start_service('druby://localhost:9001', ticker)
puts 'Press [return] to exit.'
gets
```

Not surprisingly, the client (in Listing 9.15) begins by contacting the server. It gets a reference to the stock ticker object and sets its own desired values for the high and low marks. Then the client will print a message for the user every time the stock price goes above the high end or below the low end.

We should mention the concept behind the DrbUndumped module. Very little code is actually associated with this module; basically it defines a _dump method that raises an exception when it is called. In other words, it prevents an object from being dumped.

Any object obj of a class that includes this module will thus return true for an expression like obj.kind_of? DRbUndumped. Refer to Chapter 1, "Ruby in Review," (or Chapter 5, "OOP and Dynamicity in Ruby") if this is unclear. For those familiar with Java, this is like the *opposite* of the Serializable interface.

In short, drb by default passes objects *by value* (that is, via marshalling). But by including DRbUndumped, we can pass objects *by reference*—when we want to expose an interface to an object we are managing (or when an object simply cannot be marshalled for whatever reason).

LISTING 9.15   The drb Stock Price Watcher (Client)

```
require "drb"

class Warner
  include DRbUndumped

  def initialize(ticker, limit)
    @limit = limit
    ticker.add_observer(self)   # all warners are observers
  end
end
```

LISTING 9.15   Continued

```ruby
class WarnLow < Warner
  def update(time, price)      # callback for observer
    if price < @limit
      print "—- #{time.to_s}: Price below #@limit: #{price}\n"
    end
  end
end

class WarnHigh < Warner
  def update(time, price)      # callback for observer
    if price > @limit
      print "+++ #{time.to_s}: Price above #@limit: #{price}\n"
    end
  end
end

DRb.start_service
ticker = DRbObject.new(nil, "druby://localhost:9001")

WarnLow.new(ticker, 90)
WarnHigh.new(ticker, 110)

puts "Press [return] to exit."
gets
```

There are other ways to approach this problem. But we feel that this is a good solution that well demonstrates the simplicity and elegance of distributed Ruby.

XML Parsing in Ruby

Since the late 1990s, one of the biggest buzzword technologies in Internet programming has been XML. *XML (Extensible Markup Language)* is a text-based document specification language. It enables developers and users to easily create their own, parseable document formats. XML is both machine-parseable and easily readable by humans, making it a good choice for processes that require both manual and automated tasks. Its readability also makes it easy to debug.

As is the case with most modern programming languages, there are Ruby libraries that greatly simplify the tasks of parsing and creating XML documents. There are two prevalent ways to approach XML parsing: *DOM (Document Object Model)*, a specification developed by the World Wide Web Consortium, providing a tree-like representation of a structured document, and event-based parsers including *SAX (Simple API for XML)*, which view occurrences of elements in an XML document as events that can be handled by callbacks.

9

NETWORK AND
WEB
PROGRAMMING

Two pervasive Ruby XML packages are available. The first and most widely used is
XMLParser by Yoshida Masato. XMLParser is an interface to James Clark's popular expat
library for C. It will be used in the majority of our examples because of its stability and
broader acceptance. Fairly new on the scene is Jim Menard's *NQXML* (*Not Quite XML*). The
advantage of NQXML that has many Ruby programmers excited is that it is written in pure
Ruby, which makes it very easy to modify and to install or include in software distributions.
An example of NQXML will be included at the end of this section.

A short sample XML document is presented in Listing 9.16.

LISTING 9.16   Sample XML Document

```
<?xml version="1.0" encoding="ISO-8859-1"?>
<addressbook>
    <person relationship="business">
        <name>Matt Hooker</name>
        <address>
            <street>111 Central Ave.</street>
            <city>Memphis</city>
            <state>TN</state>
            <company>J+H Productions</company>
            <zipcode>38111</zipcode>
        </address>
        <phone>901-555-5255</phone>
    </person>
    <person relationship="friend">
        <name>Michael Nilnarf</name>
        <address>
            <street>10 Kiehl Ave.</street>
            <city>Sherwood</city>
            <state>AR</state>
            <zipcode>72120</zipcode>
        </address>
        <phone>501-555-6343</phone>
    </person>
</addressbook>
```

A detailed explanation of how XML itself works is beyond the scope of this text, but there are
a few items worth noting. First, you can see that XML is made up of *tags*, which are pieces of
text surrounded by < and >. Generally, these tags have a beginning, <mytag>, and an end,
</mytag>; and they can contain either plain text or other tags. If a tag doesn't have a closing

tag, it should contain a trailing slash, as in `<mytag/>`. Tags, also called *elements*, can optionally have attributes, as in `<person relationship="friend">`, which are name/value pairs placed in the tag itself. For a more detailed introduction to XML, consult a reference.

Using XMLParser (Tree-Based Processing)

The first step in using XMLParser's DOM parsing library is to perform some parser initialization and setup. The `XML::DOM::Builder` object is a parser whose specialty is building—not surprisingly—DOM trees. In the setup portion of the code, we perform tasks such as setting default encoding for tag names and data, and setting the base URI for locating externally referenced XML objects. Next, a call to `Builder.parse` creates a new `Document` object, which is the highest level object in the DOM tree hierarchy. Finally, any successive blocks of text in the DOM tree are merged with a call to `Document.normalize` and the tree is returned. Refer to Listing 9.17.

LISTING 9.17   Setting Up a DOM Object

```
def setup_dom(xml)
  builder = XML::DOM::Builder.new(0)
  builder.setBase("./")

  begin
    xmltree = builder.parse(xml, true)
  rescue XMLParserError
    line = builder.line
    print "#{$0}: #{$!} (in line #{line})\n"
    exit 1
  end

  # Unify sequential Text nodes
  xmltree.documentElement.normalize

  return xmltree
end
```

9

What has been created so far is a first-class Ruby object that provides a structured representation of our original XML document, including the data within. All that remains is to actually do something with this structure. This is the easy part. Refer to Listing 9.18.

LISTING 9.18   Parsing a DOM Object

```
xml = $<.read
xmltree = setup_dom(xml)

xmltree.getElementsByTagName("person").each do |person|
  printPerson(person)
end

def printPerson(person)
  rel = person.getAttribute("relationship")
  puts "Found person of type #{rel}."
  name = person.getElementsByTagName("name")[0].firstChild.data
  puts "\tName is: #{name}"
end
```

With a call to our previously created setup_dom method, we get a handle to the DOM tree representing our XML document. The DOM tree is made up of a hierarchy of Nodes. A Node can optionally have children, which would be a collection of Nodes. In an object-oriented sense, extending from Node are higher level classes such as Element, Document, Attr, and others, modeling higher level behavior appropriately.

In our simple example, we use getElementsByTagName to iterate through all elements of type person. With each person, the printPerson method prints the recorded relationship and name of the person in the XML file. Of interest are the two different methods of storing and accessing data that are represented here. The relationship is stored as an attribute of the person element. For that reason, we get a handle to an object of type Attr with a call to the Element's getAttribute method, and then use to_s to convert it to a String. In the case of the person's name, we are storing it as character data within an Element. Character data is represented as a separate Node of type CharacterData. In this case, it appears as a child of the Node that represents the name element. To access it, we make a call to firstChild and then to the CharacterData's data method. For a more detailed treatment of XMLParser's DOM capabilities, refer to the samples and embedded documentation provided with the XMLParser distribution.

Using XMLParser (Event-Based Processing)

As mentioned earlier, a common alternative to DOM-based XML parsing is to view the parsing process as a series of events for which handlers can be written. This is SAX-like, or *event-based* parsing. In Listing 9.19, we'll reproduce the functionality of our DOM example using the event-based parsing method that XMLParser provides.

LISTING 9.19   Event-Based Parsing

```ruby
require 'xmlparser'

class XMLRetry<Exception; end

class SampleParser<XMLParser

  private

  def startElement(name, attr)
    if name == "person"
      attr.each do |key, value|
        print "Found person of type #{value}.\n"
      end
    end
    if name == "name"
      $print_cdata = true
      self.defaultCurrent
    else
      $print_cdata = false

    end
  end

  def endElement(name)
    if name == "name"
      $print_cdata = false
    end
  end

  def character(data)
    if $print_cdata
      puts ("\tName is: #{data}")
    end
  end

end

xml = $<.read

parser = SampleParser.new
def parser.unknownEncoding(e)
  raise XMLRetry, e
end
```

LISTING 9.19   Event-Based Parsing

```
begin
  parser.parse(xml)
rescue XMLRetry
  newencoding = nil
  e = $!.to_s
  parser = SampleParser.new(newencoding)
  retry
rescue XMLParserError
  line = parser.line
  print "Parse error(#{line}): #{$!}\n"
end
```

To use XMLParser's event-based parsing API, you must define a class that extends from `XMLParser`. This class has a method, `parse`, which is responsible for the main logic of tokenizing an XML document and iterating over its pieces. Your job when writing an extension to `XMLParser` is to define methods that will be called by `parse` when certain events take place. This example defines three such methods: `startElement`, `endElement`, and `character`. Not surprisingly, `startElement` is called when an opening XML tag is encountered, `endElement` is called after finding a closing tag, and `character` is called for a block of character data. The XMLParser API defines 23 events like these, which can be defined if needed. Undefined events (events for which no method has been explicitly overridden by the end developer) are ignored. For a complete list of events, see the README file in the XMLParser distribution.

Admittedly, this example does not lend itself well to event-based parsing. The `$print_cdata` global variable is a hack to maintain state across events. Without `$print_cdata`, the `character` method would have no way of knowing if it had encountered character data inside a `person` tag or any other arbitrary spot in a document. This illustrates an interesting constraint in the event-based parsing model: It's up to you, the developer, to maintain the context in which these events are fired. Whereas DOM provides a neatly organized tree, event-based parsing triggers events that are totally unaware of each other.

Now that we've presented two different approaches to parsing XML, you might be asking yourself how to choose between them. For most people, DOM is the more intuitive solution. Its tree-based approach is easy to comprehend and easy to manage. It is ideal when viewing XML as a document in the truest sense of the word. The primary disadvantage of DOM is that it parses and loads the entire document into memory before any operations can be performed. This can have ramifications on the performance and scalability of an application. If speed is an issue, event-based parsing enables a program to react to each element as it is read. For example, if a program had to read XML data from a slow data source (an international network link, for example), it might be advantageous to start operating on the data as it streams in, rather than loading the entire document and parsing it after the fact. From a scalability perspective, event-based parsing can also be more efficient. If you wanted to parse an extremely large file, it might be better to parse while scanning through it, rather than allocating memory to store the entire file before parsing and operating on its data.

Using NQXML

For those with a need or desire to work with a pure Ruby solution to XML parsing, Jim Menard's NQXML is currently the only thing going. Presented in Listing 9.20 is an example of its (Not Quite) DOM-parsing capabilities.

LISTING 9.20 Pure Ruby XML Parsing

```
require 'nqxml/treeparser'
   xml = $<.read

   begin
     doc = NQXML::TreeParser.new(xml).document

     root = doc.rootNode
     root.children.each do |node|
       if node.entity.class == NQXML::Tag
         if node.entity.name == "person"
           rel = node.entity.attrs['relationship']
           puts "Found a person of type #{rel}."
         end
         node.children.each do |subnode|
           if subnode.entity.class == NQXML::Tag &&
                 subnode.entity.name == "name"
             puts "\tName is: #{subnode.children[0].entity}"
           end
         end
       else
         puts node.entity.class
       end
     end

   rescue NQXML::ParserError
     # Do something meaningful
   end
```

Structurally, the program is very similar to the XMLParser DOM example previously presented. NQXML closely—but loosely—follows the DOM way of doing things, so developers familiar with DOM should have little difficulty adjusting to the sometimes different class and method names of NQXML. NQXML also offers a SAX-like streaming parser that relies more heavily on Ruby's iterators than the callback methods of XMLParser.

Summary

In this chapter, you've seen networking at a pretty low level, and at the level of well-known application interfaces like telnet and SMTP. You've seen how distributed Ruby works, and you've been through a simple example of a `drb` application. You've seen ways to use Ruby for Web development, both server-side and CGI, and you've even taken a look at XML parsing in Ruby (tangentially related to Web development).

This might be one of the primary areas in which Ruby is used. Although it's not a networking or Web language as such, we feel that more applications in the future will be Web-based, Net-capable, or otherwise based on distributed computing.

Whether your primary use of Ruby is Net-related or not, we are confident that you have already found it to be a powerful and useful language. We also hope that this book has added to your knowledge and your programming pleasure, and we hope it has been a worthwhile contribution to the Ruby community as a whole.

From Perl to Ruby

That pearl is from a mine unknown to thee,
That ruby bears a stamp thou canst not see…

—*The Rubaiyat*, Omar Khayyam
    (trans. Whinfield)

There are other references and books you can read to help you understand Ruby, so this section is going to focus on differences between Ruby and Perl. We provide some tips and warnings for the Perl programmer along the way.

Ruby will lead you to change your focus. You will notice a change in the syntax and organization of your programs. You will use objects to organize your methods. The object model has a cleaner approach, fewer surprises, and a dynamic flexibility you will not find in Perl. Yet there are enough similarities that you should be able to do a number of things in Ruby that look similar to how you do them in Perl.

Ruby One-Liners

First, use the command line to get a feel for Ruby. Most of the same options from Perl are available. Here's an example:

```
ruby -e '$x="hi"; print $x,"\n"; print 5+2;'
```

This should look no different from what Perl allows. Our next little example does the same thing in a somewhat contrived way, to demonstrate a little of Ruby's syntax:

```
ruby -e 'x=%q|hi|; print "#{x}\n"; print x+"\n"; print 5.+(2)'
```

Perl obviously won't like this, yet Ruby is perfectly fine with it. We'll explain.

Scope

The variable x is missing a prefix. In fact, Ruby does not require a prefix, and the prefixes it does allow are used for indicating *scope* and not data type. They are simply references to a strongly typed object, as defined by a particular class.

The $ prefix indicates *global* scope, not a scalar. However, nonprefixed variables starting with a *lowercase* letter are *local* in scope, and you can't refer to them until you put them in scope via assignment. There is no scope declaration via my or local, and there is no nesting or over-riding of variables.

> **NOTE**
>
> Local variable names are similar to method identifiers; when both are defined, you need to use parentheses with the method. Because using parentheses with methods is optional, there is a possibility of a mix-up.

Nonprefixed variables starting with an *uppercase* letter are *constants* and have class-wide scope. This is the only type of variable that may be accessed globally via the familiar :: scope operator, which is used to gain access inside of classes and modules. Method names do not count as variables.

The @ and @@ prefixes used inside object methods and classes denote variables belonging to a particular object or a whole class. They have nothing to do with arrays.

Variables

A variable, regardless of scoping, simply holds a reference to an object of a particular type (class). You cannot know this type by looking at the variable. It is like a Perl scalar holding a reference to a strongly typed object—with automatic referencing and dereferencing. There is no backslash (\) operator. Assignment has the connotation of simply making a reference. There is no equivalent to "typeglobs," nor is there a central symbol table, but there are methods for accessing environment bindings and the various variables and constants they contain.

> **NOTE**
>
> Multiple variables can hold a reference to the same object and may be used to alter the object referenced by another variable, leading to potentially surprising side effects.

Parallel assignment is controlled via the special * syntax (and the same rules also apply to parameter passing with blocks and methods). Here's an example:

```
a, *b = [1, 2], "a", "b"    # a=[1,2], b=["a","b"]
a, b, c = b, *a             # a=["a","b"], b=1, c=2
```

Data Types

Ruby has built-in classes for nil (which tests as false), true, false, integers (including big integers), floats, strings, ranges (which are *not* stored in array form), arrays, hashes, regexes, files, and more.

You will have to stop using 0, "", and "0" to test for false. Instead, you will be checking against false or nil.

Use string[0,1].downcase for lcfirst, and string[0] for ord. Note the unfamiliar meaning of subscripts:

```
"ABC"[0,1].downcase  # "aBC"
"A"[0]               # 65
```

Unlike Perl, Ruby does not automatically convert other object types when performing tasks such as concatenation. You can use the to_s method, which is usually defined for other objects, to convert them before working with them. Here's an example:

```
"abc" + 123.to_s      # "a b c123"
```

Ruby does not support ++ or —, although there is succ, which works with both numbers and strings by default.

Arrays and hashes use different literals but the same accessor method. There is no $# feature for arrays; use -1 as the index to the last item of an array. A hash key need not be a string: The => syntax does not "stringify" the left-hand side, and "barewords" are not used in Ruby:

```
arr = ["some", 123]; hsh = {"b"=>"hi", 99=>arr}
arr[2] = "stuff"
hsh["key"] = "value"
meth { .... }              # Method with associated block!
```

> **NOTE**
>
> nil can be used as both a key and value in a hash as well as a value in an array.

Ruby doesn't support "autovivification" for arrays, hashes, or any other indexed objects (although some people have written code to support this). Ordinarily you must assign a relevant object to a variable before accessing values. You can use the ||= syntax to assign conditionally.

File handles are taken care of by the File class.

File test operators have been implemented with the test method. Note that this method is missing Perl's -B, -t, and -T tests, and it adds ?G, ?-, ?=, ?<, and ?> . Also, ?s returns nil, not zero (if the file size is zero), and ?M returns the modification time, not the file age.

Quoting

Double-quoted strings allow for escape characters, just as in Perl. Ruby does *not* support \l, \u, \L, \U, \E, or \Q. It does have some extras, such as "\s" (space), "\v" (vertical tab), "\C-" (same as "\c["), "\M-" (meta-x or alt-x), and "\M-\C-".

> **NOTE**
>
> The \s in "\s" means a single space " ", but in the regexes' /\s/ and /[\s]/ it refers to the regular expression character class for whitespace.

Ruby uses %, %q, %w, %r, and %x in place of Perl's q, qq, qw, qr, and qx. Unlike Perl, Ruby still allows a space to be used as the delimiter for these.

You may also notice that string interpolation is done with the #{} syntax, but this is not just for variables—it is a general form that evaluates any expression. Perl has both ${} and @{} for more complex interpolation, but Ruby's approach to this actually allows for more concise scripts.

Ruby also has here-docs, just as Perl has. Indented here-docs are built in as a feature:

```
print <<-`eos`
  whois #{gets.chomp}
eos
```

In the preceding example, you also see one of the handy uses of #{}.

String Operators

Next you should notice that the plus sign (+) is used in place of the dot (.) for string concatenation. As a matter of fact, the eq, ne, gt, lt, ge, le, cmp, and x operators are not used in Ruby either. Instead, use ==, !=, >, <, >=, <=, <=>, and * (no list context equivalents).

In fact, you can use these same operators (and others) for any object that defines them as a method.

Dot Syntax

Now let's look at a little code fragment: 5.+(2). This reveals two things in Ruby: + is just a method call, and . (dot) is the syntax for dispatching a method.

Numbers are also objects (instances of a class). As such, you can send method calls to them. Ruby will look in the object's class for an implementation of the method sent to it. Compare this to Perl's -> operator (not used in Ruby).

You normally have to include the dot when dispatching methods, but Ruby makes it optional for operators that are implemented as methods. However, by using the dot with numeric operators, you override the precedence rules. Here are some examples:

```
5 + 2 * 3 + 1 * 4        # 15
5.+ 2.* 3.+ 1.* 4        # 19
5.+(2).*(3).+(1).*(4)   # 112
```

About Command-Line Options

Most of the Perl command-line options work the same way for Ruby. There are a few things to note, however. For example, autosplit results are assigned to $F instead of Perl's @F, and there are no -D, -P, -u, -U, and -V flags. Note that -T optionally takes a value to set the safe level, -I uses $LOAD_PATH ($:) instead of @INC, and -S uses either RUBYPATH or PATH. Also, there are some additional options: -C and -X are used to change directories before executing the script, -r is used to "require" named libraries, and -K specifies a language code set.

TIP

There is a debug feature as well as an enhanced interactive mode called irb.

Another Code Example

Here is another example to serve as an introduction to discussing some more differences:

```
perl -e 'while(<>){ last if /^x/; print }; print "done\n";'
ruby -e 'while gets; break if /^x/; print; end; puts "done"'
```

Again, these code fragments behave essentially the same.

Loop Constructs, Conditionals, and Modifiers

It should be no surprise that Ruby has looping constructs such as while, until, and for. However, there are no braces, because braces are used in Ruby for iterator blocks that introduce a new scope. Instead, the body is delimited by the end keyword.

Loop control in Ruby is similar to Perl, except break is used in place of last. There is no continue and no goto, but you can simulate goto with continuations or catch/throw. A new keyword, retry, is useful both for making your own iterators and for recovering from an exception when used in the rescue portion of a begin/end block.

TIP

Exception information is stored in the $! variable. The $@ variable holds the stack backtrace for it.

The foreach loop from Perl is translated this way:

```
foreach $item (@arr){ some_code }    # Perl
for item in arr; some_code; end      # Ruby
```

Ruby also has if/elsif/else/end, unless/else/end, and case/when/else/end. These also do not use braces.

> **NOTE**
>
> These statements evaluate the "truth value" of a given condition. Remember that `""`, `"0"`, and `0` will all be true because only `false` and `nil` are false in Ruby.

Modifiers work the same way as in Perl, except there is no `foreach` modifier.

Blocks

Ruby has more than one kind of block. The `begin`/`end` block is most often used with `rescue` and `ensure` to handle exceptions. It lets you group statements for control, and it may also be nested. Aside from the lack of scope, it seems to be the closest thing to Perl's brace-delimited blocks because it may stand by itself, and it supports flow control, such as `next`.

The `do`/`end` or `{}` block, on the other hand, *must* be associated with a method (otherwise, it is treated as a hash literal). This block is both a closure and an iterator. Its parameter list is used for parallel assignment of passed arguments and is required if you plan to use them—there is no equivalent to Perl's `@_` variable. Here's an example:

```
obj.iterator_method {|x,y| statements_in_here }
# associated iterator closure
```

> **NOTE**
>
> Anything assignable may be put in the parameter list, including an existing variable. If it is a local variable that does not yet exist, it will be created and kept local to the block. Otherwise, it is *not* local to the block.

There are also built-in iterator methods such as `each`, `loop`, `upto`, `step`, and `times`.

> **NOTE**
>
> The Ruby `do` keyword is very different from Perl's `do`.

Regexes

Both `\b` and `\s` are interpolated differently in double quotes and in `%r` or `//` regex literals.

There is no equivalent to (?<=, (?<!, (?{}, or (?().

Ruby does not have the /s modifier, and the /m modifier works like Perl's /sm combination.

TIP

You can simulate Perl's /s with Ruby's \A and \Z, and you can simulate Perl's /m by using /m with [^\n] in place of the dot in Ruby.

There is no /g modifier. Use String#gsub for s///g and String#scan for m//g. Also, use String#index for Perl's pos(). By the way, the pound (#) notation as used here is not part of the Ruby language but is rather a bit of slang to denote an instance method as opposed to a class method. You can use \G with the scan, gsub, and index methods.

Use String#sub for s///, use // for m//, and use String#tr for tr///. Use String#tr_s for tr///s, use String#delete for something close to tr///d, and use ^ at the start of the character list for tr///c.

There is no study equivalent. Use Regexp#quote for quotemeta. There are no /c, /e, and /ee modifiers. The following translation can be used for /e:

```
$text="lower to upper"; $text =~ s/(\w+)/uc($1)/ge;      # Perl
text="lower to upper"; text.gsub!(/(\w+)/){$1.upcase}  # Ruby
```

The =~ operator is a method defined for both the Regexp and String classes, and it returns the position of the first match.

For example, the following will *not* assign $1 and $2 to x and y:

```
x,y = (var =~ /(.)(.)/)
```

Instead, use String#scan, which returns an array of all matches. Use a subscript to access the *n*th group of matches, like so:

```
x,y = var.scan(/(.)(.)/)[0]
```

Back references are available, although you are warned to be careful about quoting them properly.

The Regexp#match method produces another type of object, of class MatchData, containing more detailed results.

Output

The print method uses $_ as a default argument. See puts and p, new output methods that don't utilize $_.

Printing to a file handle is different:

```
f = File.new("myfile.txt","w")
f.print "My text here.\n"
f.close
```

Unlike Perl, chomp and chop do not return what was removed but rather what remains. The argument to chomp indicates what should be removed, defaulting to the current record separator.

Also, note that split also behaves slightly differently.

Special Variables

Ruby has special built-in variables inspired by Perl, but some have differing meanings. For example, $" is used for %INC, $: is used for @INC, and $* and ARGV are used for @ARGV. What's more, $@, $=, $~, $<, $>, and $; are also used differently in Ruby. You can still use $!, $&, $+, $`, $', $1..$9, $/, $\, $,, $., $0, $$, $?, and $_ pretty much the same. ENV is used for %ENV, and $0 would be used for $ARGV. There is nothing for $^-type built-ins, except you can use RUBY_PLATFORM for $^O, and you can use $-w for $^W. Also, RUBY_VERSION can be used for $]. No features in Ruby correspond to Perl's $|, %SIG, @_, $-, $#, $=, $~, $%, $:, $;, and $[. Use the m modifier for $* and use Ruby's $, for $". As with Perl, Ruby has English equivalents available for these. Information on processes accessed via Perl's $(, $), $<, and $> can be obtained from the built-in Process module's gid, egid, uid, and euid methods.

NOTE

Some built-in variables, such as $_ and $~, do not actually behave as globals. Also, $_ doesn't always behave as Perl's equivalent does.

More Examples

Here's another pair of examples for comparison:

```
#!/usr/bin/perl
@list = `ls -l *.htm?`;
open(FH, ">list.txt") or die "Error opening file: $!\n";
foreach (@list){print FH; }
close FH;

#!/usr/local/bin/ruby
list = `ls -l *.htm?`
```

```
File.open("list.txt","w") { |fh|
  list.each {|line| fh.print line }
}
```

The results of the shell command are put into a single string in Ruby, including the newlines. Later, the each iterator retrieves each line from that string.

There is no close statement used here because the File.open method automatically closes it upon completion of the associated block. It also automatically raises an exception in case of an error.

Modules, Etc.

There are no do, no, package, and use keywords for modules. Also, modules in Ruby do not need to be in a separate specially named file. However, a separate file may contain one or more modules and can be loaded with require or load. You can then optionally "include" a named module into your namespace, but you can't selectively import individual methods or constants. Ruby modules are not aggregations of functions but rather sets of methods and constants inseparable from each other. There is no exact equivalent to the Perl AutoLoader module. There is autoload, which lets you register a file to be required when a Ruby module is first accessed.

You cannot access just any variable via the :: scope operator but only constants and methods.

Ruby still has Perl's BEGIN{} and END{}, but because modules and classes do not need to be allotted one per file and because there's no equivalent to Perl's Exporter, they are not really used the same way.

Classes, Objects, and Methods

There are no bless, ref, tie, tied, and untie keywords relating to classes. Also, existing classes, including the built-in ones, are easily extended at any time. Here's an example:

```
class String          # pre-existing built-in class
  def char_at(pos)    # new method being added
    self[pos,1]
  end
end

"abcdef".char_at(3)   # "d"
123.char_at(1)        # error
```

A method added to the built-in String class only applies for string objects.

Methods added to the Object class apply to all objects (compare this to Perl's UNIVERSAL class). If you make a method without specifying the class, it will belong to the Object class as a private method.

> **NOTE**
>
> Ruby has built-in handling of `private`, `protected`, and `public` methods.

Creating your own class is also easy—there is no need to make separate files.

You will often define your own class to represent custom objects. Ruby allows for something resembling a constructor; any method named `initialize` will be called by the class method `new` when the object is created:

```
class Foo
  def initialize
    # Code...
  end
end

obj = Foo.new     # Internally calls the initialize method
```

Also, you can nest classes for namespace control:

```
class Foo
  class Bar
  end
end

baz = Foo::Bar.new
```

Notice how this differs from Perl's file-based class organization, where `Foo::Bar` implies `Foo/Bar.pm`.

Using `include` from within a class causes the module methods to be available to all the objects of the class. This is a `mixin` in Ruby. Use this approach in place of multiple inheritance.

You can still define your classes in separate files and load them into your script with `require` or `load`. There is no `use` or `do` equivalent, but you can use `include` to import module constants and methods into your class. However, you cannot use it to individually import methods.

There is no __PACKAGE__ or __DATA__ file literal, but you can still use __END__ for the main file. See more on the `DATA` object (an instance of class `IO`). Also, there is no `INIT`.

Ruby uses a conservative mark/sweep garbage-collection (GC) algorithm and does not have an equivalent to `DESTROY`. See `finalizers`. Note that the GC algorithm is going to change soon, but this should be transparent to the programmer (other than a performance gain).

Ruby's inheritance model is smoother:

```
# Perl
package SomeClass
use AnotherClass
@ISA = ("AnotherClass")
# ...

# Ruby
class SomeClass < AnotherClass
#   ...
```

Also, overriding methods in Ruby is clearer:

```
# Perl
$self->SUPER::somemethod()    # Does lookup in @ISA

# Ruby
def somemethod
  super                       # Looks in superclass(es)
end
```

To obtain behavior similar to Perl's AUTOLOAD, see method_missing. Also, Ruby's built-in Struct class is analogous to Perl's class generator Class::Struct.

Defining Methods and procs

A *proc* is an object made from a block, which also maintains its original binding. A method is different in that it has a scope tied to the object and its class, and it has access to its class and instance variables and methods. Here's an example:

> **TIP**
>
> You can define methods ending in a ? or !.

```
def methodname(arg1, arg2="Default",
               *moreargs, &attachedblock)
# ...
# moreargs is now an array of parameters passed in if they exist
# attachedblock is now a Proc if a block was provided
end
```

Note that the block is treated as a special case; ordinarily a "starred" parameter such as *moreargs would consume all the remaining parameters passed into the method.

There is no direct equivalent to Perl's sub, but an anonymous subroutine in Perl is similar to a proc object in Ruby.

Redefining Operator Methods

By this point, you should understand that + is defined differently for number and string objects. This method takes an argument, and it is up to the implementation of the method to do the right thing with the argument. In fact, the string class method for + raises an exception if the argument is not a string. Here's an example:

```
x = "a" + 1
# TypeError: failed to convert Fixnum into String
```

It is an easy thing to modify this method in Ruby:

```
class String
  def +(arg)
    concat arg.to_s
  end
end
```

Many operators in Ruby are redefinable methods, allowing you to override the built-in equivalents. These include **, !, ~, +, -, *, /, %, <<, >>, &, ^, |, <=, ==, ===, =~, [], and []=.

Precedence

Precedence is slightly different from what we find in Perl. For example, =~ has a lower precedence, the bitwise &, ^, and | have a higher precedence, and the keyword operators have a lower precedence. Also note that the logical operators && and || are not interchangeable with and and or regarding precedence.

There is no list operator. Parentheses are used for grouping either expressions or method arguments, but not both at the same time.

Miscellaneous

Here are a few more miscellaneous notes:

- See the IO, Dir, and File classes as well as the Kernel module for using the various input and output methods. There is no warn, and Ruby's format is not the same as Perl's format. The dbm-related functionality is in the DBM module. There is no equivalent to the vec function.

- See the Process module for methods regarding processes and process groups. There is no alarm method.

A

- See the `socket` module for low-level socket methods. See the `Etc` module for methods regarding user and group info. Use the `Time` class for time-related functions.

- In Ruby, a variable set to `nil` is still considered defined. Perl's `undef` is used in various ways, but Ruby's `undef` is only useful for undefining methods and requires a parameter representing an already-defined method. See `remove_method` and `undef_method` as well. The closest equivalent to Perl assigning `undef` to a variable is Ruby assigning `nil`. Ruby's `defined?` is also different from Perl's `defined` because it checks for existence, not a `nil` value.

- Ruby's `dump` method (see `Marshal#dump`) has nothing to do with Perl's `dump` function, which has no equivalent.

- Ruby does not support form output. There are no `formline`, `reset`, `scalar`, and `wantarray` methods.

- Ruby's `eval` is not used for exception handling as it is in Perl. It supports a second argument as the binding in which to evaluate the method. Ruby also supports `class_eval` and `instance_eval`.

- Use `raise` (or `fail`) in place of `die`. Use `begin/rescue/end` in place of `eval` for catching exceptions. Use `catch/throw` for simple cases. There is no equivalent to the `Carp` module.

- Ruby does not yet have a container equivalent to Perl's `%SIG`. Signal handlers are established via the `trap` method, but you are limited in accessing them later.

- Commenting is done using the `#` symbol. Ruby also has a POD-like format called `RD`. It utilizes `=begin/=end` instead of `=head/=cut`.

- You can use `rdtool` to extract and convert to HTML or man pages. However, there is no utility fully equivalent to `perldoc`.

From Python to Ruby

Are you trying to somehow deal with the SNAKE?
—Adventure (Colossal Cave)

This appendix is for "classic" Python programmers who have already decided to try Ruby. Python is way too big for this section to be able to cover every aspect in a few pages, so the focus will be on assisting you in making a perspective shift and help you avoid misconceptions. Additionally, various tidbits will be pointed out along the way.

A good way to practice is by using `irb` to try things, which is one of Ruby's best interactive command line evaluators. This is similar to Python's built-in command line interpreter, but is a separate program.

A Different World View

Ruby can seem very similar to Python. For example, variables are untyped names holding references to typed objects. Exception handling is built-in. Scripting is encouraged for prototypes while programming extensions in C is used for speeding up bottlenecks.

But in fact, there is a different paradigm at work. Guido has said that he took a lot from Modula 3, which would explain why Python is explicitly modular and object-based, whereas Ruby is more integrated and class-based—but not in the manner of Java, for Ruby is even more dynamic than either Java or Python. It is also more complex, and Ruby has no mission to simplify readability by limiting expressibility. But you may find it easier and more pleasing to work with.

Some terminology may appear the same at first, but is understood differently in the Ruby community. For example, module, namespace, object, method, and iterator have different connotations in Ruby. Try to adjust your mindset from Python's modular object/statement approach to Ruby's integrated class/method approach.

A Different Program Model

A source file in Ruby is different from one in Python in a few ways. First, in Ruby, it is not considered a module. A module in Ruby is somewhat different. Second, Ruby interprets your source file from top to bottom and compiles it into a syntax tree instead of `bytecode`. There is no equivalent to `.pyc` files. Third, all code is evaluated as part of the top-level program in the default private context of a special class, called `Object`. For example, when you define a function at this level, you are really defining a private method in the `Object` class. Finally, if you load or require external source files or extensions, they are evaluated at the point of insertion, as in Python. But no separately associated namespace is created for the loaded files/extensions themselves—they are integrated into your code, within the current class binding.

You can reload source files simply by calling `load` again on the filename. You would use `require` for one-time loads and/or to load extensions. Refer to a Ruby reference (documenting the `$:` and `$"` variables) for related information.

Ruby does not have the notion of packages or `__init__.py` like Python, and there is not (yet) anything like Python's site or user modules. Distributing extensions and libraries can be done with Ruby's `extconf.rb`, or simply by placing a Ruby file at a known location.

Some Syntax Differences

Ruby syntax does not require indentation. The keyword end is used for demarcation of code blocks starting with `begin`, `case`, `class`, `def`, `do`, `if`, `for`, and others. Notice the absence of colons.

```
if x == 5
  puts "Five Golden Rings"
 end
```

You can use semicolons to separate statements on a single line, and lines can continue onto the next line.

```
a=[2,4,
 3]; for i in a; puts "%d
 " % i; end
```

If the breaking point is too ambiguous for Ruby, you can make it explicit by using the \ continuation character.

Ruby supports shell-type comments using #, and also special =begin and =end tags for making documentary or temporary multi-line comments. There is no built-in equivalent to Python's doc strings.

Keywords

Both Ruby and Python have these keywords: `and`, `break`, `class`, `def`, `else`, `for`, `if`, `in`, `not`, `or`, `return`, and `while`. The keyword `def` is used only for method definitions, and `in` is used only with `for` loops, not conditionals (use `include?` for that purpose).

Ruby has additional keywords not listed here. It does *not* have: `assert`, `continue`, `del`, `elif`, `except`, `exec`, `finally`, `from`, `global`, `import`, `is`, `lambda`, `pass`, `print`, `raise`, or `try` as keywords. You can use `next` in place of `continue`, and `begin/rescue/ensure` in place of `try/except/finally`. You will see `exec`, `lambda`, `print`, and `raise` as built-in methods in Ruby.

Variable Prefixes

Ruby variables are allowed to have special prefixes such as $, @, and @@ to indicate the scope of the variable. Regardless of the scoping prefix, variables may reference any object, just as in Python.

A global variable is prefixed with $ and is truly global, crossing all boundaries, whether inside a class, method, module, or loaded source file. There are some exceptions for built-in globals ($_ and $~). The use of $ for global variables eliminates the need for declarators such as Python's global.

An instance variable is prefixed with a single @. Using @myattribute replaces using self.myattribute in Python. (Actually, the self notation can be used in Ruby as well.) By its very nature, the instance variable can only be created and used from within the instance itself. You must use an accessor method in order to get or set the value from outside the instance— refer to any Ruby reference for a discussion of attr_accessor. Using @ for instance variables facilitates hiding, fast lookups, and exclusion from dot notation.

The class variable is prefixed with @@, and is shared only among all the instances of a class and its subclasses. An identifier starting with an uppercase letter (without a prefix) is called a constant, and is attached to a class or module namespace and the :: scope operator.

Finally, a non-capitalized variable with no prefix is a local variable. The point of assignment marks the beginning of its scope. It cannot be seen outside of a module, class, or method—and sometimes not outside of a closure (iterator block), either. This last case is a block-local variable, which only occurs if the local variable's scope started inside the closure.

Objects

In Python, everything is an object, but not necessarily an instance of a class. In Ruby, objects are always instances by default, and there is essentially no difference between an object's type and its class.

Each object has a unique ID. There is no is keyword in Ruby. You can use Object#equal? to compare object identities. See also Object#id. (Note: The hash symbol used like this in documentation is simply notation denoting an arbitrary instance of the named class as the receiver. In real code, you would use the variable for the actual object, followed by a dot and then the method. Using a dot in place of the hash with the named class would indicate a class method instead.)

Methods

Methods are not objects in Ruby. This is despite the fact that things such as classes, numbers, bindings, and threads are objects.

Ruby methods are not functions. Any time you see def in Ruby code, you are seeing a method definition. It has no namespace or attributes of its own. It cannot typically be nested. And again, it is not an object.

It follows that method names are not variable names. Method names should begin with a lowercase letter or underscore; they may have ! or ? suffixes. They do not use a prefix to denote scope, but you can make them private, protected, or public. (We should note that it is *possible* to capitalize a method name, but it is unconventional and could lead to minor difficulties.)

Many operators are implemented as methods, and can be directly overridden without the use of magic attributes such as __add__, __gt__, __setattr__, or __getitem__.

```
def +(arg)
  # ...
  end
def >(arg)
  # ...
  end
  # etc.
```

Combinations such as += are syntax sugar, not operators, so redefining + will affect += also.

There are specially hooked methods in Ruby: each, coerce, <=>, to_str, and to_ary, among others. See the Enumerable and Comparable modules.

Methods and Dot Notation

Dot notation in Ruby is used strictly for method dispatch. The left side is the object or variable, and the right side is the method name. The result is always an object, so you can chain method calls as in Python.

The :: scope operator is needed to access nested modules, classes, and their constants. It can also optionally be used to access a class method.

Methods can also be called without dot notation, in which case Ruby will implicitly use self as the receiver. However, the parser will influence operators implemented as methods and used without dot notation.

```
print 3 + 4 * 5  # 23
print 3.+(4).*(5) # 35
```

Method Calls and Parentheses

Ruby does not always require the use of parentheses to evaluate methods, unless it's necessary to avoid ambiguities.

```
def f(x)
  print x**2
end
f 3      # 9
```

However, if parentheses are used near a method, then Ruby will associate them with the method and expect an argument list inside. An expression is a valid argument.

```
f (2+3)*4   # 100
f((2+3)*4)  # 576
```

Method Naming Conflicts

Method names can coincide with keywords or local/constant variable names. This is usually not a problem because the dot notation makes things clear.

```
class MyClass
  def end    # keyword as method name
  puts "The End"
  end
end
obj = MyClass.new
obj.end     # The End
```

Local variables may be confused with a private method of the same name, since private methods can be called without dot notation or parentheses, so be careful.

```
def var     # method belongs to Object class by default
  "not 5"
end
puts var   # not 5
var = 5    # local variable
puts var   # 5
puts var()  # not 5
```

Knowing what Ruby will do is going to take practice—Ruby is more complex than Python.

Parameters and Default Arguments

Although varying-sized parameters lists are available with *, Ruby does not have Python's **
for keyword arguments. Currently, keyword arguments are only available in a limited sense by
passing a hash in as a single parameter. In such a case, the enclosing braces may be omitted.

Ruby allows for a special block parameter, indicated by the & prefix.

```
def doit(*args, &code)
 code.call(*args)
end
doit(1,2,3){|*x| puts "You sent me #{x.size} values." }
# Output: You sent me 3 values.
```

Ruby does not cache method definitions as Python does. Even default arguments are evaluated
for each call.

```
class Foo
 def val(); 2; end
 def show(v=val())
 puts v
 end
end

a=Foo.new()
a.show()     # 2

class Foo
 def val()
 3
 end
end

a.show()     # 3
```

procs and `iterator` Blocks

The closest thing to a Python function object in Ruby is the proc object, which is an encapsulated block of code.

```
b = proc{|x,y| x**2 + y } # same as Proc.new
p b.call(3,1)    # 10
p b[3,1]     # 10
```

The second form is a shortcut for the call, just as parentheses are for Python functions.

A block is used as an `iterator` in the CLU sense. An `iterator` in Ruby is not merely a function that iterates through a list of objects. It is a block of code that may be called from within the associated method zero or more times, and is an inherent part of Ruby's design and syntax.

```
3.times{|i| puts "#{i}. Iterator blocks are closures" }
["A","B","C"].collect{|t| t.downcase! }
```

There are many methods that make use of Ruby `iterator` blocks, and it is a powerful feature of Ruby. You can make your own methods that may or may not require a block.

```
def do_after(t,&b)   # block is required
  sleep t
  b.call
end

  do_after(5){ puts "Are we there yet?" }
def mymeth(x)      # block not required
  myblock = proc{|n| n**2 }
  if block_given?   # check for block
  print "Your block produces: ", yield(x)
  else
  print "My block produces: ", myblock.call(x)
  end
end

mymeth(3)      # My block produces: 9
mymeth(3){|x| x**3 }   # Your block produces: 27
```

Be forewarned that the `iterator` block has a hybrid scope. It is not separate from the surrounding namespace, although it encapsulates it. This means that the enclosing namespace becomes part of the block's binding as well. However, local variables defined for the first time inside a block stay local to that block.

```
def f(x); x**2; end
v = 32; b = 2
g = proc{|n| puts f(n) + b } # b is used
  g[3]        # 11
  p v         # 3 (v was changed)
  p n         # undefined
```

Note that the parameter list is merely a placeholder for parallel assignment. This means that if you put an existing variable into that list, it will be changed. Default arguments are not supported. There is an intricate balance in this matter, because blocks are also used for iterators, which remember the previously assigned value.

Statements and Expressions

There is little distinction between a statement and an expression; both return values. A statement can be made into an expression by enclosing it in parentheses, which will allow it to be used as an argument.

```
arr = [1,2, 3 if limit>2] # parse error
arr = [1,2, (3 if limit>2)] # OK
f(limit or 1)     # parse error
f( (limit or 1) )    # OK
```

In this case, the parentheses for the method are required to distinguish it from the parentheses that make the statement into an expression acceptable as an argument.

Ruby has || and &&, in addition to or and and. These are similar in meaning, but form an expression instead of a statement because they bind more tightly.

Another effect of statements having a value is that using return is optional in method definitions. The value of the last statement in the definition will be used as the return value in such a case.

In Ruby, you will use eval for evaluating both expressions and statements. Use an optional binding or proc where you would otherwise have used an optional global or local dict in Python as a namespace. There is no equivalent to Python's exec function. The exec method in Ruby is used to execute a shell command. Ruby's backtick operator is another form of expressing such shell commands.

Basic I/O

The puts method is closest to Python's print statement, since it adds a new line. Ruby's print adds the default record separator, which is usually nil. The puts method uses the result of inspect, whereas the other two use to_s. The inspect method is like Python's repr() function, and to_s is like str(). As we mentioned, backticks in Ruby are used as a shortcut for exec to run shell commands.

For input, use gets. Here is an imitation of raw_input:

```
def raw_input(prompt="")
 print prompt
 gets
end

x = raw_input("Please enter a number: ")
```

File handling is very similar to Python's approach. Open files are closed during garbage collection (GC) if they are no longer referenced. But if you use the block form of `File.open`, then Ruby will close the file for you at the end of the block without waiting for GC to occur.

```ruby
File.open("somefile") do |f|
  f.puts "#{Time.now}: line added to file"
end
  # File object f is now closed
```

This do/end is actually another syntax form of the `iterator` block.

Numbers

Ruby automatically detects and converts between small and large integers—there is no need to use a trailing L at any time. There is no j literal for imaginary numbers. Use the `Complex` class from `complex.rb` to work with complex numbers. Use `to_i` and `to_f` to convert values.

Number objects are instances of a class like the others, and you can define methods for them.

```ruby
class Fixnum
  def winner?
  self == 37
  end
end

puts "Pick a number."
if gets.to_i.winner?
  puts "Right!"
else
  puts "Sorry."
end
```

This is an example of extending a built-in class with Ruby.

Strings

String objects are instances of the `String` class, and have their own methods.

```ruby
"abc123".length  # 6
```

They are not immutable by default, but you can make them immutable via the `freeze` method. Strings are not lists of characters, and accessing a single element returns the ASCII value for the byte, not the character.

```
str = 'ABC'
puts str[0]    # 65
puts ?A      # 65
puts str[0,1]  # "A"
puts str[0].chr  # "A"
```

The numeric approach facilitates languages having multi-byte characters, such as Japanese.

Iterating over a string will by default deliver one line at a time. You can also iterate over one byte at a time, but remember that you might need to convert bytes to characters.

```
"abc".each_byte do |b| # convert to character before
  print b.chr.upcase # using string method
end        # "ABC"
```

There is no equivalent to Python's r"" raw string or the u"" Unicode string. Using double quotes has a different effect from using single quotes because they allow interpolation. Backticks are also different in Ruby, treating their contents as a shell command and evaluating them on the spot. Regular expressions likewise have special default quoting (forward slashes):

```
'a do-nothing string'    # escape single quotes and backslashes
"This is\ntwo lines."    # Notice - not like single quotes
`ls -l`          # Notice - not repr()
/^(.*?)=(.*?)$/       # regex literal
```

Ruby has special quoting constructs so you can specify other delimiters for these; refer to documentation of %q, %Q, %x, and %r.

Ruby allows for string interpolation in addition to the familiar % formatting.

```
x = 5
puts "I have %s apples" % (x-2)
puts "I have #{x-2} apples."
```

Ruby's string interpolator, #{}, can be used inside double quote constructs, regexes, and shell strings. You can use "here-docs" in place of Python's triple quotes.

```
heredoc = <<MARKER
Now I can type "freely"
Date: #{Time.now}
MARKER
```

Here-docs also come in other forms supporting single- and shell-quoted strings, as well as indented here-docs.

```
def whois(domain=nil)
 print <<-`SHELL`
 whois #{domain||gets}@networksolutions.com
 SHELL
end
```

True and False Values

The object `nil` is logically equivalent to false. Any other object is true, including the number zero (`0`), the empty string (`""`), and the empty array (`[]`). Ruby's `nil` is like Python's `None`. For historical reasons, `NIL`, `FALSE`, and `TRUE` are mapped to the lowercase equivalents.

Arrays

Arrays are like Python's `List` type. There is no `tuple` type in Ruby, but you can freeze an array for the same effect.

```
mylist = [1,2,3,4,5]
mytuple = mylist.freeze
myslice = mylist[0...3] # [1,2,3]
```

As you can see, specifying a slice in Ruby using a `Range` with `...` is like using `:` in Python. You must include both the beginning and the end. It is actually more common to use `..` and specify the list inclusively. There is no direct equivalent to Python's ellipsis or list comprehension syntax.

Use `include?` where you would have used a conditional `in` in Python.

```
if mylist.include? 4
   puts "Found."
end
```

Use the `+`, `<<`, or `push` methods from the `Array` class to accomplish `list.append` functionality.

Dictionaries Are Hashes

Use `=>` instead of `:` to indicate pairings in a hash. Hash keys can be mutable objects (see `rehash`). Inverting a hash does not automatically group duplicates into an array; you will lose entries if there were duplicate values.

```
hsh = {}
hsh['key'] = 7
hsh2 = { "A"=>65, "B"=>66 }
```

Ruby supports default values for hashes.

Classes

Defining a new class creates a new context nested in the enclosing class (class `Object` by default). Use the `::` scope operator to access nested classes/modules and their constants or class methods.

```ruby
class MyClass     # name must be capitalized
 C = "constant in MyClass"
 class Inner
 C = "in MyClass::Inner"
 end
end
p MyClass::C      # constant in MyClass
p MyClass::Inner::C   # in MyClass::Inner
```

Existing classes, both built-in and newly defined, may be reopened and altered or extended at any time (even from within a C extension). Any existing instances will be updated with the new class definitions.

```ruby
class String     # existing built-in class
 def my_method
 puts "length: #{length}" # implicit self
 end
end
"abc123".my_method    # length: 6
```

Any class may be subclassed; use the < symbol instead of parentheses. Ruby classes support single inheritance only. Modules are used to add shared functionality among classes (and objects) in place of using multiple inheritance.

Use `initialize` instead of `__init__` for the "constructor." You do not need to pass in `self` for method definitions, since Ruby automatically binds it for you. Remember dot notation is for method calls only, so prepend instance variables with the @ symbol instead of `self`.

> **NOTE**
>
> Prepending a method name with `self` within a class definition is optional, since it will be called from within the context of the actual instance by default.

Use `super` to call the same-named method from the superclass (or an ancestor thereof).

```
class MyString < String
 def initialize(str)
 @str = str    # instance variable
 super       # call String#initialize(str)
 end
end
```

Instantiate an object via the `Class#new` method. It will call any defined `initialize` method after allocating the object.

```
mystr = MyString.new("text here")
```

There is no equivalent to Python's __del__ hook, since Ruby does not use reference counting (see the section "Garbage Collection"). This may require you to organize your code differently.

Ruby has both class variables and class methods.

```
class MyClass
 @@class_variable = "Accessible to this class and subclasses"
 MyConstant = "Globally accessible via MyClass::MyConstant"
 def MyClass.class_method    # dot notation used in definition
 puts "Available as method of the class object itself"
 end
end
```

Ruby has no internal-use, class-private, or magic-attribute naming like Python's _*, __*, and __*__ forms. Ruby uses the __*__ form sometimes, but only to accommodate certain naming conflicts. For example, `Object#__send__` is an alias for `send`.

Modules

A module in Ruby is not file-based as it is in Python. It is an object with methods and attributes defined within a `module`/`end` block of code, like a class, but without the ability to be instantiated.

```
module MyModule   # Module names are constants (capitalized)
 MyConst = "Module Constant MyModule::MyConst"
 $my_global = "Unrelated to module namespace (global is global)"
 my_local = "Inaccessible from without"
 module NestedModule
 # Access via MyModule::NestedModule
 end
 class InnerClass
 end
```

```ruby
  def module_method
  # Can be accessed as MyModule.module_method
  end
  module_function :module_method
end

module AnotherModule
  # In same file...
end
```

You can define more than one module in the same source file, and even nest them inside each other to organize your namespace. Loading an external file with module definitions is the same as defining them in the source file, and there is no requirement to give these external files the same name as your module(s).

Once defined in the source file, a module is immediately available. You can access nested modules or constants via the :: scope operator, and module functions (shared public methods) via dot notation. You may also as a whole include the module into a class namespace, or extend any object with its methods. There is no provision for selectively including constants or methods of a module as Python's import allows, because it is considered to be a single unit.

When you use this mixin approach to incorporate such shared code from multiple sources, the included modules become part of the single inheritance tree, similar to a subclass. Yes, order does matter.

```ruby
class MyString < String
end

  p MyString.ancestors    # [ MyString, String, ...]

module AlterString
end

  class MyString
  include AlterString
end

  p MyString.ancestors    # [ MyString, AlterString, String, ...]
```

The mixin module is not copied but referenced, as in Python.

Threading Model

Ruby threading is built-in by default; no compiler flag is needed. All threads run within a single interpreter instance, time-sliced within its process (similar to microthreads in Stackless

Python). Such threading is generally not compatible with system-level threading, and it does not take advantage of multiprocessor systems.

Calling blocking I/O functions from within one thread will cause all threads to be blocked. There is no global interpreter lock available to help avoid this. Such situations require you to `fork`/`exec`, but note that forking from inside a thread currently causes all threads to be duplicated. In general, avoid mixing system forking with Ruby threading.

Nevertheless, threads are simple to use in Ruby. Just instantiate a thread object from the `Thread` class with an associated block of code.

```
begin
    i=0
    t1=Thread.new{ sleep 5; raise ThreadError }
    t2=Thread.new{ loop{ i+=1; puts i; sleep rand() } }
    t1.join; t2.join rescue ThreadError puts "Time's up!"
end
```

Notice that there is no need to subclass. Don't forget to join the thread instances to the main thread.

If you have Python code that uses daemon-based threads, you will not be able to convert it directly to Ruby's threads.

Ruby also has continuation objects, which are like a special form of thread. As such, they are interpreter-based and subject to some limitations.

Exception Handling

You may be used to using exceptions as a control structure in Python, but in Ruby they are meant to be for errors. Use `catch`/`throw` for a similar effect as a control structure.

In Ruby, `raise` is a method, not a statement. And while Python does not allow you to mix the `try` statement's except/else and `finally` forms, in Ruby you can combine the equivalents, `rescue`/`else` and ensure, in the `begin`/`end` block form.

```
begin
 f = File.new("somefile","r")
 # do stuff...
rescue Exception => details
 puts "Could not open file! #{details}"
rescue
 puts "Unforeseen error: #$!"
else
 puts "Finished task"
```

```
ensure
  f.close if f
end
```

The rescue clause is similar to Python's except, but there is a different exception hierarchy, which is always used. If you give a string as the first parameter, Ruby uses that as the message and uses RuntimeError as the default exception class.

Ruby does not necessarily raise the same-named exceptions as Python. For example, Ruby does not raise IOError above, which Python would have done. Consult a reference for Ruby's exception class hierarchy.

Ruby stores a reference to the resulting Exception object in the global variable $!, and you can use the => notation in the rescue clause to have it stored in another variable also. Ruby nests exceptions and does not forget them.

Ruby allows you to try to recover from an exception via either redo or retry, which are different. Care should be taken to avoid endless loops.

Garbage Collection

The garbage collector does not require reference counts. Ruby currently uses conservative "mark and sweep" for automatic garbage collection (GC), and will soon be using generational GC. There is no need to keep track of reference counts in your C extensions. Simply provide functions for the GC to use for marking objects and freeing memory.

One consequence to this approach is that you also have less control over the destruction of an object. Of course, you can use GC.start to force cleanup early, and you can also temporarily disable it to prevent code blocks from being interrupted. You can use finalizers to run a procedure after the object is destroyed, but this is not really a destructor.

Extensions

Ruby's C API is well-integrated to the point that just about anything you can do on the Ruby side can be done on the C side, including defining classes and methods at runtime.

It is easy to check types, raise errors, raise exceptions without explicit propagation and result testing, pass arguments cleanly, and associate objects and methods with classes. There is no need for reference counts, type objects, or method tables.

Some More Equivalencies

Table B.1 is a listing of a few more functions, operators, and other items. The Python entity is in the left column; in the right column you will find the rough Ruby equivalent and/or some pertinent comments.

TABLE B.1   Functions, Operators, and Other Items

Python	Ruby
`__bases__`	`ancestors`
`__getattr__`	`method_missing`
`__getitem__`, `__getslice__`	`[]`
`__import__`	`load, require` (redefinable)
`__setitem__`	`[]=`
`__class__`, type	`class,`
`__methods__`, `__members__`, `__dict__`	(various methods)
`apply(f,args)`	Functions are not objects; refer to proc objects: `proc.call(args)` or `obj.send(:method,args)`
`callable`	`respond_to?`
`cmp()`	`<=>`
`complex()`	`require "complex"` (etc.)
`filter()`	`find_all`
`isinstance`	`kind_of?`
`issubclass`	`ancestors.include?`
`len()`	`size, length`
`list()`	`to_a`
`__init__`	`initialize`
`__lt__`, etc.	`<`, etc.
`__hash__`	`Object#hash`
`__add__`, etc.	`+`, etc.
`sys.modules`	`$"`
`sys.path`	`$LOAD_PATH, $:`
`sys.argv`	`ARGV, $*`
`sys.stdin`	`$stdin`
`os.environ`	`ENV`
`if name == '__main__'`	`if $0 == __FILE__`
`if x in y:`	`if y.include? x`

TABLE B.1 Continued

Python	*Ruby*
`if:/elif:/else:`	`if/elsif/else/end`
`for i in x:`	`for i in x/end`
`break/continue`	`break/next/redo`

Other Notes

There is no `UserString`, etc., in Ruby. Use the actual classes themselves, since they can be opened and changed at any time. Use the `Regexp` class instead of importing the `re` module.

There is no `cStringIO` or `codec` module, but they seem like good candidates for porting.

See also: `GC` and `ObjectSpace` for garbage collection, `WeakRef` class (`weakref.rb`), `Config` module (`rbconfig.rb`), and the `DBM` class (`dbm.rb`).

Always remember that Ruby does not use dictionaries of objects as namespaces. When you use the Ruby equivalents of __methods__ and __members__, you will get arrays of strings representing the names of the methods or members.

There are intricate differences between Ruby's `Marshal` and Python's `pickle/marshal` modules (such as `bytecode`), but Ruby has `load` and `dump`, along with `_load` and `_dump`, which if defined will override the former.

Conclusion

In this brief introduction, we've tried to give you a perspective of how Ruby is different from Python. It should now be easier to make the transition as you work with a library reference or development guide.

Tools and Utilities

When all you have is a hammer, everything looks like a nail.

   —Abraham Maslow

The modern programmer typically has a small arsenal of tools at his disposal to make his job easier. These may include everything from simple debuggers to full integrated development environments (IDEs).

At the time of this writing, there is rather a shortage of such tools for Ruby. This situation, of course, will continue to improve as time goes on.

Everything here can be found in the Ruby Application Archive. Begin at the Ruby home page (www.ruby-lang.org), which will always link to the archive.

We present here an overview of many of the tools that are available as of summer 2001.

We've divided these items into five categories: Programming aids, RAD tools and IDEs, miscellaneous interactive tools, Ruby online documentation, and documentation aids. To learn about any of these, a Web search is your best bet for up-to-date information.

Programming Aids

Note that the debugger and the profiler are part of the standard distribution.

- The Ruby debugger—The library `debug.rb` is invoked by a `-rdebug` on the command line; this gives access to a command-line debugger similar to `gdb` and its ilk.
- YARD (Yet Another Ruby Debugger)—This is an enhanced debugger that can be used to attach to programs running remotely.
- The Ruby profiler—Using `-rprofile` on the command line will produce profiling output detailing numbers of method calls, time in seconds, and so on.
- RubyUnit—This is a unit-testing framework based on `junit`.
- Lapidary—Another unit-testing framework, this based on `sunit` instead.
- Rubicon—This test suite is primarily useful for verifying that the Ruby installation behaves as expected. If you use development versions of Ruby (rather than stable versions), you might want this package.
- swigruby—This is a Ruby-aware version of SWIG (Simplified Wrapper and Interface Generator), which glues C/C++ to Ruby.

RAD Tools and IDEs

Ruby doesn't yet have any truly mature Rapid Application Development tools or IDEs. Expect this category to grow.

- SpecRuby—This tool assists in creating Tk interfaces.
- Ruby/LibGlade—This tool by Avi Bryant assists in creating interfaces with GTK; it supersedes the older Glade/Ruby by Yasushi Shoji.
- Gem Finder—This tool by Jim Weirich is a simple graphical class browser, displaying useful information about subclasses, superclasses, methods, and so on.

Ruby Online Documentation

These are all various forms of online Ruby documentation. (By "online," we mean softcopy, not necessarily Web-based.)

- `ri`—This command line utility summarizes information about classes, modules, and methods specified as parameters.
- `myri`—This is a GTK-based GUI version of the `ri` utility.
- *Programming Ruby* by Thomas and Hunt—This book, the first Ruby book in English, is available on the Web in a downloadable form and as a Windows help file.

Miscellaneous Interactive Tools

This section covers editors, editor add-ons, and other tools.

- Support for emacs and vi—Fans (or at least users) of either of these two popular editors will find add-ons to enable automatic indentation, syntax highlighting, and so on. See the Ruby Application Archive.
- xmp—A "sample printer" that takes code and evaluates it a line at a time, placing the returned value to the right as a comment. It is useful in writing books or tutorials, or for pasting into mail or news messages.
- irb ("interactive Ruby")—This simply evaluates a line at a time and prints the results of each line. This is a useful way of trying some technique you're unsure of, or of gaining insight into how a small piece of code works.

C

TOOLS AND
UTILITIES

Documentation Aids

RD is the Ruby equivalent of Perl's POD format. There are various tools available for manipulating this format.

- RDtool—A formatter and set of utilities for RD; this is the tool most commonly used to manipulate embedded documentation within Ruby programs.
- RDBrowse—This is a small graphical application that will search the RUBYLIB path for embedded docs and display them.
- RTool—An add-on for RDTool that helps in creating and manipulating tables.

Resources on the Web (and Elsewhere)

If it's in print, it's out of date.

　　—Dave Thomas

This is a listing of resources related to Ruby. This list will quickly grow out of date, but right now Ruby is new enough that we want to make you aware of what's out there.

We've also added some additional programming books of a broader perspective. These deal with more general topics, such as modern perspectives on design and programming (and as such will remain important for a few years).

Web Page for This Book

URL: `http://samspublishing.com/`

The Web page for *The Ruby Way* has mainly two items of use to the reader. Every code fragment of significant length can be found there, so you won't have to type them in; and there is also an errata section for the errors that have crept in despite our best efforts.

For those who don't already own the book, there is also a sample chapter for preview purposes.

Web Resources for Ruby

There are too many Ruby sites to list here. We will only cover some of the more important ones. (In any case, there is an irony in producing a printed guide to an online medium. Always do a Web search for the latest information.)

www.ruby-lang.org

This is the master site, the actual home page of the Ruby language. Source downloads, CVS access, and bug tracking access can all be found here. All the latest news can be obtained here, and this site may have the shortest average path to all other Ruby sites.

www.rubycentral.com

This is another important source of information for Ruby developers. Highlights include articles, links, and downloads (including the "one-click" Windows installer). Also found here is the full text of the book *Programming Ruby* by Thomas and Hunt (readable online as well as downloadable).

www.rubygarden.org

An excellent source of news and information, including a list of all open RCRs (Ruby Change Requests). For those who like wikis, there is an ever-expanding wiki here, containing (among other things) a Ruby Style Guide.

www.ruby-talk.org

This very useful site holds the archives for the English ruby-talk mailing list.

www.rubyhacker.com

The author's Web site, always a work in progress.

www.rubymine.org

A good "front end" for Ruby news and information, often summarizing and encapsulating what is found elsewhere.

www.rubycookbook.org

This site contains a number of Ruby "recipes" for various tasks. It is similar in spirit to this book, but it evolved completely independently.

www.ruby.ch

The "Ruby Channel" created by Clemens Wyss. This includes a "live" version of the book *Programming Ruby* (with executable examples in the browser); it also includes a good tutorial and a Web-based Ruby interpreter. The content is available in English and German.

www.rubycode.com

Guy Hurst's Ruby page: News, links, and more.

www.rubycolor.org

Another Ruby portal, this one in Japanese only.

www02.so-net.ne.jp/~greentea/ruby/

A page with many useful scripts, brought to us by someone we know only as *greentea*.

Mailing Lists and Newsgroups

At the present time, there is one definitive Ruby newsgroup and several mailing lists. As the community grows, some of these may split into more specialized groups. Many of the existing ones are in Japanese only, and there are also lists in German and French.

comp.lang.ruby

This is the primary newsgroup for the Ruby language. The Japanese language group `fj.comp.lang.ruby` appears to exist still, but has very little traffic.

ruby-talk

This is the main English language mailing list for general Ruby-related matters. At the present time, it is mirrored with the newsgroup in both directions. This was not always the case, especially because the list is older than the newsgroup. For instructions on joining the list, visit the Ruby home page (`www.ruby-lang.org`).

ruby-cvs

If you really need to know about changes in Ruby on a daily basis, you can subscribe to the CVS Commit list (requests go to `ruby-cvs-ctl@ruby-lang.org`).

Japanese Mailing Lists

If you speak Japanese, you may want to know about the following four lists:

- ruby-list (the main Japanese-language list)
- ruby-dev (the list for developers working on Ruby)
- ruby-ext (the mailing list for extension developers)
- ruby-math (the mailing list for mathematical topics)

Other Mailing Lists

There are two other lists that we know of. By the time you read this, there will be more, so do a Web search.

- German list (visit `www.home.unix-ag.org/tjabo/ruby/index.php3`)
- French list (send request to `ruby-fr-ctl@ruby-lang.org`)

Ruby on IRC

There are at least three places on the Net to chat with other Rubyists. The ones we know of are as follows:

- OpenProjects: #ruby-lang
- IRCNet: #ruby-lang
- EFNet: #ruby

Other Ruby Books

There aren't many Ruby books as of September 2001. With the exception of *Programming Ruby*, all of the following titles have yet to be published as of the writing of this book. We trust there will be more soon.

- *Programming Ruby*, Dave Thomas and Andy Hunt. Addison-Wesley, 2000.

  The first Ruby book in English, sometimes known as the "Pickaxe Book" because it has a pickaxe and some ruby gems on the cover. At the time of this writing, this is the "bible" for Ruby programmers, and it will continue to be used in the future for its excellent tutorial value and reference value.

- *Ruby in a Nutshell*, Yukihiro Matsumoto. O'Reilly and Associates, 2001.

  A Ruby book from Matz himself—a translation of the Japanese *Ruby Pocket Reference*; sure to be a valuable resource.

- *The Ruby Programming Language*, Yukihiro Matsumoto. Addison-Wesley Professional, 2002.

  Another book from the creator of Ruby. This is slated to be more than twice the length of *Ruby Essentials*, giving room for more examples and discussion.

- *Teach Yourself Ruby in 21 Days*, Mark Slagell. SAMS Publishing, 2001.

  This book is targeted for beginners who want to pick up Ruby quickly.

- *The Ruby Developer's Guide*, Michael Neumann. Syngress Media, Inc., 2001.

  The author is known to be a significant contributor to the Ruby community.

Other Recommended Books

As it says in the Bible (the *real* one, not the Pickaxe Book): "Wisdom is more precious than rubies" (Prov 3:13). Many of the important truths we have learned in the computing world in the last few decades are language-independent. We've listed here a number of books not strictly related to Ruby that may still be of immense value to the Ruby programmer.

- *Refactoring*, Martin Fowler. Addison-Wesley, 1999.

  This is one of those modern classics. The author in this book offers a set of mental tools for untangling spaghetti code and making incremental improvements in program logic and structure. Any programmer can benefit from this book.

- *Design Patterns*, Erich, Gamma, et al. Addison-Wesley, 1995.

  This is the book by the "Gang of Four" that everyone has been talking about. Programmers have tended in the past to strive for code reusability more than design reusability; but this book has helped change that trend by taking a new look at program design at a high level of abstraction.

- *The Pragmatic Programmer*, Andy Hunt and Dave Thomas. Addison-Wesley, 2000.

  This is one of the more practical and thought-provoking books of the last few years, offering keen insights and useful advice relating to the design, coding, and testing of software. The authors also wrote the Pickaxe Book.

- *Object-Oriented Software Construction* 2nd Ed., Bertrand Meyer. Prentice Hall, 2000.

  This book was written by the creator of the Eiffel language, and the code in the examples is Eiffel. However, the explanation and discussion of OOP is of the very highest quality, and the principles that are taught are applicable to any OOP language. This book also explores the concept of *Design by Contract* (DBC), which is a powerful technique for improving code reliability.

- *Extreme Programming Explained*, Kent Beck. Addison-Wesley, 1999.

  The XP movement (unrelated, we stress, to Microsoft's forthcoming product) continues to gain momentum. This is one of a series of books outlining the philosophy of Extreme Programming and its no-nonsense test-first approach.

- *Learning Perl/Tk*, Nancy Walsh and Linda Mui. O'Reilly and Assoc., 1999.

  We mention this book because the Perl interface to Tk is similar to Ruby's. Until there is a real Ruby/Tk book, this is probably the closest you can get to one.

- *The Art of Computer Programming*, Donald Knuth. Addison-Wesley, 1998.

  This multi-volume work may have passed from "classic" into "legend" status by now. Much of it you will never use, but if you are a programmer, you should certainly own it. It will pay for itself.

- *Mastering Regular Expressions*, Jeffrey Friedl. O'Reilly and Assoc., 1997.

  This is probably the definitive work on regular expressions. If you want to gain a deeper understanding, get more practice, and understand some of the underlying theory, get this book.

- *The Tao of Programming*, Geoffrey James. Info Books, 1986.

  This book is priceless. It's intended to be a humorous look at programmers and computing, couched in the language of Eastern mysticism. However, you may find that some of the humor falls a little too close to home; and you may even gain some insight into your fellow programmers (or yourself).

- *The New Hacker's Dictionary*, Eric S. Raymond. MIT Press, 1996.

  This is more light reading, and yet it's deeper than that. Far from being just the work of one man, this book draws on multiple traditions of computing history, culture, and folklore. You won't learn any programming here, but you will be enlightened, entertained, and inspired. If you consider yourself a hacker in the classic sense of the word, you need this book.

What's New in Ruby 1.8

APPENDIX

E

Change is the only thing that is permanent.

> —Heraclitus

This book was written at an awkward time, right in the middle of a Ruby development cycle. Yet of course, that would be the case *whenever* the book was written.

We have found it difficult to revise all of the text at the last minute to incorporate all the latest enhancements in the Ruby language. Instead we've decided to summarize those changes here.

We've tried, where possible, to group the changes by class or module. Note that some of the changes here are marked as "experimental" (meaning that they may not be permanent). In general, we've omitted news about bug fixes and performance enhancements here, choosing to concentrate on changed interfaces.

This information will be out of date by the time you read it. As always, find the latest information on the Web.

Changes in Syntax and General Behavior

The syntax of Ruby is its most stable aspect, but it still evolves over time, with allowances made for backward compatibility. We've summarized some recent changes here, including one that is experimental.

- Multiple assignment behavior has changed. The assignment `*a = nil` will now make the conditional `a == []` true.

- Array expansion: If you assign `a = *[1]`, you now find that a is 1 (rather than `[1]` as before).

- Experimental: `break` and `next` can now take an optional expression used as a value for termination.

- `to_str` support has been added. Now almost all built-in methods which expect a `String` will call the object's `to_str` method if it is not a `String`. For example, any object with a `to_str` method can be meaningfully passed into `File.open` without manually calling `to_s` or any similar trick.

- Comparison of exception classes in a rescue clause has changed slightly. Now `Module#===` (rather than `kind_of?`) is used for the comparison. In conjunction with this, `SystemCallError#===` now returns `true` for identical errno values. In practice, this means that when multiple `SystemCallErrors` have the same errno, any one of them can be specified in the `rescue` clause and they will all be caught.

Changes in Libraries

- The `curses` library has been updated. It now has new methods and constants for mouse events, character attributes, colors, and keycodes.
- The `socket` library has four new methods in the `Socket` class: `pack_sockaddr_in`, `unpack_sockaddr_in`, `pack_sockaddr_un`, and `unpack_sockaddr_un`.
- Also in the `socket` library, the `TCPSocket` class has two optional parameters added to the `new` and `open` class methods. The optional third and fourth parameters are the address and port for the local side.

Changes in Modules and Classes

The classes and modules are naturally where the bulk of the changes lie. Some have had methods added; others have merely had method semantics shift a little. This list is mostly alphabetical by class or module name; the exception is at the bottom of the list where we've put all the miscellaneous items.

The methods named here are instance methods, unless noted as class methods.

Class `Array`

- `fetch` added.
- `insert` added. The new method `arr.insert(n, x, y, z)` acts just like `arr[n,0]` = `[x,y,z]`, but returns `self` rather than the assigned value.
- `sort!` always returns `self` without checking for modification of the array's contents. This behavior may change and should not be relied on.

Class `Dir`

- `Dir.chdir` has been extended to take a block. Like such methods as `File.open`, the operation is only in effect within the scope of the block.
- `Dir.glob` now supports metacharacters escaped by a backslash; wildcards and spaces may now be escaped at will.
- `Dir.open` now returns the block return value like `File.open`, not `nil` as in Ruby 1.6.
- `Dir.chdir` will warn only when it is invoked from multiple threads or when no block is specified.

Module `Enumerable`

- `all?` added (detects whether `all` items fit a given criterion).
- `any?` added (detects whether any item fits the given criterion).
- `inject` added (analogous to Smalltalk's `inject`).
- `sort_by` added (sorts by specified field or key).

Class `File`

- `fnmatch` added (along with constants `File::Constants::FNM_*`). See documentation for the Unix utility `fnmatch`.
- `File.lchmod` and `File.lchown` added (for symbolic links).

Class `IO`

- `IO.for_fd` added.
- `IO.read` added (see ruby-talk:9460).

Module `Math`

- `Math.acos(x)` added.
- `Math.asin(x)` added.
- `Math.atan(x)` added.
- `Math.cosh(x)` added.
- `Math.hypot(x,y)` added.
- `Math.sinh(x)` added.
- `Math.tanh(x)` added.

Class `Module`

- `include?` added.
- `included` added. This is a hook called after `Module#append_feature`.
- `method_removed` added.
- `method_undefined` added.

Class `Object`

- `singleton_method_removed` hook added.
- `singleton_method_undefined` hook added.

Class Proc

- `==` added.
- `yield` added. This is like `call` except that it doesn't check the number of arguments; the arguments are thus passed in as they are.

Class Process

- `Process.times` has been moved from `Time.times`. (The latter is still there but gives a warning.)
- `Process.waitall` added.
- The `Process::Status` class has been added. `$?` is now an instance of this class.

Class Range

- `step` added (default is 1).
- `to_ary` added. It's now possible to use a construct such as a, b, c = 1..3 without using to_a.

Class Regexp

- It's no longer legal to regard a standalone /re/ as meaning /re/ =~ $_ in a conditional. You must explicitly use the match operator ~ instead.
- `options` added.
- `Regexp.last_match` has been extended to take an optional argument.

Class String=

- `casecmp` added (case-insensitive comparison).
- `eql?` has been changed to be always case sensitive.
- `insert` added; the method call str.insert(n, s2) acts like str[n, 0] = s2, but returns itself rather than the value of the assignment.
- `lstrip`, `rstrip`, `lstrip!`, and `rstrip!` have been added to strip only the left or right sides of a string, respectively.

Class Symbol

- `intern` added.
- `Symbol.all_symbols` added.

Class Time

- The `Time` can now handle a negative `time_t` (when the platform supports it). This extends the range of dates back into the year 1901.
- `to_a` added.
- `zone` Now returns `"UTC"` under `gmtime`.

Other Classes and Modules

- `Interrupt` is now a subclass of `SignalException`, rather than `Exception`.
- `Kernel.open` has been extended so that when the third argument is a set of permission flags, the underlying call will be `open(2)`, rather than `fopen(3)`.
- `Marshal` will no longer dump anonymous classes/modules.
- The `Regexp` class has `to_ary` added for convenience in using the `match` method on the right-hand side in a multiple assignment. Previously, you had to say something like `junk, m1, m2, m3 = regex.match(str).to_a`, whereas now you can say `junk, m1, m2, m3 = regex.match(str)` (omitting the `to_a`).
- `Method#==` added.
- `NameError` and `NoMethodError` have moved; now `NoMethodError` is a subclass of `NameError`, which in turn is a subclass of `StandardError`.
- `NotImplementError` is obsolete because of its "broken English." Use `NotImplementedError` instead.
- A new module `Signal` has been added; it has the module functions `Signal::trap` and `Signal::list`.
- `SystemCallError.===` added. Refer to the note on comparison of exception classes in the rescue clause (at the top of this appendix).
- `SystemExit#status` added.

INDEX

SYMBOLS

O

X

Y-Z